Monteverdi's Musical Theatre

Monteverdi's Musical Theatre

Tim Carter

Yale University Press
New Haven and London

For information about this and other Yale University Press publications, please contact
    U.S. Office: sales.press@yale.edu   yalebooks.com
    Europe Office: sales@yaleup.co.uk   www.yaleup.co.uk

Set in Bembo by SNP Best-set Typesetter Ltd, Hong Kong
Printed in Great Britain by St Edmundsbury Press

ISBN 0–300–09676–3

Library of Congress Control Number 2002109930

A catalogue record for this book is available from the British Library

10 9 8 7 6 5 4 3 2 1

Contents

Preface

Claudio Monteverdi (1567–1643) was without doubt the most significant composer in late Renaissance and early Baroque Italy. He was also the one who most avidly and consistently pursued the new opportunities for relating drama to music that were made possible by the spectacular gains in stagecraft, dramatic poetry and musical style in Italy around 1600. And he is by common consent the first operatic master. It is surprising, therefore, that the only monograph to date on his entire corpus of theatrical music is Anna Amalie Abert's *Claudio Monteverdi und das musikalische Drama* (1954). Of course, his operas and other more or less theatrical works have been discussed within standard 'life and works' of the composer, in broader studies of the secular music, and indeed in general histories of the period or of opera itself, while *Orfeo* has been the subject of a Cambridge Opera Handbook edited by John Whenham (1986), and the late works have prompted monographs by Wolfgang Osthoff (1960) and Ellen Rosand (forthcoming). Both individually and together these works have also been the subject of important essays and articles that, in the past twenty years, have changed quite radically the ways in which they are approached and viewed. But Denis Arnold's comment that 'the heart of Monteverdi's music lies in his madrigals' (*Monteverdi*, p. 46) – plus Monteverdi's own association of the aesthetic and stylistic revolutions of the *seconda pratica* chiefly with this genre – have created a curious perspective whereby his music for the stage is persistently viewed in the context of, and as building upon, technical and expressive gains in his secular vocal chamber works. In some cases, the prism is a useful one; in others, it distorts quite significantly.

The situation may have been exacerbated by certain difficulties endemic to the repertory. Most will probably agree that Monteverdi's *Orfeo* (1607), *Il ritorno d'Ulisse in patria* (1640) and *L'incoronazione di Poppea* (1643) are somehow recognizable as operas in the modern sense of the term, even if the label is problematic given the expectations it then creates. The *Ballo delle ingrate* (1608) is usually seen as approaching opera, despite its emphasis on dance. But Monteverdi also dealt with other theatrical genres that remain to a greater or lesser degree distant from anything that might be claimed as operatic, such as *intermedi* and tournaments. Other cases, including *Tirsi e Clori* (1616) and the *Combattimento di Tancredi e Clorinda* (1624), even question the very meaning of the term 'theatrical', given their style, function and the likely context and location of their first performances. The gaps created by the several 'lost' works in Monteverdi's output – most notably two operas, *Arianna* (1608) and *Le nozze d'Enea in Lavinia* (1641) – raise further difficulties in terms of presenting a coherent overview of the composer's writing for the stage, if such an overview is at all possible or desirable. Yet despite the problems, there is a body of material here that deserves serious treatment on its own.

The bulk of this book is organized around a set of critical essays, each primarily on one of Monteverdi's chief works for the theatre – treating the term rather liberally (itself a matter of debate) – although all of what is commonly identified as his stage music is discussed to a greater or lesser degree. Because these essays are 'critical', they are therefore partial in both senses of the word. My aim has not been to give a complete account of each work, although I present the documentary and other materials useful for such an account. Nor do I offer thorough guidance on how one might understand or even interpret them, although much of what I say has a bearing on both reading and performance. But although these essays can be read separately, it is their combination – their weaving of recurring and interconnected themes – that is most important. Such cohesion (I would not say synthesis) is further encouraged by way of the opening general chapters. Here and indeed elsewhere in the book, I develop issues that have gradually become the predominant focus of my own work on music in early seventeenth-century Italy: the need to view Monteverdi in his various contexts; the problems of genre; the potential interactions between poetic texts and their musical setting; and, increasingly, the ways in which surviving musical and other materials from this period inhabit complex spaces between past and future performances. This also raises a series of broader questions concerning methodology that, in turn, explains why the longest chapter in the book concerns the 'lost' works, where Monteverdi's music does not survive, for all that one can still say a good deal about it. In general, however, my approach tends to be less philosophical or aesthetic than pragmatic; I am not so much concerned with my own, or even Monteverdi's, grand statements as with the nuts and bolts of how a seventeenth-century musician might have written for, and worked within, the theatre.

I have now been studying this repertory for over twenty years, and have been writing on Monteverdi's theatrical and other works for over ten.

Inevitably, much of this book draws upon previously published material, although nothing has been repeated willy-nilly. At times, and for reasons of space, I have been forced to refer to my earlier essays and articles for fuller documentation or argument, although I have attempted as much as possible to make the present text free-standing and as comprehensive as is necessary for my purpose. More often, I have been prompted by my own more recent work, and still more by that of others, to revise my opinions and conclusions such that previous publications are superseded to varying degrees. The attentive reader will still notice some gaps. My treatment of the Venetian operas is perhaps less contextualized, and more selective, than some might wish, largely because I have not wanted to compete, as if I could, with Ellen Rosand's forthcoming monograph on these works: in particular, I have left *Le nozze d'Enea in Lavinia* (1641) almost entirely to her. If I have not seemed to engage extensively in reading Monteverdi's works through the prism of gender studies and other critical theories in the various manners of Suzanne Cusick, Wendy Heller and Susan McClary, it is not through lack of admiration for their work. And if there are other omissions, either they are my fault or they reflect the fact that the field remains wide open for future research.

Titles follow the original styling, although sometimes common usage has prevailed (thus *Orfeo* rather than *L'Orfeo*, and *L'incoronazione di Poppea* rather than *La coronatione* . . . or *Il Nerone*). Operatic characters are styled in Italian – with the English or similar equivalent given in parenthesis where it is unclear – while English stylings are used for the mythological or historical individuals on which they are based: thus Orfeo is the protagonist of an opera concerning the life of Orpheus, and Nerone and Poppea represent Nero and Poppaea. Musical pitches are indicated according to the 'Helmholtz' system (where c' = 'middle' C). I refer to 'major' and 'minor' keys for convenience, without seeking to engage in a long debate about the anachronism of describing Monteverdi's music in 'tonal' terms; however, his modal practice does sometimes become a matter of discussion. Italian poetry is analysed conventionally, with *versi piani* (accent on the penultimate syllable; the norm), *versi tronchi* (accent on the final syllable) and *versi sdruccioli* (accent on the antepenultimate syllable) in lines of four to eleven syllables (respectively, *quaternari, quinari, senari, settenari, ottonari, novenari, decasillabi, endecasillabi*); *versi tronchi* (indicated by a superscript 't') and *sdruccioli* (superscript 's') are counted as modified *versi piani*, therefore with one syllable respectively more or less than the actual syllable count. Rhyme-schemes are indicated with lower-case letters for *settenari* and upper-case for *endecasillabi*; in the case of other line-lengths, the syllable count is shown by superscript numbers. This is also helpful for indicating conventional poetic forms such as the 3-line stanzas of *terza rima* (ABA, BCB, . . . , YZYZ) or the 8-line ones of the *ottava rima* (ABABABCC).

Extracts from librettos are given both in Italian and in translation; contemporary documents and similar material are given just in translation in cases where the original is easily accessible in the secondary literature, but otherwise in both languages. My translations tend towards the literal in terms of sense and word-order, and hence read more clumsily than might be preferred. In presenting Italian texts (both poetry and prose), I have done some light and mostly 'silent' editing in matters of orthography and punctuation for the sake of clarity; these are not in any sense philological editions. The sources of the music examples are given in their captions; sometimes I have preferred to edit them from the originals (in original note-values and with obvious errors tacitly corrected), but otherwise they are taken from the Malipiero edition. Citations in the footnotes use the short-title format; full details can be found in the list of Works Cited. In general, where secondary sources have been translated, I refer to the English version. References to Monteverdi's letters are made by date, with the recipient identified only when necessary to resolve confusion (e.g., in the case of two or more letters written on the same day); this avoids repeated page references to Denis Stevens's translation or to Éva Lax's fine edition of the originals. For the sake of convenience, and also so as not to introduce new readings into the literature except where necessary, I have followed Stevens's translation of the letters, with minor changes in styling and, where noted, in content. Elsewhere, I have relied on material in my translation of Fabbri's monograph on Monteverdi, again with modifications where necessary. All translations of early seventeenth-century operatic prefaces and dedications come from the anthology *Composing Opera*, ed. Szweykowski and Carter (with minor changes), which also contains the original texts.

Many of my friends, colleagues and students will recognize portions of this material presented in various formats. Students of Royal Holloway, University of London, of Rose Bruford College, London, and of the University of North Carolina at Chapel Hill have engaged with and responded to a good part of this text; I hope that they learnt from me as much as I from them. Delegates at the UK Biennial Conferences on Baroque Music and at the annual meetings of the US Society for Seventeenth-Century Music were always ready to lend supportive yet critical ears to my presentations. I have been aided significantly by staff in, and the resources of, the University of London libraries, the British Library and the University of Melbourne Music Library. I am also grateful to Royal Holloway for providing the time and support to bring this project to fruition by way of sabbatical leave in 2000–1, and to my former colleagues there for generating so exciting a research environment; although I have recently moved to a new position, they are still close to my heart. My text was much improved as a result of close reading by Ellen Rosand (Yale University) and John Whenham (University of Birmingham), by my editor at Yale University Press, Malcolm Gerratt, and by Ingrid Grimes. As always, my wife Annegret Fauser remains my fiercest and most formidable critic.

Tim Carter
Chapel Hill, May 2002

1

Monteverdi and the 'problems of opera'

Monteverdi lived in exciting times. Born in Cremona on 15 May 1567, he studied with Marc'Antonio Ingegneri, *maestro di cappella* of the cathedral, who gave him a solid grounding in counterpoint and composition to both secular and sacred texts. In 1590 or 1591 he moved to Mantua to join the court musicians of Duke Vincenzo Gonzaga as a player of instruments of the viol and violin families (he was called a 'suonatore di vivuola'). Mantua, one of the more dynamic musical centres in northern Italy, was host to some of the best composers and performers of the period, including, as head of the ducal chapel, Giaches de Wert (1535–96), who significantly influenced Monteverdi's maturing style. In the late 1590s Monteverdi became involved in a dispute with the Bolognese theorist Giovanni Maria Artusi over the composer's allegedly extravagant dissonance treatment. Monteverdi argued that such dissonances were entirely logical in a style devoted to expressing emotional texts, and the claim of music's subservience to words became a central tenet of the so-called *seconda pratica*, which Monteverdi contrasted with the 'first practice' of older polyphonists, where music reigned supreme. The dispute was bitter, but it seems to have done the composer no harm: in 1601 he was appointed Duke Vincenzo's *maestro della musica di camera*.

Monteverdi fully explored the implications of his 'second practice' in his Fourth and Fifth Books of polyphonic madrigals (1603, 1605), and then in his opera *Orfeo*, first performed before the Mantuan Accademia degli Invaghiti on 24 February 1607 (it was repeated on 1 March). In 1607–8, the composer was hard at work for the wedding festivities for Prince Francesco Gonzaga and Margherita of Savoy, celebrated after some delay in May–June 1608. The festivities included Guarini's comedy *L'idropica*, with spectacular *intermedi*, Monteverdi's opera *Arianna*, plus a dance-entertainment, the *Ballo delle ingrate*. *Arianna* was performed on 28 May to great success: its music is now lost, with the exception of the famous lament. But Monteverdi was exhausted by his efforts. He also resented what he felt was the shabby treatment accorded him by the court, and he disliked the unhealthy Mantuan climate. Events were further marred by personal tragedy, the death first of his wife and then of his favourite pupil Caterina Martinelli (who was to have sung the title-role in *Arianna*). Monteverdi began to look elsewhere for work – his *Sanctissimae Virgini missa . . . ac vespere*, the Mass and well-known Vespers of 1610, advertises his availability – and on 30 July 1612 he was dismissed from Mantuan service by Duke Francesco Gonzaga because, it seems, of insubordination and also of financial cutbacks. After a year in Cremona, on 19 August 1613 he was appointed director of music at the Basilica of St Mark, Venice.

Monteverdi now enjoyed the fame, responsibility and security of perhaps the leading musical position in Italy. He was also working for a republic rather than a court, and his primary responsibility was now to the Church. Yet the rupture with Mantua was by no means as complete as many have assumed, and Monteverdi remained a Mantuan subject and therefore obligated to the Gonzagas. After Duke Francesco's brief reign, the new duke, Ferdinando, continued to press Monteverdi for music for theatrical and other entertainments – and Monteverdi dedicated his Seventh Book of madrigals (1619) to Ferdinando's wife, Caterina de' Medici – even if many of these projects came to naught. By the 1620s, however, Monteverdi had revived his interest in theatrical music. In Carnival 1624 he presented the *Combattimento di Tancredi e Clorinda* under the patronage of the Venetian nobleman Girolamo Mocenigo, and he was involved in the entertainments for the wedding of Duke Odoardo Farnese of Parma and Margherita de' Medici celebrated in Parma in 1628. These courtly connections also began to extend to the Habsburgs in Vienna; Monteverdi's Eighth Book of madrigals, the *Madrigali guerrieri, et amorosi*, of 1638 was dedicated to Emperor Ferdinand III and contains several theatrical works, including the *Combattimento* and a revised version of the *Ballo delle ingrate*. At the same time, Monteverdi was becoming involved in the new 'public' opera houses that opened in Venice from 1637 onwards. He revised his *Arianna* for the Teatro S. Moisé in Carnival 1639–40. He also wrote a new opera for the same season, *Il ritorno d'Ulisse in patria*, based on Homer's *Odyssey*, which was successful enough to be revived the following year.[1] For his second Venetian opera, Monteverdi turned to Virgil's *Aeneid*, with *Le nozze d'Enea in Lavinia* (now lost) staged at the Teatro SS. Giovanni e Paolo in Carnival 1640–1. His last opera, *L'incoronazione di Poppea*,

---

1   For the location of the first performance (and probably the revival) of *Il ritorno*, once thought to be the Teatro S. Cassiano but now considered to be the Teatro SS. Giovanni e Paolo, see most recently Mancini, Muraro and Povoledo, *I teatri del Veneto*, i/1, p. 304; Rosand, 'The Bow of Ulysses', p. 379 n. 13.

was produced at the Teatro SS. Giovanni e Paolo in Carnival 1642–3. By now, court opera had been left far behind. With *Orfeo*, Monteverdi had participated in the very birth of opera. With *L'incoronazione*, he helped inaugurate a new age in the genre's history.

Monteverdi's death on 29 November 1643, at the grand old age of seventy-six, was marked by numerous tributes from his colleagues at St Mark's and in the Venetian musical world. Even before then, however, his reputation was considerable. Not for nothing did the unknown librettist of *Le nozze d'Enea in Lavinia* lavish extensive praise on the composer in the *Argomento* prefacing the libretto:

> Now you, my lords, tolerating the imperfection of my poetry, enjoy cheer-fully the sweetness of the music of the never enough praised Monteverde, born to the world so as to rule over the emotions of others, there being no harsh spirit that he does not turn and move according to his talent, adapting in such a way the musical notes to the words and to the passions that he who sings must laugh, weep, grow angry and grow pitying, and do all the rest that they command, with the listener no less led to the same impulse in the variety and force of the same perturbations. To this truly great man, this most noble art of music – and particularly theatrical music – knows itself to be so much in debt that it can confess that it is thanks to him that it has been brought to new life in the world more efficacious and perfect than it was in ancient Greece or wherever else it has ever been that the fine arts have been held in esteem. For this Signor Monteverde, known in far-flung parts and wherever music is known, will be sighed for in future ages, at least as far as they can be consoled by his most noble compositions, which are set to last as long as can resist the ravages of time any more esteemed and estimable fruit of one who is a wondrous talent in his profession.

Tempering admiration with, it seems, affection, the librettist makes a series of striking claims. Monteverdi, he says, could direct the emotions of the listener with the surest of hands, finding a miraculous union of word and sound. Through him, music – and in particular, theatrical music – had reached a perfection unparalleled even in Classical Antiquity, and his works would ring through the ages.

That was no idle prophecy. In the case of *Orfeo*, Prince Francesco Gonzaga seems to have wanted to mount a production in Casale Monferrato (where he was governor) during Carnival 1609–10; Francesco Rasi took it to Salzburg where it may have received regular performances from 1614 to 1619; the score was reprinted in 1615; there was a performance in Genoa some time (but not long) before 1646; and it was still admired across Italy in the early 1650s, or so said Girolamo Pinello in the preface to his play *La ninfa ribelle* (Genoa, Casamara, 1653).[2] According to Severo Bonini (*Prima parte de' discorsi e regole sovra la musica*, c1651–5), there was no musical household in Italy that did not own a copy of Monteverdi's *Lamento d'Arianna* (1608). *Il ritorno d'Ulisse in patria* (1640) had ten or more performances in Venice by late 1640 or early 1641; by the end of 1640, it had also been heard in Bologna; and a score somehow reached Vienna. *L'incoronazione di Poppea* (1643) was revived at least in Naples in 1651. All that in itself was remarkable in an age when memories were short and large-scale musical works often had limited currency beyond their immediate circumstance.

A reception-history of Monteverdi has still to be written,[3] although even a cursory overview offers important clues as to how changing percep-tions of his works have variously defined our approaches to them today. His influence spread through Italy and north of the Alps by way of his colleagues and pupils, including Francesco Cavalli and Heinrich Schütz, and he had a discernible impact on the *tragédies en musique* of Lully in France and even on Purcell in England. His music had a surprisingly long life in northern Europe up to the age before Bach, and even in Italy connoisseurs were performing and discussing his madrigals around the 1700s. In the eighteenth century – and apart from ongoing amateur or antiquarian interest – the focus shifted both to pedagogy, with Monteverdi cited as a model for (or against) good contrapuntal practice (for example, by Padre Martini), and to emerging notions of music history. For the latter, Charles Burney (*A General History of Music*, 1789) was, he said, 'unable to discover Monteverdi's superiority'. However, Stefano Arteaga (*Le rivoluzioni del teatro musicale italiana dalla sua origine fino al presente*, 1783) had some sense of the power of the *Lamento d'Arianna*; the revised edition (1813) of Ernst Ludwig Gerber's *Neues his-torisch–biographisches Lexicon der Tonkünstler* (first published in 1790) called Monteverdi the Mozart of his time; and Raphael Georg Kiesewetter's *Geschichte der europäisch-abendländischen oder unsrer heutigen Musik* (1834) could devote a chapter to what its English translation (1848) called the 'Epoch of Montiverde' (*sic*) 'because he accomplished more than any other composer in the several departments of the new opera and the madrigal', although only

2   For the early fortunes of *Orfeo*, see Fabbri, *Monteverdi*, trans. Carter, pp. 286–7 n. 98; Seifert, 'Beiträge zur Frage nach den Komponisten der ersten Opern außerhalb Italiens'; Kirkendale, *The Court Musicians in Florence during the Principate of the Medici*, p. 583 n. 179.
3   The following highly derivative and very incomplete account draws from Fabbri, *Monteverdi*, trans. Carter, pp. 1–5; Fortune, 'The Rediscovery of "Orfeo"'; Hust, 'Claudio Monteverdi in Darstellungen und Wertungen der ersten Hälfte des 19. Jahrhunderts'; Barlow, 'The Revival of Monteverdi's Operas in the Twentieth Century'; Rosenthal, 'Aspects of the Monteverdi Revival in the 20th Century'.

Orfeo is discussed briefly.[4] From the second quarter of the nineteenth century onwards, local historians such as Pietro Canal (*Della musica in Mantova*, the first edition of which dates from the mid 1840s) and Francesco Caffi (*Storia della musica sacra nella già cappella ducale di San Marco in Venezia dal 1318 al 1797*, 1854–5), and the German scholars Carl von Winterfeld (in *Johannes Gabrieli und sein Zeitalter*, 1834) and Emil Vogel (1887), each made important discoveries about the composer's life and works. So did such Italian librarians and archivists as Stefano Davari (1884–5) and Angelo Solerti (1903, 1905), whose work laid important documentary foundations for the study of the composer that are still of use today. But Monteverdi remained something of a historical curiosity, if famous as the 'inventor' of the dominant seventh, so Fétis claimed, or even as the 'originator of the Modern style of Composition' (according to the first edition of George Grove's *A Dictionary of Music and Musicians*, 1880), a trope that continued until 1950 (witness Leo Schrade's *Monteverdi: Creator of Modern Music*) and even beyond. Hubert Parry (*The Oxford History of Music*, vol. 3, 1902) could call *Orfeo* 'one of the most astonishing products of genius in the whole range of music'. However, Monteverdi never benefited significantly from the nineteenth-century (Catholic) revival of Renaissance music – such as the works of Palestrina – presumably because he was viewed chiefly as a secular composer.

Thus far, Monteverdi's operas had tended to be marginalized: there is no mention of them in Johann Gottfried Walther's *Musikalisches Lexicon* (1732), while even Fétis seems much to prefer the madrigals. But by the late nineteenth century, two trends came together to revive interest in these works. The first was the emergence of more or less scholarly editions, with bowdlerizations and cuts to greater or lesser degrees. François-Auguste Gevaert published the *Lamento d'Arianna* in Paris in 1868 (Ottorino Respighi also edited it in 1910), and Robert Eitner *Orfeo* (with major cuts) in Berlin in 1881. There were editions of *L'incoronazione di Poppea* by Hugo Goldschmidt (1904), Vincent d'Indy (1908) and Charles van den Borren (1914), and of the *Ballo delle ingrate* and the *Combattimento di Tancredi e Clorinda* by Luigi Torchi (in vol. 6 of his series *L'arte musicale in Italia*, 1897–1908), plus a fine scholarly edition of the Vienna manuscript of *Il ritorno d'Ulisse in patria* by Robert Haas in the series 'Denkmäler der Tonkunst in Österreich' (Jahrgang XXIX, vol. 57; 1922). The second trend was the new aesthetic status granted to opera by Wagner and his successors, in turn prompting renewed speculation on the

---

4   *History of the Modern Music of Western Europe from the First Century of the Christian Era to the Present Day*, trans. Robert Müller (London, T. C. Newby, 1848), p. 195.
Musical extracts from *Orfeo* and the *Lamento d'Arianna* (drawn from Burney, Hawkins and Winterfeld) are also included in Kiesewetter's *Schicksale und Beschaffenheit des weltlichen Gesanges vom frühen Mittelalter bis zur Erfindung des dramatischen Styles und den Anfängen der Oper* (Leipzig, Breitkopf & Härtel, 1841).

nature and origins of music-drama. Most of these early Monteverdi editions were specially prepared for, or otherwise associated with, performances in the concert hall or, increasingly, on the stage. For example, d'Indy's concert performances (in French) of *Orfeo* in Paris on 25 February and 2 March 1904 were a major achievement, even if about half of the opera was cut, including Acts I and V, and much of Act III. His edition was published in 1905 and first staged at the Théâtre Réjane on 2 May 1911. D'Indy then gave even more drastic treatment to *L'incoronazione* (24 February 1905; first staged on 5 February 1913), preserving only 'the most beautiful and interesting parts of the work'.[5] However, in the staging of *Il ritorno* on 16 May 1925, he did keep rather more of the original (minus the deities, except Minerva).

The revivals of *Orfeo* and *L'incoronazione* were situated in the pedagogical environment of d'Indy's Schola Cantorum, an institution devoted to the study of earlier music, although d'Indy claimed that he was moving beyond archaeology to restore real works of art (this soon became a trope). However, and like d'Indy himself, they were also inserted into current musical politics. It is apparent from the discussion surrounding the performance of *Orfeo* that Monteverdi could be viewed either as a crucial predecessor of Wagner or as a feasible alternative to the German tendencies then perceived in some quarters as infecting the French operatic stage. In a few cases he could be both, as in the various writings of Romain Rolland and his pupil Henry Prunières. Thus d'Indy and others were quick to associate the expressive strengths of Monteverdi's recitative with the new declamatory experiments of Debussy's *Pelléas et Mélisande* (1901). Yet the gains of the late nineteenth and early twentieth centuries also quickly made themselves felt in music histories. Romain Rolland's doctoral dissertation at the Sorbonne, *Les origines du théâtre lyrique moderne: l'histoire de l'opéra en Europe avant Lully et Scarlatti* (published in Paris in 1895) included a chapter on Monteverdi that focused mainly on biographical and aesthetic issues, and drew numerous comparisons with Wagner on the grounds that both composers shared a pioneering spirit in the face of narrow-minded critics, and a willingness to grant pre-eminence to the drama in opera. But Rolland does not yet give the impression of having had close experience of the music. Within twenty years, however, Hugo Leichtentritt's revised third edition (1909) of August Wilhelm Ambros's *Geschichte der Musik,* and Rolland's chapter on seventeenth-century Italy in the *Encyclopédie de la musique et dictionnaire du Conservatoire* (1914), could each contain full, sympathetic accounts of the scores of *Orfeo* and *L'incoron-*

5   The preface to the d'Indy edition (Paris, Bureau d'Edition de la 'Schola Cantorum', 1908) seeks to justify this focusing on 'les parties les plus belles et les plus intéressantes de l'oeuvre'. It also reveals that the initial transcription (from the Venice manuscript) was made by Mlle M. L. Pereyra, a student of the Schola Cantorum. The version is in three acts but just eight scenes.

azione, as well as other references to much of Monteverdi's writing for the stage. From that point on, to leave Monteverdi's operas out of the historical reckoning – as almost occurs in Jacques Handschin's *Musikgeschichte im Überblick* (1948) – starts to appear perverse.

The Italians had different battles to fight, both among themselves and against the rest of the operatic world. The position of Verdi, and his revolutionary credentials, were unassailable, but Puccini was a different matter: Fausto Torrefranca's vitriolic attack (*Giacomo Puccini e l'opera internazionale*, 1912) on Puccini's internationalism, and on his effeminate musical style sapping the masculine roots of a native Italian musical culture, was but the extreme of a range of reactions from the so-called Generazione dell'Ottanta against the frivolities of nineteenth-century Italian opera.[6] One response was a neo-classicism comparable to similar Renaissance revivals in all the arts. Not for nothing did the writer Gabriele d'Annunzio cite Dante, Michelangelo, Palestrina and Monteverdi as four of the greatest Italian artists; he also based a central episode of his novel *Il fuoco* (begun in 1896) around 'il divino Claudio' and a performance of the *Lamento d'Arianna*. Giacomo Orefice's edition of *Orfeo* for the Amici della Musica in Milan was given a concert performance there on 30 November 1909, and in Mantua on 5 April 1910 (it was also published in 1910). The rediscovery of Monteverdi's first opera seems to have made as much of an impact on writers in Italy as in France: the third (1910) edition of Alfredo Untersteiner's *Storia della musica*, one of the 'Manuali Hoepli' published in Milan, adds to the text of the first edition (1893) a discussion of the instrumentation and instrumental music of *Orfeo*. Orefice's edition also had surprising currency, being used for performances in New York (1912), Chicago (1913), Buenos Aires (1920) and Cairo (1928), as well as widely in Italy. It was only slightly better than d'Indy's in terms of its cuts (at least we get more of Act I) – much the same applies to Hans Erdmann-Guckel's edition for the Breslau (Wrocław) Stadttheater in 1913 – but it received a cogent scholarly critique from Gaetano Cesari in the *Rivista musicale italiana* (1910), and a younger composer of the Generazione dell' Ottanta, Gian Francesco Malipiero, rose to his challenge. Malipiero published a vocal score of *Orfeo* in London in 1923 (but the preface is dated 1920), and full scores of all the dramatic works – with a very different treatment of *Orfeo* – in his remarkable complete edition of the composer's works (1926–32, 1941–2). Each volume of the complete works is proclaimed 'Il Vittoriale degli Italiani', the series was supported by D'Annunzio, and nationalism had veered into the fascism of the age of Mussolini.

England and America each took a more genteel approach. The Orefice *Orfeo* was given a concert performance at the New York

---

6   See Wilson, 'Torrefranca vs. Puccini'.

Metropolitan Opera House on 14 April 1912, to general confusion over the archaic exercise. A performance of d'Indy's version of *Orfeo* in London at the Institut Français on 8 March 1924 preceded by some eighteen months the much more scholarly efforts of a twenty-year-old undergraduate at the University of Oxford, Jack Westrup, whose new edition of *Orfeo* received stage performances in Oxford on 7–9 December 1925, inaugurating the University Opera Society (later Opera Club). The success of the exercise was striking: H. C. Colles noted in *The Times* that 'There was no conscious archaicism. Monteverde was heard as on equal terms with the great musical dramatists from Purcell to Wagner and was proved to be of their company.' The university context is also significant: for much of the twentieth century UK and US university opera societies or the like actively encouraged new approaches to unknown works, while the scholarly environment prompted at least a modicum of restraint. Thus the first UK performance of *L'incoronazione di Poppea* was again at Oxford (6 December 1927), while for the US, the pioneering Werner Josten, professor of counterpoint and composition at Smith College, Massachusetts, directed *L'incoronazione* (27–8 April 1926, using d'Indy's edition), the *Combattimento di Tancredi e Clorinda* (12 May 1928, paired with Handel's *Serse*) and *Orfeo* (11 May 1929, again based on d'Indy, with Acts I and V missing and leaving time for Handel's dramatic cantata *Apollo e Dafne*).[7] The *Combattimento* was repeated in New York with the American stage première of Stravinsky's *Les noces* at the Metropolitan Opera House on 25 April 1929. Similarly, the first UK performance of *Il ritorno d'Ulisse in patria* was promoted by that institutional extension to Oxbridge, the BBC (it was broadcast on 16 January 1928), while *L'incoronazione* (in Redlich's edition) was directed by Michael Tippett at Morley College, London, on 17 May 1948. Here, outside the pressures of the commercial opera house, one could start to take the musical text for granted without rewriting it to suit modern taste, and the debate could then shift to matters of performance practice, chiefly whether to use modern instruments or some version of (or substitute for) older ones. It is no coincidence that it was a composer and scholar at Yale University, Paul Hindemith, who (as early as 1943) planned the first performance of *Orfeo* using original instruments garnered from museums and private collections; it eventually had its première at the 1954 Vienna Festival. In such scholarly environments, too, research and performance could benefit each from the other, as becomes clear in the distinguished work on Monteverdi by Hans Redlich from the 1930s onwards, and then Leo Schrade

---

7   I am most grateful to Richard Sherr for sending me a copy of *Baroque Opera at Smith College, 1926–1931: Record of a Pioneer Venture in Music; Monteverdi and Handel Operas as Performed under the Direction of Werner Josten* (New York, n.p., 1966), which is a remarkable collection of programmes and press-cuttings.

(with Hindemith at Yale), Anna Amalie Abert and Wolfgang Osthoff in the 1950s.

Malipiero, Hindemith and Tippett are just three of many prominent twentieth-century composers who succumbed to the fascination of Monteverdi: the list also includes Orff (whose involvement with *Orfeo*, the *Lamento d'Arianna* and the *Ballo delle ingrate* dated from 1923–5 and eventually led to the triptych *Lamenti* published in 1957), Respighi (*Orfeo*, 1935), Krenek (*L'incoronazione*, 1935), Dallapiccola (*Il ritorno*, 1942), Berio (*Combattimento*, 1966), Maderna (*Orfeo*, 1967), Henze (*Il ritorno*, 1982), Berio and collaborators (*Orfeo*, 1984) and Goehr (*Arianna*, 1995). In several cases, this engagement with Monteverdi was somehow linked to a period of creative experimentation or crisis. Many variously adapted the work, at first as a process of accommodation to taste, and later (and in particular, as 'scholarly' performances gained ground) as creative reinventions involving (re)composition, reorchestration and even, in Berio's case, a rock band and Hell's Angels. It is also symptomatic that Berio's outdoor version shared the 1984 Maggio Musicale (Florence) festival with an 'authentic' production of the opera (19 June 1984) by Roger Norrington and the dance specialist Kay Lawrence.

The fascination in particular of *Orfeo* was due no doubt to its totemic subject and also its emerging status as the 'first' great opera, while Dallapiccola and Henze were presumably attracted to *Il ritorno* because of its basis in universal myth. But Orff abandoned work on his proposed versions of *Il ritorno* and *L'incoronazione*, and in general, Monteverdi's Venetian operas, in particular *L'incoronazione*, did not always give rise to the same enthusiasm. Romain Rolland, d'Indy's assistant on the *Orfeo* project, may give one explanation in his review (1904) of the performance:[8]

> Our new school of composers might look for models and arguments here to support them in their conviction that there exists, that there must exist, a musical art superior to that which has been imposed on us for two centuries by a degenerate Italy and her pupil Germany: an art less solemn, less constrained, less subservient to the formalism of classical rhetoric, to the tyranny of the bar-line, to the conventions of a theatre of declaiming puppets; in their conviction, too, that the emancipation of music envisaged and desired by the impetuous nature of a Beethoven, or by the inspired ignorance of a Berlioz, is far from being accomplished, and that this dream of a freer, more human art is not a chimera; for, many centuries ago, the young and audacious genius of the Renaissance had, for a moment, achieved it. A moment so fleeting! Monteverdi himself does not seem

---

8 The relevant portion of Rolland's 'Chronique musicale' in *La revue d'art dramatique et musical*, 19 (1904), supplement, pp. 49–54, is translated by Wendy Perkins in *Claudio Monteverdi: 'Orfeo'*, ed. Whenham, pp. 119–25; for this extract, see pp. 123–4.

afterwards to have sought to press this revolution further. Just as we see him abandoning the large orchestra of *Orfeo* (36 instruments) and limiting himself in the *Ballo delle ingrate* of 1608 to a quartet of viols,[9] clavicembalo and chitarrone, and in the *Combattimento di Tancredi e Clorinda* of 1624 to a string quartet, clavicembalo and contrabasso da gamba, thus aiming at homogeneity, rather than richness of style, so, in his last opera, *L'incoronazione di Poppea* of 1642, he sacrifices freedom and musical beauty to beauty of line. Here we no longer have the impalpable texture of musical poetry that we admire in *Orfeo*. Here already we have the conventional grand structure of the classical Italo-German opera. Here we have beautiful arias, beautiful duos, fixed forms to which life must adapt whether it wishes to or not. All the genius in the world will try in vain to make these forms more flexible. From now on, the idea is adapted to the form, and not the form to the idea as the creators of Florentine opera had dreamed it should be.

Rolland here establishes a striking number of ideas that would be repeated in later writings on Monteverdi; indeed, his criticisms of *L'incoronazione* (he probably did not yet know *Il ritorno*) in terms of formalism, of too great an emphasis on melody at the expense of 'musical poetry', and of the domination of the aria, come close to Gary Tomlinson's in *Monteverdi and the End of the Renaissance* (1987).[10] Rolland's explanation for Monteverdi's 'failure' to pursue the revolution of *Orfeo* – the collapse of the Italian Renaissance under the oppressive strains of political and religious despotism – would also find its resonances in later scholarly accounts.

　　Rolland's main point, however, is that *L'incoronazione* is too much like a normal opera. It is surprising, therefore, that it has generated such a range of abnormal solutions on the part of performers who, one assumes, would decry or at least dismiss the composers' reinventions discussed above, yet are happy to bastardize the score by proclaiming some kind of fidelity to Monteverdi's intentions. One issue is the availability of the original sources to performers: as early as 1927, Adolf Sandberger argued in the preface to his facsimile of the 1609 edition of *Orfeo* (Augsburg, Benno Filser) that access to the sources was essential to avoid the misrepresentations of a d'Indy or an Orefice, yet to date there is still no facsimile of the Vienna manuscript of *Il ritorno* or the Naples one of *L'incoronazione*. Perhaps precisely because it was

---

9　For this oft-repeated error in the scoring of the instrumental music in the *Ballo delle ingrate*, see Chapter 6.

10　See, for example, Tomlinson's claim (p. 231) that 'Monteverdi rarely evaded the formalism of Badoaro's and Busenello's texts', and also his extended critique of Monteverdi's Venetian music in the context of Marinism. I engaged with some of the broader issues in my review in *Early Music History*, 8 (1988), 245–60.

printed in its time, mounting a decent performance of *Orfeo* has proven relatively straightforward, at least once one has found the singers, and the cornetts, sackbuts and a chitarrone or two instead of the oboes, clarinets, trumpets
and trombones commonly used before the 1960s (and still recommended in
Denis Stevens's edition of 1968). The score is reasonably complete, and the
main trend noticeable in performances from the 1980s onwards has been the
changing sound of the instruments (voices, on the other hand, have developed less, for obvious reasons). Even Raymond Leppard's *Orfeo* (1965, for
Sadler's Wells, London) was relatively 'pure'. But the same can rarely be said
for Monteverdi's Venetian operas. It is true that the musical sources for both
Il ritorno and *L'incoronazione* are problematic, with missing instrumental parts
and an air (at least in *L'incoronazione*) of work in progress. Yet what one
should do with these sources still remains a matter for debate. While many
Monteverdi enthusiasts of my generation will be grateful to Raymond
Leppard for his editions for the Glyndebourne Opera House of *L'incoronazione* (1962; published in 1966) and several Cavalli operas – it was how we
got to know (and some of us even first performed) these marvellous works
– his 1988 defence of his elaborate instrumental accompaniments (for the
London Philharmonic Orchestra), transpositions and cuts on the grounds both
of practical necessity and of some kind of fidelity to the spirit of the music
is much more problematic, and the still relatively widespread use of his edition
(or in Italy, of the similar travesty by Alberto Zedda) is indefensible, other
than as some kind of historical curiosity. Yet there remains a strong divide
between Continental European and Anglo-American traditions. Nikolaus
Harnoncourt, whose ground-breaking and reasonably 'authentic' Monteverdi
trilogy at the Zurich Opera (1975–9; produced by Jean-Pierre Ponnelle) was
subsequently widely toured, broadcast and recorded, remained ambivalent
even in 1984:

> In contrast to the all-too-liberal arrangers, there are those representing the
> opposite extreme: super purists who only want to realize the handed-down,
> skeletal score and reject any additions. This sort of loyalty to the work does
> not serve the intention of the composer, since it negates the presupposi-
> tions on which he based his work. It is just as incorrect to reveal only
> the 'skeleton' which was written down by Monteverdi as to cover it with
> inappropriate 'flesh' of a much later age – as frequently happens.[11]

The view remains common among some Continental performers, including
the estimable René Jacobs, who seems happy to mix music from different
decades by Monteverdi, Cavalli and Cesti, plus his own however stylish

---

11   In Barlow, 'The Revival of Monteverdi's Operas in the Twentieth Century', p. 198.

pastiche. Alan Curtis, on the other hand, prefers a more purist approach (in the preface to his 1989 edition of *L'incoronazione*, p. xii):

> It is high time, however, that the public be made aware of the historical facts (too often obscured by so-called musicologists), and that modern arrangements (whether or not for 'original' instruments) be no longer allowed to masquerade as 'realizations', or as having anything whatsoever to do with the composer's intentions. 17th-century opera scores are not 'sketches' in need of completion or 'skeletons' needing to be filled out. They are, in the majority of cases, full scores in need only of intelligent, sensitive editing and interpretation.

But often it seems that the argument is not so much one of fidelity to the spirit or intention of the composer as how to deal with various practical issues caused by the scale and scope of these works: there is a large theatre to fill, it does not pay to have the orchestra just sit with instruments in the lap, singers cannot be trusted to perform as actors (still less in a foreign language), and opera audiences expect musical display.

The Leppard revivals of the 1960s (he also did *Il ritorno* in 1979) coincided with a further burst of interest in Monteverdi on the part of scholars. Denis Arnold's 'Master Musicians' study of the composer (1963) preceded the quatercentenary celebrations in 1967, which generated a major conference moving between Cremona, Mantua and Venice, Denis Stevens's edition of *Orfeo*, the proposed launching of a new complete edition (the first volume appeared in 1970 but the series is still incomplete) and widespread performances of Monteverdi's works. Centenaries or their equivalents are always important staging posts in the reception-history of a composer; 1993, the 350th anniversary of Monteverdi's death, saw at least two major conferences (in Mantua and Detmold) plus, again, numerous performances, including a remarkable Utrecht Festival of Early Music that included almost all the secular chamber works and numerous others. That this was a time of rapid change in views on the composer is clear just from examining a single decade, the 1980s. This began with Iain Fenlon's archival study of *Music and Patronage in Sixteenth-Century Mantua* (1980), Denis Stevens's translation of the composer's letters (1980; revised 1995), Silke Leopold's *Monteverdi und seine Zeit* (1982; translated in 1991) and Nino Pirrotta's *Music and Theatre from Poliziano to Monteverdi* (1982; a translation of his *Li due Orfei* of 1969), passed through Ellen Rosand's key reading of *L'incoronazione di Poppea* (1985), Manfred Stattkus's definitive catalogue of Monteverdi's works (1985), Denis Arnold and Nigel Fortune's edition of *The New Monteverdi Companion* (1985), John Whenham's 'Cambridge Opera Handbook' on *Orfeo* (1986) and Gary Tomlinson's *Monteverdi and the End of the Renaissance* (1987), and ended with Alan Curtis's '*La Poppea impasticciata* or, Who Wrote the Music to *L'incoronazione*

(1643)?', his edition of *L'incoronazione*, and last but by no means least, Susan McClary's critical–feminist 'Constructions of Gender in Monteverdi's Dramatic Music' (all 1989). Thus we enter the sphere of what has, for better or for worse, become known as the 'new musicology', the trends of which have come to animate much endeavour in the field.

But it is worth taking a step backwards, not to deny more recent musicologists their due – they will be cited often enough in the following pages – but, rather, to ground their and my concerns in different ways. The scholar who perhaps most moulded Monteverdi studies since even before the quatercentenary was the remarkable Italian Nino Pirrotta. In 1963, the same year as Arnold's monograph, Pirrotta presented a lecture at the Fondazione Cini in Venice; it was published in 1971. The title, shamelessly borrowed for this chapter, was 'Monteverdi e i problemi del melodramma'. His 'problems' were not grand aesthetic ones on a Wagnerian scale such as had preoccupied the late nineteenth and earlier twentieth centuries; nor was Pirrotta concerned directly with the pragmatics of performance in the manner of the post-war early music revival. Instead, he wanted to counteract the view that 'Monteverdi was not only the greatest musician of his time . . . but also the only one with an unerring ability to see through and beyond the prejudices and illusions of that period'. Pirrotta preferred 'not to believe in [Monteverdi's] infallibility and to love him for his mistakes no less than for his intuitions and successes'. Consequently, Pirrotta sought 'to explore three moments in Monteverdi's operatic activity to see how that activity was rooted in his time and shared some of its false illusions, and how in the greatest accomplishment of his art the shadow and bitterness of defeat were not lacking' (p. 235). In other words, Pirrotta wished to dispel any lingering Romantic vision of Monteverdi as a transcendental genius, and the related claim that opera as a genre emerged fully formed and perfect in his hands. Rather, he sought to place the composer and his work for the theatre squarely in the context of his life and times. Monteverdi was a working musician, subject to the whim of his employers and the vagaries of fashion, and his operas, for all their undoubted status as masterpieces, were the product of artistic struggle where problems were exposed and not always solved.

Pirrotta's notions of struggle and even defeat problematized the early history of opera in ways akin to Rolland in 1904. But the issues he covers are more localized and grounded in their context, and for him opera is less a universal art-form than the product of specific circumstance. Pirrotta's three 'moments' in the composer's operatic activity concern *Orfeo*, *Arianna* and *L'incoronazione*; not unusually even for the 1960s, he seems to have had a blind spot when it came to *Il ritorno*. In the case of *Orfeo*, Pirrotta is anxious to demonstrate its close relationship to a work without doubt known by Monteverdi and his librettist Alessandro Striggio, *Euridice*, with text by Ottavio

Rinuccini and music by Jacopo Peri, staged in Florence in October 1600 for the festivities celebrating the wedding of Maria de' Medici and Henri IV of France, and the first 'opera' to survive complete. The Rinuccini–Peri *Euridice* does not always come off worse in the comparison. But the 'failure' in *Orfeo* lies in the last act, with its two different endings. The first, in the librettos printed for the first performances of the opera in 1607, concerns Orfeo's renunciation of women on his return from Hades, having failed the test to bring his beloved Euridice from the Underworld; Orfeo then encounters the Bacchantes who, it is implied, cause his death. The second, contained in the musical score printed in 1609, has Orfeo rescued from his despair by the god Apollo descending from the heavens, whither they both return in triumphal apotheosis. Pirrotta was uncertain which ending came first in the conception of the opera – he changed his mind at least once[12] – but either way he was inclined to see the Bacchante finale as a 'failed attempt on Monteverdi's part to rebel against both the conventions of the pastorale and the even more imperious exigencies of court life' (pp. 244–5). Thus the Apollo finale showed Monteverdi forced to succumb to courtly taste and to the need for princely glorification.

    Arianna, for the festivities celebrating the wedding of Prince Francesco Gonzaga and Margherita of Savoy in Mantua in May–June 1608, was also subject to revision at the behest of the court; Rinuccini's libretto was reviewed by the Duchess of Mantua and found to be 'quite dry' (*assai sciutta*), at which point the poet agreed to 'enrich it with some action' (Pirrotta suggests as additions the scenes involving the gods at the beginning and the end of the opera). Despite, or perhaps because of, this interference, *Arianna* was by all accounts a huge success, and its central lament for the protagonist reportedly moved the ladies in the audience to tears. Whether or not this description was just a conventional rhetorical topos, the *Lamento d'Arianna* became a totemic example of the new recitative style, copied and imitated across Italy and beyond; not for nothing is it the only part of the opera to survive. But according to Pirrotta, *Arianna* 'must have left in the artist's soul the bitter stamp of defeat' (p. 247). In part this was for personal reasons: the death in early March 1608 of Monteverdi's pupil Caterina Martinelli, intended for the role of Arianna, coming soon after the death of the composer's wife (on 10 September 1607), must have cast a pall over the opera, added to which was Monteverdi's overwork for the Mantuan festivities and his increasing sense

---

12   In 'Monteverdi and the Problems of Opera' (pp. 244–5), Pirrotta has the Bacchante ending replaced by the Apollo one; in 'Theatre, Sets, and Music in Monteverdi's Operas', first published in 1968, he suggests the reverse (p. 258) because of the presumed lack of space in the original theatre for the appropriate stage machinery for Apollo.

of frustration at being undervalued by his employers. But the 'failure' of *Arianna*, in Pirrotta's eyes, also lay in its genre – it was the first *tragedia in musica* – and in the constraints therefore placed upon the work. Although *Arianna* is more 'human' than *Orfeo*, tragedy required as its subject-matter 'the actions of public personages' rather than the 'personal vicissitudes of private persons'. The work's clichéd themes of love versus duty, and the conventional manner in which they are handled by way of messengers and choruses, produce a libretto that is 'prosaic' (Pirrotta uses the term three times in close succession) and, in the end, uneventful. This, Pirrotta suggests, explains why Monteverdi never published the complete score of what in the end was his 'failed attempt' (p. 248).

L'incoronazione di Poppea fails for different reasons again. Unlike many previous or, indeed, later scholars, Pirrotta is not so concerned with the moral questions famously raised by an opera celebrating the illicit passion of Emperor Nero for his mistress, the scheming Poppaea, and one dripping with decadence and sex. He suggests that in the magical world of Baroque opera as it was emerging in Rome and Venice, one should not expect moral probity, for all the importance of the character of Seneca in *L'incoronazione* as a proponent of reason (significantly, he dies less than half-way through the work). Nor should one expect such opera to adhere to conventional canons of verisimilitude when wonder, delight and *meraviglia* were the order of the day. Pirrotta is particularly concerned with the emergence of aria in this period as a natural expressive force, despite its seeming illogicality. Whereas the early composers (and theorists) of opera had sought to establish the recitative style as a verisimilar representation of heightened, rhetorical speech, music as music had won out because of what Pirrotta calls a 'rising wave of lyricism' used to project the rush of feeling (p. 250). Here the contrast with Rolland's view, given above, is quite striking. For Pirrotta, the 'overflowing expansion of vocal melody' in *Poppea* grows from 'the psychological "excitement" of the heart, from the ardor of passion that overflows the bonds of language'. It is the fact that *L'incoronazione* is 'a study of characters dominated by passion' that makes it a 'unique, isolated example of a true historical opera' (pp. 252–3). The 'failure' is that Monteverdi's contemporaries did not grasp its full significance: characters in later Baroque opera are 'convenient marionettes', clinging both to canons of verisimilitude and to the habit of convention to justify the use of song, rather than musical speech, on the stage.

Pirrotta's unalloyed pleasure in the sensual and musical delights of Monteverdi's last opera, and his palpable regret, if perhaps secret delight, that no one managed to repeat the experiment, strikes a refreshing note in contrast to the more Puritan ethic apparent in most scholars' attempts to deal with *L'incoronazione*. It also exposes a number of broader issues concerning the developing role of music in support of drama. Only in an aside on Act

IV of *Orfeo*, however, does Pirrotta start to articulate the problem. With reference to Orfeo's second loss of Euridice in the Underworld, Pirrotta notes what he perceives as the musical and dramatic weakness of Monteverdi's representation: 'From the very beginning [of opera] the law is established that only in the very rarest of cases does opera succeed in expressing action musically, not just the aura of affective reactions that accompany action' (p. 244). Pirrotta must have held this view as somehow axiomatic: he repeated it in another essay of 1968 with reference to Monteverdi's *Combattimento di Tancredi e Clorinda*, which he claims is more (if still not entirely) successful than contemporary operas, 'which almost never succeeded in representing the actions of characters as effectively as their affective reactions'.[13] The seeming dichotomy can easily be resolved: on the whole, and as Pirrotta's remarks on *L'incoronazione* suggest, within opera affective reaction is itself the action. Yet this and other of Pirrotta's problems raise crucial questions about what opera might have sought to do in the early seventeenth century, and what we construe it as doing now. That is one reason for the present book.

---

13   Pirrotta, 'Monteverdi's Poetic Choices', p. 289.

2

Music on the late Renaissance stage

How might one best construct a historical account of early opera? A useful example is provided by the Florentine composer Marco da Gagliano, who in October 1608 published his opera *Dafne* (Florence, Cristofano Marescotti), performed earlier that year during Carnival in Mantua. The dedication to Duke Vincenzo Gonzaga is conventional puffery, but the preface is more unusual, offering a detailed discussion of the work and its performance, and also a brief history of a new genre. According to Gagliano, the idea for the first operas came from the poet Ottavio Rinuccini who, after 'having time and time again discussed the manner used by the ancients in representing their tragedies', produced a libretto treating the mythological tale of Apollo and Daphne. This was in part set to music by the Florentine patron Jacopo Corsi, a 'lover of all learning and particularly of music', before the composer Jacopo Peri was brought in on the venture. Peri, 'most skilled in counterpoint and a singer of extreme exquisiteness', completed the score to Corsi's satisfaction, and *Dafne* was performed during Carnival 1597–8 in the presence of leading members of the Florentine nobility: 'The pleasure and wonder that this new spectacle produced in the spirits of the listeners cannot be expressed: suffice it to say that on the many occasions on which it has been performed, it has generated the same admiration and the same delight.'

Rinuccini, says Gagliano, was encouraged by this first venture, and 'having come to realize by such an experiment how apt song was to express all kinds of emotions and that not only . . . did it not lead to boredom but to incredible delight', he set to working on a new libretto, *Euridice*, designed by Corsi for the festivities celebrating the wedding of Maria de' Medici and Henri IV of France in Florence in October 1600. Here Peri 'discovered that artful manner of sung speech which all Italy admires', although only those who have heard him perform the role of Orfeo will comprehend 'the gentility and force of his arias, since he gives them such a grace and in a way impresses upon others the emotion of those words, that one is forced to weep and to grow happy according to his wishes'. Among the audience at the 1600 wedding was the Duke of Mantua, who, impressed by *Euridice*, decided to have an opera to a text by Rinuccini performed at the wedding festivities for his son, Prince Francesco, and Margherita of Savoy in Mantua in May–June 1608. For that opera, *Arianna*, Monteverdi 'composed the arias in so exquisite a way that one can truly affirm that the excellence of ancient music was revived, since he visibly moved the whole theatre to tears'. Thus Gagliano concludes his survey: 'Such is the origin of the representations in music, a spectacle truly of princes and moreover most pleasing to all, as that in which is united every noble delight, such as the invention and disposition of the tale, sententiousness, style, sweetness of rhyme, art of music, concertos of voices and instruments, exquisiteness of song, grace of dance and of gesture.' Add to that painting (for the scenery) and costume, and opera combines 'the most delightful arts which human wit has discovered'.

Gagliano writes with the enthusiasm of a neophyte, although between his lines one can detect a number of anxieties about the new genre. The comparisons with ancient theatrical practice, and also with the reputed power of ancient music to arouse powerful and extreme emotions, may just be conventional Humanist rhetoric, but they also seek to validate an entirely modern venture, and therefore one of dubious theoretical status. The priority granted the poet Rinuccini emphasizes that opera has a literary seriousness, while the repeated references to noble patrons are an obvious strategy to claim the aristocratic high ground. Gagliano also seeks to undercut common criticisms made of early opera: some might have thought it boring but Peri proved otherwise; these works may not look much on the printed page but they have a powerful effect when performed by virtuoso singers; there is more to opera than just singing, given its unique conflation of all the arts.

Gagliano's chronology comes close to modern textbook accounts of the 'invention' of opera in Florence, particularly the priority granted to Rinuccini as poet, Corsi as patron and Peri as singer–composer. It is, of course, incomplete. The omission of Monteverdi's *Orfeo* of 1607 is striking, although there is no real reason why Gagliano should have known (of) the work. There is no mention of Peri's arch-rival, the Florentine tenor Giulio Caccini, who had intervened in the performance of Peri's *Euridice* in October 1600 by having his singers sing his own, rather than Peri's, music, and who beat Peri to the press with his score (although it was first performed complete only on 5 December 1602). Caccini may have been a pioneer of new forms of song for solo voice and continuo accompaniment – in particular in his collection *Le nuove musiche*, published in Florence in 1602 – but it seems that he was not to be given much credit in the history of opera. Also absent from Gagliano's account is Emilio de' Cavalieri, whose pastorals with music of the

1590s – *Il satiro* and *La disperatione di Fileno* (1590), *Il giuoco della cieca* (1595) – were felt, at least by Cavalieri himself, to have made some impact on emerging theatrical practices in Florence. Moreover, his 'sacred' (or perhaps better, 'moral') music–drama, the *Rappresentatione di Anima, et di Corpo*, was the first full-length opera to be performed (in Rome, February 1600) and published (by Niccolò Muti in Rome, September 1600). Gagliano's prejudices against Caccini reflect contemporary twists in Florentine musical politics: the musical Accademia degli Elevati, recently established (in 1607) by Gagliano, was under threat from a rival camp headed by Caccini, and further antagonisms were becoming apparent in Florence precisely at the time of the publication of *Dafne* because of competing claims for the music for the festivities celebrating the wedding of Prince Cosimo de' Medici and Maria Magdalena of Austria in October 1608. As for Cavalieri, he was history (he had died in 1602), and anyway, 'sacred' opera has always been left on the margins, as the fate of Agostino Agazzari's obscure *Eumelio*, performed in Rome in 1606, also reveals.

Some sixteenth-century precedents

Gagliano's agenda, and his claim for novelty, discouraged him from discussing the earlier musical practices of the Renaissance theatre that established the ground for both the theory and, still more, the practice of early opera. Music had been used in the theatre long before opera took the stage: it had a crucial role to play within the politics of splendour that lay at the heart of courtly endeavour. In the fifteenth and sixteenth centuries, the north Italian courts used well-established ways of articulating moments of princely celebration, and various forms of entertainment were available to the Renaissance court and academy. Tragedies and comedies, whether classical or classically inspired, gave vent to the Humanist-inspired emulation of ancient Greece and Rome that was so powerful a force in the Renaissance as a whole. Given the acknowledged place of music on the classical stage, these performances also allowed composers to emulate the renowned music of antiquity (hence Andrea Gabrieli's choruses for the translation of Sophocles' *Oedipus tyrannus* performed at the opening of Palladio's Teatro Olimpico in Vicenza in 1585). Pastoral plays, too, displayed the trappings of classical authority: important precedents were set by two entertainments from the late fifteenth century, Angelo Poliziano's *Fabula d'Orpheo* (Mantua, *c*1480) and Niccolò da Correggio's *Fabula di Cefalo* (Ferrara, 1487), and the trend was confirmed in Tasso's *Aminta* (1573) and, later, Guarini's *Il pastor fido*. But more important was the fact that the pastoral's celebration of the Age of Gold – an idyllic time of prosperity and peace – was readily susceptible to allegorical interpretation.

This made the genre a powerful tool in the hands of Renaissance princes and their propagandists.

More effective still as propaganda were the entr'acte entertainments known as *intermedi*, performed within spoken plays. What started life as a set of simple episodes more or less loosely linked to the main drama so as to provide relief from the action, to allow time to change scenery and to generate a sense of temporal perspective, was expanded and elevated by the Florentines to an art form where stage spectacle and propaganda came together in unique ways. The performance of a play with lavish *intermedi* became a particular feature of Medici wedding festivities, beginning with those for the marriage of Duke Cosimo de' Medici and Eleonora of Toledo in 1539, through those for the wedding of Grand Duke Ferdinando de' Medici and Christine of Lorraine in 1589, to the festivities for Prince Cosimo de' Medici and Maria Magdalena of Austria in 1608 and beyond (and thus until well after opera took to the stage). They normally drew their subject-matter from mythology, with or without coherent plots; they always involved spectacular scenery – including heaven, sea, pastoral and underworld scenes – and stage machines; and they were invariably set entirely to music, so as to emphasize the magical stage-effects (and also to cover the noise of the machinery).

The Medici had strong reasons for using the theatre in so political a way: their absolute power as Dukes (from 1569, Grand Dukes) of Tuscany had only recently been consolidated, and any Italian state had to negotiate complex political and other relationships between the main European superpowers of Spain, France and the Holy Roman Empire. The point is clear from perhaps the greatest set of Florentine *intermedi*, those of 1589. Grand Duke (from 1587) Ferdinando de' Medici's intention was to emphasize a new start both to foreigners and to native Florentines, who liked the new Grand Duke as much as they hated his predecessor, his elder brother Francesco de' Medici. Ferdinando's marriage to Christine of Lorraine also marked the beginning of a shift in Medici foreign policies away from Spain towards France that would reach its culmination in the 1600 wedding of Maria de' Medici and Henri IV of France. The 1589 wedding had all the usual elements: the triumphal entry of the bride into the city; a sumptuous ceremony in the cathedral; banquets, balls and various indoor and outdoor entertainments, including spectacular jousts and tournaments; a naval battle in the flooded courtyard of the Pitti Palace; a *sacra rappresentazione*; and two performances of Girolamo Bargagli's play *La pellegrina*, with magnificent *intermedi* (the latter were repeated during a performance of another comedy, *La pazzia d'Isabella*, performed by Isabella Andreini and her *commedia dell'arte* company known as the Gelosi).[1]

---

1   Saslow, *The Medici Wedding of 1589*, discusses the events, with important literary and
    iconographical material.

The theme of the *intermedi*, devised by the prominent Florentine nobleman Giovanni de' Bardi, was the power of music, with all its potential for political allegory (the cosmic harmony of the spheres reflected in the harmony of the state): the third and fifth dealt specifically with the mythological musicians Apollo and Arion. To match the theme, the composers involved in the production produced a rich musical display.

Thus in the first *intermedio* ('The Harmony of the Spheres'), Harmony descends on a cloud in front of a blue backcloth representing the heavens, singing a solo song accompanied by lute ('Dalle più alte sfere'). The backcloth is raised to reveal the star-filled heavens, with the Sirens on four clouds ('Noi che cantando le celeste sfere', for two 4-voice choirs). During a 6-part sinfonia for lutes, viols, trombones, flute(s) and harps three large clouds appear, the central one containing Necessity with the three Fates, and the right and left clouds bearing the planets, while in the heights is seen a circle of heroes with a boy at their head. The boy, the Fates and the Sirens sing in dialogue ('Dolcissime Sirene' for two 6-voice choirs; 'A voi, reali amanti' for six 5-voice choirs), and then the Sirens ascend and all sing together a final 6-voice madrigal ('Coppia gentil d'avventurosi amanti'). So the entertainment continued to the final dance at the end of the sixth *intermedio*, the celebrated 'Ballo del Granduca', where the gods paid homage to Florence and its court in what became a prototypical example of a new genre, combining singing with dancing in elaborate choreography.

The desire, and need, to make a stunning visual and aural impact is clear right from the start in Armonia's opening song, delivered by the virtuoso soprano Vittoria Archilei. The text was by Bardi, and the music by either Emilio de' Cavalieri or Antonio Archilei (the attribution conflicts in different sources):[2]

Dalle più alte sfere	From the highest spheres
di celesti Sirene amica scorta,	as friendly escort to the heavenly Sirens,
son l'Armonia ch'a voi vengo,	I am Harmony who comes to you, o
o mortali;	mortals;
poscia che fino al ciel battendo l'ali	for the winged messenger has brought to heaven
l'alto fiamma n'apporta:	tidings of great import,
che mai sì nobil coppia il sol non vide,	that never has the sun seen so noble a pair

---

2   Although Cavalieri is more likely. Antonio Archilei, husband of the singer Vittoria, would conventionally have claimed authorship of music sung by his wife even if he was not in fact the composer; for a later example, see Carter, 'Intriguing Laments', p. 50 n. 37.

qual voi, nova Minerva e forte   as you, new Minerva and brave Alcides
    Alcide.   [Hercules].

The text is in the form of a conventional madrigal (free-rhyming *settenari* and *endecasillabi*), although the rhetoric is of a type that would soon be adopted in operatic prologues. Hence we find strong indicators of place ('Dalle più alte sfere') and character ('son l'Armonia'; the use of the first-person 'I' is typical), plus customary references to the audience ('voi . . . mortali') and to the noble patrons of the performance ('nova Minerva e forte Alcide', i.e., Christine of Lorraine and Grand Duke Ferdinando), much as in the prologue to Monteverdi's *Orfeo* (see Chapter 5). The music is highly ornamented (Ex. 2-1), thus establishing an association between virtuoso embellishment and supernatural power that becomes an operatic topos even in later periods. The audience must have been amazed by what it first saw and heard literally out of the blue.

The subject-matter of these entertainments, and likewise of the first operas, is significant. Like a good number of their successors through the cen-

Ex. 2-1 Emilio de' Cavalieri (or Antonio Archilei), 'Dalle più alte sfere' (*intermedio* 1, 1589), Armonia (voice and bass line only).

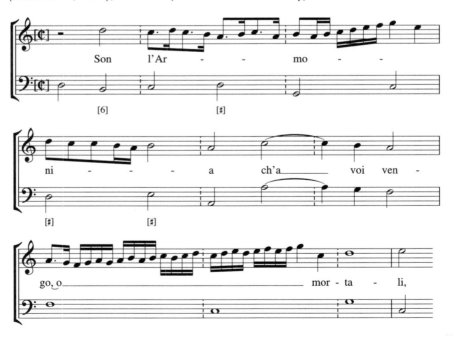

Les fêtes du mariage de Ferdinand de Médicis et de Christine de Lorraine, Florence 1589, ed. Walker, p. 4.

turies, the Florentines turned to classical myth both as a source of inspiration (it had long been thus for the Renaissance Humanists) and as an attempt to justify their new revelation of music's power: Apollo and Orpheus, the protagonists of the first operas, were renowned for their musical prowess. Such subjects could also counter the accusation that having characters sing, rather than speak, was essentially irrational: verse, not prose, and music, not speech, formed the natural language of the gods. But the use of myth also made early opera more than mere entertainment. Those involved in these works believed that they were making a powerful statement both about their times – when the arts had reached such a peak that Orpheus himself could be brought back to life – and about their princely patron, the Apollo/Sun-King around whom the political, social and cultural world revolved.

Peri's Euridice

Those in charge of the 1589 *intermedi* included Giovanni de' Bardi (he also wrote some of the words and music), the architect and scene designer Bernardo Buontalenti, the poet Ottavio Rinuccini, and Emilio de' Cavalieri, a Roman musician who had come to Florence with Ferdinando and was now court superintendent of the arts. Among the performers were Giulio Caccini and Jacopo Peri, each of whom also composed a solo song, as well as the young Alessandro Striggio (playing the viol), son of the Mantuan madrigalist (also Alessandro) and later to be the librettist of *Orfeo*. Funds for the performance were provided by a consortium of Florentine noblemen, including Jacopo Corsi, whose wealth generated by the silk industry and from banking, coupled with his own artistic interests, made him one of the most influential patrons in Florence towards the end of the century.

A good number of these individuals were variously involved in the experiments that led to the emergence of opera in the next decade. For example, Bardi headed the so-called 'Camerata', a group of artists and dilettantes who met in the 1570s and 1580s to discuss the state of the arts, particularly music. Their general dissatisfaction with the failure of modern music to achieve the emotional power attributed to music in Classical Antiquity provided an important impetus for the more practical experiments of the following decade. When Bardi left Florence for Rome in 1592, Corsi exploited his own position to use his patronage as part of a conscious strategy for family advancement, staging entertainments for the court and gaining significantly from the connections and other benefits that ensued. Rinuccini and Peri were closely associated with Corsi in business as well as in the arts, and their collective idea of applying music to drama in the reputed manner of performances of Greek tragedy seems to have taken root in the mid 1590s (Peri claimed 1594). The first result of their collaboration was *Dafne* – the subject-matter harks back to the third of the 1589 *intermedi* – which was given a relatively private performance in Corsi's palace probably in early 1598; it was repeated there before visitors from the court as a Carnival entertainment in 1599, and then performed once (perhaps twice) in 1600. The music, part of which was by Corsi, is almost entirely lost.[3] Then Corsi offered a second music-drama to the court for the celebrations of a wedding which he had played a considerable part in organizing, that of Maria de' Medici and Henri IV of France in October 1600: *Euridice* was performed in the Pitti Palace on 6 October, and Peri's score was published in Florence by Giorgio Marescotti in early 1601 (the dedication to Maria de' Medici is dated 6 February).

The musical style of these early operas owed some debt to the ideas of members of the Bardi circle. Its chief theorist, the lutenist Vincenzo Galilei, held strong views on the defects of the music of his time:

> Today the singing in harmony of many voices is considered the summit of perfection; among the ancients solo singing had this reputation. And if the singing of many together was also esteemed, it was the singing of one melody and not of so many. Today the quantity of consonances is greatly prized, and unisons are undervalued, while then the first were prized and the second deprecated. Today, touching many and diverse notes is in esteem; then, few and the same notes, and they did not use more notes in singing than in speaking, except enough to distinguish the two. Today many varied time-values are used, both slow and fast. Then there were used only the long and the short as is customary naturally in speaking, although I believe that instruments when played alone used more. Today runs of *gorgia* [= embellishments] and many other artifices are prized which the ancient, the better composers especially, preferring simplicity, deplored as lascivious and effeminate. Today by imitation of the words is understood not the complete thought and the meaning of the words and of the whole text, but the significance of the sound of one only. Today it is customary to repeat many times the same words, and verses are pronounced in singing in such a way that often one cannot distinguish them from prose. These repetitions were condemned by the ancients as impertinent . . . The music of the ancients, besides returning the infirm to health, tempered disordered appetites, while today our music with its lasciviousness corrupts and contaminates them. In great esteem today is canonic imitation, which, because of its interference with the comprehension of the words, it is obvious the ancients did not use in connection with words but rather in instruments when words were absent. Today one syllable is dragged under many notes.

---

3   What survives is transcribed in Porter, 'Peri and Corsi's *Dafne*'.

Each syllable of the ancients ordinarily only had one note, and rarely more than two, so that words could be articulated and heard with the greatest facility. The end of music today is nothing but the delight and pleasure of the senses. Among the ancients it was to move and dispose the soul to virtue.[4]

This diatribe against modern vocal polyphony (as heard in contemporary Masses, motets and madrigals) draws upon several strands of Renaissance Humanist thought on music and its ethical responsibilities that derive ultimately from Plato's *Republic*; no less typical are the gendered discourse (modern music is 'lascivious and effeminate') and the explicit preference for ancient practice that becomes enshrined in the major treatise to emerge from Bardi's Camerata, Galilei's *Dialogo della musica antica, et della moderna* (Florence, Giorgio Marescotti, 1581). But as Galilei well knew, the chief difficulty was to uncover precisely what ancient musical practice had been: it was extensively described in numerous classical sources, but no usable example of ancient music survived.

Perhaps inevitably, Jacopo Peri adopted a pragmatic solution to the problem, as he recounts in his preface to *Euridice*:

Seeing that it was a question of dramatic poetry and that therefore one should imitate with song him who speaks . . . I decided that the ancient Greeks and Romans (who, according to the opinion of many, sang their tragedies throughout on the stage) used a harmony which, going beyond that of ordinary speech, fell so short of the melody of song that it assumed an intermediate form . . . Therefore, rejecting every other type of singing heard up to now, I set myself to discovering the imitation necessary for these poems, and I decided that that type of voice assigned to singing by the ancients, which they called Diastematic (that is, sustained and suspended) could in part speed up and take an intermediate path between the suspended and slow movements of song and the fluent, rapid ones of speech, thus suiting my intention (just as they, too, adapted it in reading their poetry and epic verse), approaching the other [voice] of speech, which they called Continuous . . . Similarly, I realized that in our speech some words are intoned in such a manner that harmony can be founded upon them, and that while speaking we pass through many others which are not intoned, until we return to another capable of movement to a new consonance. Taking note of these manners and accents that serve us in grief, joy and similar states, I made the bass move in time to these, now faster,

---

4 Vincenzo Galilei, *Il primo libro della pratica del contrapunto intorno all'uso delle consonanze* (c1591), Florence, Biblioteca Nazionale Centrale, MS Ant. di Galileo 1, translated in Palisca, *The Beginnings of Baroque Music*, pp. 217–19.

now slower, according to the affection, and I held it firm through the dissonances and consonances until, passing through various notes, the voice of the speaker arrived at that which, being intoned in ordinary speech, opens the way to a new harmony. I did this not only so that the flow of the speech would not offend the ear (as if stumbling upon the repeated notes because of the more frequent chords) or that it might not seem in a way to dance to the movement of the bass, and especially in sad or serious subjects, since happier subjects require by their nature more frequent movements, but [I did this] also because the use of dissonances would either diminish or mask the advantage thereby gained because of the necessity of intoning every note, which the ancient musics perhaps had less need of doing. And therefore, although I would be reluctant to claim that this was the type of song used in Greek and Roman plays, nevertheless I have believed it to be the only type that our music can give us to suit our speech.

That final sentence undercuts the presumed antiquarian tendencies of early opera. Certainly Peri and Rinuccini, like Cavalieri, were anxious to associate their endeavours with the classical revival, but these Humanist overtones seem designed more to give a veneer of academic respectability to an essentially modern (and modernist) enterprise. Indeed, in the prologue to *Euridice*, the allegorical figure Tragedy admits that she is here not to sing of typically tragic events: instead, 'behold, I change my gloomy buskins and dark robes, and I awaken in hearts sweeter emotions' ('ecco i mesti coturni e i foschi panni / cangio, e desto ne i cor più dolci affetti'). Of course, this was entirely appropriate for the occasion of the performance, and for what must have been the same reason, Rinuccini modified the outcome of the myth, allowing Orfeo to lead Euridice successfully from Hades. Also, *Euridice* owes more to the pastoral than to classical tragedy – we are in the world of shepherds and shepherdesses in an Age of Gold – while its subject-matter also refers to the tradition of the Florentine *intermedi*, even if the staging was on a smaller scale and without elaborate machines.[5]

In his preface, Peri describes a declamatory style midway between speech and song, where rhythm and pitch contour follow some kind of 'natural' delivery of the text, while the rate of harmonic change (and therefore the bass movement) both matches the emotion and underpins the metrical stresses of the poetry. This more or less squares with his practice in *Dafne*, so far as we can tell, and in *Euridice*. However, his theoretical requirements are sometimes subverted by musical constraints. The Pastore's opening recitative in *Euridice* reveals the basic principles (Ex. 2-2). Here, the rhythmic and

5   On the staging and other issues, see Palisca, 'The First Performance of *Euridice*'.

Ex. 2-2 Jacopo Peri, *Euridice*, [scene 1], Pastore del Coro.

Peri, *Le musiche . . . sopra L'Euridice* (Florence, Giorgio Marescotti, 1600), pp. 2–3.

pitch accents (respectively, in italic and underlined in the text below), plus the harmonic repetitions or changes (working at the semibreve; marked in bold), all follow the accentuation of the text (in *versi piani*, as here, with the standard primary accent on the penultimate syllable). They also aid a 'rhetorical' delivery:[6]

> *Nin*-fe ch'i <u>bei</u> crin **d'o**-ro
> (Nymphs who fine hair of gold)

6   For a complementary reading of this passage, based on its relationship to actual speech-patterns, see Hill, 'Toward a Better Theory of Recitative'.

scio-glie-te *lie*-te̯al-lo scher-zar de **ven**-ti,
(loosen happily to the play of the winds,)
e *voi* ch'al-mo te-*so*-ro
(and you who the divine treasure)
den-tro chiu-*de*-te̯a bei ru-*bi*-ni̯ar-*den*-ti,
(close within fine, fiery ribbons,)
e *voi* ch'al-l'al-ba̯in *ciel* to-*glie*-te̯i *van*-ti,
(and you who from dawn in the heavens snatch the prize,)
tut-te ve-ni-te̯o pa-sto-*rel*-le̯a-*man*-*ti*.
(all come, o shepherdess-lovers.)

The two highest notes (*e'*) in the passage are on the first syllables of 'liete' and 'tutte', in both cases presumably for emphasis, while the high *d'* on 'ciel' ('heavens') is word-painting. Peri also manipulates the melodic contour, with its circling around *b* and gradual descent to the final cadence on *g*, to match the quite complex syntax comprising three vocatives ('Ninfe . . . , e voi . . . , e voi . . .') followed by an imperative ('tutte venite . . .'). As is appropriate, only the first and last lines start at the beginning of a bar; the others begin on an upbeat to match the accentuation. Peri holds the bass firm 'through the dissonances and consonances', changing harmony only at metrically or otherwise important words (chord repetition provides a subsidiary articulation). Harmonic change coincides with the main accent on the penultimate syllable of each line when such a syllable is contained within a noun ('d'oro', 'venti', 'tesoro', 'vanti') but not when within an adjective ('ardenti', 'amanti'; the latter is a noun in effect used adjectivally). Such penultimate accents should produce trochaic (long–short) endings to lines – which Peri achieves in the case of 'd'oro' and 'venti' – although there is an inherent tendency for them to become spondaic (long–long), as on 'tesoro' and 'vanti' (even if the singer taking a breath would shorten the second long), or even iambic (short–long). Peri sometimes seeks to avoid the problem, for example by eliding the melodic cadence on 'ardenti', but he cannot prevent the improper end-accent created by the final cadence on 'amanti'. Nor can he cope with Rinuccini's enjambment, although he sometimes tries to maintain the flow across lines. But none of these problems is unusual for composers setting *versi piani*, where the long–short line-endings tend to conflict with the weak–strong musical cadences. In terms of affect, the Pastore's speech is fairly 'happy', although the music certainly does not 'dance to the movement of the bass'; that would probably have required a different verse structure (see below). Nevertheless its relatively tuneful nature – which modern scholars would tend to call 'arioso' – serves well enough to underline the emotion.

Peri modifies the technique when it comes to 'sad or serious subjects', of which there are plenty in *Euridice*. Dafne's narration of Euridice's death is much less melodic, with its monotone opening, narrow range and static, sustained harmony (Ex. 2-3a), even if some might deem it (like the poetry) a little too leisurely for comfort. But while this beginning is fairly neutral in narrative terms, things change significantly at the moment of crisis (Euridice bitten by a snake; Ex. 2-3b), with a shift from *cantus mollis* (a 1-flat system) to *cantus durus* accompanied by a strong sharpward move, 6-3 chords, dissonances (a diminished fifth on 'fiori'; a minor seventh on 'dente'), complex harmonies, striking shifts (a major triad on G to one on E for 'punsele il piè') and awkward word-setting. This is quite intense in Peri's necessarily narrow terms – he only has one voice and the continuo – and he draws upon an expressive palette not so different from contemporary polyphonic madrigals. It is also striking that the rate of harmonic change speeds up, from one chord for two lines of text at the beginning (although this is not maintained consistently) to two or more chords per line. This is not 'dancing to the movement of the bass' by any means – the increasing harmonic rhythm is instead prompted by the need for a greater expressive intensity – but it does provide another example of a problematic match between theory and practice in response to intuitively musical concerns.

The passages from *Euridice* that do 'dance to the movement of the bass' are most often associated with portions of the libretto that use more structured verse. Rinuccini's libretto, as with most pastoral plays of the period, is mostly in *versi sciolti*, mixing *settenari* and *endecasillabi versi piani*, which may be loosely structured by rhyme but which are essentially free, except where some recurring refrain might bind together various sections of text. In some parts of his libretto, however, we find fixed verse forms and/or strophic structures that may also use other line-lengths such as *ottonari*, *quinari* and *quaternari* (see Table 2-1); these other line-lengths, and in particular *ottonari* and *quaternari*, are particularly associated with Rinuccini's contemporary, Gabriello Chiabrera, who in this period was developing their use for lyric canzonettas and *scherzi*. The fixed forms include the *terza rima* and the *ottava rima*, and also the strophic quatrains (normally ABBA) typical of operatic prologues. All these are normally set strophically (i.e., with the same music for each stanza) or by way of strophic variation, with more or less the same bass line, and therefore harmonic scheme, but with the melody altered to suit the changing text. The *ottava rima* may also be set strophically internally, splitting the eight lines of the stanza into two groups of four, or four groups of two.

As for the Chiabrera-derived 'canzonetta' structures, Rinuccini tends to reserve them for the end-of-'scene' choruses that divide his librettos into

Ex. 2-3 *Euridice*, [scene 2], Dafne.

Le musiche . . . sopra L'Euridice (1600), pp. 14–15.

[a] Through that delightful wood where watering the flowers slowly moves the spring of the laurels . . .

[b] when, ah harsh, bitter fate, a snake cruel and spiteful which lay hidden amid the flowers and the grass punctured her foot with so evil a tooth . . .

Table 2-1 'Structured' verse in early opera librettos

(End of scene/act choruses are given in italic. Scene numbers reflect divisions as follows: *Dafne*, 4 scenes by chorus (5 in 1608 version); *Euridice*, 5 scenes by chorus; *Arianna*, 8 scenes (Solerti).)

	Rinuccini, *Dafne* (1598; with additions in 1608)	Rinuccini, *Euridice* (1600)	Striggio, *Orfeo* (1607)	Rinuccini, *Arianna* (1608)
Terza rima	Scene 4, Apollo: 'Non curi la mia pianta, o fiamma, o gelo' (3 stanzas)	Scene 5, Orfeo: 'Gioite al canto mio, selve frondose' (2 stanzas)	Act III, Orfeo: 'Possente spirto e formidabil nume' (6 stanzas)	
Ottava rima	Scene 2, Amore: 'Chi da' lacci d'Amor vive disciolto' (1 stanza)		Act IV, Spirito, Altro spirito: 'O degli habitator de l'ombre eterne' (1 stanza)	
Other strophic: 11	Prologue, Ovidio: 'Da' fortunati campi, ove immortali' (ABBA; 7 stanzas)	Prologue, Tragedia: 'Io che d'alti sospir vaga e di pianti' (ABBA; 7 stanzas)	Prologue, Musica: 'Dal mio Permesso amato a voi ne vegno' (ABBA; 5 stanzas) Act III, Caronte: 'O tu ch'innanzi mort'a queste rive' (ABBA; 3 stanzas)	Prologue, Apollo: 'Io che ne l'alto a mio voler governo' (ABBA; 6 stanzas)
11 + 7	Scene 3, chorus: 'Non si nasconde in selva' (aabCdEe, with last line as refrain; 4 stanzas)	Scene 1, chorus: 'Al canto, al ballo, a l'ombra, al prato adorno' (AbbA; 4 stanzas, with 1st also acting as refrain)	Act III: 'Nulla impresa per huom si tenta in vano' (ABaBCddCEE; 3 stanzas (only 1 set in score))	Scene 2, chorus: 'Fiamme serene e pure' (aaBccB; 4 stanzas) Scene 4, chorus: 'Avventurose genti' (aBbAcC; 4 stanzas) Scene 5, chorus: 'Misera giovinetta' (abABCbCdD; 2 stanzas)

Table 2-1 *Continued*

	Rinuccini, *Dafne* (1598; with additions in 1608)	Rinuccini, *Euridice* (1600)	Striggio, *Orfeo* (1607)	Rinuccini, *Arianna* (1608)
11 + 5	Scene 2, Tirsi: 'Nel puro ardor de la più bella stella' (ABCDd^5, also with internal rhymes; 2 stanzas)			Scene 6, chorus: '*Su l'orride paludi*' (abbacc; 5 stanzas)
7		Scene 4, chorus: '*Poi che gli eterni imperi*' (ababcc; 5 stanzas)	Act II, Pastore, etc.: 'Mira ch'a se n'alletta' (abba; 6 stanzas)	Scene 2, chorus: 'Se d'Ismeno in su la riva' ($a^8b^8b^8a^8$; 3 stanzas)
8	[scene 1 (1608), chorus: 'Se lassù tra gli aurei chiostri' ($a^8b^8a^8b^{8e}$; 4 stanzas, with last 2 lines of 1st acting as additional refrain)] Scene 1, chorus: '*Almo dio, che 'l carro ardente*' ($a^8b^8c^8a^8b^8c^8$; 4 stanzas) Scene 2, chorus: '*Nudo arcier, che l'arco tendi*' ($a^8b^8b^8a^8c^8c^8$; 5 stanzas)	Scene 2, chorus: '*Cruda morte, ahi pur potesti*' ($a^8b^8a^8b^8$; 7 stanzas, with last 2 lines of 1st also acting as additional refrain) Scene 3, chorus: '*Se de' boschi i verdi onori*' ($a^8b^8c^8a^8b^8c^8$; 3 stanzas)	Act II, Orfeo: 'Ecco pur ch'a voi ritorno' ($a^8b^8b^8a^8$; 1 stanza) Act II, Orfeo: 'Vi ricorda, o boschi ombrosi' ($a^8b^8b^8a^8$; 4 stanzas) Act V (score), chorus: '*Vanne Orfeo felice a pieno*' ($a^8b^8a^8b^8c^8c^8$; 2 stanzas)	Scene 3: '*Stampa il ciel con l'auree piante*' ($a^8b^8b^8a^8$; 7 stanzas, with 1st also acting as refrain)

8 + 4	Scene 4, chorus: *'Bella ninfa fuggitiva'* ($a^8a^4b^8c^8c^4b^8$. 8 stanzas)	Scene 5, chorus: *'Biondo arcier, che d'alto monte'* ($a^8a^4b^8c^8c^4b^8$; 8 stanzas)		Scene 8, chorus: 'Spiega omai, giocondo nume' ($a^8a^4b^8c^8c^4b^8$; 2 stanzas)
5 + 7			Act I, chorus: 'Lasciate i monti' ($a^5a^5b^7c^5c^5b^7$; 3 stanzas)	
irregular		Scene 4, Orfeo: 'Funeste piaggie, ombrosi orridi campi' ('Lagrimate al mio pianto, ombre d'inferno' appears 3 times)	Act IV, Orfeo: 'Qual honor di te fia degno' (a^8baB; 3 stanzas) [end of Act V (libretto), chorus: *'Evohè, padre Lieo'* ($a^8a^4b^8b^8a^8cc$; 5 statements of 1 stanza during scene)]	
Versi sciolti with refrain	[Scene 4 (1608), chorus: *'Piangete, ninfe, e con voi pianga Amore'* (appears 5 times)]	Act I, Pastore: 'In questo lieto e fortunato giorno' (1st 5 lines come back at end of speech) Act II, Messaggera: 'Ahi caso acerbo, ahi fat'empio e crudele' (text appears 5 times in act) Act III, Orfeo: 'Ahi sventurato amante' ('Rendetemi il mio ben, Tartarei numi' appears twice)		Scene 6, Arianna: 'Lasciatemi morire' ('Lasciatemi morire' and 'O Teseo, o Teseo mio' appear variously)

sections (four in *Dafne* and a classical five in *Euridice*) in the absence of formal act or scene divisions.[7] Here Rinuccini follows contemporary theorists such as Angelo Ingegneri in his *Della poesia rappresentativa & del modo di rappresentare le favole sceniche* (Ferrara, Vittorio Baldini, 1598):

> Choruses can also be given to pastorals and comedies, but not out of necessity, as in tragedies, for these two types of poetry imitate private actions which take place in the town and in the woods, with no-one else having knowledge of or curiosity in the events except those who take part in them . . . Therefore, if choruses are to be placed in pastorals, it will not be enough, as some are wont to do, to place the word 'Choro' at the end of each act and provide a canzone for them to sing. Rather, it will be best to find an opportunity to introduce them into the action, such as, for example, festivities, weddings, dances, games, outdoor pastimes, amusements or other entertainments . . . Once these choruses have been introduced at a suitable occasion, they can be either stable or mobile, as the very occasion demands, and can intervene to speak with the actors or not . . . The author will do well if, wanting a chorus in his play, he handles it in such a manner that it enters and leaves realistically, and even better if he makes it divide the acts with short and charming *canzone* . . .[8]

Thus Rinuccini's structured end-of-'act' *canzone* or canzonettas distinguish the *coro stabile* (the stable chorus), which responds to and comments on what has occurred, from the *coro mobile* (the mobile chorus; but it may be the same individuals) that participates in the action either collectively or by way of singular representatives (a nymph, a shepherd, etc.). The shorter line-lengths and regular accentuation produce repetitive musical rhythms and hence structured melodies: particularly characteristic are the triple-time hemiola patterns associated with *ottonari* and *quaternari* that can, in turn, become associated with dancing, as with 'Biondo arcier, che d'alto monte' at the end of *Euridice*, which embraces a *ballo* (Ex. 2-4).[9]

7   Solerti's editions of *Dafne* and *Euridice* (in *Gli albori del melodramma*, ii, pp. 75–99, 115–42) divide them each into six scenes on the basis of the entrance of new characters, but a division by choruses is more appropriate; it is also usually reinforced typographically in the early prints of these works by decorated or otherwise distinguished initials. The expanded version of *Dafne* set by Gagliano (1608) has an additional end-of-'scene' chorus, producing the standard 5-part division.

8   In Carter, *Jacopo Peri*, pp. 142–3.

9   The original time-signature (**C**) and barring (marked by slashes above the stave in Ex. 2-4) every four or eight minims (rather than in groups of three) is entirely typical for this period, given that barlines do not generally indicate metrical stress; see Aldrich, *Rhythm in Seventeenth-Century Italian Monody*, *passim*. There may be implications for tempo, since 'properly' barred triple times were perhaps taken faster.

Ex. 2-4 *Euridice*, [scene 5], chorus.

Le musiche . . . sopra L'Euridice (1600), p. 50.

Blonde archer who from the high mountain a golden spring [lets forth . . .]

Structured verse outside prologues and end-of-'scene' choruses has more interesting implications. It is nearly always associated with some kind of formal song, be it one that acts diegetically within the action (i.e., the character actually sings) or one that is plausible in certain conventional circumstances: a god is singing; a moral precept is presented; the occasion prompts a generic association (a song of celebration, or a lament). This of course raises the problem of verisimilitude that perennially bedevils opera: even if one can accept musical recitative as a representation of heightened speech, and therefore appropriate on the stage, song is another matter altogether, given that singing, rather than musically 'speaking', is inherently inverisimilar except under special circumstances. Rinuccini's librettos reveal both the technique and the anxieties. In *Dafne*, Apollo's *terza rima* 'Non curi la mia pianta, o fiamma, o gelo' is a formal lament, while Amore's *ottava rima* 'Chi da' lacci d'Amor vive disciolto' is a moral precept.[10] In *Euridice*, Orfeo's *terza rima*, 'Gioite al canto mio, selve frondose', is sung by a mythical demigod (and also a famed musician) and is cued almost diegetically in the text ('Rejoice in my *song*, leafy woods . . .'); Tirsi's 'Nel puro ardor de la più bella stella' is implicitly established as a diegetic song (a shepherd sings at the celebration of a wedding), although Rinuccini seems uncomfortable enough over the situation to provide a text in ambiguous *endecasillabi* (subdivided by internal rhymes), apart from a final *quinario*. Three out of four of these passages (the exception is Apollo's lament) are set musically in triple time, the conventional signifier of 'song' even at this early stage in opera's history. However, *endecasillabi* are not well suited to triple-time setting because of the placing of the internal accents, as Orfeo's rather ungainly 'Gioite al canto mio, selve frondose' reveals (Ex. 2-5; compare the easier setting of *ottonari* in Ex. 2-4). Song also tends to require text repetition, which in turn needs some facilitation by the librettist: in the case of Orfeo's song, the appeal to Echo permits the repetition of the final line.

Song may be a threat to verisimilitude, but it is also a *sine qua non* of opera: there always comes a point where speaking (whether musically or not) shifts to singing, and that point is usually one of heightened emotional expression. So powerful is the impulse, and so embedded is it within the genre, that composers may even have to overrule the librettist to give way to it. Towards the end of *Euridice*, the shepherd Aminta rushes in to announce the safe return from Hades of Orfeo with Euridice (Ex. 2-6):

Non più, non più lamenti,	No more, no more laments,
dolcissime compagne,	sweetest companions,
non fia che più si lagne	let no one complain further
di dolorosa sorte,	of grievous fate,
di fortuna o di morte: il nostro Orfeo,	of fortune or of death: our Orfeo,
il nostro semideo,	our demigod,
tutto lieto e giocondo	all happy and glad
di dolcezza e di gioia	of sweetness and of joy,
nuota in un mar che non ha riva o fondo.	swims in a sea which has neither shore nor bottom.

This text is in *versi sciolti*, albeit with short lines and recurring rhymes (it is, in effect, a poetic madrigal: abbcDdefE). Peri, however, sets the opening in a clearly accented (if not barred) triple time that then shifts to duple, to *tripla*

10   For the allocation of this *ottava rima* stanza to either Venere or Amore, see Reiner, 'La vag'Angioletta', pp. 44–7. However, Amore seems more likely; see Carter, *Jacopo Peri*, p. 140 n. 6.

Ex. 2-5 *Euridice*, [scene 5], Orfeo.

Le musiche . . . sopra L'Euridice (Florence, 1600), pp. 46–7.

Rejoice in my song, leafy woods; rejoice beloved hills and everything around. Let Echo resound from the hidden valleys.

Ex. 2-6 *Euridice*, [scene 5], Aminta.

Le musiche . . . sopra L'Euridice (1600), p. 42.

(for word-painting on 'Tutto lieto e giocondo') and then back to duple. This is hardly a diegetic song; but it is an inherently musical moment.

Other entertainments in Mantua and Florence

Monteverdi may have been in Florence for the 1600 festivities as part of the retinue of Duke Vincenzo Gonzaga; certainly Alessandro Striggio the younger was there.[11] And even if neither of them saw the rehearsals or small-scale per-

11   For Striggio and perhaps Monteverdi in Florence in 1600, see Carter, 'Artusi,
     Monteverdi and the Poetics of Modern Music', p. 179 n. 14.

formance of *Euridice*, they undoubtedly had access to the printed libretto and musical score that appeared shortly after; this much, at least, is clear from the echoes of *Euridice* in their *Orfeo*. But Monteverdi's own stage experience prior to *Orfeo* was far broader, in large part thanks to Mantua's rich theatrical traditions. Vincenzo Gonzaga's father, Duke Guglielmo, not quite the ascetic Counter-Reformation zealot that some believe, made considerable headway in establishing a permanent theatre, and permanent players, in the city. He was aided not least by the activities and initiative of Leone de' Sommi as playwright and *corago* ('director' comes closest in English, but the term embraces the creative management of all aspects of a production). In a letter to Pietro Martire Cornacchia of 6 July 1567, Luigi Rogna gives some sense of Mantua's theatrical life:

> The crowd of people of all kinds gained every day by one and the other of these two troupes of comedians is unbelievable. Consider, Your Lordship, that the artisans [*artisti*] and the Jews leave their work aside to go and hear them, nor does one pay less than half a *reale* per person. The gentlemen stand there the whole day, and some of the lord officials, such as the Lord Steward [*il signor massaro*] and some of the Lord Masters of the Receipts [*signori maestri dell'entrate*], also go there. I leave aside speaking of the gentlewomen, for whom are reserved the windows and certain other places.[12]

Rogna refers to the presence of two *commedia dell'arte* troupes, to the wide range of social and other classes permitted attendance at theatrical entertainments (but to the restrictions placed on women), and to seemingly mixed modes of production and finance combining courtly patronage (however defined) with a paying audience. For the most part, these characteristics persisted throughout the reign of Duke Vincenzo, reinforced by his own special, personal interest in the stage. Although the court theatre within the Palazzo Ducale built by Giovan Battista Bertani in 1549 had burnt down in 1588, it was rebuilt at least partially by 1591 and then gradually remodelled, reaching completion in time for the grand performances of Guarini's *Il pastor fido* in 1598. Duke Vincenzo also created a taut infrastructure of artists and artisans, carefully managed by court functionaries (Federico Follino), architects and stage designers (Antonio Maria Viani, Gabriele Bertazzolo), and secretaries and sometime librettists (Alessandro Striggio and Ercole Marigliani (or Marliani)) to serve his apparent love of spectacle. As with the Medici, the Gonzagas exploited the theatre within the so-called politics of prestige – not least, to impress foreign visitors – and also as an instrument of social control in

---

12 Mantua, Archivio di Stato, Archivio Gonzaga, *busta* 2577, fol. 23r, in Buratelli, *Spettacoli di corte a Mantova tra Cinque e Seicento*, p. 181.

repressive political and religious times: the issue takes on a particularly hard edge in the case of the regular performances at Carnival by members of the Jewish community, which was in effect held to ransom to provide financial and other support for entertainments in return for more liberal treatment in the ghetto. In addition, Duke Vincenzo forged close relationships with *commedia dell'arte* players, including Tristano Martinelli (Arlecchino) and Pier Maria Cecchini (Fritellino), plus Giovanni Battista Andreini (Lelio) and his wife Virginia (Florinda), whose various companies could be 'lent' to other courts in Italy and abroad (Paris, Vienna) if the time and price were right (often they were not) or if there was diplomatic advantage to be gained. Their careers variously intersected with Monteverdi's throughout his life, and often in fruitful ways.

Archival records in both Florence and Mantua offer surprisingly little information on the day-to-day matters of staging even the grandest court entertainments:[13] presumably things usually ran smoothly enough not to have to become a matter of record (and conversely, documents destined to be stored in archives tend often to note particular problems or crises). Thus one usually has to seek oblique evidence for the kinds of issues that must regularly have been handled by the court artists as a normal part of their jobs. For example, the playright Muzio Manfredi was unusually fussy in writing to the singer, lutenist and dancer Isacco Massarani ('Isacchino hebreo') on 19 November 1591 concerning the potential staging at court of his play *Semiramis*. Massarani, a castrato in court service since about 1580, deserves significant recognition for his role in establishing particular patterns for sung and danced entertainments in Mantua, and he probably did not welcome Manfredi's advice:

In the [*favola*] *boschereccia* that have I sent to your Lord Duke, the four canzonettas of the chorus are without doubt sung, but they are also danced. And since it will be your job to create the dances, I tell you that the first should have little movement and no gesture; the second, little movement as well, but some small gesture of desire; the third has to be like the second, but varied in terms of its sections [*purché variato di partite*]; the fourth should have somewhat greater movement than the others, and gestures of grief and scorn. At the end there is a fairly lively *moresca*, done with spears and darts; and I say 'fairly lively', and not too much so, given the concern one should have for the nymphs. The final dance of Hymen is lively in terms of movement and gesture, and not very slow. I know that you are a capable man, and so I will not tell you any more.

13 An exception is the 1589 Florentine *intermedi*, where the *provveditore delle fortezze*, Girolamo Seriacopi, who was in charge of the practicalities of the staging, kept quite detailed notes; see Matteini, *L'officina delle nuvole*.

Nor, one suspects, did the distinguished composer Giaches de Wert welcome a similar letter sent the next day:

> Just as I write to Messer Leone [de' Sommi] and Messer Isacchino, giving the one some instruction concerning the costumes and the other concerning the dances, thus I beg Your Lordship that the songs [*canti*] of the four canzonettas of the chorus should follow their affects, and should be so free of fugal artifice [*e siano tanto sinceri d'artificio fugato*] that the words should not be lost in terms of their understanding, noting that all the chorus should sing, now together, now in two groups, correspondingly in the stanzas and in the refrains, and always dancing and with several instruments. As for the dance of Hymen, even though it should have a great noise of voices and instruments, I would be grateful if even its words could be understood, and likewise those of the madrigal in praise of the goddess, even if, given that this is to be done without any instrument, it might have some brief little imitation [*alcuna brieve fughetta*] because of its joyfulness.[14]

Both Massarani and Wert were involved in the extensive preparations that dominated Mantuan theatrical activity in the 1590s, the repeated attempts to stage Guarini's *Il pastor fido*. Guarini's pastoral play was controversial because of its mixing of genres and general rule-breaking: it created an academic scandal in several ways similar to the Artusi–Monteverdi controversy of the same period. *Il pastor fido* was also notoriously difficult to stage. Written in the 1580s, it had been mooted for performance during the 1589 Florentine wedding festivities but was dropped, and then taken up by Vincenzo Gonzaga, who sought unsuccessfully to mount a production for Carnival 1591–2 – then in June 1592 and in mid-1593 – with music by Wert and Francesco Rovigo.[15] Particular performance difficulties seem to have been caused by the sung and danced *Giuoco della cieca* in Act III which, like Cavalieri's 1589 *ballo* 'O che nuovo miracolo', had been devised in the unusual order choreography–music–text. Other problems included the boy playing Amarilli having his voice break at a crucial stage in the rehearsals, causing a frantic search for a

---

14   These letters (in Archivio Gonzaga, *busta* 2231, unfoliated) are in Buratelli, *Spettacoli di corte a Mantova tra Cinque e Seicento*, pp. 159, 176 n. 84.
15   However, the Carnival 1591–2 celebrations were disrupted by the death of Cardinal Gian Vincenzo Gonzaga on 22 December 1591. For these various attempts to stage a play that Vincenzo Gonzaga had wanted to perform since at least 1584, see Ancona, *Origini del teatro italiano*, ii, pp. 537–75. This supersedes Rossi, *Battista Guarini ed 'Il pastor fido'*, pp. 223–35, although Rossi's appendix does provide Guarini's accounts of the two sets of *intermedi* summarized below. The Mantuan productions are also discussed in Fenlon, *Music and Patronage in Sixteenth-Century Mantua*, i, pp. 146–57.

replacement. Eventually, there were three performances of the play in 1598: one towards the end of June, one in early September (for the visit of Juan Fernandez de Velasco, Governor of Milan); and the last on Sunday 22 November in honour of Margaret of Austria, whose marriage to Philip III of Spain had just been celebrated in Ferrara:

> The morrow after being Sunday, the 22. of Nouember [1598] there was done nothing except at night: about 5. of the clocke there was vpon a great round Theater (wherein euery one might stand) played an excellent Comedy, which dured from the said fiue of the clocke vntill 3. houres after midnight, without any one beeing wearied with seeing or hearing, for the great singularities of inexplicable artifices which were shewed in the same: which vnto all seemed so admirable, so rare and so excellent, that in the iudgements of them all, it should seeme impossible, (as long as the world shal stand) to represent a Comedy more excellent and pleasant, where (ouer and aboue the said artifices and admirable rarieties,) there was betweene euery enterlude, heard most rare musicke of many partes, with diuers instruments, accompanied with angelical & delicate voyces, insomuch that it seemed rather a diuine, the[n] humane thing, or at least wise, that the voices of heauen had intermixed themselues with the entire perfection of that of men, and the spirits of this age. Being in fine a thing so rare, that it is impossible to set the same in writing, except the author therof, or the inuentor of the artifices should doe it himselfe: The said comedy, besides the castle of artificial fireworkes, and besides the triumphall arkes which were in good number excellent well made, and ouer and aboue the present of the litter, did cost aboue 25000. crownes of gold . . .[16]

The details of the three 1598 performances remain hazy, although it is clear that there was music in the play (for the *Giuoco della cieca*, by Giovanni Giacomo Gastoldi)[17] and also between the acts. We have notes by Guarini himself for two different sets of four *intermedi* (between the five acts) for his play, at least one of which may have been used in Mantua in 1598. The first, which Guarini originally designed for the 1591–2 production, was probably adopted for the performance in September 1598: the theme is the music of (respectively) the earth, sea, air and heavens, reflecting the harmony of the four elements. The second set (we do not know if or when they were

---

16   Anon., *A Briefe Discourse of the Voyage and Entrance of the Queene of Spaine into Italy* (London, n.p., n.d.), p. 10. According to the title-page, the text is translated from the French and Dutch by 'H.W'.

17   Gastoldi's setting of the *Giuoco della cieca* was published in his *Il quarto libro de madrigali a cinque voci* (Venice, Ricciardo Amadino, 1602), headed 'rappresentato alla Regina di Spagna nel Pastor fido'; the first two sections are in Newcomb, *The Madrigal at Ferrara*, ii, pp. 22–30.

performed) is more conventionally mythological, with a prologue for Hymen, the first two *intermedi* dealing with the fall and rise of Phaeton, the third with the Muses, and the last the appearance of the gods. Guarini's prescriptions for these *intermedi* are remarkably precise in terms of scenery, costume and, in particular, music (although none survives): he knew his business, and like any *corago*, he would have expected his instructions to be followed by the Mantuan musicians. Thus his notes for the first set specify: (*intermedio* 1) music for four nymphs (who take the soprano and tenor parts), two satyrs (bass) and four women who play string instruments; (2) a double-chorus of marine nymphs and sirens, who sing and/or play soft wind instruments (muted cornetts, recorders, dulcians, a German fife); (3) 8-part instrumental music performed by the four chief winds (each playing a 'trombone squarciato') and the four collaterals (cornetts); (4) the seven planets each playing their respective instruments, while a large number of backstage voices and instruments produce a very full sound ('desiderando io che questa sia pienissima musica et concerto numeroso'). The second set has: (*intermedio* 1) a solo madrigal ('Se pur è tuo voler, Giove, e mia colpa') sung by an unnamed woman (Ovid's earth-goddess? – compare *Metamorphoses*, II); (2) a madrigal ('Sorgi, Fetonte, homai, sorgi del sole') sung by five nymphs, plus (it seems) another madrigal sung by the nymphs with backstage instrumental accompaniment; (3) the Muses miming to backstage instrumental music; (4) a madrigal ('Vieni, gloria del Tebro [?Hebro]') sung by six nymphs, to which the backstage instruments responded, making a very full concert of voices and instruments ('un concerto di voci et di stromenti pienissimo').

The November 1598 performance of *Il pastor fido*, however, had a different set of *intermedi* depicting the wedding of Mercury and Philology, a thinly veiled allegory for Philip III and Margaret of Austria. As the curtain rose, the city of Mantua was seen, with Venus and the stars Hesperus and Julia in a cloud; they sang a madrigal to Margaret. Nymphs and shepherds then entered, and Mincio and Manto (and her son Ocno), representing the city of Mantua, rose from the waters. The scene then changed to reveal the Arcadian set of the play. The first *intermedio* was set in the Elysian Fields: Juno entered on an airborne chariot drawn by peacocks, and Iris announced the marriage of Mercury and Philology, with sixteen poets accompanying her song. The scene then changed to the Inferno, with the River Lethe and Charon on his boat, ferrying Pluto on his way to celebrate the wedding; Pluto then ascended to the heavens on a cloud, while the poets sang in praise of the bridal pair. In the second *intermedio*, an earthquake caused the scene to change to reveal clouds and sea. Four winds appeared, then Discord, angry for not having been invited to the wedding. A group of Indian fishermen invoked Venus to give them corals and pearls to present as wedding gifts. From the sea emerged Glaucus, tritons and other marine deities, and a large whale with a triton (playing a cornett) on its back, then Neptune in a chariot drawn by dolphins, who then rose to the heavens on a cloud. Similar underground rumblings marked the beginning of the third *intermedio*, a rugged mountain scene revealing Berecynthia, then, on his horse-drawn chariot in the air, Apollo, who summoned the Muses and praised Philology. All then ascended to the heavens, where the Graces sang and Jupiter embraced the bride. The fourth *intermedio*, set in a city, involved the appearance of the twelve months, and then Fame and Time discussing the happy event. The heavens opened to reveal the marriage pair and gods, with Peace on high, ending with a canzonetta in praise of the bride and groom. For the final *licenza*, all the gods appeared in the heavens, while on earth shepherds and corybants invoked Hymen in song and dance, ending with a *moresca*.[18]

The themes and stage effects here were to have some impact on future entertainments both in Florence and in Mantua. Thus we find a close relationship between them and Chiabrera's *Il rapimento di Cefalo* in the 1600 Florentine festivities, and also the *intermedi* accompanying Guarini's comedy *L'idropica* for the wedding of Prince Francesco Gonzaga and Margherita of Savoy in 1608. Presumably all the Mantuan musicians were on call for the 1598 performances; in 1593, Guarini had already warned Duke Vincenzo that his play and their *intermedi* required so large a number of singers and instrumentalists that some would have to be borrowed from Ferrara, Verona and Venice.[19] Given that Monteverdi was surely involved in the November performance of *Il pastor fido* and the other music offered during Margaret of Austria's visit to Mantua,[20] he is unlikely to have been in Ferrara, where

18   For the November 1598 *intermedi*, see Ancona, *Origini del teatro italiano*, ii, pp. 570–2, drawing on Neri, 'Gli "intermezzi" del "Pastor fido"', which in turn relays the account in Giovanni Battista Grillo, *Breve trattato di quanto successe alla maesta della regina D. Margarita d'Austria N.S. dalla città di Trento . . . sino alla città di Genova* (Naples, Costantino Vitale, 1604). Ancona reports that the texts of these *intermedi* can also be found in Gian Donato Lombardo da Bitonto ('Il Bitontino'), *Prati de' prologhi* (Vicenza, Heredi di Perin libraro, 1602), which I have not seen.

19   See Guarini's letter to the duke of 22 March 1593 in Ancona, *Origini del teatro italiano*, ii, p. 560: 'Ricordo all'*Altezza* Vostra che non habbiamo musici a bastanza, perché ci vanno concerti molti et vari et pieni, et molti chori et di voci et d'instrumenti, et che però bisognerà provvedere molto a buon hora per concertarli et esercitarli. Ferrara, Verona et Vinegia ne darà quanti saprà volere et desiderare . . .'.

20   In addition to his long account of the *intermedi* (*Breve trattato . . .* , pp. 41–56), Grillo describes other musical performances in Mantua, including on 20 November trombones and cornetts in the Piazza del Duomo and a motet for voices and instruments in several choirs in the cathedral (p. 37), on the 22nd a sung Mass (p. 41), and on the 23rd chamber music comprising 'various musical concertos, [with] voices and instruments' (p. 56: 'se ne ritornò a casa, dove sentì varij concerti di musiche, voci, & instrumenti, che di già erano stati preparati').

Margaret had stayed the week before, when performances of his madrigals at the house of Antonio Goretti prompted the first flurries of the Artusi–Monteverdi controversy. And certainly Guarini's play had an impact on Monteverdi's music: witness the large number of madrigals setting texts from *Il pastor fido* from this decade by him and other Mantuan composers, even if they were intended for performance in the chamber rather than the theatre.[21]

Although most of the entertainments discussed in this chapter were designed for special celebrations, they were replicated on a smaller scale in countless court festivities. Given, too, that such works served most to define the theatrical horizons of any librettist or composer in late Renaissance and early Baroque Italy, it is not surprising to find early 'operas' adopting features of the *intermedi* or incorporating elements of theatrical or even social dancing. The entertainments for the wedding of Henri IV and Maria de' Medici in Florence in 1600 are a case in point. The main theatrical work, staged on 9 October, was Gabriello Chiabrera's *Il rapimento di Cefalo*, with music in the main by Giulio Caccini (mostly lost, apart from some extracts included in Caccini's *Le nuove musiche* of 1602). Although *Il rapimento* was sung throughout and has a coherent dramatic thread – thus it is as much an opera as any other such work in this period – it embraced numerous elements of the *intermedio* tradition, including spectacular stage-effects (three different pastoral sets, one maritime, and two different versions of the heavens) and machines (the clouds came in for particular praise), monologues by mythological and allegorical figures, and florid musical song, while the whole concluded with a sung and danced *ballo*. Even *Euridice* was not performed as a self-contained entity; it was followed by two hours of social dancing.[22] Any theatrical composer or performer of this period had to be flexible, adaptable and ready to turn a hand to a range of different tasks. Not much changes in the theatre of later periods.

But the 1600 Florentine entertainments were not a success. Members of the audience pronounced the new recitative boring and 'like the chanting of the Passion', and Giovanni de' Bardi commented that the court artists 'should not have gone into tragic texts and objectionable subjects'. The wedding of Maria de' Medici and Henri IV was a considerable political coup, and presumably the Florentine court was keen to mark it with a new musicodramatic genre. But opera seems to have been fundamentally ill-suited to a

---

21 Tomlinson (*Monteverdi and the End of the Renaissance*, pp. 115–18) effectively demolishes the long-standing notion that Monteverdi's Book V *Pastor fido* settings were intended for, and used in, the 1598 performances of the play, although even he cannot resist the sense that they were somehow for the stage.

22 Palisca, 'The First Performance of *Euridice*', p. 437.

public ceremony intended to glorify the Medici in the national and international arena. Significantly, at the wedding of Prince Cosimo de' Medici to Maria Magdalena of Austria in 1608, the Florentines turned their back on opera and reverted to the traditional format of a comedy with *intermedi* (Michelangelo Buonarroti's *Il giudizio di Paride*) – the 1589 festivities were used as a model – wishing, they said, to avoid the mistakes made in 1600. The course of early opera's history did not run smooth. It also turned elsewhere.

3

Monteverdi and his librettists

One might plausibly write a history of opera on the basis not of its composers but, instead, of its librettists. Arguably, they were the driving force behind many of the genre's developments in subject-matter, plot and even structure, the last by virtue of close correlations between poetic and musical form that quickly became established through convention and accepted practice. Not for nothing did Marco da Gagliano grant priority to the poet Ottavio Rinuccini in his account of the invention of opera, while in the 1630s and 1640s, the Florentine theorist Giovanni Battista Doni went still further, awarding Rinuccini the prize for the musical achievements of Peri and even Monteverdi: without his eloquent verse, Doni argued (with a theorist's typical prejudice against practical musicians), these composers would have had little or no opportunity to make their mark. Relationships between composers and librettists have not always been smooth in the history of opera. But this is not to say that poets and musicians might not collaborate on their endeavours, or that the text and music of an opera could not involve the pooling of shared ideas. The issue here is not necessarily the aesthetic priority of text over music, for all that in some periods this was a matter of significant debate. Rather, it is simply a fact of operatic life that a composer usually cannot begin work on an opera until some kind of libretto has been written. If we are to understand Monteverdi's theatrical works, we would do well to start with their texts.

The need to acknowledge the role of the librettist is all the more acute for opera in the seventeenth, eighteenth and even early nineteenth centuries, when the poet not only came high in the hierarchy of the complex modes of production that defined the 'opera industry' but also often had a range of production responsibilities beyond just the text. For all that the poet–*corago* might delegate work to architects, painters, dancing-masters and musicians, he needed a thorough working knowledge of all aspects of stage practice. He was also the first point of contact in any theatrical endeavour.

Thus Monteverdi's letters reveal the composer negotiating with his librettists on both general and detailed matters of structure, content and performance; less often, and usually only in the case of last-minute crises, did he engage in such matters directly with his patrons.

In part, that was a matter of social hierarchy. Monteverdi's librettists either were of aristocratic rank or had positions granting them greater access to the ear of authority. Both Alessandro Striggio (?1573–1630) and Ercole Marigliani (also styled Marliani; c1580–1630) were secretaries in the Gonzaga court, with Striggio rising further within the court administration (by 1628 he was a chancellor); Ottavio Rinuccini (1562–1621) was a free-floating courtier in Florence and also at the court of Maria de' Medici in Paris; Giulio Strozzi (1583–1652) and Giacomo Badoaro (1602–54) would no doubt have regarded themselves as in or close to the Venetian upper class; and Giovanni Francesco Busenello (1598–1659), who trained as a lawyer in Padua, seems to have been a man of some wealth and therefore leisure. Striggio's father (also called Alessandro) was a musician, and Striggio himself appears to have had some skills as a performer which may have aided his association with Monteverdi. But none of these librettists would have regarded himself as a professional poet, or indeed a professional anything, given that their pre-capitalist societies had different notions of work, obligation, duty and reward. They might have regarded themselves more broadly as men of letters, and each was educated to the elevated level that granted participation in the stand-ard outlet for intellectual activity in this period, the academy. Thus Striggio was closely involved in the Mantuan Accademia degli Invaghiti (the forum in which Monteverdi's *Orfeo* was first performed), while Badoaro, Busenello and Strozzi were variously associated with the Accademia degli Incogniti, a group of some importance for emerging trends in Venetian 'public' opera. Similarly, apart from court festivity or other official celebration, it was the academy that provided the chief outlet for theatrical works that in turn took on many fea-tures of academic discourse and debate.

Some clues as to what Monteverdi expected of a good libretto can be found in his letters and in other documents, particularly after he had estab-lished his presence on, and experience of, the stage. His well-known dismis-sive comment on Scipione Agnelli's *Le nozze di Tetide* (in his letter of 9 December 1616) – '*Arianna* led me to a just lament, and *Orfeo* to a righteous prayer, but this play leads me I don't know to what end' – suggests that at least in the case of opera he wanted strong characters, powerful dramatic situa-tions and a clear sense of direction in the plot. One of the reasons he liked Giulio Strozzi's *La finta pazza Licori*, Monteverdi said, was because of its opportunities for sound-effects and of its fast-changing action that offered musical variety (see Chapter 8). But he had few hopes of Rinuccini's *Narciso*, given its unvaried casting (too many sopranos and tenors) and its 'sad and tragic' ending.[1] As for poets' responses to Monteverdi, the unknown librettist of *Le nozze d'Enea in Lavinia* prefaced his scenario with a long apologia for his text (chiefly on the grounds of its non-conformance to classical rules) that gives some glimpse of the way in which he had to arrange the plot and the verse to the composer's requirements. Thus 'changes of emotions, which always appear good in such poems, also greatly please our Signor Monteverde since he has the opportunity with emotional variety to show the wonders of his art'. Furthermore,

And thus to accommodate myself to the characters and to the emotions which must be expressed by them, I have availed myself of several poetic metres, such as to say giving *versi sdruccioli* to low characters, and the short and *verso tronco* to those who are angry, knowing well that the good Tuscan tragedians have not used other than the 7-, 11- and sometimes the 5-syllable line, even though, since the ancient Greeks and Romans in their tragedies used, in addition to the iamb, the trimeter, tetrameter and others, I do not know why at least the 6- and 8-syllable line should be prohibited to us; beyond which, musical tragedies are due that licence which the others performed simply [i.e., spoken] do not have. And if in such verses there is needed that lightness and majesty which I confess they lack, it is indeed [due to] this dearth of wit, but also shortness of time and a multiplicity of tasks, which have not allowed me apply the study necessary to find graceful and unusual words, and to consider the metaphors so that they should succeed in their proper proportion, contenting myself rather with producing a modest, low [style] than one too inflated, as modern practice tends in great part. Beyond which, if music requires lightness, it also seeks clarity since, using its divisions and partitions, with many metaphors and other figures one comes to render the sentiment obscure; for which reason I have avoided thoughts and conceits taken from the abstruse, and I have rather aimed for the emotions, as Signor Monteverde wishes, to please whom I have also changed and left aside many things from what I first wrote.

Giacomo Badoaro remarked of Monteverdi's setting of *Il ritorno d'Ulisse in patria* that he scarcely recognized the work as his.[2] And Monteverdi liked

---

1 For *Narciso*, see Monteverdi's letter of 7 May 1627. Rinuccini's libretto was probably written for Florence in 1608 with the intention of providing a showpiece for Giulio Caccini's *concerto di donne* (hence the predominance of sopranos); see Carter, 'Rediscovering *Il rapimento di Cefalo*'.
2 For Badoaro's dedication to Monteverdi of the libretto of *Il ritorno* (at least, the copy in Venice, Museo Civico Correr, MS Cicogna 564), see Osthoff, 'Zu den Quellen von Monteverdis "Ritorno di Ulisse in patria"', pp. 73–4. Rosand's reading (in 'The Bow of Ulysses', pp. 377–9) may exaggerate the conventional tropes of deference.

working with Giulio Strozzi not only because of the poet's enthusiasm for the composer but also (so he told Striggio on 20 June 1627) because he 'is a worthy subject, courteously and willingly following my ideas'; this is a 'convenience' which makes it 'very much easier' for Monteverdi to set his verse to music.

We also have little information on the working processes involved in bringing a libretto and its setting to fruition. Published sources – even those close to a given performance – always become influenced by the various agendas of publication, be they commemorative, eulogistic, descriptive or prescriptive. Thus they become increasingly detached from the events they seek to represent. For example, by the time Busenello's libretto for *L'incoronazione di Poppea* was included in an edition of his 'complete works' (*Delle hore ociose*, published in Venice in 1656), it was far removed from the handwritten text that the librettist must have presented to Monteverdi prior to composition; at the very least, Busenello would have recast his text for its new 'literary' environment, whether or not taking into account (or reacting against) what Monteverdi might have done to his verse in the music. Even manuscripts seemingly close to a production (and therefore in some sense 'working' texts) have a problematic relation with what might actually have been performed, as recent debates over the textual and musical sources for *L'incoronazione* reveal. At times there may be sufficient internal evidence within a source even at one or more stages removed from (the preparations for) a performance from which to draw some conclusions about actions that might have been undertaken in response to changing patronal demand, to problems of staging or casting, or even just to a perceived need for revision in pursuit of a more effective result: *Arianna* is a case in point. For the most part, however, the myriad of alterations and accommodations that must have been made as a performance approached have been erased from the record.

However, even the more polished surviving sources somehow have embedded within them the results of a wide range of activities that led to their production, be those activities (pre-)compositional, the outcome of rehearsal and performance, or a matter of subsequent deliberation. These works are the product of work by the constellation of artists and artisans involved in the complexities of contemporary modes of operatic production, and viewed in that light they become both less and more than masterpieces fixed for posterity. To decipher such corporate labour requires insight and imagination, true, but also a pragmatic, commonsensical approach to how the theatre might have operated in the early seventeenth century (not that different, one suspects, from how it operates now), an approach that has often been lacking in recent scholarship. One is also helped by an understanding of conventional generic and other procedures that became fixed remarkably early on in opera's history.

In terms of the libretto, we have already seen (in Chapter 2) how Rinuccini consolidated poetic conventions that have strong musical implications, with free-rhymed 11- and 7-syllable *versi sciolti* for recitative (sung speech) and more structured verse (using forms such as the *ottava rima* and *terza rima*, strophic patterns, other line-lengths, etc.) for 'songs', whether sung by an individual character or by the chorus. We have also seen that Peri 'overruled' his librettist (Aminta's 'Non più, non più lamenti') when it suited him to do so. Rinuccini's principles remain remarkably standard, for Italian librettos at least, through the nineteenth century and beyond (in effect, until poetry is replaced by prose): recitative is poetically free (to a greater or lesser extent), while songs, which would come to be called arias, are structured in various possible ways. The presence and dramatic function of song (rather than sung speech) may vary, at least until aria becomes a *sine qua non* of the genre. Thus Rinuccini's *Arianna* contains far fewer examples of structured verse (and almost none outside the end-of-scene choruses) than his *Dafne* and *Euridice* (see Table 2-1). Presumably this is because of questions of genre – Rinuccini designated *Arianna* a 'tragedia', the most serious of the theatrical genres – and also because the characters are, on the whole, mortals who have less justification to sing. But it may also reflect some initial uncertainty about the structures most appropriate for librettos. Gabriello Chiabrera's *Il rapimento di Cefalo* (1600), for example, contains remarkably little structured poetry, and its text is entirely in *settenari* and *endecasillabi*. This is ironic, given that from the late seventeenth century onwards, it was common to blame Chiabrera for the introduction of inappropriate canzonetta forms into what should be elevated verse.

There are few contemporary theoretical statements on the nature of theatrical poetry for music in early seventeenth-century Italy; presumably such verse was variously viewed either as beneath contempt or as undifferentiated by its rules from its spoken dramatic counterpart. And when such statements do begin to appear, the die had already been cast: the author of *Il corago* (*c*1630), for example, takes it for granted that opera librettos will contain canzonetta forms of various shapes and sizes, and indeed gives a lengthy series of examples covering a wide range of possibilities.[3] But of those directly involved in early Florentine opera, only Emilio de' Cavalieri (through his mouthpiece, Alessandro Guidotti) makes significant reference to the matter in the preface to his *Rappresentatione di Anima, et di Corpo*:

---

3   See *Il corago, o vero Alcune osservazioni per metter bene in scena le composizioni drammatiche* [Modena, Biblioteca Estense, γ.F.6.11], ed. Fabbri and Pompilio, pp. 70–9. A tradition has emerged of attributing *Il corago* (by a Florentine, it would seem) to Ottavio Rinuccini's son, Pierfrancesco, which is not implausible but appears to have little concrete justification.

The poem should not be more than 700 lines in length, and it is appropriate that it should be written in an easy style and full of short lines, not only 7-syllable ones but also those in five and eight syllables, and from time to time in *versi sdruccioli*. And having close-spaced rhymes, because of the beauty of the music, makes a graceful effect. And in the dialogues the statements and responses should not be very long, and the narratives of single characters should be as short as possible.

It is not clear whether this is written in response to, or as an implied criticism of, Rinuccini's *Euridice* (the dedication of the *Rappresentatione* is dated 3 September 1600), although presumably Cavalieri knew *Dafne* well enough. *Euridice* is longer (790 lines) than Cavalieri recommends (the first version of *Dafne*, at 445 lines, is shorter), it has more *endecasillabi* than he would presumably have liked (and certainly more than in the text of the *Rappresentatione*),[4] it does not contain *versi sdruccioli*, the rhymes are not always close-spaced (again, in contrast to the *Rappresentatione*), the dialogues are not short, and the narratives (for Dafne, Arcetro and Aminta) are very long indeed. Although Striggio drew extensively on Rinuccini's example when writing the libretto of *Orfeo*, he also seems to have shared Cavalieri's views: his libretto is about the right length (although it depends on which finale one chooses), he prefers *settenari* to *endecasillabi*, he has *quinari* and *ottonari* and also *versi sdruccioli* (at the end of Orfeo's lament in Act V), the dialogues are faster paced, and there is only one, relatively short, narration. There are also more opportunities for songs within the acts (again, see Table 2-1), particularly in the strophic sequences articulating the first half of Act II.

In *Orfeo* as in *Euridice*, however, the bulk of the business is carried out in *versi sciolti*, and with a particular rhetoric that reveals both the strengths and weaknesses of early opera as drama. Take Striggio's handling of Orfeo's passage from Hades, the moment in the libretto that, according to Pirrotta (see Chapter 1), proves his general law 'that only in the very rarest of cases does opera succeed in expressing action musically, not just the aura of affective reactions that accompany action'.[5] This is a key point in the opera, marking the abrupt transition between Orfeo at the height of his powers – he has just persuaded the gods of the Underworld to release Euridice – and his plunge from grace because of his inability to exercise the Humanist virtue of self-control: pride literally comes before a fall.

[Un spirito del coro]
Ecco il gentil cantore   7   Here is the gentle singer

4   The proportion of *endecasillabi* to *settenari* in *Dafne* is roughly 50/50, and in *Euridice* roughly 70/30; see Carter, *Jacopo Peri*, p. 161.
5   Pirrotta, 'Monteverdi and the Problems of Opera', p. 244.

	Italian		English
	che sua sposa conduce al ciel	11	who leads his bride to the sky
	superno.		above.

Orfeo

	Italian		English
	Qual honor di te fia degno	8	What honour is worthy of you,
	mia cetra onnipotente,	7	my all-powerful lyre,
5	s'hai nel Tartareo regno	7	if you in the Tartarean kingdom
	piegar potuto ogni	11	were able to soften every harsh
	indurata mente?		mind?
	Luogo havrai fra le più belle	8	You will have a place among the
			most beautiful
	imagini celesti,	7	celestial images,
	ond'al tuo suon le stelle	7	whence at your sound the stars
10	danzeranno co' gir'hor	11	will dance in steps now slow,
	tard'hor presti.		now fast.
	Io per te felice a pieno	8	Through you, I entirely happy
	vedrò l'amato volto,	7	will see my beloved's face,
	e nel candido seno	7	and within the white breast
	de la mia donn'oggi sarò	11	of my lady shall I today be
	raccolto.		gathered.
15	Ma mentre io canto, oimè,	11	But while I sing, alas who assures
	chi m'assicura		me
	ch'ella mi segua? ohimè	11	that she follows? Alas, who hides
	chi mi nasconde		from me
	de l'amate pupille il dolce	11	the sweet light of my beloved's
	lume?		eyes?
	Forse d'invidia punte	7	Perhaps struck by envy
	le dietà d'Averno	7	the gods of Avernus
20	perch'io non sia qua giù	11	so that I might not be wholly
	felice a pieno		happy above
	mi tolgono il mirarvi,	7	take from me the sight of you,
	luci beate e liete,	7	o blessed, happy eyes,
	che sol col sguardo altrui	11	which with just a glance can
	bear potete?		make another happy?
	Ma che temi mio core?	7	But what do you fear, my heart?
25	Ciò che vieta Pluton	11	That which Plutone forbids, Amor
	comanda Amore.		commands.
	A nume più possente	7	A god more powerful
	che vince huomini e dei	7	which defeats men and gods
	ben ubbidir dovrei.	7	should I indeed obey.
	Qui si fa strepito dietro la		*Here a noise is made off-stage.*
	tela.		
	Ma che odo, oimè, lasso?	7	But what do I hear, alas, alack?

30	S'arman forse a' miei danni	7	Armed perhaps to my disadvantage
	con tal furor le furie innamorate	11	with such fury are the enamoured Furies
	per rapirmi il mio ben, ed io 'l consento?	11	to snatch away my beloved from me, and do I allow it?
	Qui si volta Orfeo.		*Here Orfeo turns.*
	O dolcissimi lumi io pur vi veggio,	11	O sweetest eyes, I now see you,
	io pur . . . ma qual eclissi ohimè v'oscura?	11	I now . . . but what eclipse, alas, obscures you?

Un spirito

35	Rott'hai la legge, e se' di grazia indegno.	11	You have broken the law and are unworthy of grace.

Euridice

	Ahi vista troppo dolce e troppo amara:	11	Ah, sight too sweet and too bitter:
	così per troppo amor dunque mi perdi?	11	thus through too much love do you lose me?
	Et io misera perdo	7	And I, wretched, lose
	il poter più godere	7	the power to enjoy further
40	e di luce e di vita, e perdo insieme	11	both light and life, and also I lose
	te, d'ogni ben più caro, o mio consorte.	11	you, dearest above all things, o my husband.

Un spirito del coro

	Torn'a l'ombre di morte	7	Return to the shadows of death,
	infelice Euridice,	7	unhappy Euridice,
	né più sperar di riveder le stelle,	11	and hope no more to see again the stars,
45	ch'omai fia sordo a' preghi tuoi l'inferno.	11	for the Inferno will be forever deaf to your prayers.

Orfeo

	Dove te 'n vai mia vita? Ecco io ti seguo.	11	Where do you go, my life? Lo, I follow you.
	Ma chi me 'l nieg'ohimè: sogn'o vaneggio?	11	But who stops me: do I dream or imagine it?
	Qual occulto poter di questi orrori	11	What hidden power of these horrors
	da questi amati orrori	7	from these beloved horrors

50	mal mio grado mi tragge,	11	against my will drags me away
	e mi conduce		and leads me
	a l'odiosa luce?	7	to the hateful light?

The poetry is not Striggio's best: lines such as Euridice's 'e di luce e di vita, e perdo insieme / te, d'ogni ben più caro, o mio consorte' (ll. 40–1), or Orfeo's awkward repetition in 'questi orrori . . . amati orrori' (ll. 48–9; though I suspect that the latter may be a mistake in the source), are scarcely elegant, if that is a desirable quality. But the layout of the scene works well enough for musical purposes. The spirit announces the appearance of Orfeo leading his bride. The reference to 'gentil cantore' reminds us that Orfeo is a singer and therefore is entitled to sing a song, which he duly does – 'Qual honor di te fia degno' – praising his lyre (represented by the two violins in the instrumental ritornello preceding and separating the stanzas) and then joyfully anticipating his reunion with Euridice. This is an aria in the technical sense of a strophic setting of strophic poetry: Striggio provides three strophes, a^8baB (the opening *ottonario* is a further cue). It is also one in the stylistic sense of a tuneful melody over an active bass line, in the manner of the canzonettas of the 1607 *Scherzi musicali*.[6] But as Orfeo experiences his first doubts – that his singing (note the confirming reference 'io canto') has lulled him into a false sense of security – the text returns to the 7- and 11-syllable *versi sciolti* of recitative which continue to the end of the passage. Monteverdi responds accordingly (Ex. 3-1), setting the text in the recitative style with the music subordinate to the affective declamation of the words. Orfeo has explicitly moved from singing to 'speaking', and he, the spirits and Euridice remain speaking until the end.

But who is being addressed by whom? As Orfeo airs his mistrust of the Underworld deities, casts his lot in favour of a god more powerful than Plutone – Amor – and fatally misconstrues the off-stage noise (it is a warning to Orfeo, but he takes it as a threat to Euridice), he seems to be talking to himself out loud: the only second-person pronouns (tu/te, voi/vi) or verbs are those referring to his lyre, to Euridice's eyes, and to his heart. When Orfeo turns to gaze upon Euridice he addresses her 'dolcissimi lumi' (again), and as Euridice fades from view, she addresses him (although the bulk of her speech is concerned with 'io'), and then Orfeo her. But he does so for only one line, reverting to first- and third-person constructions as he describes the 'occulto

---

6   Strictly speaking, it is a strophic variation, with the melody varied (slightly) in each strophe over the same bass: these variations seem prompted by different patterns of accent in successive strophes, and also by the need to highlight, or even paint, specific words. The slight general awkwardness of the melody, with its irregular accentuation, may be due to the text's inclusion of *settenari* and an *endecasillabo*.

Ex. 3-1 *Orfeo*, IV, Orfeo.

Monteverdi, *L'Orfeo, favola in musica* (Venice, Ricciardo Amadino, 1609), p. 79.

poter' dragging him away from the scene. The spirits, too, direct their remarks to Orfeo only when absolutely necessary, preferring instead to make sententious pronouncements. For the most part, the characters on stage, if they speak at all (Plutone and Proserpina remain silent), seem hardly aware of each other.

There is a typical operatic paradox in this scene, that its most action-filled moments are marked by non-musical events (the off-stage noise; Orfeo turning back). But it cannot be the lack of action *per se* that concerns Pirrotta here: a fair amount happens in a relatively short space of time, and this action seems expressed musically in so far as such a thing is possible within a style that has limited semiotic (rather than just mimetic) powers. Thus Orfeo's song is halted by his recitative, and the latter is paced and structured in a manner close to heightened, if rather leisurely, declamation that also emphasizes appropriate words melodically (for example, the diminished fifths on 'oimè'). *Pace* Pirrotta, too, the scene contains strikingly little affective reaction: neither Orfeo nor Euridice has time to articulate a lengthy response to what has just happened (and later, there is no Gluckian 'Che farò senza Euridice' for Monteverdi). What might explain Pirrotta's comment, however, is the fact that often here (and for that matter, in much opera) the characters seem to act less as participants in the events on stage than as narrators of them. They do not so much interact dramatically or react affectively as provide comment, outlining and explaining their actions and reactions for the benefit of the audience. As they address themselves, so they address us, inviting us to contemplate their fate.

None of this is very different from contemporary spoken drama. In both cases, too, the inclusion of the audience may be a crucial part of the equation, explaining why, as Aristotle noted, the modes of epic and drama come close together, for all their structural differences in terms of content and technique. But the tendency to address objects (a lyre, eyes), while not foreign to drama or epic, also reflects the influence of lyric poetry – in particular in this case, it seems, that of Tasso – and it is the combination of lyric, epic and nascent dramatic techniques that give a work like *Orfeo* its characteristic flavour, to which we respond with a mixture of involvement and contemplation, the latter perhaps outweighing the former. Whether this is because of the nature of the genre and its mythological subject, or because of the types of musical styles operating within opera in its earliest stages, remains an issue for debate.

Orfeo sings because he is a musician; as many have noted, the choice of subject-matter of the first operas was a deliberate attempt to circumvent the problems of verisimilitude arising from the act of singing. But as the plots of later operas extended their reach through mythology, epic and history, the question of why characters should sing became both more acute and, by virtue of acceptance of the convention, less troublesome. The author of *Il corago* noted that 'If we take as characters people close to our times, and of manners more obviously similar to ours, all too clearly this manner of sung speech soon presents itself to us as improbable and not lifelike [*inverisimile*].' But Giacomo Badoaro was less concerned, if we are to believe the preface to his *Ulisse errante* (set by Francesco Sacrati in 1644):

> Today, no one worries, to increase the delight of the spectators, about giving way to something not lifelike, which does not damage the action. Thus we see that to give more time for the changes of scene, we have introduced music, in which we cannot avoid something not lifelike – that men should carry out their most important business in song. Moreover, so as to enjoy all kinds of music in the theatre, we are accustomed to hearing pieces for two, three and more voices: this produces something else not lifelike – that talking together men should without thinking happen to say the same things. Therefore it is no wonder that, devoting ourselves to pleasing modern taste, we have rightly moved away from the ancient rules.

Similarly, Francesco Sbarra admitted in the preface to his *Alessandro vincitor di se stesso* (1651):

I know that some people will consider the *ariette* sung by Alexander and Aristotle unfit for the dignity of such great characters . . . nevertheless it is not only permitted but even accepted with praise . . . If the recitative style were not mingled with such *scherzi*, it would give more annoyance than pleasure. Pardon me this licence, which I have taken only in order to make it less tiresome for you.[7]

Even at the outset of opera, the recitative style had been found tedious, and by the 1620s there were strong moves to find alternatives. But while the increasing confidence of librettists and composers in permitting song may have pandered to audience tastes, it also reflects the notion that music should be more than just a form of heightened speech. Thus there is a significant amount of structured verse in Giacomo Badoaro's libretto for *Il ritorno d'Ulisse in patria* and in Giovanni Francesco Busenello's for *L'incoronazione di Poppea* (see Table 3-1).[8] Not for nothing was Busenello acutely aware of the requirements of modern opera:

Since I must write, and have written, poetry which must be sung, and where the measures and metres, the endings and syllabifications have regard for music, the strophes, the antistrophes and the epodes of the Greeks do not come into consideration, one cannot decipher here the hymns of Orpheus, the idylls of Theocritus and of Anacreon, much less Pindaric odes and the like . . . and even granted that the poetry of the ancient Greeks was sung . . . that music was different from ours.[9]

---

7   These three passages are in Rosand, *Opera in Seventeenth-Century Venice*, pp. 428 (compare *Il corago*, ed. Fabbri and Pompilio, p. 63), 410, 421; Rosand also translates the latter two (pp. 44–5) amid a discussion (pp. 39–45) of the broader issues.

8   There is also a larger number of 1- or 2-line verbal refrains, and still more musical ones. But it is not always possible to tell whether these are the librettist's or the composer's. Rosand discusses Monteverdi's 'powerful brand of editing' in *Opera in Seventeenth-Century Venice*, pp. 250–6, although she and I disagree somewhat on various aspects of these librettos. For example, she claims that Badoaro is 'perhaps the most ascetic of all early Venetian librettists when it came to arias' (p. 250), and that Busenello's text is 'less conservative than Badoaro's' (p. 255). This is not borne out by Table 3-1 or, indeed, in the following discussion.

9   From the *Lettera scritta dal signor Gio. F. Busenello ad un suo virtuoso amico richiedendolo del suo parere intorno al di lui dramma 'La Statira'*, in Brizi, 'Teoria e prassi melodrammatica di G. F. Busenello e "L'incoronazione di Poppea"', p. 57: 'dovendo io scrivere et havendo scritto poesia che dev'esser cantata e che le misure e i numeri, le desinenze et le assillabazioni riguardano la musica, le strofe, le antistrofe e gl'epodi dei Greci qui non vengono in taglio, gl'Hinni d'Orfeo, gl'Idilli di Teocrito e d'Anacreonte qui dedur non si possono, molto meno le odi pindariche e altro simile . . . e posto anche che le poesie degli antichi Greci fossero cantate . . . altra era quella musica della nostra'.

Table 3-1 'Structured' verse in Monteverdi's settings of *Il ritorno d'Ulisse in patria* and *L'incoronazione di Poppea*

(Excludes occasional short lines or *versi tronchi* and *versi sdruccioli*, refrains, etc.)

	Badoaro, *Il ritorno d'Ulisse in patria* (1640); passages in square brackets not set in score	Busenello, *L'incoronazione di Poppea* (1643)
11		I.4, Arnalta: 'La pratica coi regi è perigliosa' (ABB; 5 stanzas)
		I.8, Pallade/Seneca: 'Seneca, io miro in cielo infausti rai' (ABBA; 2 stanzas; patterning continues in I.9)
11 + 7	I.12, Iro: 'Pastor d'armenti può' ($a^t b^t B^t c^s C^s$; 2 stanzas)	I.1, Ottone: 'Caro tetto amoroso' (aBB; 4 stanzas)
	[II.5, Pisandro: 'Tutta di pompa illustre' (abBcc; 3 stanzas, 1 for each of the Proci)]	1.11, Ottone/Poppea: 'Ad altri tocca in sorte' (aBaBCC; 7 stanzas)
	II.8, Proci: 'Han fatto l'opre nostre' (abB; 3 stanzas [plus additional 1 for Eurimaco])	II.5, Nerone: 'Son rubin preziosi' (aabbCC; 1 stanza)
	III.7, Nettuno: 'So ben quest'onde frigide' ($a^s a^s B^t$; 2 stanzas)	II.6, Ottone: 'Sprezzami quanto sai' (abB; 3 stanzas)
		II.8, Nutrice: 'Il giorno femminil' ($a^t B^t c^t c^t deE$; 2 stanzas)
		III.8, Nerone: 'Per capirli negl'occhi' ($ab^t cb^t DeD$; 1 stanza)
7	I.6, Feaci: 'In questo basso mondo' ($ab^t[=b^{4t}b^{4t}]c^t C^t$; 1 stanza)	II.10, Poppea: 'Or che Seneca è morto' ($ab^t ab^t$; 1 stanza; last 3 lines also recur later in scene)
	I.13, Eumete: 'Come lieto t'accoglio' ($ab^t ab^t c^t c^t$; 1 stanza)	II.10, Arnalta: 'Oblivion soave' (abb; 3 stanzas; a 4th stanza is implied but continues differently)
	III.7, Giunone: 'Ulisse troppo errò' ($a^t b^t b^t a^t$; 1 stanza)	
8	I.8, Minerva: 'Cara e lieta gioventù' ($a^8 b^{8t} b^8 a^{8t}$; 2 stanzas separated by speech for Ulisse)	I.5, Nutrice: 'Se Neron perso ha l'ingegno' ($a^8 b^8 a^8 b^8 CC$; 2 stanzas (2nd stanza interrupted by Ottavia); lines 3–4 of 2nd stanza ('Fa riflesso al mio discorso . . .') become refrain later in scene)
	I.10, Melanto: 'Ama dunque ché d'Amore' ($a^8 b^{8t} a^8 b^{8t}$; 1 stanza; also recurs as refrain in score, although libretto gives new text)	II.3, Famigliari: 'Questa vita è dolce troppo' ($a^8 b^8 a^8 b^8$; 2 stanzas, plus 2-line refrain ('Io per me morir non vò . . .') in *ottonari tronchi*)

Table 3-1   *Continued*

	Badoaro, *Il ritorno d'Ulisse in patria* (1640); passages in square brackets not set in score	Busenello, *L'incoronazione di Poppea* (1643)
	II.1, Eumete/Ulisse: 'Verdi spiagge, al lieto giorno' ($a^8b^8b^8a^8$; 1 stanza)	II.4, Valletto/Damigella: 'Sento un certo non so che' (whole scene mixes sestets and quatrains in *ottonari piani* and *tronchi*, ending in *senari*)
		III.8, Nerone/Poppea: 'Pur ti miro, pur ti godo' ($a^8a^8b^8b^8c^8c^8d^{8t}d^{8t}$; 1 stanza)
6	Prologue, Fortuna: 'Mia vita son voglie' ($a^6a^6b^6c^6d^6c^6$; 1 stanza)	II.4, Valletto/Damigella: 'O caro godiamo' ($a^6a^6b^6c^6b^6$; 1 stanza)
5 + 11	I.2, Melanto: 'Duri e penosi' ($a^5a^5b^{5t}c^5c^5b^{5t}DD$; 2 stanzas, with same last line)	II.10, Amore: 'O sciocchi, o frali' (a^5a^5BB; 4 stanzas)
	III.7, coro in cielo, coro marittimo, *tutti*: 'Giove amoroso' ($a^5a^5b^{5t}$ / $c^5c^5b^{5t}$ / DD)	
	III.10, Ulisse, Penelope, *a2*: 'Non si rammenti' ($a^5a^5b^{5t}$ / $c^5c^5b^{5t}$ / D^tD^t)	
5 + 7	II.1, Telemaco: 'Lieto cammino' (a^5b^5ab; 1 stanza)	
5	[I.3, nereids, sirens: 'Fermino i sibilli' ($a^{5s}b^{5s}c^{5t}$ / $d^{5s}d^{5s}c^{5t}$; continues in *senari doppi* and *quinari*)]	
	I.8, Ulisse/Minerva: 'Ninfe serbate' ($a^5b^5b^5a^5a^5$; 1 stanza)	
	II.1, Telemaco/Minerva: 'Gli dei possenti' ($a^5b^5a^5$; 1 stanza)	
	II.4, Eurimaco: 'Peni chi brama' ($a^5b^{5t}c^5b^{5t}$; 1 stanza)	
	[II.6, Moors: 'Dame in amor – belle e gentil' (2 5-line stanzas of *quinari tronchi doppi*)]	
	II.12, Pisandro: 'Com'intrattabile' ($a^{5s}a^{5s}b^{5t}c^{5s}c^{5s}b^{5t}$; 1 stanza)	
3 + 6	II.4, Eurimaco, Melanto: 'Godendo / ridendo' ($a^3a^3b^{6t}$; 2 stanzas)	

Here Busenello also hints at an expansion in the range and type of poetic techniques to prompt a more formal musical setting. As a result, the content of Table 3-1 is fairly approximate: it does not take account of the occasional brief appearance of shorter line-lengths (*quaternari, quinari, senari, ottonari*) or sequences of *versi sdruccioli* and *versi tronchi*, the latter even when quite extended.[10] Moreover, it does not reveal the tendency of Busenello, in particular, to structure seeming *versi sciolti* by parallelisms, especially between characters in a dialogue.[11] Finally, the table passes over some problematic cases. For example, it is difficult to classify a passage such as Amore's in the prologue of *L'incoronazione* (here *versi tronchi* and *sdruccioli* are marked with a superscript 't' or 's' respectively):

Che vi credete, o dee,	7	How can you believe, o goddesses,
divider fra di voi del mondo tutto	11	that you can divide between you
		of the whole world
la signoria e 'l governo,	7	the sovereignty and government,
escludendone Amore,	7	while excluding Amore,
nume ch'è d'ambe voi tanto	11	a power which is so much greater
maggiore?		than both of you?
Io le virtudi insegno,	7	I teach the virtues,
io le fortune dono,	7	I grant fortunes,
questa bambina età	7^t	this childish age
vince d'antichità	7^t	is older than
il Tempo e ogn'altro dio:	7	Time and every other god:
gemelli siam l'eternitade ed io.	11	eternity and I are twins.
Riveritemi,	4^s	Worship me,
adoratemi,	4^s	adore me,

10 Compare Poppea's concluding speech in III.5 ('Per te ben mio, non ho più cor in seno'), with four *settenari tronchi* within nine lines of *versi sciolti*, or Arnalta's at the end of III.7 ('Chi lascia le grandezze, / piangendo a morte va / ma chi servendo sta, / con piu felice sorte, / come fin degli stenti ama la morte'). A still more extended example, Ericlea's 'Ericlea, che vuoi far' (*Il ritorno*, III.8) is discussed in Rosand, *Opera in Seventeenth-Century Venice*, pp. 251–2 (and also in eadem, 'The Bow of Ulysses'). Rosand considers this (and a similar passage involving fewer *versi tronchi*, Ulisse's 'O fortunato Ulisse' in *Il ritorno*, I.9) a case where Monteverdi has edited Badoaro's text to provide greater opportunity for aria-structures involving triple time and refrains. There remains some question, however, of whether *versi tronchi* are not themselves sufficient (or at least, plausible) prompts for 'aria' independent of strophic or similar structures and other standard cues.

11 For example, in *L'incoronazione*, I.8, Pallade's four *endecasillabi*, rhyming ABBA, are matched by the immediately following four lines for Seneca. A similar technique operates in the following scene for Nerone and Seneca, giving their legalistic debate a poetic tautness that does much to flavour the scene.

| e di vostro sovrano il nome | 11^s | and grant me the title of your |
| datemi. | | sovereign. |

This text comprises mostly *versi sciolti*, although the end of each sentence is marked with a rhyming couplet. But towards the end we find *versi tronchi* (as Amore pronounces a maxim) and *versi sdruccioli* (a set of imperatives). These have quite strong musical implications. The weak–strong endings of *versi tronchi* are better suited to musical cadences than the strong–weak endings of *versi piani*. As for *versi sdruccioli*, their dactylic accentuation is very suggestive of triple time, as Monteverdi accepts (at 'Riveritemi'). The general fluidity here, however, helps explain, and perhaps even prompts, the fuzzy boundaries now adopted by Monteverdi and his Venetian contemporaries between shorter (and even longer) triple-time passages and surrounding recitative. Yet for all the difficulties, Table 3-1 still reveals some useful trends, especially in comparison with Table 2-1. Fixed forms such as the *ottava rima* and *terza rima* have disappeared, partly because they are by now old-fashioned, and partly because there are fewer diegetic songs (or the near equivalent) in these works. It is also noticeable that older metrical patterns (in particular, the Chiabreran 8-4-8-8-4-8) have been abandoned for a much wider range of structures. This variety both within and outside closed poetic forms is rich in musical possibilities, and since the bulk of these strophic and related texts is given to individual characters rather than (as with Rinuccini or Striggio) to a chorus, the consequence is inescapable: these librettos are designed to provide a significant number of formal arias, distinguished both poetically and musically.

In the case of *Il ritorno*, and in keeping with notions of decorum, arias are given to gods and allegorical figures (Fortuna, Giunone, Minerva, Nettuno), shepherds or otherwise 'lowly' characters (Eumete, Eurimaco, Melanto) and those who debase themselves by their actions (the Proci, Iro). In terms of those characters for whom aria might seem less appropriate, Telemaco, though noble, is a youth and so one might excuse his song. Apart from at the end of the opera, Ulisse sings in aria only with Minerva (a goddess) and Eumete (a shepherd), and for the most part only when he is in disguise; indeed, the fact that he sings in triple time enhances his disguise.[12] Penelope hardly ever sings in aria styles – as we shall see (in Chapter 9), there is a dramatic point to be made from this – except, again, towards the end. But within those limits Badoaro's libretto, at least in Monteverdi's redaction, is notable for the number of aria-like passages, the variety of their metres and forms, the emphasis on *versi tronchi*, and also, curiously, the number of single-stanza structures. Whether or not Monteverdi instructed his librettist in what was needed, he was himself 'instructed' quite precisely in terms of what

12   The point is Rosand's; see *Opera in Seventeenth-Century Venice*, pp. 120–1.

to do with his music, for all that he could make other choices when he wished.

Take the opening of the score's Act II. Here, the goddess Minerva brings Ulisse's son Telemaco back to Ithaca, riding through air on a divine chariot. They encounter the old shepherd Eumete accompanied by Ulisse (in disguise), Eumete greets Telemaco, heralding his return as a sign of renewed fortune, Eumete and Ulisse invoke nature, and Telemaco responds.

Telemaco

	Lieto cammino,	5	Happy journey,
	dolce viaggio,	5	sweet voyage,
	passa il carro divino	7	the divine chariot passes
	come che fosse un raggio.	7	as if it were a ray of light.

Minerva / Telemaco

5	Gli dei possenti	5	The powerful gods
	navigan l'aure,	5	navigate the breezes
	solcano i venti.	5	and plough the winds.

Minerva

	Eccoti giunto alle paterne ville,	11	Now you have reached your father's domains,
	Telemaco prudente.	7	prudent Telemaco.
10	Non ti scordar già mai de' miei consigli,	11	Never forget my counsels,
	ché se dal buon sentier travia la mente	11	for if your mind strays from the right path,
	incontrerai perigli.	7	you will encounter dangers.

Telemaco

	Periglio invan mi sguida,[13]	7	Danger leads me astray in vain
	se tua bontà m'affida.	7	if your grace is entrusted to me.

Eumete

15	Oh gran figlio d'Ulisse,	7	O great son of Ulysses,
	è pur ver che tu torni	7	is it indeed true that you return
	a serenar della tua madre i giorni,	11	to brighten your mother's days,
	e pur sei giunto al fine	7	and have you come at last
	di tua casa cadente	7	of your fallen house

---

13 Malipiero's 'guida' is an error; the reading is clear both in the Vienna score and in Cicogna 564. There are other minor differences between this scene in the libretto and in the score, although the basic structural (and metrical) outlines are the same.

20	a riparar l'altissime ruine?	11	to repair the most noble ruins?
	Fugga, fugga il cordoglio e cessi il pianto;	11	Let grief flee, flee, and weeping cease;
	facciam, o pelegrino,	7	let us, o stranger,
	all'allegrezze nostre honor col canto.	11	honour our joy with song.

Eumete/Ulisse

	Verdi spiagge, al lieto giorno	8	Green shores, to the happy day
25	rabbellite herbette e fiori,	8	embellish yourself with grasses and flowers,
	scherzin l'aure con gli amori,	8	let the breezes play with the cupids,
	ride il ciel al bel ritorno.	8	let the sky smile on the fair homecoming.

Telemaco

	Vostri cortesi auspici a me son grati.	11	Your kind auspices are welcome to me.
	Manchevole piacer però m'alletta,	11	However, an incomplete pleasure charms me,
30	ch'esser calma non puote alma ch'aspetta.	11	for a soul that is waiting cannot be tranquil.

Telemaco's quatrain of two *quinari* and two *settenari* (ll. 1–4) praising his 'happy journey' is followed by three *quinari* (ll. 5–7) for him and Minerva invoking the power of the gods, and then a group of *settenari* and *endecasillabi* (ll. 8–14) as Minerva tells Telemaco that he is in his homeland. These *versi sciolti* continue as Eumete greets Telemaco (ll. 15–23); then the text shifts to rhymed *ottonari* (ll. 24–7) when Eumete and Ulisse urge the return of spring as happiness comes to Ithaca. Finally, Telemaco acknowledges their welcome (ll. 28–30) in *endecasillabi*, with a final rhyming couplet. These changes in metre and rhyme reflect the dramatic function of the various sections of the text: the free-rhymed 7- and 11-syllable *versi sciolti* (ll. 8–23, 28–30) represent action–dialogue, with one character speaking to another, while the sections in other line-lengths and more regular patterns involve more passive statement or commentary. It is significant in the light of the discussion of the episode from *Orfeo*, above, that reaction and commentary are here allocated so clearly to the more structured portions of the text that distinguish 'aria' from recitative.

There may be a passing similarity between this scene and the celebratory opening of Act II of *Orfeo*. But there are also striking differences, including the greater variety of line-lengths (*quinari* join *ottonari* as conventional cues for aria), and the fact that the text is faster paced, with shorter exchanges between the characters. This compression in part produces a more naturalistic dialogue – note, too, that the characters address each other directly – but it also prompts more space for musical expansion; thus there is a greater amount of text repetition for emphasis. Telemaco's first quatrain becomes a duple-time aria extended, by repetition of the first two lines at the end, into a rounded ABA form. The duet for Minerva and Telemaco (ll. 5–7) adopts a suave triple time, a style also used in the duet for Eumete and Ulisse (ll. 24–7). But when the text first shifts to dialogue in *versi sciolti* (l. 8), as Minerva tells Telemaco that she has brought him to his father's domains, the music changes to declamatory recitative. This is what one would expect. For the most part, too, the triple-time passages are reasonably verisimilar: Eumete specifically invites Ulisse join him in song (for 'Verdi spiagge, al lieto giorno'), while in the case of Telemaco's opening 'aria' and the following brief duet with Minerva, one can plausibly sing while travelling through the air in a divine chariot.

But there is one exception to this close matching of the structures of text and music, Eumete's speech greeting Telemaco as the 'great son of Ulysses' in lines 15–23. The *versi sciolti*, and the fact that Eumete is directly addressing another character, would seem to prompt recitative: only the last line, 'honour our joy with song', with its reference to 'canto', suggests literal imitation (Monteverdi acts accordingly, preceding it with one line of 'recitative' to make the point). But the beginning of Eumete's speech is set in a triple-time aria style, overriding the text (Ex. 3-2). This is certainly an appropriate gesture – Eumete's joy at seeing Telemaco bursts the bounds of speech – but the effect is produced solely by Monteverdi. Thus he exerts his right to prevail over his librettist in producing drama through music. He may as a result have caused himself problems, for in constructing an aria from verse devised for recitative (with long lines and a lack of patterning), he ends up mangling the text: 'Oh gran figlio, gran figlio d'Ulisse, oh, oh, oh, oh gran figlio d'Ulisse . . . e pur sei giunto, sei giunto al fine, al fine . . .'. But even this has its point, as Eumete's song both grows from psychological excitement – hence the verbal incoherence – and represents it by way of affective codes to which we, the audience, have learnt to respond. In turn, we no longer just contemplate a given dramatic situation or emotional state; rather, we are forced to share and feel it.

The process is nowhere more cool and calculating than in Monteverdi's last opera, where song is Poppea's chief tool for achieving her seduction both of Nerone and of the listener. But this is far more apparent in the score than in the libretto, which is in fact relatively restrained. As Table 3-1 reveals, the pattern in *L'incoronazione* is similar to that of *Il ritorno*: arias are given principally to gods (Pallade, Amore), to 'comic' characters (Arnalta, Nutrice), and to lower-class lovers (Valletto and Damigella, the counterparts

Ex. 3–2 *Il ritorno d'Ulisse in patria*, II.1–2.

Vienna, Österreichische Nationalbibliothek, MS 18763, fol. 53r.

of Eurimaco and Melanto). For all their apparent propensity to sing in triple time, Nerone and Poppea have few structured texts (the most obvious is the final duet, as with Ulisse and Penelope in *Il ritorno*), and whether they debase themselves by their (musical) actions – as with, say, the Proci or Iro in *Il ritorno* – remains a matter for debate. The major surprise is Ottone, whose formal arias in I.1, I.11 (shared with Poppea) and II.6 are out of character, although they strongly contribute to representing him as a rather pathetic, even emasculated figure: if Orfeo's songs were a sign of strength, Ottone's are most definitely one of weakness.

　　Busenello's verse is more formal and classically polished than Badoaro's (or at least, than Badoaro's as edited by Monteverdi) – it also tends to avoid the shorter line-lengths – and the formal arias are positioned clearly, and also well defined (with two or more stanzas). He may have been willing to break the standard rules of poetry – as his various prefaces suggest – just as he was willing to rewrite history to suit his purpose. In this case, however, the result is to make *L'incoronazione* appear in several ways quite old-fashioned, and also more realistic; one wonders whether the presence of 'historical' characters on stage encouraged a more straightforward adherence to conventional notions of (musical) speech. Yet the greater structural neutrality of the bulk of Busenello's text seems to have prompted Monteverdi to treat it very flexibly indeed. Take, for example, Act I scene 3, where Poppea adopts various wiles to keep Nerone in her arms, and to achieve the repudiation of his wife Ottavia, extending from physical embraces to an aural stimulation that is in effect the song of sex. This is the text as in Busenello's *L'incoronatione di Poppea . . . opera musicale rappresentata nel Teatro Grimani l'anno 1642* (Venice, Andrea Giuliani, 1656; a fascicle of Busenello's *Delle hore ociose*), with only minor editing:

Poppea			
	Signor, deh non partire,	7	Sire, ah do not leave,
	sostien che queste braccia	7	let these arms
	ti circondino il collo,	7	surround your neck,
	come le tue bellezze	7	just as your beauties
5	circondano il cor mio.	7	surround my heart.
	Appena spunta l'alba, e tu che sei	11	Dawn has scarce broken, and you who are
	l'incarnato mio sole,	7	my sun incarnate,
	la mia palpabil luce,	7	my one palpable light,
	e l'amoroso dì della mia vita,	7	and the loving day of my life,
10	vuoi sì repente far da me partita?	11	wish so suddenly from me to depart?
	Deh non dir	4ᵗ	Ah, say not
	di partir,	4ᵗ	'depart',
	che di voce sì amara a un solo accento,	11	for at the single sound of so bitter a word,
	ahi perir, ahi spirar quest'alma io sento.	11	ah, I feel my soul languish and die.
	Nerone		
15	Poppea, lascia ch'io parta.	7	Poppea, let me leave.
	La nobiltà de nascimenti tuoi	11	Your noble birth
	non permette che Roma	7	does not permit that Rome
	sappia che siamo uniti	7	should know that we are united
	in sin ch'Ottavia non rimane esclusa	11	until Ottavia remains exiled
20	col repudio da me. Vanne, ben mio.	11	with my repudiation. Go, my love.
	In un sospir che vien	7ᵗ	In a sigh that comes
	dal profondo del sen,	7ᵗ	from the bottom of my heart,
	includo un bacio, o cara, et un'à dio;	11	I include a kiss, my dearest, and a farewell;

	si [= ci] rivedrem ben tosto,	11	we will see each other again soon,
	idolo mio.		my idol.

Poppea

25	Signor, sempre mi vedi,	7	Sire, you always see me,
	anzi mai non mi vedi:	7	or rather, you do not see me:
	perché s'è ver che nel tuo	11	for if it is true that I am in your
	core io sia,		heart,
	entro al tuo sen celata,	7	and hidden in your breast,
	non posso da tuoi lumi esser	11	then I cannot by your eyes be seen.
	mirata.		
30	Deh non dir	4ᵗ	Ah, say not
	di partir,	4ᵗ	'depart'
	che di voce sì amara a un solo	11	for at the single sound of so bitter
	accento,		a word,
	ahi perir, ahi spirar quest'alma	11	ah, I feel my soul languish and
	io sento.		die.

Nerone

	Adorati miei rai,	7	My adored eyes,
35	deh restatevi homai.	7	ah, stay now.
	Rimanti, o mia Poppea,	7	Remain, o my Poppea,
	cor, vezzo, luce mia.	7	my heart, delight, light.
	Non temer, tu stai meco a	11	Fear not, you are with me at all
	tutte l'hore,		hours,
	splendor negl'occhi, e deità	11	the splendour of my eyes, the
	nel core.		goddess in my heart.
40	Se ben io vò,	5ᵗ	Although I go,
	pur teco io stò;	5ᵗ	yet I stay with you;
	il cor dalle tue stelle	7	my heart from your eyes
	mai mai non si disvelle.	7	can never, ever be torn.
	Io non posso da te viver	11	I cannot live apart from you
	disgiunto		
45	se non si smembra l'unità del	11	just as the unity of the point
	punto.		cannot be divided.

Poppea

Tornerai?		You'll return?

Nerone

Tornerò.		I'll return.

Poppea

Quando?		When?

Nerone
> Ben tosto.   11   Soon.

Poppea
Me 'l prometti?   Do you promise?

Nerone
> Te 'l giuro.   7   I swear it.

Poppea
E me l'osserverai?   7   And will you respect your oath?

Nerone
E s'a te non verrò, tu a me   11   And if I do not come to you, you
    verrai.   shall come to me.

Poppea
50 À dio, Nerone, à dio.   7   Farewell, Nerone, farewell.

Nerone
À dio, Poppea, ben mio.   7   Farewell, Poppea, my love.

Here the text is mostly in free-rhyming 7- and 11-syllable *versi sciolti*, with occasional *versi tronchi* (ll. 11–12, 21–2, 40–1). The implication is that this verse should be set as some kind of recitative. Three lines are repeated (ll. 11–14 = 30–3), which may suggest some kind of refrain although it does not seem to have a strong structural force. But Busenello tends to proceed fairly natural-istically, as if this were an actual real-life dialogue – again, the characters speak to each other – rather than one designed for music, even if the opening speeches are too drawn out and (again typically) some of the conceits seem overly artificial and mannered ('Sire, you always see me, or rather, you do not see me: for if it is true that I am in your heart, and hidden in your breast, then I cannot by your eyes be seen'). The sense of naturalism increases still more towards the end of the scene, as the erotic pace speeds up and lines are breathlessly divided between the two characters.

But this is not Busenello's text as it appears in Monteverdi's score. Here the long opening speeches for each character are broken up by transposing lines, reallocating them, and creating significant interruptions and reiterations, with further text repetition to heighten the feverish atmosphere:

Poppea
1   Signor, signor, deh non partire,   Sire, Sire, ah do not leave,
2   sostien che queste braccia   let these arms
3   ti circondino il collo,   surround your neck,

4	come le tue bellezze	just as your beauties
5	circondano il cor mio.	surround my heart.

Nerone

15	Poppea, lascia ch'io parta.	Poppea, let me leave.

Poppea

1	Non partir, non partir, Signor, deh non partire.	Do not leave, do not leave, Sire, ah do not leave.
6	Appena spunta l'alba, e tu che sei	Dawn has scarce broken, and you who are
7	l'incarnato mio sole,	my sun incarnate,
8	la mia palpabil luce,	my one palpable light,
9	e l'amoroso dì della mia vita,	and the loving day of my life,
10	vuoi sì repente far da me, da me, da me partita?	wish so suddenly from me, from me, from me to depart?
11	Deh non dir	Ah, say not
12	di partir,	'depart',
13	che di voce sì amara un solo accento,	for at the single sound of so bitter a word,
14	ahi, perir, ahi spirar quest'alma io sento.	ah, I feel my soul languish and die.

Nerone

16	La nobiltà de nascimenti tuoi	Your noble birth
17	non permette che Roma	does not permit that Rome
18	sappia che siamo uniti	should know that we are united
19	in sin ch'Ottavia . . .	until Ottavia . . .

Poppea

(19)	In sin che, in sin che . . .	Until what, until what . . .

Nerone

19	. . . in sin ch'Ottavia non rimane esclusa . . .	. . . until Ottavia remains exiled

Poppea

(19)	Non rimane, non rimane . . .	Remains, remains . . .

Nerone

19	. . . in sin ch'Ottavia non rimane esclusa	. . . until Ottavia remains exiled
20a	col repudio da me.	with my repudiation.

Poppea

20b	Vanne, vanne, ben mio, ben mio; vanne,	Go, go, my love, my love; go, go, my love, my love; go my love.

vanne, ben mio, ben mio;
vanne, ben mio.

Nerone

21	In un sospir, sospir che vien	In a sigh, a sigh that comes
22	dal profondo del sen,	from the bottom of my heart,
21	in un sospir, sospir che vien, sospir che vien	In a sigh, a sigh that comes, a sigh that comes
22	dal profondo del sen,	from the bottom of my heart,
23	includo un bacio, o cara, o cara, et un'à dio;	I include a kiss, my dearest, my dearest, and a farewell;
24	ci rivedrem ben tosto, sì, sì, ci rivedrem, ci rivedrem ben tosto, idolo mio;	we will see each other again soon, yes, yes, we will see each other again, we will see each other again soon, my idol;
24	ci rivedrem ben tosto, idolo mio.	we will see each other again soon, my idol.
	(etc.)	*(etc.)*

The music is a heady mixture of recitative and 'aria' (although the aria passages can be very short), the shifting styles prompted not so much by the metrical structure of the poetry (as is largely the case in *Il ritorno*) as by its affective content and rhetorical potential. Poppea begins in a languid recitative, but one structured by repetitions and sequential extensions in her melodic line, and moving to sensuous chromaticism and exotic accidentals. Monteverdi's reordering of the text permits Nerone to speak sooner, allowing for a more plausible exchange, and also then enables Poppea, by her eager interruptions, to emphasize how she is managing the situation (Ex. 3-3). She is allocated Nerone's 'Vanne, ben mio' for the first appearance of triple time in the scene: this makes sense – why should Poppea leave her own palace?[14] – but it also gives her the upper hand in telling Nerone just what to do. His response, 'In un sospir che vien', follows Poppea's musical cue, being cast as a formal triple-time aria with an introductory sinfonia. Poppea's 'Signor, sempre mi vedi' is also in the manner of a formal aria, but in duple rather than triple time, and preceded by a sinfonia. Nerone responds in triple time ('Adorati miei rai'), shifting to recitative, and Monteverdi then gives Poppea's repetition of 'Deh non dir di partir . . .' more or less the same music as before. Again Nerone enters in triple time at 'Non temer', moving to duple time at

14 This suggests, in turn, that the 1656 reading may be an error (I thank John Whenham for the observation). If so, it is a persistent one: 'Vanne, ben mio' is given to Nerone in Curtis's edition, even though the Venice manuscript is unambiguous at this point (and is followed by Malipiero).

Ex. 3-3 *L'incoronazione di Poppea*, I.3.

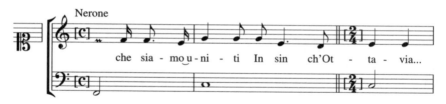

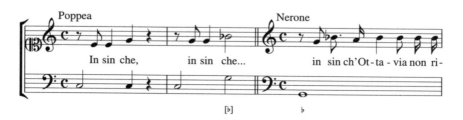

Venice, Biblioteca Nazionale Marciana, MS 9963 (It. IV.439), fols. 14v–15r.

'splendor negl'occhi', with semiquavers (imitated in the bass) linked to 'splendor' as word-painting. Monteverdi inserts and adds repetitions of Poppea's questioning 'Tornerai?' in Nerone's speech, breaking it up with exquisite sequences and dissonances. Yet again Nerone enters in triple time at 'Io non posso da te', while the final 'à dio' repetitions are singled out by Monteverdi in long notes and with sensuous semitonal movement. It is a remarkable scene. And the arias are not at all mimetic – there is scant verisimilitude in a Roman emperor, even a musician such as Nero, singing to and with his mistress – but are chiefly representative of sensual excess. Yet this music does more than just signify passion. Poppea's one quasi-formal aria, 'Signor, sempre mi vedi', is in a sturdy duple time, whereas Nerone tends to sing in a more languid triple time. Poppea seems much more in control of the scene, and she is by far the dominant musical personality.

It is perhaps inevitable that a chapter beginning with the libretto, and one privileging the structural and expressive power of a poetic text to a greater extent than is customary in most studies of opera, should nevertheless still end with the music. Although the art of the libretto might usefully be viewed independently from that of the music designed to accompany it, any opera or similar work necessarily places in a symbiotic relationship the text and its musical voicing. That relationship may be harmonious, at times it may be dissonant, but either way, the finished product does not easily permit the separating out of its constituent elements. Yet an awareness of the nature of those elements, and of their opportunities and constraints, is vital for any understanding of the final result. In the end, opera may or may not be an inherently musical genre, but one ignores its text at one's peril.

4

The art of the theatre

As we saw in Chapter 2, for all the novelties of early opera, the genre inserted itself within a long-standing tradition of Renaissance theatrical endeavour. It also drew upon its modes of staging, production and performance. Classical tragedies, comedies and pastorals, *intermedi* and even the less formal renditions of the *commedia dell'arte* all had their impact, even if opera posed additional complications by virtue of its continuous music. Thus one can glean some ideas for performing operas and related works from general treatises on the theatre from the sixteenth century, such as Leone de' Sommi's dialogues or Angelo Ingegneri's *Della poesia rappresentativa & del modo di rappresentare le favole sceniche* (Ferrara, Vittorio Baldini, 1598). Ingegneri, in particular, deals with pastoral plays, which he rates in significance far above tragedies and comedies (after all, he was Ferrarese and a colleague of Tasso and Guarini); he offers important information both on the design of the play and on sets, machines, costume (for pastoral plays, simple and graceful), acting (including the importance of facial expression and gesture), the various roles of the chorus (both stable and mobile), and on the place and nature of music in the end-of-act choruses and *intermedi*.

A similar sequence of topics provides the structure for the treatise *Il corago* (*c*1630), which ostensibly deals with all types of plays, but admits that those with music throughout are now the most popular and effective.[1] Much of its advice is eminently sensible: composers should have the complete text before starting to compose, and understand it well; distribute the emotional highpoints carefully, not peaking too soon; play the music to the poet for his advice and approval; write homophonically in ensembles, or if polyphony is required (for the sake of variety), have the verses recited first by a solo voice; vary the harmony and mode; draw on the experience of similar entertain-

---

1 The following recommendations are abstracted from *Il corago*, ed. Fabbri and Pompilio, pp. 80–4 (composers), 90–2 (performers), 125–6 (*corago*).

ments in Florence, Mantua and Ferrara; seek appropriateness, rather than novelty for its own sake; copy out selected emotional passages from other dramatic works as exemplars; use semitones for expression, but not too many; model the recitative on the declamation of a good actor; provide instrumental interludes and ritornellos to allow for stage movement; observe the poetic sense, not the metre, in recitatives, treating verse as prose; know the singers and their ranges; use few continuo instruments so as not to obscure the voice (harpsichords and *violoni* are preferred and the number of instruments depends on the number of singers); use simple accompaniments in recitative, whereas the harmony can be fuller in livelier passages; avoid unisons with the voices; make the accompaniment move more when the voice has one or more sustained notes; have the instruments play before or after the voice, but always just before the voice enters so as to give the note; and modify the use of instruments according to the distance between singers and instrumentalists. As for performers, they should slow down their gestures to match the musical pace; punctuate the music according to the sense (which requires rehearsal); deliver the words slowly except where the text requires otherwise; move around the stage when permitted by instrumental passages; use natural gestures and movements (in the case of the *coro mobile*), and also move in unison; follow the practice of a good actor; if they lack stage presence, be placed in machines, which should move slowly; gesture more if they are representing gods and marine and infernal deities; not sing immediately on entering the stage, but instead take time to reach a good position; respect the rank and station of their character; not turn their back on the audience; enunciate clearly, especially the final syllables and consonants; and use gesture like an actor. And just before the performance begins, the *corago* should ensure that all the actors are in costume and in place; those working the machines are ready; tailors and costumiers are available to help with costume changes; the musicians have tuned their instruments; the machines are well oiled, move freely and have been checked for sabotage; the actors and stage-hands stand clear of the scenery in the wings; individuals are given sole responsibility for lighting to ensure illumination and also for safety. Even in a modern theatre, none of this would go amiss.

Staging, sets and costumes

Opera and other forms of music theatre in the early seventeenth century could be performed in various environments: a room adapted for a single performance, an open or covered courtyard, some other outdoor space, or a dedicated theatre that might (or might not) also provided the room needed for musicians. Matters tended to be more flexible in courtly contexts – where there was also less need to provide for different social ranks (apart from the privileged position normally granted the ruler and his immediate circle) – than in the sphere of 'public' opera, which almost by definition tended to occupy a building designed solely for theatrical use. Although few theatres have survived in or near their original states – the Teatro Farnese in Parma and the Gonzaga theatre in Sabbioneta are partial exceptions – one can make some assessment of the conditions, and also the acoustic, experienced by performers and audience. Most court theatres had a rectangular or U-shaped auditorium with amphitheatre-type seating on rising steps around the walls. The model was classical, although it also served a modern purpose, leaving the floor space free to accommodate both a dais for the prince, positioned to achieve the best sight-lines for the perspective of the stage, and a location for theatrical and social dancing. Venetian opera houses, however, tended to have tiers of boxes – permitting greater social distinctions and also privacy – with standing-room (later, benches) in the *parterre*. Even a one-off adapted space presumably required some form of stage for the performers, while by this period purpose-built theatres tended to have a proscenium arch which served both to hide the stage machinery and to create a barrier between stage and auditorium, even if this barrier might be (and in court theatres, usually was) bridged by one or more sets of stairs to allow freedom of movement into the space for dancing. Lighting was by candles and mirrors; sets and machines were moved by ropes and pulleys. Given the tendency to use wooden materials – hence the danger of fire – and the types of dress worn by theatre-goers, the acoustic would tend towards dryness and emphasizing the upper frequencies, although some kind of resonating system could be used to enhance the sound (as with the large urns in the Uffizi theatre in Florence). Theatrical works were normally performed straight through, without intervals. This placed additional constraints on stage movement. It must also have made things uncomfortable for the audience: not for nothing did the ducal entourage attending the performance of Tasso's *Aminta* with spectacular *intermedi* in Parma in 1628 (for the wedding of Duke Odoardo Farnese and Margherita de' Medici) miss Act III of the play to take refreshment, returning just in time for the next *intermedio*.

For all the limitations, remarkable things could be achieved. In the prologue for Guarini's *L'idropica* (with music by Monteverdi), performed for the festivities celebrating the wedding of Prince Francesco Gonzaga and Margherita of Savoy in May–June 1608:

When all the people which the theatre could hold were gathered together . . . and once the torches were lit in the theatre, the usual trumpet fanfare was given from behind the stage. At the third statement of the fanfare, the large curtain which concealed the stage disappeared with such speed, at the blink of an eye, that although it rose upwards few could see how it had been removed. With the stage revealed to the spectators, one saw on its sides many palaces and towers standing out, partitioned by loggias and porticos done with such realism that everyone quickly recognized the scene for the city of Mantua, which was illuminated in such a way that without seeing any light lit therein was revealed the splendour not of torches or other illumination but of the pure rays of the sun. Nor was anything lacking therein, so that the spectators would have believed that there it was day, and that the sun was then shining naturally (so well planned were the shadows and the light from those reflections), if they had not known that night had already fallen. This curtain had not disappeared before one saw in the air three most beautiful enclosed clouds, constructed with such artifice that they appeared no different from those made in the sky by the vapours of the earth, and with the stage-floor covered by pleasant waters it was so like real life that indeed it seemed that there lay a most placid lagoon. One saw the lagoon bubble in the middle and from it emerge the head of a lady who, rising little by little, revealed herself through her costume and attributes to be Manto, daughter of Tiresias and founder of Mantua, who was raised up in so measured a fashion that by the time the trumpets had finished sounding she stood on a little island bathed by those waters; and pausing among some reeds that were placed thereupon, to the sound of several instruments which were behind the stage she sang the following words, which enraptured the minds of all the audience . . .

When Manto began to sing the fourth stanza, the three clouds which were in the sky opened suddenly, and in the middle one saw Hymen with torch in hand, who, for his garments rich in gold which he had around him and for the reflections of some lights which with much artifice had been hidden within that cloud, was so resplendent that he resembled a heavenly god. In the cloud which was on the right, the Three Graces were seen, so well placed and so beautiful that they seduced the sight of the onlookers; and in the left [cloud] were Fecundity and Peace, both with lit torches in their hands adorned with flowers and gold, which let forth sweetest perfumes.

When Manto had finished singing the aforesaid stanza, she began to sink into the same waters from whence she had risen, and at the same time the clouds began to move downwards very slowly, the deities that were therein singing the words that follow to the greatest delight of the audience . . .

This song was composed with such measure that at the end of its final strains the clouds found themselves on the stage, leaving behind them the buildings which represented the city and covering all sight of them, whence Hymen, placing his foot on the little island, sang the verses written below . . .

While Hymen sang the second quatrain, the Graces, having left the cloud and walking slowly along the little island, seated themselves on his right, with Fecundity and Peace doing the same on the left, whence the three clouds, remaining empty, wondrously dissolved in the blink of an eye; and of those three there was made one, but of another shape, for it seemed a dense fog which engulfed all the view of the stage behind the little island. Once Hymen had finished singing, he approached Fecundity and Peace, and no sooner did he take his seat at their side than the island split apart, dividing itself into two equal parts, one of which moved towards one part of the stage, and the other towards the other, carrying those deities off-stage through the waves, and at that same point the waters and the cloud disappeared, and the scene representing the city of Padua remained clear for the play to come.[2]

Such effects appear regularly in accounts of early seventeenth-century theatrical performances; no less common are descriptions of lavish costumes with characters identified by conventional attributes whether worn or held.[3] But while this kind of staging was common for *intermedi*, most early operas seem to have been on a simpler scale. That was partly a reflection of their relative value in the scale of court entertainments; it was also partly because of the tendency to use more intimate performance spaces. *Orfeo* was done on a 'narrow stage' (though we still do not quite know where),[4] probably with just two sets (one pastoral and one Underworld, as with Peri's *Euridice*) and one machine (for the descent of Apollo in the revised ending). According to Angelo Ingegneri, pastoral sets were fairly generic:

But when dealing with the pastoral, so long as the whole is rustic, anything will do. Here, too [as in tragedies and comedies], it is as well to get

2   Follino, *Compendio delle sontuose feste* (1608), in Fabbri, *Monteverdi*, trans. Carter, pp. 87–8. The role of Manto was sung by Angela Zanibelli.
3   The best examples are the costume drawings for the Florentine 1589 *intermedi*, reproduced and discussed in Saslow, *The Medici Wedding of 1589*.
4   In the dedication to Prince Francesco Gonzaga of the 1609 score of *Orfeo*, Monteverdi said that it had been done 'sopra angusta Scena'. This has sometimes been transcribed as 'augusta Scena' on the grounds that it is a typographical error (an 'n' inverted as a 'u') and that 'august' would better suit the rhetoric of a dedication. However, the 'n' in 'angusta' does not seem to be an inverted 'u': the two characters are different in Amadino's font. There does remain the possibility, however, that Amadino or his typesetter misread the original. On the location, see Besutti, 'The "Sala degli Specchi" Uncovered'. We do not know whether the second performance on 1 March 'before all the ladies [*dame*] resident in the city' was in a different space from the first, although it has sometimes been assumed that a change in venue is what prompted the revised ending.

as close as one can to the likeness of that region in which the action takes place, be it Arcadia or somewhere else. And in all cases, the woods, the mountains, the valleys, the rivers, the springs, the temples, the stables and above all the perspectives even of such things in the distance should offer a wondrous grace . . .[5]

The Underworld set was also probably a much pared-down version of such scenes in the *intermedi*. As for the prologue, it was probably done in front of the pastoral set, given Musica's closing reference to birds, burbling streams and breezes.

    Arianna was staged in a temporary theatre, reportedly before an audience of 6,000 (which seems very unlikely).[6] According to Follino's official description there was just one set:

> This work was very beautiful in itself, and for the characters who took part, dressed in clothes no less appropriate than splendid, and for the scenery, which represented a wild rocky place in the midst of the waves, which in the furthest part of the prospect could be seen always in motion, giving a charming effect.[7]

The single set was in part due to tragedy's requirement of unity of place,[8] but one assumes that economies of scale were also involved, as well as, perhaps, a space unsuited for theatrical endeavour. Similarly, the machines seem to have been limited. A cloud machine was used for the opening:

> It was Apollo who, representing the prologue, gave the introduction to so beautiful a play. He was sitting on a very beautiful cloud (which at the removal of the great curtain which covered the scene was seen in open air of brightest splendour), which, moving down little by little (while from within the stage was heard a sweet consort [*concerto*] of various instruments), reached in a short space of time the stage, and leaving Apollo on that part

5   Ingegneri, *Della poesia rappresentativa*, p. 62: 'Ma se trattasse di Pastorale, quando il tutto sia rustico, ogni cosa servirà: avegnache anco quivi sia bene l'accostarsi il meglio che si possa alla similitudine del sito di quella regione, sia Arcadia, od altra, dove si presuppone che il fatto succeda. Et in ogni caso le selve, i monti, le valli, i fiumi, le fontane, i Tempi, le Capanne, e sopratutto le prospettive etiandio di tai cose lontane, daranno gratia maravigliosa . . .'. For *Orfeo* and two sets, plus other matters of staging, see *Claudio Monteverdi: 'Orfeo'*, ed. Whenham, pp. 42–7.

6   The figure is given by Follino, who also claimed that the main theatre held 5,000. The Estense ambassador estimated an audience of 4,000 for *Arianna*, which still seems too high; see Povoledo, 'Controversie monteverdiane', p. 365.

7   This and the following extract is from Follino, *Compendio delle sontuose feste* (1608), in Fabbri, *Monteverdi*, trans. Carter, pp. 85–7.

8   Although *Il corago* (ed. Fabbri and Pompilio, p. 31) argues that the rule of unity of place is irrelevant because it does not suit the modern need for spectacle, and that the ancients' use of it was simply a reflection of their primitive practices.

of the rock broaching the sea, it disappeared in a moment. Whence he, finding himself on foot on that mountainous rock, stepping forth majestically, placed himself forwards somewhat, and having finally stopped within view of the spectators, he began to sing with a very suave voice the verses that follow, with the said instruments accompanying throughout his beautiful song.

But Venere and Amore (for the first scene) probably just entered from the wings (Follino says that they 'were seen to appear'), and certainly Bacco and Arianna did so at the end for the final *ballo* (Bacco's earlier arrival is just narrated), although Venere then emerged from the sea and the heavens opened to reveal Giove.

The *Ballo delle ingrate*, also performed in the 1608 festivities, was given in the same permanent theatre as *L'idropica* but the space now operated as a ballroom, with room for dancing in front of the stage. The entertainment began with social dancing by the court until a 'terrifying noise' startled the dancers and directed their attention to the stage. After the swift ascent of the curtain,

> in the middle of the stage one saw the large mouth of a wide and deep cavern, which, stretching beyond the confines of the scene, seemed that it went so far beyond it that the human eye could not reach to discern its end. That cavern was surrounded within and around by burning fire, and in its darkest depths, in a part very deep and distant from its mouth, one saw a great abyss behind which there rotated balls of flames burning most brightly and within which there were countless monsters of the Inferno so horrible and frightening that many did not have the courage to look upon it. It seemed a horrifying and monstrous thing to see that infernal abyss full of such fire and so monstrous images, but it caused the people to wonder all the more to see in front of that fiery mouth from the outside part, where some small misty and gloomy light shone, beautiful Venus who held her beautiful son Cupid by the hand, who, to the sound of sweetest instruments which were behind the stage, sang with a very suave voice the verses written below in dialogue with Amore.[9]

After the arrival of Pluto, 'formidable and awesome in sight, with garments as are given him by poets, but burdened with gold and jewels', and the *ingrate* (eight men and eight women), the latter descended from the stage and performed their *ballo*:

---

9   For this and the following descriptions, see Follino, *Compendio delle sontuose feste* (1608), in Fabbri, *Monteverdi*, trans. Carter, pp. 89–92.

These condemned souls were dressed with garments in a very extravagant and beautiful style, which draped to the ground, made up of a rich cloth that was woven precisely for this effect. It was grey in colour, mixed with most subtle threads of silver and gold with such artifice that to look upon it it seemed to be ashes mixed with flashing sparks; and thus one saw the dresses, and likewise the cloaks (which hung from their shoulders in a very bizarre manner), embroidered with many flames made of silk and gold, so well arranged that everyone judged that they were burning; and between the said flames, there could be seen scattered in most beautiful order garnets, rubies and other jewels which resembled glowing coals. Their hair was also seen to be woven with these jewels, which, part cut short and part spread around with wondrous art, seemed destroyed and burned; and although it was all covered with ashes, nonetheless it showed between the ash and the smoke a certain splendour, from which one could well recognize that at another time they were blondest of blondes like gold thread; and their faces, showing signs of a former beauty, were changed and palled in such a way that they brought terror and compassion together on looking upon them.

After the dancing, the ingrates returned through the mouth of the Inferno, which then (according to Federico Zuccari) transformed into a beautiful garden with many nymphs and shepherds performing graceful dances and cheerful songs.

The Venetian theatres with which Monteverdi became associated towards the end of his life – including the Teatro S. Moisé and Teatro SS. Giovanni e Paolo – were more fixed than most court theatres; the repertory system currently being put into place prompted a formulaic approach to matters of staging, sets and, one assumes, costume, as well as economies of scale in terms of complex machinery (except in the Teatro Novissimo under Giacomo Torelli). Both *Il ritorno* and *L'incoronazione* are fairly undemanding in terms of staging; the same would seem to have applied to *Le nozze d'Enea in Lavinia*, which also appears to have had few sets (chiefly the bank of the Tiber). This suited the Venetian theatres and also eased the demands for touring (*Il ritorno* was performed in Bologna later in 1640, and *L'incoronazione* was toured at least to Naples, in 1651). *Il ritorno* has three sets (see Table 4-1), one a palace ('Reggia'), one maritime ('Marittima') and one woodland ('Boschereccia'), none of which requires particular identifying features. Their distribution is one of the arguments in favour of the division of *Il ritorno* into five acts (as in the libretto) rather than three (as in the Vienna score, where traces of the 5-act division still remain), given the evident continuity of scene and action from Act I scene 11 to Act II scene 3. These sets square with what seem to have been the typical resources of a Venetian theatre. The opera which

Table 4-1 The layout of *Il ritorno d'Ulisse in patria* in its 3-act and 5-act versions

('x' indicates when a character sings; 'o' when a character is present but silent.)

	Reggia			Marittima						Reg.				Boschereccia			Reg.					Bos.		Reg.		??	Reg.				Mar.		Reg.		
Libretto	Act I									Act II							Act III					Act IV				Act V									
Score	Act I													Act II												Act III									
	1	2	3	4	5	6	7	8	9	10	11	12	13	1	2	3	4	5	6	7	8	9	10	11	12	1	2	3	4	5	6	7	8	9	10
Penelope (12 scenes)	x									x								x	o	x				x	x			x	x	x				x	x
Ericlea (4)	x																																x	o	x
Melanto (4)		x								x							x											x							
Eurimaco (6)		x															x	o	o	o?	x														
Feaci (3)				o	o	x																													
Ulisse (14)					o	o	x	x	x				x	o	x	x						x	x		x										
Nettuno (3)				x	x																											x			

Giove (2)																		x	
Minerva (7)				x	x							x			x	x		x	x
Eumete (12)				x	x	x	o	x	x		x	x			x	x		x	o
Iro (3)					x			x			x								
Telemaco (7)						x	x	x			x	x	x		x			x	x
Antinoo (5)								x	o	o	x								
Pisandro (5)								x	o	o	x								
Anfinomo (5)								x	o	o	x								
Giunone (2)															x	x			
Coro (a4) in cielo (1)															x				
Coro (a4) marittimo (1)															x				

Note: I.3 is a chorus of nereids and sirens; II.6 is a *ballo* of Moors; III.2 is Mercurio (and the silent shades of the suitors) in a 'deserto'. Act II scene 12 is divided into two in the libretto (Act IV, scenes 2, 3) at the entry of Pisandro and Anfinomo (who therefore are not present for the fight between Iro and Ulisse).

inaugurated the Teatro S. Cassiano as an opera house in 1637, *Andromeda*, with a libretto by Benedetto Ferrari and music by Francesco Manelli, required precisely the same settings and similar machines. Their *La maga fulminata* (S. Cassiano, 1638) added only an inferno set; while the first opera at the Teatro SS. Giovanni e Paolo, Manelli's *Delia* (1639; to a libretto by Giulio Strozzi) had a sea scene, a wood, a cave, an inferno and a garden, plus just one cloud machine.[10] In the case of *Il ritorno*, the careful sequence of these sets, and the no less careful introduction of characters, suggests that the maritime and woodland sets alternated in the background, while the 'palace' was somehow created (with flats or a backcloth) in the interior.[11] In terms of machines and the like, *Il ritorno* needs a ship turned to stone in I.6, an airborne chariot for Minerva and Telemaco in II.1, a bolt of fire and the earth opening to engulf Ulisse in II.3, Giove's eagle flying overhead in II.8, and Minerva in the heavens in II.12. Also, one assumes that the heavens and the sea opened up to reveal the gods in I.5–6 and III.6–7. The location of the prologue is unclear; it could plausibly have been in front of the main curtain, if there was one.

L'incoronazione is no less formulaic (see Table 4-2), for all that the Teatro SS. Giovanni e Paolo was a fairly large theatre. The sequence of sets suggests a similar technique to *Il ritorno*. The prologue is done (according to the 1643 *scenario*) within a 'scena di tutto cielo' – presumably a backcloth – with Fortuna, Virtù and Amore in a machine. The opera itself has a generic 'City of Rome' in the background and flats and/or backcloths for Poppea's palace, Seneca's villa, Poppea's garden and Nerone's palace.[12] Presumably, the 'City of Rome' set also had some kind of canal for the boat carrying Ottavia off to exile in III.6 (she addresses the oarsmen). The distribution of sets pro-

---

10 See the details in Mancini, Muraro and Povoledo, *I teatri del Veneto*, i/1, pp. 141–2 (S. Cassiano), 312.

11 Ibid., p. 304. Povoledo ('Controversie monteverdiane', pp. 382–3) suggests the reverse – i.e., the palace in the background and the maritime and woodland sets in the foreground – although the arrival of Minerva's chariot in II.1 then seems problematic. Either way, III.2, for Mercury and the shades of the suitors in a desert, may have been omitted not just because it was 'melancholic', as the score says, but also because it required an additional set, and one, moreover, within the 'Reggia' set which was in place immediately before (II.11–12) and after (III.3–5).

12 See Day, 'The Theater of SS. Giovanni e Paolo and Monteverdi's *L'incoronazione di Poppea*'; Mancini, Muraro and Povoledo, *I teatri del Veneto*, i/1, pp. 305, 312–13. In his edition of *L'incoronazione*, Alan Curtis creates a range of difficulties by not accepting the obvious (p. xxiii): 'After a Prologue in the Heavens, the mortal action takes place within a single day: outside Poppaea's palace [I.1–4]; in Rome (the imperial apartments? [I.5–13]); in the garden of Seneca's villa [II.1–3]; back in Rome (the same, or other, imperial apartments? [II.4–9]); in Poppaea's garden [II.10–12]; in Rome (a street? public place? at court?) [III.1–7]; and finally in Nero's palace [III.8].'

duces the seemingly odd result of having apparent interior scenes played out-
doors, but this is not unusual for contemporary drama, and it is also necessary to define a 'neutral' space that permits the logical introduction of quite
different characters in sequence; for example, were Ottavia and Nutrice's I.5
played in a private apartment, as one might expect, it would be implausible
to have Nerone and Poppea appear therein in I.10, or Ottone and then
Drusilla in I.10–13. As a result, particular scenes may be cast in a different
light, including the legalistic debate between Nerone and Seneca in I.9, which
now takes place in a relatively public forum, and similarly the drinking scene
between Nerone and Lucano in II.5. Presumably the machinery of the prologue was also used to have Pallade airborne in I.8, and likewise Mercurio in
II.1, Amore in II.11–12, and Venere, Amore and the Coro di Amori in III.8c.
But that apart, the opera demands nothing special in terms of stage effects,
just as one would expect from its subject-matter.

It would be dangerous to accept at face value the accounts of these
and similar entertainments in printed descriptions, which often, at least in the
case of court festivity, were prone to exaggeration for the sake of propaganda.
Also, it is hard to see how a work such as Monteverdi's *Proserpina rapita* (1630),
staged in the upstairs salon of Girolamo Mocenigo's palace in Venice, could
have included all the special effects required by its libretto, with one character turned into a mountain, another into a river, Venere and Amore on a
cloud, Mount Etna opening to reveal Plutone, and so forth. It seems clear
that early seventeenth-century audiences were highly receptive to theatrical
suggestion. But even if contemporary descriptions are not wholly to be
trusted, they do serve a purpose, capturing something of what contemporaries
wanted and were willing to believe.

Some other performance matters

We have already seen (in Chapter 2) that Marco da Gagliano's preface to his
Dafne (1608) reveals a number of anxieties about the new genre. Not only
does he ground opera in its recent history; he also offers a number of instructions for performance that seek to alleviate the concerns and potential confusions of those unfamiliar with the genre. Although his remarks are mostly
specific to *Dafne*, they provide useful hints for the performance of similar
works that are more detailed than the general instructions in *Il corago*. They
can be summarized as follows (roughly in sequence).

In terms of the addition of vocal embellishments, Gagliano condemns
the haphazard use of '*gruppi, trilli, passaggi* and *esclamazioni*', recommending
that they be restricted to due time and place, namely 'the songs of the choruses' and specific vocal arias; he praises in particular the graceful renditions

Table 4-2 The layout of *L'incoronazione di Poppea* (Venice manuscript)

('x' indicates when a character sings; 'o' when a character is present but silent. For additions in Naples manuscript, see Table 10-2.)

Locations by act and scene:
- **Act I** — Poppea's palace (1–4); City of Rome (5–13)
- **Act II** — Seneca's villa (1–3); City of Rome (4–8); Poppea's garden (9–12)
- **Act III** — City of Rome (1–7); Nerone's palace (8a–8d)

	I‑1	I‑2	I‑3	I‑4	I‑5	I‑6	I‑7	I‑8	I‑9	I‑10	I‑11	I‑12	I‑13	II‑1	II‑2	II‑3	II‑4	II‑5	II‑6	II‑7	II‑8	II‑9	II‑10	II‑11	II‑12	III‑1	III‑2	III‑3	III‑4	III‑5	III‑6	III‑7	III‑8a	III‑8b	III‑8c	III‑8d
Ottone (12 scenes)	x	x	o?							o	x	x	x						x	x		x			x				x							
Soldati (3)	o		o																																	
Poppea (12)			x	x						x	x												x	o	o					x			x	o	o	x
Nerone (11)			x						x	x								x															x	o	o	x
Arnalta (8)				x							o												x		x		x	x	o	x		x				
Ottavia (4)					x	x														x											x					
Nutrice (3)					x	o															x															
Seneca (7)						x	x	x	x					x	x	x																x				

Personaggio	1	2	3	4	5	6	7	8	9	10	11	12	13	14	15	16
Valletto (3)	x					x			x							
Pallade (1)		x														
Drusilla (7)			x						x	x	x	x	x	x		
Mercurio (1)				x												
Liberto (1)					x											
Famigliari (1)						x										
Damigella (1)							x									
Lucano (1)								x								
Amore (3)										x	x					x
Littore (3)												x	x	o		
Consoli/Tribuni (1)															x	
Coro (a3/4) di Amori (1)																x
Venere (1)																x

of the *ottava rima* stanza 'Chi da' lacci d'amor vive disciolto' by the soprano Caterina Martinelli and the *terza rima* stanza 'Non curi la mia pianta, o fiamma, o gelo' by the tenor Francesco Rasi. Otherwise, 'where the tale does not require it, leave entirely aside all ornament, so as not to act like that painter who, knowing how to paint cypresses well, painted them everywhere'. The singer should also 'seek to chisel out the syllables so as to make the words well understood, and this is always the chief aim of the singer in every occasion of song, especially in reciting, and be persuaded that true delight arises from the understanding of the words'. Gagliano notes particularly the importance of the role of the messenger (Tirsi) narrating Dafne's metamorphosis: 'The part . . . is most important: it requires expression of the words above everything else.' It was played by Antonio Brandi (a Florentine): 'His voice is a most exquisite contralto, the delivery and grace of his singing marvellous, and not only does he make you understand the words, but also with gestures and with movements it seems that he insinuates in the spirit an I-don't-know-what profit.'

The ideal position of the instruments was a matter of some debate in this period. According to Gagliano, 'be advised that the instruments which must accompany the solo voices should be situated in a position to look the actors in the face, so that hearing each other better they can proceed together'. The instrumentalists in Peri's *Euridice* had been situated behind the stage ('dentro alla scena'), and probably likewise in Monteverdi's *Arianna*. They were on a platform to the side for the *Ballo delle ingrate*. In Parma in 1628, Monteverdi and his assistant Antonio Goretti spent some time trying to solve the problem of where to put them, eventually adapting an area in front of the stage – between two sets of stairs leading down to the auditorium – in what came close to an orchestra pit. Such pits were in use elsewhere by the 1620s, if not earlier: they had obvious advantages in terms of co-ordinating the singers and the musicians, although the pit also separated the stage from the auditorium in ways that created difficulties for those court entertainments, such as *balli*, that often required freedom of movement from one to the other.

Gagliano then covers the manner of realizing the continuo: 'Ensure that the harmony is neither too much nor too little, but such that it controls the song without impeding the understanding of the words. The manner of playing should be without embellishments, taking care not to double the consonance that is sung, but those which can most help it, always keeping the harmony lively.' He also discusses instrumental sinfonias and ritornellos: 'Before the curtain falls, to make the listeners attentive, one should sound a sinfonia made up of various instruments which serve to accompany the choruses and to play the ritornellos.' In the case of *Dafne*, that sinfonia (not given in the score) was to last 15–20 bars before the entrance of Ovidio to deliver the Prologue.

Gagliano's performance instructions for the prologue itself would work well enough for similar pieces in the repertory:

note that he [Ovidio] should match his step to the sound of the sinfonia, not however with affectation as if he were dancing but with gravity, in such a manner that the steps are not discordant with the sound. When he has arrived at the position where it seems appropriate to him to begin, let him commence without other movements; and above all let the song be full of majesty, gesturing more or less according to the elevation of the conceit, noting, however, that every gesture and every step should fall on the beat of the sound and of the song. He should rest after the first quatrain, taking three or four steps, that is, for as long as the ritornello lasts, but always in time. Note that the movement should begin on the accent on the penultimate syllable; let him begin again in the position where he finds himself. He could sometimes join together two quatrains to show a certain *sprezzatura*. The costume should be that which is appropriate to a poet, with the laurel crown on the head, lyre at his side and bow in hand. Having delivered the last quatrain, with the Prologue re-entering within, let the chorus appear on stage . . .

No less useful is his advice for managing the chorus. The chorus in *Dafne* is made up of nymphs and shepherds, 'more or fewer according to the capacity of the stage', although Gagliano says later in the preface that they should comprise 16–18 individuals.[13] They should make appropriate expressions and gestures according to the shifts in the dramatic action. The normal position for the chorus is in a half-moon (a position which has a classical precedent). Characters that speak 'should not be confused with those of the chorus but should stay four or five paces in front, more or less, according to the size of the stage'. Members of the chorus speaking as individuals must stand 'two or three paces' in front of the others. The chorus should move and respond in unison, and also interact with each other. Gagliano spends some time discussing the performance of the choral lament on the death of Dafne, 'Piangete, ninfe, e con voi pianga Amore': 'when they sing together the duo "Sparse più non vedren di quel finoro", looking each other in the face at those exclamations has great force. Similarly, when they all sing "Dov'è, dove è 'l bel viso", moving according to the motions of the chorus produces no little grace, and [likewise] when united together they repeat "Piangete, ninfe, e con voi pianga Amore".' Individual characters should also walk in time to

13 According to *Il corago* (ed. Fabbri and Pompilio, p. 98), the chorus should be no fewer than twelve and no more than twenty-four. As we shall see, however, there is a strong case for assuming that the choruses in *Orfeo* were sung with just one or at most two to a part.

the music, with specific actions choreographed to match the words. Gagliano then gives further detailed instructions for the handling of particular passages in *Dafne*, including Apollo's battle with the python (where a dancer dressed as Apollo can substitute surreptitiously for the singer should the latter either be incapable of imitating battle or be rendered too breathless to sing). In general, the best movement for the choruses is 'successively to the right, left and rear, but avoiding altogether the affectation of dance'.

Finally, Gagliano reveals some of the tricks of the theatrical trade. In terms of the python, 'The serpent needs to be big, and if the painter who makes it will know how – as I have seen – to make it move its wings [and] spew fire, it will make a better sight. Above all it should writhe, with its operator placing his hands on the ground, so that he goes on all fours.' Gagliano also explains how Apollo can appear to crown himself with a laurel branch using a trick devised 'by Messer Cosimo del Bianco, a man most diligent above and beyond his profession, and one of great invention as regards scenery, costumes and similar things'. And he suggests a useful way of having Apollo seem to play the *lira da braccio*, the bowed string instrument commonly associated with the god by way of a misplaced classical association:

> Nor do I wish to ignore the fact that since Apollo, in singing the *terze rime* 'Non curi la mia pianta, o fiamma, o gelo', must place the *lira* to his breast (which he must do with good attitude), it is necessary to make it appear to the auditorium that from Apollo's *lira* appears a more than ordinary melody. So let there be placed four string players (*da braccio* or *da gamba* matters little) in one of the exits close by, in a position where, unseen by the audience, they see Apollo, and as he places his bow on the *lira* they should play the three notes written, taking care to draw equal bow-strokes so that it appears one stroke only. This trick cannot be recognized except by the imagination of someone who knows about these things, and it brings no little delight.

A fair amount of all this advice is applicable to *Orfeo* – not surprisingly, given that it shares several thematic elements with *Dafne* – and one wonders whether Francesco Rasi, who played Apollo in *Dafne*, also used the same *lira da braccio* trick in, say, the final stanza of 'Possente spirto e formidabil nume' ('Sol tu, nobile dio, puoi darmi aita', with its 'halo' of string sound) in Act III of *Orfeo*. Gagliano's guidelines also offer, *mutatis mutandis*, a number of hints for Monteverdi's later stage works.

Here, however, the chief editorial and performance problems are caused by the instrumental parts, whether the constitution of the continuo group (which Monteverdi had gone to some length to clarify in *Orfeo* by way of rubrics in the printed score, varying it according to character and situation) or the nature and scoring of the instrumental sinfonias and ritornellos indicated sketchily, in different ways, in both *Il ritorno* and *L'incoronazione*. Some difficulties are posed by the single instrumental chords indicated in *Il ritorno* at the beginning of I.1 and I.4 in lieu of a 'sinfonia' (compare the single chord provided in Act IV of *Orfeo* as Orfeo crosses the Styx), although a hint may be provided by the written-out string fanfares over a simple tonic–dominant–tonic progression at Ulisse's killing of the suitors in II.12. Similarly, in the case of *L'incoronazione*, much of the instrumental music in the Venice manuscript (mostly in three parts) and in the Naples one (mostly in four) has missing or inconsistent upper parts. Moreover, although the bass lines are often the same or similar, these upper parts, where given, can vary quite significantly, suggesting that the original materials used various short-hand forms of notation, and that the instrumentalists had a degree of latitude in what they played. One assumes that additional instrumental music could have been added in the later operas as the need arose: for example, to cover stage movement or set changes; for the latter, not a single one of the changes in either *Il ritorno* or *L'incoronazione* (except immediately after the prologues) is provided with a sinfonia or introductory ritornello, although there is instrumental music for the descent of Minerva and Telemaco in *Il ritorno*, II.1. It is worth noting, however, that neither Gagliano nor, in fact, any other major source of the period would seem to justify the extended addition of instrumental accompaniments to arias or other items in Venetian operas, whether editorially or by way of spontaneous improvisation in performance.

Monteverdi's singers

Singers have a crucial role to play in any opera – any theatre composer needed to cater quite precisely for their talents and ambitions – and yet they tend to get forgotten in historical accounts of the repertory. While this pragmatic requirement has begun to be acknowledged in studies of opera in the eighteenth and nineteenth centuries, there is still often a reluctance to accept that any 'great' art form such as opera could be so strongly determined – some might say contaminated – by its modes of production. The tantrums of the *prima donna* may be accepted as a necessary evil, or even part of the mystique of the profession, but the image of Handel threatening to pitch out of the window a spoilt and too demanding virtuoso soprano (Francesca Cuzzoni) appeals nicely to our prejudice that, in the end, the composer could and should keep firm control of the art work flowing through his pen. Monteverdi, too, could get into legal and other difficulties with singers.[14]

14 For a late example, see Beth Glixon, 'Scenes from the Life of Silvia Gailarti Manni'.

However, a composer's relationships with his performers could be collaborative rather than combative: indeed, such collaboration was necessary to the smooth running of any production and, for that matter, was surely in the composer's best interests – if, that is, he had any say in the matter. The history of opera provides many examples – from Handel and Senesino to Britten and Peter Pears – of composers pushing, and being pushed by, their preferred singers to scale greater heights of virtuosity and dramatic expression. Presumably, Monteverdi was no exception in working with the grain of specific voices to produce his most characteristic music.

The tenor Francesco Rasi is a case in point. He had studied with Giulio Caccini, becoming well schooled in the new arts of Florentine solo song, and his abilities seem firmly embedded in the title-role of *Orfeo*. Monteverdi also catered specifically for what appears to have been his favourite party-trick of including elaborate vocal or instrumental echo effects in his virtuoso performances. The *intermedi* accompanying the performance of Guarini's *Il pastor fido* in Mantua in June 1598 included 'Rasi with the chitarrone, who sang most wondrously, to whom responded two echoes with marvellous excellence', while for the second *intermedio* of Guarini's *L'idropica*, staged in Mantua in June 1608, Giovanni Giacomo Gastoldi provided a piece (for Rasi?) in which the mythological character Glaucus 'sang in this manner, making his voice resound so that various instruments were heard in due order one after the other repeating in sound his closing phrases as an echo from various parts [of the stage]'.[15] Rasi also made great play of impersonating the famed musicians of Classical Antiquity. For example, in February 1608 he accompanied Duke Vincenzo and Prince Francesco to Turin (for the actual wedding ceremony with Margherita of Savoy) and took part in an entertainment staged there:

> From a part of the wood entered by way of a river a majestic Arion carried by a dolphin, which, while it frisked through the water, approaching the spectators gave place to the song of the most famous Rasi, who to the harp made the woods echo with celestial harmony.[16]

15   For the 1598 performance, see Parisi, *Ducal Patronage of Music in Mantua*, p. 188 n. 80: 'il Rasi con il Chitarrone che cantò mirabili*ssimamente*, a cui rispondavano duo Echo con meraviglosa [*sic*] eccellenza'. One model was Jacopo Peri's 'Dunque fra torbid'onde' for the fifth of the 1589 Florentine *intermedi*. For Glaucus, see Follino, *Compendio delle sontuose feste* (1608), in Solerti, *Gli albori del melodramma*, iii, p. 219: 'cantò di questa maniera, rimbombando la sua voce in modo che s'udivano diversi stormenti ordinatamente l'un dopo l'altro replicare in forma d'eco da varie parti col suono i suoi ultimi accenti'. Perhaps significantly, too, the text for Glaucus – 'Or che se 'n va rinchiuso in forme nove' – uses the same poetic form (*terza rima*) as Orfeo's 'Possente spirto e formidabil nume'.

16   Kirkendale, *The Court Musicians in Florence during the Principate of the Medici*, p. 573: 'Da un ridotto della selva uscì per entro il fiume un maestoso Arione portato da

The potential association with Orfeo's great Act III set piece, 'Possente spirto e formidabil nume', is clear, particularly in the light of the prominent part for double-harp in its third stanza. The influence also extends to the musical style: the opening of 'Possente spirto' is very like other theatrical songs known to have been sung by Rasi in Florence and Mantua (see Ex. 4–1; and note also Ex. 5–5).[17]

Similarly, *Arianna* seems to have been strongly influenced by the late recruitment of the famous singer–actress Virginia Andreini, replacing in the title-role Monteverdi's unfortunate pupil Caterina Martinelli, who had died of smallpox some three months before the première. Indeed, the evidence suggests that the central lament in the opera – the only part of it to survive – was a later addition to the work's original design, made specifically to exploit Andreini's renowned theatrical talents (see Chapter 8). Other female singers with whom Monteverdi worked closely include Settimia Caccini, the younger daughter of Giulio, who may have performed in *Andromeda* and who certainly ravished the ears of audiences in Parma at the 1628 wedding entertainments.[18] Anna Renzi, too, may have had an Andreini-like influence on the role of Ottavia in *L'incoronazione*, which conforms to a character-type often represented by her on the Venetian stage during her long theatrical career. So famous was her performance as Ottavia that it was enshrined in contemporary verse:

Poi cominciasti afflitta   Then, afflicted, you began
tue querele canore   your melodious complaints
con tua voce divina   with your voice divine
'Disprezzata regina',   'Disprezzata regina',
e seguendo il lamento   and continuing your lament
facevo di dolore   you forced, out of grief,
stillar in pianto, e sospirar Amore.   Amor to burst into tears and sigh.
Sò ben'io, che se vero   Well do I know that,

un delfino, qual mentre andava guizzando per le acque avvicinandosi a i spettatori diede luogo al canto del famosissimo Rasis, qual sopra l'arpa fece eccheggiare le selve di celeste armonia.'

17 The text of 'Indarno Febo il suo bell'oro eterno' (Ex. 4–1(c)) is from Gabriello Chiabrera's *Il pianto d'Orfeo* (Solerti, *Gli albori del melodramma*, iii, pp. 89–100, see p. 93), which the poet may have presented to Mantua for staging in 1608.

18 For Settimia Caccini, see Kirkendale, *The Court Musicians in Florence during the Principate of the Medici*, pp. 337–46. She married the Lucchese musician Alessandro Ghivizzani (ibid., pp. 333–7) shortly before they entered the Medici payroll on 3 November 1609. Enzo Bentivoglio had been involved in attempts to engineer a marriage between Settimia and Girolamo Frescobaldi in early 1609; see Newcomb, 'Girolamo Frescobaldi 1608–15'.

Ex. 4-1 (a) Giulio Caccini, *Il rapimento di Cefalo*, V, final chorus ('Ineffabile ardore'), stanza 4 ('This air was sung, with some of the *passaggi* as given and some according to his own taste, by the famous Francesco Rasi, noble of Arezzo, most obligated servant of His Highness [the Duke] of Mantua'); (b) *Orfeo*, III, Orfeo, 'Possente spirto e formidabil nume' (unornamented version); (c) Francesco Rasi, 'Indarno Febo il suo bell'oro eterno' (*Vaghezze di musica*, 1608).

Giulio Caccini: *'Le nuove musiche' (1602)*, ed. Hitchcock, pp. 109–10; Monteverdi, *L'Orfeo, favola in musica* (Venice, Ricciardo Amadino, 1609), p. 52; Rasi, *Vaghezze di musica per una voce sola* (Venice, Angelo Gardano & fratelli, 1608), fol. 2r.

[a] For moving through the ethereal plains, the sun here below turns the night's shade to day . . .

[b] Powerful spirit and fearsome god . . .

[c] In vain Phoebus his beautiful gold eternal . . .

---

fosse stato il cordoglio,	had the grief been true,
e l'historia funesta,	and the dolorous tale,
alla tua voce mesta,	hearing your mournful voice,
alle dolce parole, ai cari detti,	your sweet words, your endearing expressions,
si come i nostri petti	just as they filled our breasts
colmaro di pietade, ah sò ben'io,	with pity, ah, well do I know that
Neron s'havrebbe fatto humile, e pio.	Nero would have been rendered humble and compassionate.[19]

Other singers associated with Monteverdi are more shadowy. The prologue to *Orfeo* was delivered by the Florentine castrato Giovanni Gualberto Magli, another pupil of Caccini, who also took at least one other role (and perhaps two) in the opera, and its relatively simple style was presumably designed to allow free rein with embellishment in the style of the 'new music'. We do not (yet) know the name of the virtuoso bass(es) for whom Monteverdi revised the role of Plutone in the *Ballo delle ingrate* and who played Nettuno in *Il ritorno* and Seneca in *L'incoronazione*; the three roles share significant similarities of range, tessitura and writing, such that they may have been written for the same singer, possibly the bass for whom Monteverdi also wrote the virtuosic 'Ab aeterno ordinata [*sic*] sum' in the *Selva morale e spirituale* of 1640–1. One itches to identify the singers who played Testo in the *Combattimento* (Monteverdi's son, Francesco?), Penelope and Ulisse, or Nerone

---

19 Rosand, *Opera in Seventeenth-Century Venice*, p. 385 (with minor modifications), citing *Le glorie della Signora Anna Renzi romana* (Venice, Giovanni Battista Surian, 1644), p. 25. 'Disprezzata regina' is, of course, the opening of Ottavia's first scene in *L'incoronazione* (I.4). Compare also the association between Renzi and lament in a contemporary account of Francesco Sacrati's *Bellerofonte* (1642) in Rosand, *Opera in Seventeenth-Century Venice*, p. 101. Such books praising singers were not unusual: compare Domizio Bombarda's *Teatro delle glorie della S^a Adriana Basile* (Venice, Evangelista Deuchino, 1623), the enthusiasm of which was prompted by the visit to Venice of this well-known virtuoso soprano in May 1623.

and Poppea (Anna di Valerio?),[20] and those who delighted audiences with their portrayal of 'character' parts (Caronte in *Orfeo*; Iro in *Il ritorno*; Arnalta in *L'incoronazione*), or for that matter, just the alto with the wide range (*d–a'*) who sang in the Act III and Act IV choruses in *Orfeo*, and also, it seems, in the *ballo Tirsi e Clori*. Yet although they remain nameless, their voices resound through the music.

A careful look at the distribution of roles in *Orfeo*, *Il ritorno* and *L'incoronazione*, plus their range and nature, produces striking results that must surely reflect the prior planning of both librettist and composer working under typical constraints. It is almost certain that *Orfeo* was designed to be performed by an all-male cast (with castratos taking the female roles); one year later, in 1608, Federico Follino noted in his account of the festivities for the wedding of Prince Francesco Gonzaga and Margherita of Savoy that only for these performances, and for the first time, had Duke Vincenzo Gonzaga allowed his female singers to appear on the public stage.[21] One can also reasonably assume that the seventeen (at least) solo roles in *Orfeo* were not taken by seventeen different singers, but that some doubling occurred. This was another fact of theatrical life. Monteverdi's letter of 6 January 1617 concerning the abandoned *Le nozze di Tetide* deals with the practicalities of having the virtuoso Adriana Basile take two roles in the piece – as Venere and as one of the three sirens – and therefore having time for a quick costume change. In the work eventually performed in the 1617 Mantuan festivities, Santi Orlandi's *Gli amori d'Aci e Galatea*, Margherita Basile was also expected to take two roles;[22] while during the preparations for the 1628 Parma festivities, the less experienced singers panicked over late changes of multiple casting. The author of *Il corago* explicitly recommends against doubling roles – a sure indication that it occurred regularly – on the grounds that audiences quickly recognized singers' voices, although he noted that if doubling was to occur, the music should be sufficiently well contrasted (suggesting, perhaps, that often it was not).[23]

20   For Di Valerio, see Curtis, '*La Poppea impasticciata*', pp. 41–2 n. 28 (which also discusses other possible singers in *L'incoronazione*); Fabbri, 'New Sources for "Poppea"', p. 19. For Nerone, Pirrotta's argument ('Forse Nerone cantò tenore') that the role may originally have been taken by a tenor has not been widely accepted.

21   See Follino's account of the *intermedi* for *L'idropica* in *Compendio delle sontuose feste* (1608), pp. 73–4 (Solerti, *Gli albori del melodramma*, iii, p. 208). The use of castratos (or boys) to take female roles was not unusual. In the case of the early performances of Peri's *Euridice*, for example, the parts of Venere and Proserpina were taken by castratos, Dafne (the messenger) by a boy, Tragedia first by a woman and then by a castrato, and Euridice by a woman; see Palisca, 'The First Performance of *Euridice*', p. 445.

22   Davari, 'Notizie biografiche del distinto maestro di musica Claudio Monteverdi', p. 117.

23   *Il corago*, ed. Fabbri and Pompilio, p. 67.

Table 4-3   A possible allocation of roles in *Orfeo*

(In column 4, entries in parenthesis indicate usual tessitura.)

Singer	Role	Appearance	Clef and range
Soprano A (Giovanni Gualberto Magli)	Musica	Prologue	C1: $f'-d''$ $(a'-d'')$
	Euridice	I; IV	C1: $d'-d''$ $(g'-d'')$
Soprano B	Ninfa	I	C1: $d'-d''$ $(f'-c'')$
	Proserpina	IV	C1: $c'-f''$ $(f'-c'')$
Soprano C	Messaggera	II	C1: $c'-e''$ $(f'-c'')$
	Speranza	III	C1: $c'-e''$ $(f'-c'')$
Alto A	Pastore	I; II	C3: $c'-a'$
Tenor A (Francesco Rasi)	Orfeo	I; II; III; IV; V	C4: $Bb-f'$
Tenor B (?Pandolfo Grande)	Pastore	II (upper part)	C4: $d-f'$
	Spirito	IV	C4: $d-e'$
	Eco	V	C4: $b-e'$
Tenor C (?Francesco Campagnolo)	Pastore	I; II (lower part)	C4: $d-f'$
	Spirito	IV	C4: $f\sharp-eb'$ (but marked to be transposed up a tone, i.e., for Alto)
	Apollo	V	C4: $d-eb'$
Bass A	Caronte	III	F4: $F-bb$
Bass B	Plutone	IV	F4: $A-a$
Bass C (but could be Bass A)	Spirito	IV	F4: $c-a$

Close analysis of the vocal range and writing associated with each solo role in *Orfeo*, plus a modicum of common sense (characters on the stage in the same or nearly adjacent scenes cannot be taken by the same singer), reveals how such doubling might work (see Table 4-3).[24] There are also

24   I present a much more detailed argument, with supporting evidence, for this scheme in my 'Singing *Orfeo*'. The allocation of the soprano roles is based largely on pairings prompted by similarities of range, tessitura and style of writing, although others are possible, and whatever the case, the scheme seems to have been altered at the last minute because of difficulties over the original singers. For a different allocation gained independently of, and prior to, mine, while proceeding from a similar premiss, see Kelly, *First Nights*, pp. 2–59, at p. 35 (drawing on his '"*Orfeo da camera*"'). Kelly's 9-performer scheme has separate singers for Orfeo (Rasi) and Euridice (Girolamo Bacchini; who in fact was no longer in Mantuan service), plus Soprano 1 (Magli; Musica, Messaggera, Speranza, chorus in Act V), Soprano 2 (Ninfa, Proserpina, chorus in Acts I, II and V), Alto (Pastore in Acts I and II, duet and trio in Act I, chorus in Acts I–IV), Tenor 1 (Pastore in Acts I and II, duets in Acts I and II, Spirito, Apollo, chorus in Acts I–IV), Tenor 2 (Pastore in

grounds for believing that there was not a separate chorus: in fact, the chorus parts in *Orfeo* can be allocated to the solo singers on similar principles, leaving only a very few unaccounted for, and perhaps taken by supernumeraries (instrumentalists not being used at a given point?) singing from the wings. The allocation permits the choruses to be done often two to a part, at least in the case of the upper voices. The process also reveals some quite striking decisions made at the design stage: for example, the bass parts in the Act I choruses have a much wider range (thus, for Bass A) than those in Act II (for Bass B), leaving Bass A one act in which to change costume to enter as Caronte in Act III, while Bass B then has time to prepare for the role of Plutone. It also reveals the kinds of problems that always emerge when trying to turn theory into theatrical practice. Monteverdi faced several last-minute difficulties with the sopranos – indeed, Magli had to be hurriedly recruited from Florence – that seem to have caused him to reallocate some of their roles (which probably emerged not as indicated in Table 4-3); performers becoming somehow incapacitated or worse at the last minute was not uncommon, as the Gonzagas discovered in 1591–2 in the ill-fated preparations for *Il pastor fido*, and would again experience in 1608 over Monteverdi's *Arianna*. Similarly, an annotation in the 1609 score of Act IV of *Orfeo* makes it clear that the Apollo finale was a later addition, replacing the one with the Bacchantes. This prompted Monteverdi to remove one tenor (Tenor C) from Act IV – his speech was transposed up a tone into an alto range – so that he would have time to change costume as Apollo.[25] It is possible, too, that one perceived advantage of the new Apollo finale was that it may have given Monteverdi's former pupil, Francesco Campagnolo, an opportunity to shine next to the virtuoso tenor Francesco Rasi. But there is more. The solo roles in *Orfeo*, plus the vast majority of the choruses, can be taken by three sopranos, one alto, three tenors, and two basses – that is, nine singers, to which should probably be added a second alto (the one with the large range) for at least some of the choruses. If one removes the tenor Francesco Rasi (Orfeo) from the reckoning, the resulting ensemble (SSSAATTBB) is the same as the one for which Monteverdi wrote the madrigal 'Questi vaghi concenti' concluding the Fifth Book of madrigals (1605) and in a similar style to parts of *Orfeo*. This rather strange piece is written for two choruses – SSATB, SATB – the constitution of which reflects quite precisely what seems to have been the standard complement of (male) singers at the Mantuan court (three castratos and two of each other voice). The conclusion is both inescapable and,

Acts I and II, duets in Acts I and II, Spirito, chorus in Acts I–V), Bass 1 (Plutone, Eco, chorus in Acts III and IV), and Bass 2 (Pastore in Act I, Caronte, chorus in Acts I–V).

25   The final chorus in the score of Act V, 'Vanne, Orfeo, felice a pieno' also does not fit the vocal ranges used earlier, suggesting again a later addition.

in the end, obvious: *Orfeo* was designed and written for a fixed body of male court singers (and, it can be shown, instrumentalists) which Monteverdi headed as *maestro della musica di camera* of Duke Vincenzo Gonzaga.

One of the advantages of working with such an ensemble was the speed with which things might be done. Monteverdi's letters repeatedly emphasize the need for adequate rehearsal of his works, but he was also grateful if the performers took just a few minutes to look over a new piece of music and try it out prior to performing it: many performances of chamber and sacred works, then, may have come close to sight-reading. For stage works, more learning was required, if only to commit parts to memory. But Giovanni Gualberto Magli did not do badly in the case of *Orfeo*. Brought in at a late stage, he had been sent the prologue and other music by post on 17 January 1607. He left Florence on or after 5 February, by which time he had learnt the prologue (twenty lines of text) but not the rest, much to the consternation of Prince Francesco Gonzaga. However, he seems to have learnt a significant amount of new music after his arrival in Mantua on 16 February prior to the performance on the 24th. In 1608, the singer–actress Virginia Andreini reportedly learnt the part of Arianna in six days; even if this may not have included the lament, it was still an impressive feat. Other female singers perhaps made a harder job of it. The young Angela (Angioletta) Zanibelli had some difficulty learning her music for the 1608 Mantuan festivities in time, and she seems to have been coached by ear (could she read music?) and perhaps also phonetically.[26] But in the case of Monteverdi's later stage works for Mantua, the proximity between his sending the last portions of music from Venice and the performance suggest that time-scales could often be very tight indeed. One also assumes that under the repertory system that emerged in Venetian 'public' operas, singers were expected, and able, to learn new music relatively quickly.

As for *Il ritorno d'Ulisse in patria* and *L'incoronazione di Poppea*, the stage movement of their characters works very differently from *Orfeo*. In *Orfeo*, there would seem to be very little mobility within each act, except where a new character enters mid-way through (for example, Messaggera in Act II, Caronte in Act III, Apollo in Act V), and the action therein remains quite unified. Both *Il ritorno* and *L'incoronazione*, however, adopt the dynamic of contemporary spoken drama, with the successive entrances and exits of characters creating a linear sequence the coherence of which is granted chiefly

---

26 For Zanibelli, Marchesa Isabella Bentivoglio noted on 26 December 1607 that she was barely literate and needed to learn music by ear (see Reiner, 'La vag'Angioletta', pp. 37–8). Her own curious corruption of one of her lines in the final *intermedio* for *L'idropica* in her letter of 11 April 1608 (ibid., p. 60) suggests that she may not have seen the text written down. For other examples of how singers learnt new music, see Hill, *Roman Monody in the Circle of Cardinal Montalto*, i, pp. 128–9.

by overlapping (the process is clear in Tables 4-1 and 4-2). So, within a given scene-complex (a sequence of scenes played on a single set), at least one character will tend to be present in two or more contiguous scenes before making an exit, while a change of set permits the process to begin anew. For example, in the second scene-complex of Act I of *L'incoronazione* (I.5–13), Ottavia is on stage in I.5 (with Nutrice) and I.6 (with Seneca and Valletto), Seneca is on stage in I.6 then I.7 (alone), I.8 (with Pallade) and I.9 (with Nerone), Nerone is on stage in I.9 then I.10 (with Poppea), Poppea is on stage in I.10 then I.11 (with Ottone), and Ottone is on stage in I.11 then I.12 (alone) and I.13 (with Drusilla); subsidiary continuities are maintained by characters being on stage but silent (Nutrice in I.6, Ottone in I.10, Arnalta in I.11). This would in effect become the typical dynamic of later Baroque *opera seria*, where each main character exits with a da-capo aria. A complete change of personnel between two scenes in a given scene-complex is both unusual and quite difficult to handle smoothly (see *Il ritorno*, I.1–2; *L'incoronazione*, II.4–6). Both operas are quite similar from this structural point of view; they also, curiously enough, have their monologue scenes in much the same places (for *Il ritorno*, I.1, I.7, I.12, III.1, III.8; for *L'incoronazione*, I.1, I.7, I.12, II.6, III.1, III.6, III.7). While these broad principles determine the pacing of the drama, they also affect the performers, whose presence on the stage will depend on the weight of their role and also, one assumes, in some sense on the ranking of the singer: as one might expect, Ulisse and Penelope have the most scenes on stage in *Il ritorno*, while in *L'incoronazione* it is Poppea, Nerone and, more surprisingly, Ottone. Given that these main characters must return at various points in the action (a further difference from *Orfeo*, where only Orfeo appears in all five acts), their performers are not free to double up roles. This is not to say, however, that other doublings might not have occurred.

In Venice, Monteverdi had a much bigger pool of singers on which to draw, ranging from the *cappella* at St Mark's over which he had control as director (and whose members regularly earned extra income by extensive freelance performance), to other musicians employed in the city's churches, confraternities and other institutions, to the women who were now increasingly taking to the stage. Although Duke Vincenzo Gonzaga was notoriously reluctant to let his female singers perform in the theatre on the grounds of both prestige and propriety, the Venetians had less compunction over the issue, in part because of the more liberal climate there but also because of the role of the theatre at the more respectable end of the sex-industry that formed a major part of the city's tourist trade. As yet, we know far too little about the organization of the 'public' opera houses emerging in Venice from 1637 and precisely how singers were recruited, whether individually or as a company, and whether for a work, a season or a theatre (all were possible and no doubt practised). Thus it is hard and perhaps unreasonable to claim that *Il ritorno* and

L'incoronazione were written for specific companies, in whatever sense, in the same way that *Orfeo* was designed for the corpus of Mantuan court musicians. Yet if one performs a similar exercise on Monteverdi's last two operas as on *Orfeo*, above, the results are highly suggestive.

Table 4-4 lists the thirty roles in *Il ritorno* distributed according to range and voice-type between fourteen singers (three sopranos, two mezzo-sopranos, one alto, six tenors and two basses). In the case of Act III scene 7, I have assumed, not unreasonably, that the 'coro in cielo' and the 'coro marittimo' can include the named roles participating in this scene. I would not claim that this is definitely how *Il ritorno* was performed in 1640, but it could certainly be performed thus now (with one slight difficulty, discussed further below). The number reflects what seems to have been a speedy expansion to a more or less standard norm of the forces employed in Venetian opera: Francesco Manelli's *Andromeda* (Teatro S. Cassiano, 1637) involved seven singers (including the composer) and probably three dancers, with, it seems, four singers doubling roles; Francesco Sacrati's *Bellerofonte* (Teatro Novissimo, 1642) had 9–13 singers, depending on how roles were doubled.[27] The number also reflects the standard constitution of a *commedia dell'arte* troupe (12–15 players). What is also striking in the case of *Il ritorno* is the overall expansion in voice ranges compared with those of (most of) the roles in *Orfeo*, particularly in the case of the sopranos: although we cannot be sure who sang in *Il ritorno*,[28] they must have been competent. There is a problem with the role of Eumete, who seems to be a tenor (C4 clef) up to Act II scene 2, and then (from Act II scene 7) a soprano castrato (C1 clef).[29] The shift comes between Acts II and III in the (probably original) 5-act version, which may suggest in turn that the sole surviving manuscript of *Il ritorno* conflates (and renders in three acts) two previous redactions of the opera for (at least some) different performers. Melanto's role also suspiciously shifts

27 For *Andromeda* and *Bellerofonte*, see Rosand, *Opera in Seventeenth-Century Venice*, pp. 71, 101. In the latter's *Descrittione* (1642), the singers are mostly unnamed ('un soprano di Parma', 'un basso Senese' . . .) and it is not always clear whether reference is made to the same singer in connection with different roles.

28 In the revival of *Il ritorno* in Bologna in 1640, Giulia Paolelli played Penelope, and Maddalena Manelli Minerva; see Rosand, *Opera in Seventeenth-Century Venice*, p. 18 n. 24. However, we do not know whether they sang these roles in Venice. Giovan Battista Marinoni (1596–1657), a tenor at St Mark's from 1623 until early 1642, may have earned his sobriquet 'Giove' from taking that role in *Il ritorno* (another Giove, in Francesco Manelli's *Andromeda* of 1637, had been sung by Giovanni Battista Bisucci; see *The Letters of Claudio Monteverdi*, trans. Stevens, p. 332).

29 As a result, Eumete's part from II.7 onwards needs to be transposed if the role is to be taken by a tenor. The recent English National Opera production took II.7 down an octave, II.10, 12 down a fifth, III.4, 5 in part down a fifth and in part down an octave, and III.9 down an octave.

Table 4-4   A possible allocation of roles in *Il ritorno d'Ulisse in patria*

(In column 3, entries in parenthesis indicate a character on stage but not singing; in column 4, entries in parenthesis indicate usual tessitura.)

Singer	Role	Appearance	Clef and range
Soprano A	Fortuna	Prologue	C1: $c\sharp'\!-\!g''$ ($g'\!-\!e''$)
	Minerva	I.8, 9; II.1, 9, 12; III.6, 7	C1: $c'\!-\!g''$
	Coro in cielo 2	III.7	C1: $f'\!-\!e''$
Soprano B	Amore	Prologue	C1: $d'\!-\!g''$; sings upper part in trio in Prologue.
	Giunone	III.6, 7	C1: $d'\!-\!a''$
	Coro in cielo 1	III.7	C1: $e'\!-\!f''$
Soprano C	Melanto	I.2, 10; II.4; III.3	C1: $a\!-\!f''$ ($d'\!-\!d''$); one g'' in I.2; II.4 is pitched quite low.
	Coro marittimo 1	III.7	C3: $d'\!-\!a'$
Mezzo-soprano A	Humana Fragilità	Prologue	C1/C3: $c'\!-\!c''$ ($c'\!-\!a'$)
	Ericlea	I.1; III.8, (9), 10	C1: $c'\!-\!e''$
Mezzo-soprano B	Penelope	I.1, 10; II.5, (6), 7, 11, 12; III.3, 4, 5, 9, 10	C1: $b\flat\!-\!d''$ ($c'\!-\!c''$); one a in II.5.
Alto A	Feaci 1	I.(4), (5), 6	C3: $d'\!-\!a'$
	Anfinomo	II.5, (6), (7), 8, 12	C3: $a\!-\!a'$; one g in II.12.
	Coro in cielo 3	III.7	C3: $a\!-\!a'$
Tenor A	Eurimaco	I.2; II.4, (5), (6), (?7), 8	C4: $c\!-\!g'$ ($a\!-\!f'$); II.8 is strangely low.
	Coro marittimo 3	III.7	C4: $f\!-\!d'$
Tenor B	Feaci 2	I.(4), (5), 6	C4: $f\!-\!f'$
	Iro	I.12; II.12; III.1	C4: $d\!-\!g'$ ($d\!-\!d'$); lower than Eumete.
	Coro in cielo 4	III.7	C4: $d\!-\!f'$
Tenor C	Ulisse	I.(4), (5), (6), 7, 8, 9, 13; II.(1), 2, 3, 9, 10, 12; III.10	C4: $c\!-\!g'$ ($f\!-\!f'$); in general, lower than Eumete, Iro and Telemaco.
Tenor D	Eumete	I.11, 12, 13; II.(1), 2, 7, 10, 12; III.4, 5, 9, (10)	(a) I.11, 12, 13; II.2 – C4: $c\!-\!g'$. He seems to be the highest tenor of the group; II.2 is higher (around $g\!-\!g'$) than I.11–13 (around $d\!-\!d'$). (b) II.7, 10, 12; III.4, 5, 9 – C1: $c'\!-\!e''$

Table 4-4   *Continued*

Singer	Role	Appearance	Clef and range
Tenor E	Giove	I.5; III.7	C4: *d–g′*
	Pisandro	II.5, (6), (7), 8, 12	C4: *e–g′* (*g–g′*); one *d* in II.12
	Coro marittimo 2	III.7	C4: *e–f′*
Tenor F	Telemaco	II.1, 2, 3, 11; III.5, 9, 10	C4: *c–g′* (*g–e′*); second half of II.11 is in C1.
Bass A	Tempo	Prologue	F4: *F–d′* (*G–g*)
	Feaci 3	I.(4), (5), 6	F4: *F–b♭*
	Antinoo	II.5, (6), (7), 8, 12	F4: *E–d′* (*A–a*)
Bass B	Nettuno	I.5, 6; III.7	F4: *C–d′*
	Coro marittimo 4	III.7	F4: *F–c′*

downwards in terms of range (but within the same clef), particularly in Act II scene 4 (III.1 in the 5-act version). However, the other clef changes (including Humana Fragilità in C1 and C3 clefs in the prologue) are less problematic, being linked more to issues of tessitura. And most of the roles fall quite nicely into regular patterns: it would seem that only the singers playing Penelope, Eumete, Ulisse, Telemaco and Nettuno took just one role in the opera, while the others had two or more and/or sang in the choruses.

The distribution of roles in Table 4-4 permits sufficient time for costume changing where necessary, but not as much, on the whole, as in *Orfeo*: performers in the 'public' theatre probably had to work harder and faster than in the court. However, this distribution does not reflect an entirely economical use of the resources to hand, given that the following do not sing in all three acts: Soprano B (not in Acts I or II), Mezzo-soprano A (not in II), Tenor F (not in I), Bass A (not in III, unless in the *coro marittimo*), Bass B (not in II). Monteverdi's relatively sparse use of instruments in the opera would also seem rather profligate, unless the obbligato parts were variously taken by different members of the continuo group, changing instruments as the need arose. Musicians may be happy to be paid just to sit around the dressing-room doing nothing, but for an impresario wanting value for money, it is better to have them performing as much as possible. In part, the situation in *Il ritorno* may reflect a design flaw on the part of the librettist: Badoaro seems content to let characters drift in and out of the action just as they are required to further the main plot, rather than in order to develop sub-plots (Iro is perhaps the exception). Thus Ericlea, the prototype world-weary nurse (compare Nutrice and Arnalta in *L'incoronazione*), is not seen between I.1 and III.8; Eurimaco disappears unnoticed at the end of Act II (presumably because he is allied with the suitors); and Eumete – a surprisingly large role for a 'secondary' character – peters out in III.9. This is one reason why *Il ritorno* can sometimes seem to lack direction.

The most effective and appropriate allocation and distribution of singers to roles – often in the context of cast changes and new hirings at the last minute – must have been a matter of concern to any librettist and composer.[30] And Giovanni Francesco Busenello, the librettist of *L'incoronazione*, was acutely aware of the economic and other demands of the theatre. *L'incoronazione* is much tauter than *Il ritorno* in terms of its design and pacing, and also of the apparent distribution of the singers (see Table 4-5, following the Venice manuscript, with added notes on the Naples one where necessary). Here the twenty-nine roles can feasibly be taken by six sopranos, one mezzosoprano, two altos, two or three tenors and two or three basses: that is, 13–15 singers. This is much the same as the number for *Il ritorno*, although the distribution of voices is different: *Il ritorno* is more tenor-orientated, while it is the sopranos that dominate *L'incoronazione* and indeed give the opera its characteristic flavour. It is worth noting that even with the minimum number of singers – involving some very fast but not impossible costume changing for Tenor A and Bass B towards the beginning of Act II[31] – the consuls and tribunes in III.8 could each be doubled, respectively by Tenors A and B, and Basses B and C. Again, the singers of the main roles – Poppea, Nerone, Ottone, Arnalta and Ottavia – were probably not expected to do anything else,[32] although the bass taking the role of Seneca may have come back on towards the end of Act III as a tribune (if they were doubled). Lesser roles, however, seem to involve quite systematic doublings distributed within and

30   Compare Pietro Andrea Ziani's letter to Giovanni Faustini of 28 November 1665 concerning *Alciade* (1666), in Rosand, *Opera in Seventeenth-Century Venice*, p. 437.
31   One issue is whether the bass playing Mercurio in II.1 can enter as Famigliare 3 in II.3. That may have been a plan which then proved difficult: in the Venice manuscript, Mercurio's part is marked to be transposed up a fifth ('alla quinta alta'), i.e., for tenor (*c–g'*) and so, perhaps, for Tenor A, who still has time to change as Lucano for II.5. At that point, however, Tenor A cannot sing both Mercurio and Liberto.
32   But this assumes that in the case of the Naples manuscript, Amore would sing Coro di Amori 1 in the 3-part choruses in III.8 (and Venere another part in the 4-part one). If Amore does not take part in the chorus, then the singer of Ottavia would probably have to do it. These kinds of problem may help explain the omission of the Coro di Amori in the Venice manuscript (although the chorus is included in the rubric for the final scene): Anna Renzi might not have been prepared to demean herself by taking such a secondary role. The issue may also have a bearing on the ordering of Act III scenes 6 (Ottavia) and 7 (Arnalta), which are reversed in the Venice and Naples manuscripts (but in the present order in most of the librettos). For the different versions of the end of Act III, see the chart in Curtis, '*La Poppea impasticciata*', pp. 36–7.

Table 4-5 A possible allocation of roles in *L'incoronazione di Poppea*

(In column 3, entries in parenthesis indicate a character on stage but not singing; in column 4, entries in parenthesis indicate usual tessitura.)

Singer	Role	Appearance	Clef and range
Soprano A	Fortuna	Prologue	C1: *c'–g''* (*a'–e''*)
	Valletto	I.6; II.4, 8	C1: *c'–g''* (*g'–e''*)
	Venere (and additional part in *a*4 Coro di Amori)	III.8c	C1: *c'–e''*
Soprano B	Virtù	Prologue	C1: *d'–g''*; higher than Fortuna; but lower than her in the duet.
	Drusilla	I.13; II.8, 9; III.1, 2, 3, 4	C1: *d'–g''* (*a'–f''*)
	Coro di Amori 2	III.8c	C1: *c'–e''*
Soprano C	Amore (and Coro di Amori 1)	Prologue; II.11, 12; III.8c	C1: *d'–d''*; to *f''* in II.11–12; *c'–e''* in III.8.
	Pallade	I.8	C1: *d'–f''*
	Damigella	II.4	C1: *e'–f''*; Naples version (ed. Curtis, p. 261) has *c♯'* and *d'*.
Soprano D	Poppea	I.3, 4, 10, 11; II.10, 11, 12; III.5, 8a, (8b), (8c), 8d	C1: *d'–g''* (*g'–g''*); Naples insert to I.4 (ed. Curtis, p. 267) has *a''*, and the part here seems pitched slightly higher; Naples insert to III.8 (ed. Curtis, p. 287) also has brief *a''*.
Soprano E	Nerone	I.3, 9, 10; II.5; III.3, 4, 5, 8a, (8b), (8c), 8d	C1: *d'–g''* (*g'–e''*); three *c's* in III.4 (bar 135), and two in III.8 (bar 110); Naples insert to II.5 (ed. Curtis, p. 274) has one brief *a''*, and the part here seems pitched higher than normal.
Soprano F (Anna Renzi)	Ottavia	I.5, 6; II.7; III.6	C1: *c'–g''* (*e'–e''*); Naples insert of II.6, and insert to II.7 (ed. Curtis, pp. 278–86) seem pitched slightly higher.

Table 4-5 *Continued*

Singer	Role	Appearance	Clef and range
Mezzo-soprano A	Ottone	I.1, 2, (3?), (10), 11, 12, 13; II.6, 7, 9, 12; III.4	C2: a–c'' (c'–a'); C3 in III.4; Naples insert to I.12 (ed. Curtis, p. 269) goes up to d'' and the part here seems pitched slightly higher.
Alto A	Arnalta	I.4, (11); II.10, 12; III.2, 3, (4), 7	C3: a–a' (c'–g'); has one b' in III.3, and several gs only in III.7 (the which scene overall seems to have a lower tessitura); Naples insert to I.12 (ed. Curtis, p. 271) also has $g\sharp$, although this seems pitched at Arnalta's usual level.
Alto B	Nutrice	I.5, (6); II.8	C3: a–bb' (c'–a')
	Famigliare 1	II.3	C3: a–bb'
	Coro di Amori 3	III.8c	C3: g–b'
Tenor A	Soldato 1	I.(1), 2, (3)	C4: c–g'
	Lucano	II.5	C4: d–g'; also has one a'
	Consoli/Tribuni 1	III.8b	C4: c–eb'
Tenor B	Soldato 2	I.(1), 2, (3)	C4: c–g'
	Famigliare 2	II.3	C4: e–g'
Tenor C (unless Tenor A with quick change in Act II)	Liberto	II.2	C4: d–f' (e–c'); Naples insert to II.2 (ed. Curtis, p. 272) goes up to a', and in general the part here seems pitched higher.
Bass A (but could be Bass B with quick change in Act II)	Mercurio	II.1	F4: G–d' (c–c')
Bass B	Famigliare 3	II.3	F4: A–c'
	Littore	III.2, 3, (4)	F4: A–d'; Naples insert to III.4 is in C1: g'–g''.
	Consoli/Tribuni 2	III.8b	F4: G–d'
Bass C	Seneca	I.6, 7, 8, 9; II.1, 2, 3	F4: E–d' (A–a)

between the acts, some of which produce in fact quite interesting dramatic possibilities, as when the singer of Virtù comes on as the 'virtuous' Drusilla, or the same person plays Amore and the flirtatious Damigella. Again, there is no guarantee that this is how *L'incoronazione* was done.[33] But the plausibility, and indeed the success, of Table 4-5 is enhanced by the fact that with a cast of thirteen singers, and assuming that the consuls and tribunes were doubled, each singer is on stage in each act. Whoever performs in this casting of *L'incoronazione* gives good value for money.

Paying close attention to vocal ranges, and characteristic voice-types, pays clear dividends. The next step would be to undertake a similar exercise for other operas staged at particular theatres in Venice, season by season. This would help judge, say, whether the particular characteristics of the vocal scorings of *Il ritorno* and *L'incoronazione* are in any way typical of productions in their theatres and therefore in some sense representative of one or more companies:[34] the obvious place to start is *La finta savia*, with a libretto by Giulio Strozzi and music by Filiberto Laurenzi and others, which shared the stage with *L'incoronazione* at the Teatro SS. Giovanni e Paolo in the 1642–3 season (Anna Renzi played Aretusa, and Anna di Valerio, Aventina). Then one might track individual singers through different works and different theatres: for example, the singer who first performed Penelope must have had a very characteristic voice which might presumably be found in other operas of the period. One can also gauge the effect of subsequent revisions and revivals, as with the additions in the Naples score of *L'incoronazione*, which often seem to be pitched slightly higher than the same roles in the Venice manuscript, suggesting that they were intended for a different team of singers.[35] Of course,

33   As for other possibilities, Curtis claims that in the Naples version, the same singer took the roles of Nutrice, Arnalta and Soldato 1; see the preface to his edition of *L'incoronazione*, p. xiii. He also suggests (p. xiv) the following doublings for modern performances: Drusilla, Pallade and perhaps Virtù; Fortuna and perhaps Ottavia, Nerone or Venere; Lucano, Soldato 1 and Consoli e tribuni 1; Soldato 2, Famigliare 2 and Consoli e tribuni 1; Seneca and Consoli e tribuni 2; Mercurio, Littore and Consoli e tribuni 2, and perhaps Famigliare 3; Famigliare 1 (whom Curtis argues is Seneca's wife) and Venere, Fortuna or Ottavia, or Ottone in travesty. We agree (more or less) on most of the male characters, but not on the female ones.

34   If *Il ritorno* had its première in the Teatro SS. Giovanni e Paolo (see Chapter 1), it would have shared the stage with Manelli's *Adone*, while the Teatro S. Cassiano (probably) mounted the première of Cavalli's *Gli amori d'Apollo e di Dafne*. The revival of *Il ritorno* in 1640–1 coincided with Monteverdi's *Le nozze d'Enea in Lavinia* – the Teatro S. Cassiano staged the première of Cavalli's *Didone* – although the main competition in the 1640–1 season was Sacrati's *La finta pazza* at the Teatro Novissimo.

35   Related to this is the vexed issue of the pitch-level of Ottone's part in I.1 and I.11 in both manuscripts, which, according to Curtis ('*La Poppea impasticciata*', *passim*), indicates both revision and transposition to suit a higher voice.

this is not an exact science – much of the above is speculative – and it would probably also be a mistake to relegate an individual singer to just one type of vocal or dramatic character, even if there would be precedents for that within the specialist roles of the *commedia dell'arte*. But none of this is inconsistent with what one might reasonably expect of the workings of the early seventeenth-century theatre; certainly it was the way of the theatrical world for centuries to come.

In his letters, Monteverdi was often critical of singers, complaining of the quality of the voice, weakness in ornamentation, and in the case of one Mantuan tenor who probably sang in *Orfeo* (Pandolfo Grande), unclear diction.[36] For all the undoubted virtuosity of many of the performers under his direction, like any group of professionals they had strengths and weaknesses. Moreover, any composer wishing to get on with his colleagues, to please his employers and to produce musical results had to cut his suit to fit the cloth, showing the forces under his command in their best light while accepting their defects and being ever ready to cope with last-minute crises. Monteverdi was surely no exception. The status of his operas as the first 'great' examples of the genre means that they are rarely studied in this more practical light; thus their careful design and even content made to suit his performers have not hitherto been fully appreciated. Not that these works suffer as a result; indeed, one is forced to recognize still more Monteverdi's remarkable achievement as a man of the theatre.

36 So Monteverdi complained in his letter to Duke Vincenzo Gonzaga of 9 June 1610. For the broader issues, see Wistreich, ' "La voce è grata assai, ma . . ." '.

5

Orfeo (1607)

Orpheus with his lute made trees,
And the mountain tops that freeze,
    Bow themselves, when he did sing:
To his music, plants and flowers
Ever sprung; as sun and showers
    There had made a lasting spring.

Every thing that heard him play,
Even the billows of the sea,
    Hung their heads, and then lay by.
In sweet music is such art,
Killing care and grief of heart
    Fall asleep, or hearing, die.

(Shakespeare, *Henry VIII*, III.1)

Treating Monteverdi's operas and related works as being of and for the theatre does not diminish their stature. Nor is an awareness of the niceties of Italian metrics or of the pragmatics of early seventeenth-century staging a necessary prerequisite for any aesthetic appreciation of these pieces, for all their relevance for and influence upon compositional and performative decisions apparently made by Monteverdi and his collaborators. Presumably, he expected his audience to enjoy the theatrical experience unaware of the accommodations, compromises and even crisis-management involved in bringing these works to life.

Presumably, too, Monteverdi expected his audience to engage with issues of meaning generated by his musical theatre. Those meanings are unlikely to have been quite the same then as now, and it is the task of the historian to create appropriate frames of reference within which his works might plausibly have been viewed and understood by competent members of their first audiences. We are helped by various more or less obvious signposts in the works themselves; we are hindered by the unclear nature of early seventeenth-century theatrical and musical semiotics. Much hangs on the question of how precisely the music both informs and shapes our under-standing. In the case of *Orfeo*, for example, there are affecting moments in the score, such as the arrival of Messaggera in Act II to tell of the death of Euridice, and also impressive ones, including Orfeo's virtuosic showpiece aria 'Possente spirto e formidabil nume' at the centre of the work in Act III. Yet the music of *Orfeo* also often seems to resist involvement. The problem is not just the modern lack of contextual and cultural referents, but also the fact that Monteverdi was working in a period of profound stylistic change, where things might not always be what they seem. Constructing meaning is an exer-cise both challenging and fraught with danger. But it is an essential part of the theatrical experience.

Interpreting the myth

The plot of *Orfeo* is relatively straightforward. After the prologue delivered by Musica, Act I opens with the celebration of the forthcoming wedding of Orfeo and Euridice. The festivities continue in Act II until the fateful entry of a messenger, relating Euridice's death from a snake-bite while gathering flowers in the field. Orfeo laments and resolves to die with her. In Act III, the allegorical figure Speranza (Hope) leads Orfeo to the gates of Hades, where he encounters Caronte (Charon) and sings his famous plea 'Possente spirto', eventually succeeding in crossing the River Styx. In Act IV, Proser-pina persuades Plutone to release Euridice to demonstrate that pity rules even in the Inferno; Plutone agrees, but imposes the condition that Orfeo must lead Euridice earthwards without looking back. Orfeo fails the test. Act V opens in the fields of Thrace, with Orfeo lamenting his fate, until (in the score) his father, Apollo, descends to raise him to the heavens where Orfeo will see Euridice in the stars.

The stories embedded in early operas were matters of collective knowledge in an educated society that also placed some faith in the hidden truths of classical myth. When the members of the Accademia degli Invaghiti in Mantua, with Prince Francesco Gonzaga at their head, heard that their colleague Alessandro Striggio was planning to mount a *favola in musica* based on the tale of Orpheus, they would probably have expected something more nuanced than the standard theatrical fare of Carnival in Mantua.[1] They would

---

1 We know from Carlo Magno (see his letter given below) that two days before
   Orfeo, a 'comedia' was performed in the court theatre. This was presumably the

have appreciated the emulation of a recent Florentine precedent, Peri's
Euridice, while perhaps also being happy to welcome Orpheus back to his
true home, given that Poliziano's *Fabula d'Orpheo* (c1480) had been closely
associated with another Francesco Gonzaga in Mantua over a century before.
Poliziano's play was still alive in most literary memories, and educated
academicians would have needed no introduction to the main classical sources
of the Orpheus legend on which it was based: Ovid's *Metamorphoses*, X–XI
(Striggio's main source, too) and Virgil's *Georgics*, IV (on which Striggio draws
for his account of the Inferno). They would have known the outcome of
the myth told by Ovid and Virgil, represented by Poliziano, and hinted at by
Striggio in the libretto's finale to *Orfeo*:[2] Orpheus returns from Hades empty-
handed having failed Pluto's test, he renounces women and/or creates a
counter-cult against Dionysus (Bacchus), and he is murdered by a horde of
Bacchantes who leave his head and lyre, still lamenting the loss of Eurydice,
to float down the River Hebrus and end up in Lesbos. (However, Striggio's
finale contains nothing particularly violent or contentious: on seeing the Bacchantes approach, Orfeo makes off; they say that he will get his punishment
in the end, and meanwhile that they will sing in praise of Bacchus, which
they do at some length.) Striggio's Mantuan colleagues would also have
known the alternative endings to the tale, principally the celestial apotheosis
of Orpheus' lyre at the intercession of Apollo and the Muses as recounted by
Hyginus in his *Astronomia*, II.7 (compare the second stanza of Orfeo's 'Qual
honor di te fia degno', given in Chapter 3). And they would probably have
realized that the two endings were not necessarily incompatible. Even Ovid
has Orpheus and Eurydice happily reunited in Elysium – mortal death has
no sting in most classical and Christian cultures – while Bacchus punishes the
women for their crime.

But our academicians would still have needed some kind of guidance on how best to read Striggio's own interpretation of the myth as
measured against these various sources. The most obvious signposts towards
an interpretative framework for Monteverdi's operas are offered in their prologues; these are what the audience first hears, and therefore they adopt a
privileged position in establishing points of reference from which subsequent
actions can be judged. The notion of a somehow separate introductory scene
serving to clarify and enhance the perceptual and conceptual frame of the

regular Carnival production mounted by the Mantuan Jewish community (see
Buratelli, *Spettacoli di corte a Mantova tra Cinque e Seicento*, Chapter 4); we do not
know to what extent it involved music and thus how its production schedule might
have affected the preparations for *Orfeo*.
2   See Sternfeld, 'The Orpheus Myth and the Libretto of "Orfeo"'. Striggio's
'Bacchante' finale is in *Claudio Monteverdi: 'Orfeo'*, ed. Whenham, pp. 35–41; *The
Operas of Monteverdi*, ed. John, pp. 57–8.

drama, often by securing some manner of collusion with the audience, was well established in Renaissance drama. Here, and later, the prologue could variously invoke the audience's favour, outline the work's aesthetic intent, introduce its characters and plot, and pay homage to a patron. The resulting mixture of invitation, exhortation, explication, justification and dedication was particularly useful for works which were (or claimed to be) novel, and thus, where an audience's anxieties might need to be assuaged. Renaissance pastorals were a case in point, given their uncertain theoretical status: Poliziano's *Fabula d'Orpheo* has a prologue recited by Mercury, Cupid introduces Tasso's *Aminta* (1573), and the river Alfeo Guarini's *Il pastor fido*. Similar motives inspired the prologues in early opera: Rinuccini opted for the straight-forwardly classical Ovid in *Dafne* (1598), Tragedy in *Euridice* (1600) and Apollo in *Arianna* (1608) to explain the rationale behind the entertainment to come. The choices reflect the insecurity of early opera over its dubious aesthetic foundations: Tragedia in *Euridice* is careful to explain how and why she has abandoned her classical garb for more attractive ends. They also reflect the fear that contemporary audiences might find the notion of sung drama un-acceptable. Rinuccini responds by producing sententious verse in rigorous quatrains. This is matched by the formalist settings of his composers, who generally employ an improvisatory style evoking the aristocratic recitation of epic verse to improvised formulas that was common in the Renaissance courts. The generic associations, plus of course the speakers and their senti-ments, claim credibility for an essentially incredible genre.

The prologue to *Orfeo* is delivered by Musica, prompting a different focus to the work:

Dal mio Permesso amato a voi ne vegno,	From my beloved Permessus I come to you
incliti eroi, sangue gentil de regi	renowned heroes, noble blood of kings
di cui narra la Fama eccelsi pregi	of whom Fame speaks the highest praises
né giunge al ver perch'è tropp'alto il segno.	and yet does not reach the truth, for the target is too high.
Io la Musica son, ch'ai dolci accenti	I am Musica, for to sweet accents
so far tranquillo ogni turbato core,	I know how to make tranquil every troubled heart,
et hor di nobil ira, et hor d'amore	and now with noble anger, and now with love
poss'infiammar le più gelate menti.	I can inflame the coldest minds.

Io su cetera d'or cantando soglio	I, singing on a golden lyre, am wont
mortal orecchio lusingar tal'hora,	now to charm mortal ears
e in questa guisa a l'armonia sonora	and in this way in the sonorous harmony
de la lira del ciel più l'alme invoglio.	of the lyre of heaven I enfold souls.
Quinci a dirvi d'Orfeo desio mi sprona,	Thus desire spurs me to tell you of Orfeo,
(etc.)	*(etc.)*

After the obligatory (and obligatorily discreet) reference to the Gonzagas, Musica proclaims her ability to calm the soul, to arouse it to anger and to love – pre-empting the three musical *genera* of the preface to the *Madrigali guerrieri, et amorosi* of 1638 – and also to invoke the harmony of the spheres. We are thus invited to witness, and consequently to assess, a demonstration of these claims. The neo-Platonic resonances are obvious, and the tone is coolly calculating: in the last stanza of the prologue birds, streams, breezes and even we, the audience, are enjoined to sit still in quiet contemplation.

While the power of music may be one obvious theme embedded within the dramatic and musical structure of *Orfeo*, there are others that might usefully be kept separate: there is no reason why early operas should not be polyvalent, and perhaps even inconsistently so. For example, Striggio provides other signposts to a reading of *Orfeo*, in particular by way of his end-of-act choruses. Their presence is conventional in terms of punctuating the action; so, too, is their discursive nature (and those ending Acts I, II and IV are in *versi sciolti*), for all that Rinuccini tended to adopt a different model (strophic verse), and that Monteverdi seems to have felt it necessary to reduce their length. Less typical, and more problematic in production terms, is Striggio's apparent tendency to confuse the chorus's mobile and stable functions (the terms are Angelo Ingegneri's) in terms of participating in and commenting on the action. Thus the choruses at the ends of Act I and II both proffer a moral and engage with present and future action: in Act I, the chorus comments on Orfeo's situation and cues his return to the stage for Act II; in Act II, the chorus picks up on the lamenting refrain established in the middle of the act by Messaggera ('Ahi caso acerbo . . .'), and also discusses recovering Euridice's body and (cut from the score) preparing her funeral.

Extracting the moral from these choruses is rendered still more problematic by their often allusive nature. The difficulties of reading the Act III chorus are typical, and are exacerbated by Monteverdi having cut its second and third stanzas. The first stanza (the only one in the score) reads, and has usually been interpreted, as a conventional Humanist statement of the power of man:

Nulla impresa per huom si tenta in vano,	Nothing undertaken by man is done in vain,
né contr'a lui più sa natura armarse:	nor does nature any longer know how to arm herself against him.
ei de l'instabil piano	He of the unstable plain
arò gl'ondosi campi, e 'l seme sparse	ploughed the wavy fields, and sowed the seed
di sue fatiche, ond'aurea messe accolse.	of his toils so that he reaped a golden harvest.
Quinci perché memoria	Thus so that the memory
vivesse di sua gloria,	might live on of his glory,
la Fama a dir di lui sua lingua sciolse,	Fame loosened her tongue to speak of him,
ch'ei pose freno al mar con fragil legno,	that he curbed the sea with his fragile boat,
che sprezzò d'Austr'e d'Aquilon lo sdegno.	that he scorned the fury of the South and North Winds.

But this is no general proclamation: rather, the unspecified 'he' to whom the text refers is Jason, whose arduous sea voyages allowed him to reap a 'golden harvest': that is, the Golden Fleece. The second stanza similarly praises the nature-defying feats of Daedalus, who conquered the air with his artificial wings, and the third begins with what seems to be a reference to Phaeton, who (at least briefly) tamed fire by driving the Sun's chariot; Orpheus then completes the cycle through the four elements (water, air, fire, earth) with his feat of conquering the Inferno, excelling even these other heroes. But everyone would have heeded the implied warning. Jason, Daedalus and Phaeton may have defied nature by way of art, but only to reach variously sticky ends: Jason's second wife, Creusa, was killed by the vengeful Medea, Daedalus lost his son Icarus, and Phaeton was dragged to a watery death. In each case, pride came before a fall, just as will be the case with Orfeo in Act IV. If the Act III chorus is a grand Humanist plea, it is one tinged with reservation.

The sequence of morals running through these choruses follows a logical plan that relates to the dramatic action while also adding nuance to its meaning (parentheses indicate material cut from the score): first, man should not give in to despair because things always get better, just as spring follows winter (while overcoming difficulties is a test of character from heaven that will lead to even greater reward); second, man should not place his faith in happiness, which is fragile;[3] third, men have achieved great things (none

---

3   In fact, this is the moral proclaimed by the penultimate chorus in Act II ('Non si fidi huom mortale') before Messaggera's final speech, which seems displaced (see below).

more so than Orpheus), but, it is implied, one should avoid hubris; fourth, virtue is a prize from heaven (and it can often be clouded by emotion opposed to reason), yet although Orpheus conquered the Inferno, he was conquered by himself, and only those who can control their emotions are worthy of victory; and fifth, they that sow in tears shall reap in joy. The last, a quotation from Psalm 126 (AV 127),[4] emphasizes the potential Christian symbolism also apparent in the Apollo finale, which rounds off the Lent–Easter–Ascension allegory (and Carnival, when *Orfeo* was performed, was traditionally a period of pre-Lent celebration and contemplation). Yet in a syncretic fashion typical of the Renaissance, the allegory also melds with a pre-Christian ethic of human behaviour in the face of fate.

These two strands directing a reading of *Orfeo*, one fixed by the prologue and the other by the choruses, in fact match the two separate messages that sixteenth-century commentators identified in the tale of Orpheus. One concerned the power of eloquence:

> The story of Orpheus shows us how much strength and vigour eloquence can have, like she who is the daughter of Apollo who is none other than Wisdom. The lyre given to Orpheus by Mercury is the art of speaking properly, which, like the lyre, moves the affections with sounds, now high, now low, of the voice and of the delivery, so that the woods and the forests are moved by the pleasure that they derive from hearing the well-ordered and clear speech of a wise man.

This is, in effect, the point of the prologue. The second, however (elaborated in the choruses), concerns the moral and other imperatives of human behaviour:

> Through Orpheus, who having regained Eurydice loses her through turning back, we see the state of the soul, which man loses whenever he abandons reason and turns back: that is, to pursue blameworthy and earthly concerns.[5]

Keeping these messages separate resolves the apparent paradox that can cloud any interpretation of *Orfeo*, that an opera seemingly extolling the power of music should appear to end in failure, saved only by a contrived *lieto fine*.

---

4   *Claudio Monteverdi: 'Orfeo'*, ed. Whenham, p. 192 n. 39.
5   The first reading is from Gioseppe Orologgi's annotations on Giovanni Andrea dell'Anguillara's Italian reworking of Ovid's *Metamorphoses* (*Le Metamorfosi di Ovidio: ridotte da Gio[vanni] Andrea dell'Anguillara in ottava rima con le Annotationi di M. Gioseppe Horologgi, e gli argomenti & postille di M. Francesco Turchi* (rev. edn, Venice, Francesco de' Franceschini, 1568; the first edition dates from 1561)); the second comes from Lodovico Dolce's translation of Ovid. Both are cited and discussed in Sternfeld, 'The Orpheus Myth and the Libretto of "Orfeo"', p. 21.

Orfeo's failure is not one of eloquence: in effect, Musica gets Orfeo through the gates of Hades. Rather, it is one of moral fibre: Orfeo lacks the ability and experience to control his emotions by way of reason.

This also helps explain another apparent paradox. Orfeo's Act III showpiece 'Possente spirto e formidabil nume' is a great plea to at least one god of Hades.[6] It charms Caronte and delights his heart ('Ben mi lusinga alquanto / dilettandomi il core', he says), but Caronte resists the urge to pity Orfeo and therefore denies him access to Hades: pity, he says, is not a response worthy of his godly valour. Orfeo breaks into a much more impassioned speech ('Ahi sventurato amante') that leads to a heartrending plea: 'Rende-temi il mio ben, Tartarei numi' ('Restore to me my beloved, gods of Tar-tarus'). He then plays his lyre (represented here by a 5-part string sinfonia), which sends Caronte to sleep, leaving Orfeo free to row himself across the River Styx. The apparent failure of 'Possente spirto' is not due to a lack of rhetorical power: nothing could move Caronte, and pity is more a female virtue (as we discover at the beginning of Act IV when Proserpina pleads Orfeo's case). More to the point, falling asleep – that is, being enchanted into another world – is an entirely positive response to (Orphic) music, as Shake-speare reveals: it is not a sign of weakness, still less a comic moment. Orfeo enters Hades with his art intact; it is his virtue that will prove lacking.

Plutone's test imposed on Orfeo is one precisely of virtue. The ques-tion, expressed by one of the spirits of the Underworld, is whether Orfeo will or will not be overcome by 'giovenil desio' ('youthful desire'). Orfeo fails both because he is still young and also because he gives way to emotion, the 'affetto humano' that according to the Act IV chorus (but cut by Monteverdi) threatens virtue by opposing itself to reason. Apollo re-emphasizes the point at the end of Act V: in the course of his lament in the fields of Thrace, his son Orfeo has given way to extreme emotions unworthy of a generous heart, and he needs to learn the lesson of experience, that nothing on earth lasts. But there is another villain hiding in the wings. Orfeo's desire and the 'affetto' to which he succumbs are the attributes of earthly love. Amor as a character (as distinct from an emotion) does not appear in the opera, but he is regu-larly invoked therein. In Act I, the Pastore invites Orfeo to sing some happy

---

6   Philip Pickett claims that it is in fact addressed to Apollo; see his '*Armonia celeste*', p. 153. However, the argument fails the test of Occam's Razor, and there are serious flaws in his claims that the opening of the sixth stanza, 'Sol tu, nobile dio, puoi darmi aita' ('Only you, noble god, can give me aid'), is addressed to the Sun (= Apollo; thus 'Sun, you, noble god, can give me aid'). Pickett argues that Monteverdi makes the meaning clear to the initiated by having Orfeo start on a G. True, G can be solmized as *sol* (which is Pickett's point), but not in the flat system as here, where it must be *re*. Pickett's reading also creates a ghastly collision of three vocatives that would surely have offended Striggio's sensibilities.

song ('qualche lieta canzon') given to him by Amor, and Euridice is reluctant to articulate her feelings for Orfeo but invites him to ask Amor just how happy she is. In Act V, Orfeo tells Apollo that his extreme grief has been prompted by scorn and love, although he is now willing to listen to his father's reason. And the mistake that Orfeo makes in Act IV is to believe that there is a god greater than Plutone:

Ma che temi, mio core?	But what do you fear, my heart?
Ciò che vieta Pluton comanda Amore.	That which Plutone forbids, Amor commands.
A nume più possente	A god more powerful
che vince huomini e dei	which defeats men and gods
ben ubbidir dovrei.	should I indeed obey.

As Ovid pointed out, Eurydice does not have much cause for complaint: Orpheus' only sin is that he loved her too much. Yet Orfeo's appeal to Amor becomes his downfall, and it is only by committing himself instead to the path of 'true virtue' – and, by implication, celestial love – that he will find the 'delight and peace' advocated by Apollo as the two ascend singing to heaven ('Saliam cantand'al Cielo / dove ha virtù verace / degno premio di se, diletto e pace'). Earthly love is left to be praised by the Bacchantes and hence is silenced in the performable version of *Orfeo* that survives.[7] That Amor is a fickle master is a common theme of early opera (Rinuccini's *Dafne* elaborates the same premiss); it also one that dominates Monteverdi's later theatrical output.

Yet although it is necessary to distinguish the two main threads of the Orpheus tale as presented in *Orfeo* – the power of (musical) eloquence and the perils of earthly love – they remain intertwined. As Musica suggests in the prologue, music is inextricably associated with the language and expression of love, both in late Renaissance cultural practice (witness the amorous texts set in polyphonic madrigals) and specifically in the songs cued in the libretto of *Orfeo*. Thus music's dangerously seductive power has to be controlled if events are to reach a properly moral conclusion. Musica herself shows the way forward by the sequence of her argument, from temperance (calming the soul) to passion to celestial harmony, that is, in turn, related to the sequence both of Striggio's end-of-act choruses and of Orfeo's own journey towards his virtuous apotheosis in Act V. This may in part explain why *Orfeo* seems to lose musical interest as it heads towards its conclusion. The more

---

7 In the speech just before the libretto's final chorus, a Bacchante notes that without Bacchus (i.e., wine), the 'alma Dea che Cipro honora' ('kind goddess whom Cyprus honours') would remain 'cold and insipid'. The unnamed goddess is Venus, mythological mother of Cupid.

celestial the harmony becomes, the less it has need of worldly words. Similarly, the more Orfeo relies on the sound of his lyre, the less he needs specifically to sing: not for nothing is Caronte finally tamed by a 5-part string sinfonia. In Act IV, Orfeo should perhaps have paid heed to one lesson of Act III – the efficacy of pure sound – instead of singing a song in praise of his lyre. Love may inspire one to sing, but at times it is better to be silent.

'Tutti li interlocutori parleranno musicalmente'

What most seems to have surprised our academicians anticipating the première of *Orfeo* is the fact that Striggio's *favola* was, precisely, 'in musica'. As Carlo Magno wrote from Mantua to his brother Giovanni in Rome on 23 February 1607,

> The play [*Comedia*] was performed yesterday in the usual theatre and with all the customary splendour. Tomorrow evening the Most Serene Lord the Prince [Francesco] is to sponsor a [play] in a room in the apartments which the Most Serene Lady [Margherita] of Ferrara had the use of. It should be most unusual, as all the actors are to sing their parts; it is said on all sides that it will be a great success. No doubt I shall be driven to attend out of sheer curiosity, unless I am prevented from getting in by the lack of space [*l'angustia del luogho*].[8]

While Striggio ranges effortlessly and with allusive abandon through the ramifications of the Orpheus tale and its various possible interpretations, he seems to have been much more anxious about the presence of continuous music, such that he packs his libretto with musical terminology ('cantare', 'cantore', 'canto', 'accenti', 'concenti', 'suono', 'note'); even Dante's famous inscription on the gates of Hades, 'Lasciate ogni speranza voi ch'entrate' is rendered, Speranza says, in 'queste note'. Indeed, almost all of the formal songs in the opera – cued by strophic verse – are explicitly or implicitly diegetic within the action, as characters are regularly invited to sing songs, to play instruments, and even to dance. As a consequence, Striggio and Monteverdi's Orfeo is much more a musician than the restrained poet–singer of Peri's *Euridice*.

Striggio also seems anxious to fix and locate the plot as efficiently as possible. The very opening of Act I is characteristic:

In questo lieto e fortunato giorno	On this happy and fortunate day
c'ha posto fine a gl'amorosi affanni	which has brought an end to the amorous sufferings

8   *Claudio Monteverdi: 'Orfeo'*, ed. Whenham, p. 170. This letter is also discussed in Fenlon, 'Monteverdi's Mantuan *Orfeo*'.

del nostro semideo,	of our demigod,
cantiam, pastori, in sì soavi accenti	let us sing, shepherds, in such suave accents
5 che sian degni d'Orfeo nostri concenti.	that our concents are worthy of Orfeo.
Oggi fatta è pietosa	Today is made pitying
l'alma già si sdegnosa	that soul once so scornful
de la bell'Euridice,	of the fair Euridice,
oggi fatto è felice	today is made happy
10 Orfeo nel sen di lei per cui già tanto	Orfeo on the breast of her for whom already so much
per queste selve ha sospirato e pianto.	through these woods has he sighed and wept.
Dunque in sì lieto e fortunato giorno	So, on this happy and fortunate day
c'ha posto fine a gl'amorosi affanni	which has brought an end to the amorous sufferings
del nostro semideo,	of our demigod,
15 cantiam, pastori, in sì soavi accenti	let us sing, shepherds, in such suave accents
che sian degni d'Orfeo nostri concenti.	that our concents are worthy of Orfeo.

A comparison with the leisurely beginning of Rinuccini's *Euridice* (see Chapter 2) is revealing. Striggio tells us a great deal in just eleven lines of verse (then five repeated): this is a happy and fortunate day in the life of a demigod who is released from the pains of love; the speaker is one of a group of shepherds able to sing in sweet accents; the demigod's name is Orfeo, whose own singing is a paragon the shepherds seek to match; the name of his once scornful but now amenable bride is Euridice; the scene is woodland that once rang to sighs but will now do so to music. Thus we are given indicators of time, place, character, past history and the propriety of song.[9]

Act II similarly opens with a reference to the woodland scene (Orfeo's 'Ecco pur ch'a voi ritorno / care selve e piagge amate'), while in Act III Orfeo identifies his companion as Speranza and the location as the sunless kingdom of Hades ('a questi mesti e tenebrosi regni / ove raggio di sol giammai non giunse'), and also explain why he is there, to see again those eyes (i.e., Euridice) that alone are capable of bringing him light. Speranza further points out the 'dark marsh' and the boatman who ferries souls across the Styx. Act V begins with Orfeo signalling his return to the fields of Thrace

---

9 For a broader discussion of these issues, see Calcagni, 'Monteverdi's *parole sceniche*'.

and to the spot where he had been struck down by the news of Euridice's death (so, the set of Acts I–II). As Whenham rightly argues, careful stage designers and directors can glean a great deal of evidence on the settings of, and movement in, the opera simply by a close reading of the libretto. Monteverdi's instrumental sinfonias and ritornellos perform a similar function, identifying space (the shift to 'Underworld' cornetts, trombones and regals in the sinfonia between Acts II and III), the passage of time, and perhaps even thematic ideas. The last seems suggested by the recurrence of Musica's ritornello from the prologue at the end of Act II and between Acts IV and V, unless this is just associated with the removal and reappearance of the pastoral set. One rather curious exception in the libretto is the opening of Act IV, where Proserpina does not introduce herself but only addresses an unspecified 'Signor', and tells of Orfeo wandering through the fields of Hades, calling out for Euridice (an action not played out in the libretto),[10] and who had recently lamented so sweetly. The scene needs no explanation (it is the same set as for Act III), but the lack of introduction for Proserpina and Plutone suggests that they had also been seen on stage at some time during Act III and had already been identified, as it were, by default (and, we may assume, by their costume).

   These various indications of place and character presumably reflect Striggio's desire to keep everything clear; a similar impulse is apparent in his frequent use of demonstratives ('Ecco Orfeo') and imperatives ('Mira, deh mira Orfeo') which direct the characters' and the audience's attention. But they may also suggest a pared-down production that left a great deal to the audience's imagination; thus their point is to describe as much what is not on the stage as what is. Carlo Magno feared not being admitted to the première of *Orfeo* because of the 'lack of space', and his phrase 'l'angustia del luogo' (literally, 'the narrowness of the place') finds an echo in Monteverdi's dedication (to Prince Francesco Gonzaga) to the 1609 edition of the score, where he says that a work which had been 'performed in music on a narrow stage' (*sopra angusta Scena musicalmente rappresentata*) was now to appear in the 'great theatre of the universe' (*nel gran Teatro dell'universo*), a conventional metaphor for publication. Although Monteverdi's 'angusta Scena' here may simply be set in opposition to 'gran Teatro', Magno's comment would seem to suggest little space for a large stage with significant scenery and similar apparatus. One wonders, too, just how much room there was for the large orchestra (forty or more instruments) that Monteverdi specifies in his score with such care and unusual precision, comprising string and wind consorts

---

10   In his penultimate speech in Act III ('Ahi sventurato amante'), Orfeo refers to
     himself calling out Euridice's name in vain, but he does not in fact do so in
     'Possente spirto'.

playing behind the stage (they are usually indicated as playing 'di dentro') and with varied continuo groups on one or other side in the wings (and on both for the opening of Act V). Certainly the issue of space has been considered to have had an impact on the revised 'Apollo' finale, which, it has been suggested, was created for a performance in a larger theatre;[11] however, we do not know whether the second, and in the end last, performance of Orfeo in 1607, on 1 March, before 'all the ladies resident in the city', was done in the same space as the first, even if the 'Apollo' finale might seem more friendly to women than the 'Bacchante' one.

We lack the pre-production materials for Orfeo that might fully solve the problem of when and why the apotheotic lieto fine was added to Act V, although as I argued in the discussion of the casting of the opera in Chapter 4, it was probably after Monteverdi had completed the score of at least the first half of Act IV — that is, after the Spirito's speech which is marked to be transposed up a tone in the 1609 score, thereby freeing up a tenor to change costume as Apollo. Indeed the two printed librettos of 1607 and the score of 1609 offer little insight into the kinds of reworkings and adjustments that must have occurred during the course of composition. Given that the librettos record aspects of the vocal scoring ('Due Pastori', etc.), they must have been prepared with some knowledge of the score, and thus probably do not reflect the text initially given to the composer for musical setting, unless Striggio was particularly precise about such details. However, and apart from the altered finale, there are some minor differences between the text in the libretto and the one in the score, suggesting both that further revisions occurred after the libretto went to press, and that Striggio at times edited his libretto for literary consumption.[12] Although most of the variants can plausibly be regarded as slight adjustments for ease of sense (in particular, by clarifying the syntax) or musical setting (by improving the word order), some are more significant. For example, in cases of subsequent revisions to the libretto the changes may not always have been for musical reasons. At the end of Act IV in the 1607 librettos, Proserpina begs Plutone that he should 'd'Orfeo dolente il lagrimar consoli / e fa che la sua Donna in vita torni / al bel seren de i sospirati giorni' ('console the tears of grieving Orfeo, and have his wife return to life, to the fine serenity of sighed-for days'); the score instead has 'fa ch'Euridice torni / a goder di quei giorni / che trar solea vivend'in fest'e in canto / e del miser'Orfeo consola 'l pianto' ('have Euridice return to enjoy those days which she was wont to pass in feasting and singing, and console

11   Whether the second performance or, so Iain Fenlon suggests, a planned third one (which never materialized) in early March for the proposed visit of the Duke of Savoy; see Claudio Monteverdi: 'Orfeo', ed. Whenham, pp. 17–18.
12   See the partial list of variants in Gallico, Monteverdi, pp. 63–4 n. 17.

the lament of the wretched Orfeo'). The libretto's suggestion that Euridice should 'return to life' might have offended strict Counter-Reformation sensibilities, prompting the more straightforward reading in the score. As for literary revisions, Striggio seems to have been concerned about the final chorus of Act I, 'Ecco Orfeo cui pur dianzi' ('Here is Orfeo . . .'). This cues the entrance of Orfeo at the beginning of Act II, where he responds '*Ecco* pur ch'a voi ritorno' ('Here now I return to you'), but the chorus lacks the 'Ecco' in the 1607 librettos. Either the 'Ecco' was added by Monteverdi (it is emphatically built into the score),[13] or it was removed by Striggio from his original because of the collision of diphthongs required to make this a *settenario*.

Further peculiarities in the libretto permit some speculation about its earlier states. In Act I, the Pastore's invitation to sing 'some happy song which Amor gave you' ('qualche lieta canzon che detti Amore') would seem to prompt something different from Orfeo's 'Rosa del ciel, vita del mondo e degna'; also, the celebration of untroubled love here and in Euridice's utterly compliant response does not quite square with claims elsewhere of their hitherto fraught relationship.[14] Indeed, one could at this point pass straight to Orfeo's Act II 'Vi ricorda, o boschi ombrosi', which is certainly a 'happy song'; it would also work more smoothly in tonal terms. In Act II, the same (alto) Pastore's request to Orfeo after 'Vi ricorda, o boschi ombrosi' ('Segui pur co 'l plettro aurato / d'addolcir l'aria in sì beato giorno'; 'Now continue with the golden plectrum to sweeten the air in so blessed a day') seems uncomfortably placed, and it has a strange triple-time musical setting, for all that something needs to happen before Messaggera enters. Later in the act, Messaggera's final speech, 'Ma io ch'in questa lingua', sits oddly (there are also some tonal disjunctions) between two choruses, the first of which already begins the moralizing typical of the end of an act; this passage either may have been a late addition, or may originally have followed immediately after Orfeo's exit (hence, prior to the chorus), and subsequently have been shifted to allow for some kind of contrast. In Act III, the final Caronte–Orfeo exchange ('Ben mi lusinga alquanto' – 'Ahi sventurato amante') may be an addition – Caronte's music is rather rough and ready, continuing the strophic variations of his previous speech even though the text is not strophic – and thus 'Possente spirto' may originally have been immediately preceded and followed by the sinfonia that, the second time round, sends Caronte to sleep. Finally, in Act V, an isolated *quinario* in line 12 of Orfeo's lament (and also an

13 *Claudio Monteverdi: 'Orfeo'*, ed. Whenham, p. 53.
14 'Rosa del ciel', in turn, seems to have been a fairly self-conscious reference to the *impresa* of the Accademia degli Invaghiti – an eagle with its eyes fixed on the sun (plus the motto 'Nihil pulcherius', 'Nothing more beautiful'); see Fabbri, *Monteverdi*, trans. Carter, p. 69.

unusual repetition of an end-word) immediately preceding the passage involving Eco suggests that something was altered here, too, and thus it is possible that the echo-scene, a pastoral convention, was itself a later thought.[15] Indeed, a close reading of Striggio's text gives the impression of there being embedded within it a smaller-scale work that has variously been expanded at particular points to provide further characterization, a better pacing of the action, additional dramatic interest or even just musical variety.

None of this would be unusual, since the librettist and composer worked together (one assumes) to plan out the work and then put flesh on its bones. Nevertheless, the final product is tautly structured, and remarkably so in comparison with the Rinuccini–Peri *Euridice*, which both Striggio and Monteverdi must have had to hand. Striggio packs a great deal into 650 or so lines of poetry, not only by paring down the 'poetic' qualities of his verse in favour of balder statements, but also by compressing events in ways that bring the double benefit of dramatic concision and of allowing the music more space and time to make its effect. Thus, although the text of *Orfeo* is significantly (about 140 lines) shorter than that of *Euridice*, the piece lasts almost the same time in performance. In *Euridice*, it takes twenty-nine lines of verse (divided into ten speeches) to get from the entrance of the messenger (Dafne) to the beginning of her narration of Euridice's death; Striggio covers the same ground in sixteen lines (but the same number of speeches). The narration itself takes thirty-three lines in *Euridice* and twenty in *Orfeo*. In both cases, Striggio follows more or less precisely the same rhetorical sequence as Rinuccini, and even borrows phrases from him, while also framing the whole scene with a fairly direct quotation.[16] However, the compressed dialogue, and also the fact that Euridice's death is announced before the narration begins, produces a much more focused result that is given still more point by Messaggera's powerful opening, 'Ahi caso acerbo', that comes to dominate the act as a plangent refrain.

15   The problem occurs in line 12: '. . . / [11] per farvi per pietà meco languire / [12] al mio languire. / [13] Voi vi dolesti, o monti, e lagrimaste / . . .'. In fact, this could have led straight into the 'Bacchante' scene: '. . . / per farvi per pietà meco languire / al mio languir. Ma ecco stuol nemico / di donne amiche à l'ubriaco nume / . . .'. Echo effects were a standard device in pastoral plays, and there were also numerous previous examples in theatrical and other music, including Peri's *Dafne* and Cavalieri's *Rappresentatione di Anima, et di Corpo*; see Sternfeld, *The Birth of Opera*, Chapter 7.

16   The two narrations are compared in Carter, *Music in Late Renaissance and Early Baroque Italy*, pp. 208–14. For the music, see Tomlinson, *Monteverdi and the End of the Renaissance*, pp. 133–6. In *Euridice*, Dafne enters with 'Lassa, che di spavento e di pietate / gelami il cor nel seno' ('Alas, from terror and pity, my heart freezes in my breast'). In *Orfeo*, Messaggera has an emphatic 'Lassa' towards the beginning of her scene, and her narration concludes with her saying how she stood 'piena il cor di pietade e di spavento' ('my heart full of pity and terror').

A comparison of Monteverdi's and Peri's music gives a similar impression. Those scenes directly parallel between the two scores reveal an obvious musical debt. Thus Messaggera's narration is very similar to Dafne's in *Euridice* in terms of pacing, melodic profile, harmonic movement and even specific chordal progressions at dramatic moments (such as the oft-cited shift from a major triad on G to one on E). There are further similarities between their handling of Orfeo's stunned reaction to the news (in Peri, 'Non piango e non sospiro'; in Monteverdi, 'Tu se' morta mia vita, ed io respiro?'), and of the sectional choral lament concluding the scene. However, Monteverdi manages to outdo Peri at just about every point (in part aided by some memorable lines in the libretto): his conclusion to Orfeo's lament, 'À dio terra, à dio cielo, e sole à dio', is far more striking both poetically and musically than Rinuccini's and Peri's 'non son, non son lontano, / io vengo, o cara vita, o cara morte' (see Ex. 5-1).

The carefully structured ascent of 'À dio terra . . .' is typical of Monteverdi's recitative, where melodic lines tend to rise, fall, or stay on one pitch, all in striking contrast to the gentle circling around a note that typifies Peri's recitative. In fact, Monteverdi may not have found *Euridice*, and the styles involved therein, entirely congenial. Rather than merely outdo Peri in his emulation of, competition with, and perhaps even homage to, *Euridice*, Monteverdi instead seems to have gone back to first principles in forging his own approach to drama through music. And although it is obvious that he understood the workings of Peri's recitative, he also drew upon other forms of 'musical speech' developed in the genre of the polyphonic madrigal by his Ferrarese and Mantuan predecessors and contemporaries. It may be no coincidence that as the opera progresses (and thus departs from the dramatic scheme of *Euridice*), the second model would seem to take over from the first, producing quite different results.

As Tomlinson has noted,[17] Monteverdi's own previous experiences of representing musical speech drew on the declamatory polyphonic styles adopted by Luca Marenzio, and still more by Giaches de Wert, in their late settings of texts from Guarini's *Il pastor fido*. The influence of Wert on Monteverdi was especially profound and provided one impetus for his own *Pastor fido* settings in his Fourth Book of five-voice madrigals (1603) and even more so in his Fifth (1605). While these settings were not theatrical in the sense that they were to be used on the stage, they nevertheless provide some kind of ersatz theatrical experience within the chamber, as Guarini's lament-

---

17 *Monteverdi and the End of the Renaissance*, Chapter 5. Tomlinson also discusses the influence of this style on the *Lamento d'Arianna* – which he regards as the peak of Monteverdi's early dramatic writing for solo voice – but not, curiously, on *Orfeo*, against which he seems to entertain a range of prejudices stemming, at least in part, from his unnecessarily negative view of Striggio's libretto.

Ex. 5-1 (a) *Orfeo*, II, Orfeo; (b) Jacopo Peri, *Euridice*, [scene 2], Orfeo.

Monteverdi, *L'Orfeo, favola in musica* (Venice, Ricciardo Amadino, 1609), p. 40; Peri, *Le musiche . . . sopra L'Euridice* (Florence, Giorgio Marescotti, 1600), p. 17.

[a] Farewell earth, farewell heaven, and sun, farewell.
[b] I am not, I am not far away, I come, o dear life, o dear death.

ing shepherds and shepherdesses are given poignant voice, rehearsing the emotional high points of a play well known in Mantuan circles. The notion of having five voices 'speak' as one character is not a problem within the conventions of the polyphonic madrigal, although it was to become so as the aesthetic of the *genere rappresentativo* (where voice and character are equivalent) started to take effect. However, it does place constraints upon the naturalistic representation of speech, given the need to manipulate and vary the 5-voice texture.

   The musical model for Marenzio, Wert and Monteverdi was the canzonetta, with its strongly directed harmonies and slightly plodding rhythms
(the latter could, however, be mitigated in performance, especially if
done by solo voice and instrumental accompaniment). A comparison between
Monteverdi's own early 3-voice canzonettas (published in 1584) and the
Pastor fido settings in the Fifth Book makes the point clear (Ex. 5-2). The

Ex. 5-2 (a) Monteverdi, 'Io mi vivea com'aquila mirando' (*Canzonette a tre voci*
(Venice, Giacomo Vincenti & Ricciardo Amadino, 1584)); (b) Monteverdi, 'Ferir
quel petto, Silvio?' (5th part of 'Ecco, Silvio, colei che in odio hai tanto', *Il
quinto libro de madrigali a cinque voci* (Venice, Ricciardo Amadino, 1605)); (c)
Orfeo, IV, Proserpina.

Ex. 5-2 *Continued*

Sia   be - ne - det - to il   dì   che   pria   ti   piac - qui,

Be - ne - det - ta   la   pre - da e'l dol - c'in - gan - no,

Claudio Monteverdi: Tutte le opere, ed. Malipiero, x, p. 11; ibid., v, p. 38; *L'Orfeo* (1609), p. 76.

[a] I lived as an eagle gazing [ever upon the opulent light of my beautiful sun . . .]
[b] Blessed be the day that I first burned [for you], blessed the [tears and torments . . .]
[c] Blessed be the day that I first pleased you, blessed the hunted and the sweet deceit . . .

3-voice 'Io mi vivea com'aquila mirando' (Ex. 5-2(a)) is typical:[18] the first two lines of text are set homophonically to characteristic cadence formulas, while the third expands contrapuntally to mark the emotional point of the setting. Both the characteristic long–short–short rhythms and the cadential progressions recur in numerous passages in the Fifth Book, as in Ex. 5-2(b); here the 'speaker' is Dorinda. This provides the musical basis for many of the more *arioso* passages in *Orfeo*: Ex. 5-2(c) is particularly close, inspired, it seems, by a textual reference. Here the rhythmic patterns, the melodic structure and the harmonic direction give a greater sense of shape and articulation than in Peri's more formless recitative.

But even where formlessness might be a virtue, Monteverdi tends to follow the models of the Fifth Book. Euridice's poignant speech in Act IV of *Orfeo* (Ex. 5-3) owes a great deal both to the gestures of the late sixteenth-century madrigal – witness the dissonances, and the harmonic swerves to 'paint' 'dolce' in the very first phrase – and to the pseudo-declamation in his

18 The text by Guarini elaborates (entirely coincidentally, one assumes) the same image as the *impresa* of the Accademia degli Invaghiti (described above), although in this case the 'sun' upon which the eagle gazes is the poet's beloved.

Ex. 5-3 *Orfeo*, IV, Euridice.

Ahi___ vi - sta trop - po dol - ce

e trop-po a-ma - ra: Co-sì per trop-po a - mor dun-que mi

per - di? Et io mi - se - ra per - do Il po - ter più go - dere

L'Orfeo (1609), p. 81.

Ah, sight too sweet and too bitter: thus through too much love do you lose me? And I, wretched, lose the power to enjoy further [both light and life . . .]

Pastor fido settings: compare the four-square rhythms, the frequent rests, the (over-)long notes for emphasis, and the tendency for the melody to adopt a jagged profile at extreme moments. Indeed, one could quite easily add a further four voices to this line (the long notes and the rests help by leaving space for other entries) to produce something that would not be out of place in the Fifth Book. And although Monteverdi's setting of 'Et io misera perdo' may be profoundly affecting, it is far removed from even the most heightened declamatory speech, and thus from how Peri might have handled such words.

Structure and expression

A great deal of the analytical literature on *Orfeo* has been devoted to Monteverdi's apparent pursuit of musical structure. On the one hand, there are the frequent strophic settings and strophic variations: for the former, witness the opening sequence of Act II; and for the latter, the Prologue, the final cho-ruses of Acts I and II, and particularly Orfeo's 'Possente spirto e formidabil

nume', where each *terza rima* stanza except the last is set to a highly embellished vocal line, over a more or less repeating bass. On the other hand, we
find larger-scale symmetries, as in the disposition of the various separate
musical numbers in Act I, which are laid out symmetrically around Orfeo's
'Rosa del ciel, vita del mondo e degna', with the choruses 'Vieni, Imeneo,
deh vieni' and 'Lasciate i monti' repeated in reverse order towards the end of
the act. Such symmetries might even be found in the whole opera, with
'Possente spirto' as its centrepiece. Most of these structures are implied in the
libretto, but there seems little doubt that Monteverdi exploited them further
of his own accord: his decision to set Striggio's non-strophic choruses at the
ends of Acts I and II by way of strophic variation is revealing. He also operated these techniques at quite low levels where their presence is scarcely a
matter of musical or dramatic concern: Caronte's 'O tu ch'innanzi mort'a
queste rive' in Act III is set as strophic variation (following the three quatrains of the text), as are the pairs of lines of the first quatrain (but not, curiously, the second) of the *ottava rima* stanza shared between two spirits in Act
IV ('O degli habitator de l'ombre eterne'). Elsewhere, textual and musical
refrains ('Ahi caso acerbo, ahi fato empio e crudele'; 'Rendetemi il mio ben,
Tartarei numi') further serve to provide local coherence.

But there are other issues on the analyst's agenda. First, the structural
elements in *Orfeo* are presumed to anticipate techniques in later Baroque
opera, therefore enhancing the status of *Orfeo* as a work founding an entire
theatrical tradition; it has become common to note almost gleefully the way
in which the Pastore's speech opening Act I (the text of which is given above)
has its first five lines repeated at the end, producing in the music an ABA
structure that in turn prefigures the da-capo aria. Second, there is an aesthetic
presumption that if music is to add anything to drama, it does so not just by
imitating the ebb and flow of the action through musical speech, but also by
crystallizing the emotional issues within various formal paradigms. In other
words, some kind of musical structure is viewed as essential for both affective and effective expression. This may be a dangerous position to take for
opera in its very early history. It is also a problematic strategy for dealing with
Orfeo, not least because it results in large parts of the work (particularly in
the last two acts) being in effect ignored.

Monteverdi's models for the 'songs' and related numbers in *Orfeo* can
be found in his own music and in that by other Mantuan and Florentine
composers. The 5-voice 'Lasciate i monti' in Act I is a sung and danced *balletto* in the manner of Gastoldi; it also goes through the standard musical
metres – duple, *sesquialtera* (in effect, slower triple) and *tripla* (faster triple) –
required by the usual sequence of dance steps. Orfeo's Act II aria 'Vi ricorda,
o boschi ombrosi' is a triple-time dance-song on the model of some of the
arias in Giulio Caccini's pioneering collection of solo songs, *Le nuove musiche* (Florence, I Marescotti, 1602), with the hemiola patterns commonly

associated with Chiabreran *ottonari*; Caccini's 'Belle rose porporine' is a convenient example. Monteverdi had already assimilated these styles in works
before *Orfeo*, not least in his collection of 3-voice *Scherzi musicali* published
by Ricciardo Amadino in Venice on 21 July 1607, but also with repertory
variously dating back to 1599.[19] Thus Orfeo's 'Ecco pur ch'a voi ritorno',
opening Act II, bears more than just a family resemblance to one of the
scherzi, 'Lidia spina del mio core' (Ex. 5-4), for all the similarities to parts of
Euridice in the same tonal-type (compare Ex. 2-4).

Other passages in *Orfeo* seem to draw more upon improvisatory practices. The threefold toccata opening the opera (and reworked in the introit of
the 1610 Vespers, 'Deus in adiutorium . . . Domine ad adiuvandum') invokes
a standard device to initiate Mantuan theatrical performances – we have
already seen (in Chapter 4) the example of Guarini's *L'idropica* of 1608 – and
reworks typical fanfare motifs associated with trumpet signals on the battlefield. The strophic-variation arias, on the other hand, and most noticeably in
the prologue and in 'Possente spirto', draw upon standard improvisation formulas such as the *arie da cantar terze rime*, using stock melodic–harmonic progressions (e.g., the Romanesca) as a basis for declamatory and/or embellished
singing. Any court singer would have had these simple formulas at his
fingertips, and Francesco Rasi used them frequently (see Ex. 4-1). But
Monteverdi goes one stage further: he provides two versions of the vocal line
in 'Possente spirto', one plain and the other richly embellished. There are parallels in contemporary solo song collections, where simple and embellished
lines are given, the former either for those amateurs unable to sing difficult
ornaments or for those singers who wished to improvise their own. For
example, Bartolomeo Barbarino gives both simple and embellished vocal lines
in his *Secondo libro delli motetti . . . a una voce sola* (Venice, Bartolomeo Magni,
1614), stating that the simple versions are for those who are skilled in counterpoint and who have the vocal ability to add of their own accord *passaggi*
and the other things required of good singing. Likewise, in the preface to
Enrico Radesca da Foggia's *Il quinto libro delle canzonette, madrigali et arie, a tre,
a una, et a due voci* (Venice, Giacomo Vincenti, 1617), its compiler (Ludovico
Caligaris) explains that he has asked Radesca not to notate *passaggi*, first, so
that the singer lacking the ability to sing them would not be prevented from
performing these works, and second, because *passaggi* are never performed as
written down. However, he continues, singers are free to add *passaggi* as they
wish. It is not clear whether the embellished version of 'Possente spirto'

---

19 For the influence of canzonetta structures in *Orfeo*, and also the dating of the
    contents of the 1607 *Scherzi musicali* (based on comments in Giulio Cesare
    Monteverdi's 'Dichiaratione'), see Ossi, 'Claudio Monteverdi's *ordine novo, bello et
    gustevole*'.

Ex. 5-4 (a) *Orfeo*, II, Orfeo; (b) Monteverdi, 'Lidia spina del mio core' (*Scherzi musicali a tre voci* (Venice, Ricciardo Amadino, 1607)).

L'Orfeo (1609), p. 27; *Claudio Monteverdi: Tutte le opere*, ed. Malipiero, x, p. 56 (note-values doubled; original time-signature, **C**).

[a] Here now I return to you, dear woods and beloved fields . . .
[b] Lidia, thorn in my heart, wherefore Love tortures and strikes me . . .

reflects Monteverdi's attempt to notate Rasi's performance, his memory of that performance, or indeed what he wished Rasi had performed. There is no doubt, however, that Rasi was well equipped to handle such virtuosic writing: his own song collections, the *Vaghezze di musica* (Venice, Angelo Gardano & fratelli, 1608) and *Madrigali di diversi autori* (Florence, Cristofano Marescotti, 1610), contain richly notated embellishment on a par with the kinds of passages found in 'Possente spirto' (Ex. 5-5).

Ex. 5-5 (a) *Orfeo*, III, Orfeo, 'Possente spirto e formidabil nume'; (b) Francesco Rasi, 'Ardo ma non ardisco il chius'ardore' (*Vaghezze di musica*, 1608).

L'Orfeo (1609), p. 58; Rasi, *Vaghezze di musica per una voce sola* (Venice, Angelo Gardano & fratelli, 1608), fol. 6r.

[a] To you have I turned my path . . .
[b] [and let] the tomb of your ashes [be] my breast.

Table 5-1   The sequence opening Act II of Orfeo

Section	'Key'
Sinfonia	g–(internal cadences on B♭, C, d)–g
Orfeo: 'Ecco pur ch'a voi ritorno'	g–(B♭, F)–g
Ritornello [I]	C–(F, B♭)–C
Pastore: 'Mira ch'a se n'alletta'	F–(g, B♭)–C
Ritornello [I]	C–(F, B♭)–C
Pastore: 'Su quell'herbosa sponda' (= 2nd stanza of 'Mira ch'a se n'alletta')	F–(g, B♭)–C
Ritornello [II]	g–(d, F, B♭)–g
Due pastori: 'In questo prato adorno'	g–(F, V/g, c)–g
Ritornello [II]	g–(d, F, B♭)–g
Due pastori: 'Qui Pan, dio de' pastori' (= 2nd stanza of 'In questo prato adorno')	g–(F, V/g, c)–g
Ritornello [III]	C–(G, D, G)–C
Due pastori: 'Qui le Napee vezzose'	C–(G, D, G, C; i.e., same bass as Ritornello III)–G
Ritornello [III]	C–(G, D, G)–C
Coro: 'Dunque fa degno Orfeo' (= 2nd stanza of 'Qui le Napee vezzose')	C–(G, D, G, C)–G
Ritornello [IV]	G–(D, C, a)–G
Orfeo: 'Vi ricorda, o boschi ombrosi'	G–(a, G, C, G, a)–G

Over half of Orfeo (in temporal terms) is taken up with strophic songs, choruses and instrumental music, weighted strongly in favour of the first three acts. This is one reason why it is such a musical feast. One difficulty of closed formal structures within a dramatic context, however, is the consequent tendency to halt the flow as one 'song' ends prior to something else beginning. The opening of Act II reveals both the problems and their possible solutions. The libretto has one stanza of ottonari for Orfeo, then six of settenari for the shepherds and nymphs, leading to Orfeo's strophic 'Vi ricorda, o boschi ombrosi', again in ottonari: Monteverdi sets the middle six stanzas in pairs (see Table 5-1).[20] But despite the sectionalization, emphasized by changes of musical metre, Monteverdi attempts to maintain the pace by eliding endings and beginnings: each vocal section begins on an upbeat that completes the last 'bar' of the previous instrumental passage. He also makes the individual sections tonally open rather than closed, ranging through the various possible tonalities of a given system. As a result, the sequence from

20   In my indication of tonal structures in Table 5-1, 'major' keys are given in upper case and 'minor' keys in lower. Here and elsewhere I ignore the probable tierce de picardie cadences concluding 'minor'-key sections on a major rather than minor triad. They are a foreground feature rather than any indication of 'key', although they, too, can aid continuity (as when a major triad on G concluding a 'G minor' piece becomes the dominant of 'C major').

the opening sinfonia to the end of 'Vi ricorda, o boschi ombrosi' forms a cohesive musical unit because of these elisions, the tonal structure, and indeed the constant tactus; it is very noticeable when the pattern breaks, at the Pastore's 'Mira, deh mira Orfeo che d'ogni intorno'.

The process is aided by Monteverdi's tendency to construct his songs and ritornellos from short phrases, each ending with a cadence (which may then be weakened in various ways) that can move in any number of directions, or for that matter may be omitted. Thus the 'D minor' ritornello preceding the prologue consists of four clear-cut phrases, in effect the same music, cadencing on the notes D, A, F and D. Each vocal stanza of the prologue except the last starts in D minor but ends in A minor; the subsequent statement of the ritornello is then foreshortened (starting at phrase 2) to begin in A minor and conclude in D minor. The final stanza starts as usual in D minor but ends on the dominant of A minor (thus, in suspense, marking Musica's instruction for everything to be still); there follows a complete (4-phrase) statement of the ritornello which, by starting in D minor, in one sense breaks Musica's spell and permits the action proper to begin as the Pastore enters with 'In questo lieto e fortunato giorno' (also in D minor).

These cadence structures can also be viewed in a slightly different light in the context of voice-leading patterns that comprise bass arpeggiations and linear melodic descents, each prolonged in various ways. While the terminology might seem Schenkerian (it is), it reflects the normal condition of Renaissance modes, where an octave scale is divided into a fifth (*diapente*) and a fourth (*diatessaron*), with the fifth acting as a primary definer of the modal type according to its pitch (on any one of six pitches in the 12-mode system) and its position (below or above the fourth, marking the difference between authentic and plagal modes respectively).[21] Thus a melodic descent through the *diapente* (and the harmonic support associated with it) will provide a clear modal marker and also a strong form of closure, while cadences on notes within the *diapente* (or in the *diatessaron*) will be in some sense weaker. The opening of Act II provides several obvious examples of melodies constructed on both short- and long-term descending fifths that are embellished in various ways, as in Ex. 5-4(a), where the simple fifth descent in bars 2–4 of 'Ecco pur ch'a voi ritorno' reflects the descending fifth (with an initial ascent) that is the background for the whole song, fixing its modality as G-Dorian. This procedure is typical of Monteverdi and can be found throughout *Orfeo*, as well as in many of his madrigals.

21   My technique owes a significant debt to McClary, *The Transition from Modal to Tonal Organization in the Works of Monteverdi*, while the following references to systems can be clarified by reference to Chafe, *Monteverdi's Tonal Language*, *passim*. For neo-Schenkerian approaches to this repertory, see also Chew, 'The Perfections of Modern Music'; Carter, '"An air new and grateful to the ear"'.

Also, any given note of a descent through the *diapente* or *diatessaron* can in effect be prolonged by a subsidiary *diapente* or other descent either from or to that note. If those subsidiary descents are strongly articulated (e.g., with cadential support under 2–1), they will create modal mixture or, in a (loose) sense, modulation; this explains the tonal sequence of the opening of Act II detailed in Table 5-1, as well as the internal cadences within each section. The technique can also be used to provide some kind of continuity across what might appear to be extreme dislocation. The opening of Act II establishes the note D (supported harmonically by G in the flat system) as the head-note of a *diapente* descent (in G-Dorian). This gradually becomes supplanted by E (an upper neighbour-note to D) as the head-note of possible descents to C (3–2–1), to G (6–5–4–3–2–1; see 'Qui le Napee vezzose') or to A (5–4–3–2–1); all three possibilities are exploited in 'Vi ricorda, o boschi ombrosi' (hence its internal cadences on A minor, G and C). The Pastore's subsequent 'Mira, deh mira Orfeo' re-establishes the E in the context of 'C major' (hence, 3–2–1). Messaggera's abrupt entrance ('Ahi caso acerbo') is marked by an extremely disruptive harmonic shift (a major triad on C followed by a 6–3 chord on C♯). Yet she, too, enters on E, now the head-note of two *diapente* descents to A (5–4–3–(2); 5–4–(3)–2–1), although they are disrupted in various ways (Ex. 5-6). One can then follow the various descents (foreground, middleground and background) through the rest of the act to discern the working out, as it were, of the conflict between *diapente* descents from D (through B♭; the 'flat' system) and E (through B♮; the 'sharp' system). As the final chorus reveals, that conflict is left unresolved, although the recurrence of Musica's ritornello at the end of the act (prior to the 'Underworld' sinfonia) attempts a mediation through its 'D minor' (the 'natural' system). It does not take much analytical skill to decipher these structures, and it scarcely even requires a good ear to feel the effect of those recurring, piercing top Es. Without some kind of analysis, however, the unremittingly painful relationship between Messaggera's 'Ahi caso acerbo' and the previous opening of Orfeo's seemingly optimistic 'Vi ricorda, o boschi ombrosi' passes for naught.

Any discussion of meaning, expression and structure in *Orfeo* hinges on the question of how strongly the work as a whole and its constituent parts (text, music, staging) might direct our reading of it. Most scholars have commented, usually with some relief, on what they perceive as the predominantly and inherently musical focus of much of what Monteverdi seems to do here, although as the above discussions have suggested, the music's contribution to the semiotic process is at times somewhat rudimentary, and at others fairly weak, for all its subtleties and strengths in other ways. Scholars have also used this focus to compare *Orfeo* favourably with Peri's *Euridice*, the music of which seems far less rich and expressive. It is certainly true that *Euridice* is an acquired

Ex. 5-6 *Orfeo*, II.

L'Orfeo (1609), p. 36.

Pastore: . . . to sweeten the air in so blessed a day. *Messaggera*: Ah bitter misfortune, ah wicked, cruel fate, ah injurious stars, ah greedy heaven.

taste, while *Orfeo* offers a far better musical and even theatrical experience. Whether one views that as a strength or a weakness will depend on one's aesthetic presuppositions concerning the nature of early opera, if not opera in general. I imagine that the more purist among the Florentines would have been less than impressed by Monteverdi's approach to the libretto. Yet at least one of Monteverdi's contemporaries found in *Orfeo* a perfect match between text and music. When the Mantuan theologian Cherubino Ferrari met Monteverdi in Milan in August 1607, he read the libretto and heard the score of *Orfeo*, and wrote to Duke Vincenzo Gonzaga (22 August) that

> certainly both poet and musician have depicted the inclinations of the heart so skilfully that it could not have been done better. The poetry is lovely in conception, lovelier still in form, and loveliest of all in diction; and indeed no less was to be expected of a man as richly talented as Signor Striggio. The music, moreover, observing due propriety, serves the poetry so well that nothing more beautiful is to be heard anywhere . . .[22]

But the presumed ideal, and often idealized, marriage of music and drama in *Orfeo* seems threatened by impending divorce even in the prologue ('Io la Musica son . . .'), and the often competing demands of structure and expression create tensions that would become embedded within opera as a genre. How Monteverdi coped with those tensions – he never resolved them – and even rendered them thematic in his later works becomes a matter for further thought.

22 In *Claudio Monteverdi: 'Orfeo'*, ed. Whenham, p. 172.

6

The *balli*

Calling *Orfeo* an 'opera' is in one sense just a matter of modern convenience; for Striggio it was a 'favola' (a 'fable', 'tale' or 'play'), and for Monteverdi a 'favola in musica'. However, the term also invokes a strong historiographical agenda, placing the work squarely within the early history of a genre of profound significance for the Western art tradition, and also within the Baroque period, often construed as marking the beginning of 'modern' music. This forces narrative accounts of music theatre in Italy in the first half of the seventeenth century down certain unpalatable paths. A wide range of disparate works from different times and places are located in one procrustean bed, while others are marginalized for seeming tangential to the main course of music history. We also tend to view the reluctance of the north Italian courts to embrace wholeheartedly the notion of drama represented in music – always just one of a range of options for princely entertainment – and their concomitant objections to operatic recitative as an inevitable result of inherent courtly conservatism. But for all its appeal to *letterati* and *cognoscenti*, opera often took a back seat because of the nature of the dramatic action, of the musical style(s), and of the audience's involvement or lack thereof. Thus the history of opera in Italy in the first third of the seventeenth century is fairly sporadic and haphazard. Opera's status both as a genre and as an institution becomes more stable only after the opening of the first 'public' opera house in Venice in 1637, when newer styles and forms meshed with more consistent modes of production.

Early seventeenth-century commentators had no less difficulty in finding appropriate generic labels for different forms of entertainment, whether old or new. The term 'favola' is itself loaded, even if it is usually best defined by a negative (something that is not, by strict definition, a tragedy or a comedy). Although 'favola' was often qualified (*favola pastorale, favola boschereccia, favola marittima*, etc.), it was usually associated with pastoral, and therefore not just with a certain type of subject-matter but also with a mixed dramatic mode, as in the (pastoral) tragicomedy. Most early operas belong to the pastoral tradition in terms of their characters, plot and even favourite devices. As for the generic implications of the presence of one or other kind of music, most contemporary theorists would have solved the problem by regarding the matter as incidental rather than fundamental: thus music is not a defining feature, but essentially a decorative one. Those who were *parti pris* (such as Marco da Gagliano or the author of *Il corago*) might well feel that involving music brought the theatre to the peak of perfection, by virtue of the resulting synthesis of all the arts. But in the end, it was a secondary issue, akin to (and usually debated on similar terms to) the long-standing argument of whether or not to use prose or poetry in spoken drama.

Another art form usually implicated in early opera and related entertainments, but often ignored today, is that of dance. In Chapter 6 of *Il corago*, we learn that there are three ways of delivering a drama: through speech, through song, and through ballet or mime. In the end, the author offers guidance only on the first two, promising to treat pantomime in a succeeding treatise which seems not to have survived. Thus his comments (in Chapter 18) on *balli* as an (essentially decorative) element of opera are fairly cursory, even if he does make some interesting remarks on classical dances in honour of mythological gods such as Apollo, Bacchus and Diana, who were also celebrated in dance in the early seventeenth century. But he does scant justice to the powerful role of dancing in contemporary courtly theatrical and other entertainments. Even the most mundane social dancing emphasized, like all courtly activities, the cohesion and distinction of an élite class and itself tended towards the theatrical in its use of gesture and costume. When used on the stage, theatrical dancing could combine intricate choreography with scenic extravagance to provide climactic moments of splendour and celebration revolving, often literally, around the ruler and his family. Both on and off the stage – or moving between the two – the spectacle pleased both the eye and the ear, the complex geometrical patterns creating not just a display of *virtù* but also a rich metaphor of cosmic, civic and corporal harmony adopted for precise political ends. And as with the use of music in early opera, dance had a kudos accrued by classical precedent. When the Florentine theorist Giovanni Battista Doni extolled the combination of singing and dancing in his *Trattato della musica scenica* (1633–5), he did so on the grounds of the best practice of Classical Antiquity.[1] Sung *balli*, in particular, not only displayed

---

1   See Kirkendale, *L'Aria di Fiorenza*, pp. 43–4. According to Doni, the theatrical poet 'might usefully in composing his choruses . . . use metre and rhyme such that they would be capable of a fine sung and danced air [*una bell'aria di Canto, e di Ballo*], in which consists the greater part of the excellence of the ancient music'. For the broader issues, see Alm, 'Humanism and Theatrical Dance in Early Opera'; Fenlon, 'The Origins of the Seventeenth-Century Staged *ballo*'; Baroncini, ' "Sinfonie et balli

greater virtuosity by way of solving the poetic, musical and choreographic problems involved; they also invoked the combination of oration, harmony and rhythm that for Plato (in *The Republic*) had defined the art of music.

Doni's commendation was an act of pro-Florentine propaganda: his ideal had been achieved, he said, by a musician in service at the court of Grand Duke Ferdinando I de' Medici, Emilio de' Cavalieri, who was 'not only an extremely expert musician but also a most graceful dancer'.[2] Doni also linked his praise to one specific work by Cavalieri, the final *ballo* of the *intermedi* accompanying Girolamo Bargagli's comedy *La pellegrina* in the festivities for the wedding of Ferdinando and Christine of Lorraine in Florence in May 1589. The *ballo* concluding the sixth and final *intermedio* drew on the Platonic theme (elaborated in *Laws*, II) of the gods descending from the heavens to give mortals the gift of harmony and rhythm (i.e., music and dance). The choreography, then the music, of 'O che nuovo miracolo' was by Cavalieri, and the text was added after their composition by the Lucchese poetess Laura Guidiccioni de' Lucchesini.[3]

'O che nuovo miracolo' alternates a sung/danced *ballo* for 5-part choir (representing mortals) – later known as the 'Aria di Fiorenza' – with trio sections (called 'risposta') for three sopranos (the gods), sung by Vittoria Archilei (also playing the Spanish guitar), Lucia Caccini (Neapolitan guitar) and Margherita della Scala (tambourine). The priority of the choreography in the creative process is matched by the detailed description of it in the 1591 edition of the music: it specifies twenty-seven individual dancers, including seven principal ones – four (*sic*) women and three men (the latter also danced during the trio sections sung by the three women) – while others remained in the heavens. Guidiccioni was prompted to produce verse predominantly in *settenari* (with prominent *versi sdruccioli* in the *ballo*) and *endecasillabi*: the text is not stanzaic (reinforcing the notion that it was written to pre-existing choreography and music), although the overall structure of the music, for all its apparent complexity, is regular in its sectionality and in its scheme of repetitions. This music also involves an alternation between duple (**C**) and triple (O3) time, the latter of two kinds in what the choreography refers to as 'tempi di Gagliarda' (in effect, 3/2) and 'tempi di Canario' (6/4).

allegri"'. Much of my discussion here draws on my 'New Light on Monteverdi's *Ballo delle ingrate*'.

2   Doni, *Lyra barberina*, ii, p. 95, in Fenlon, *Music and Patronage in Sixteenth-Century Mantua*, i, p. 159.

3   The music was published by Cristofano Malvezzi in his *Intermedii et concerti, fatti per la commedia rappresentata in Firenze nelle nozze del Serenissimo Don Ferdinando Medici, e Madama Christiana di Loreno, Gran Duchi di Toscana* (Venice, Giacomo Vincenti, 1591); for a modern edition, see *Les fêtes du mariage de Ferdinand de Médicis et de Christine de Lorraine*, ed. Walker, pp. lvi–lviii, 140–54.

It is not clear to what extent Cavalieri and his colleagues were drawing on Ferrarese models for the final *ballo* in the 1589 *intermedi*. The so-called *Balletto delle donne* (or *della duchessa*) at the court of Duke Alfonso II d'Este of Ferrara used elaborate costumes and choreography, combining singing and dancing with great artistry. For example, on one evening in Carnival 1584–5,

> there was a gathering in the *gran sala*. Twelve dancers with astounding plumes, ordered by the duke himself, performed the *balletti*. It was said to be a most beautiful thing to see; but the violins, harpsichords and organs could only be heard with difficulty. The words, composed by Signor [Battista] Guarini, were extremely pleasing, and the music, by [Ippolito] Fiorino, served them well. The dancing was so well matched to both that it was celestial.[4]

It does seem, however, that Cavalieri was seeking to steal a march on a Ferrarese play (with subsequent Mantuan connections) that had been mooted for performance in the 1589 festivities: Guarini's *Il pastor fido*, with its notoriously difficult *Giuoco della cieca* (III.2) that had also, reportedly, been conceived in the order choreography–music–text (see Chapter 2). Here the exigencies of the choreography prompted a different approach to the verse structure. There are four sung/danced choruses (for a 'coro di ninfe') each preceded and separated from the next by dialogue; in contrast to Guidiccioni's (loosely) regular line-lengths and non-stanzaic structure, these four choruses are each (loosely) stanzaic with irregular line-lengths (in general, 4-line stanzas; 8-7-5-11). Luzzasco Luzzaschi's original music for the *Giuoco della cieca* does not survive, so it is impossible to tell how this verse structure reflected metrical or other contrasts within the music. But *ottonari*, *settenari* and *quinari*, whether together or separately, were to become particularly characteristic of later sung *balli*: their strong, regular rhythms, soon to be associated with the Chiabreran canzonetta, were ideal for matching with dance steps.

The significance of 'O che nuovo miracolo' and the *Giuoco della cieca* lies not just in their attempt to combine song and dance, or in their various structural solutions to the problems posed thereby for both text and music, but also in their incorporation of dance thematically within some manner of dramatic action, rather than as a tacked-on conclusion to it. Certainly that also seems to have been the thrust of subsequent entertainments (all now lost) that Cavalieri and Guidiccioni provided for the Medici court: *Il satiro* and *La disperatione di Fileno* (1590), and a new version of the *Giuoco della cieca* (1595). The last two, at least, would have had sung dancing integrated

---

4   Fenlon, *Music and Patronage in Sixteenth-Century Mantua*, i, p. 154 (modified). For Ferrarese *balletti*, see also Newcomb, *The Madrigal at Ferrara*, i, pp. 35–45.

within the action, if we are to believe the advice in Alessandro Guidotti's preface to Cavalieri's *Rappresentatione di Anima, et di Corpo* (Rome, Niccolò Muti, 1600):

> After there has been some solo singing, it is good to have the choruses sing, and to vary frequently the modes, and that now the soprano should sing, now bass, now contralto, now tenor, and that the arias and the music should not be similar, but varied with many proportions, that is, *tripla, sestupla* and *binario*, and adorned with echoes and with as many inventions as one can, such as, in particular, dances, which liven up these representations as much as possible, as in effect has been judged by all the onlookers. In the case of the dances, or *moresche*, if they are made to appear somewhat outside common practice, it will be more delightful and novel, as for example the *moresca* for battle and the dance on the occasion of play and frolic, just as in the pastoral of *Fileno* three satyrs come to battle, and on this occasion they perform the combat singing and dancing to the tune of a *moresca*. And in the *Giuoco della cieca* four nymphs dance and sing while they frolic around the blindfold Amarilli, obeying the rules of blind-man's buff.

The alternation of duple time with slower and faster triple times in 'O che nuovo miracolo' and praised by Guidotti also became standard.[5] Thus the optional final *ballo* for Cavalieri's *Rappresentatione* has a text, 'Chiostri altissimi e stellati', comprising six 6-line stanzas in *ottonari*. Each stanza is set for a 5-voice chorus shifting from duple (**C**) to triple (3/2) time, separated by an instrumental ritornello (one version in **C**3/2 and the other in **C**6/4). The performance instructions in the preface prescribe dancing both in the chorus and in the ritornellos:

> one starts the dance with *riverenza* and *continenza*; and then follow other slow steps, with interweavings and passes [*trecciate, & passate*] by all the couples with gravity. In the ritornellos, there should be four, who dance exquisitely a leaping dance with caprioles [*un ballo saltato con capriole*], and without singing. And thus one continues with all the stanzas, always varying the dance, and the four *maestri* who dance could vary, at one time a galliard, another a canary, another the courante, which go well with the

---

5   The time signatures for such triple-time sections vary widely between 3, 3/2 and 6/4 (each preceded, or not, by **C** or **₵**), as does the chief unit of notation (semibreve, minim or semiminim). The proportional relationships between them (or with contiguous duple-time sections) is also a vexed issue; for some of the arguments, see Bowers, 'Proportional Notations in Monteverdi's "Orfeo" ', although his solutions cannot always be danced. The pattern also has some influence on later opera sinfonias, as with *L'incoronazione di Poppea*.

ritornellos. And if the stage is not big enough for four dancers, at least two should dance, and make sure that the said dance is composed by the best *maestro* one can find.

The stanzas of the dance should be sung by all both on and off the stage, and one should use as many instruments as one can in the ritornellos.

'O che nuovo miracolo' became something of a totem for later Florentine entertainments: the main entertainment staged for the wedding of Maria de' Medici and Henri IV of France in October 1600, *Il rapimento di Cefalo* (with music by Giulio Caccini and others), had a final sung *ballo*; the last chorus of Peri's *Euridice*, performed at the same festivities, combined singing with dancing; and the provision of a sung *ballo* on the model of the 1589 *intermedi* was a cause of much concern for the organizers of the *intermedi* accompanying *Il giudizio di Paride* (by Michelangelo Buonarroti *il giovane*), which formed the centrepiece of the festivities for the wedding of Prince Cosimo de' Medici and Maria Magdalena of Austria in October 1608. The Mantuans also seem to have jumped on the bandwagon, having already successfully solved the problems over the *Giuoco delle cieca* in 1598. Indeed, the festivities in Mantua in 1608 for the wedding of Prince Francesco Gonzaga and Margherita of Savoy – which competed directly, and knowingly, with the 1608 Florentine celebrations – appear to have involved a concerted attempt to explore new ways of using dance on the stage both within opera and as a more socially and culturally acceptable alternative.

Monteverdi's early balli

Monteverdi must have worked on stage music for Mantua (at least as a performer) ever since his arrival there as an instrumentalist among the court musicians in 1590 or 1591. But his appointment as Duke Vincenzo Gonzaga's *maestro della musica di camera* on the death of Benedetto Pallavicino in 1601 presumably focused his work as a composer of theatrical and similar entertainments: in 1607 (in the 'Dichiaratione' to the *Scherzi musicali a tre voci*), his brother noted how busy the composer was in writing for tournaments, *balli* and comedies.[6] His first known stage work in this capacity was indeed a *ballo* – commonly given the title *Gli amori di Diana ed Endimione* – intended, it seems, for Carnival 1604–5. Nothing of it survives, and we have only an

---

6   Compare also Gabriele Zinano's comment in a letter from Naples of 17 February 1604 (in Fabbri, *Monteverdi*, trans. Carter, p. 55) referring to the fame of Mantua's 'comedies, music, *balli*, tournaments'.

incomplete, preliminary account of it in a letter from Monteverdi to Duke Vincenzo Gonzaga, written some time in December 1604:

> Ten days ago I received from the courier a letter from Your Most Serene Highness commanding me to compose two *entrate*, one for the stars that have to follow on the moon, the other for the shepherds who come on after Endymion; and likewise two dances, one for the aforementioned stars alone, and the other for the stars and shepherds together.
>
> And so, with a most eager desire to obey and carry out Your Most Serene Highness's commands as promptly as possible . . . I set to work first on the music for the stars. But not finding among the instructions how many there must be to dance it, and wishing to compose it on an alternating plan, as it would in my opinion have been novel, delightful and pleasing – that is, having first of all a short and cheerful air played by all the instruments and likewise danced by all the stars; then immediately the five *viole da braccio* taking up a different air from the first one (the other instruments stopping) and only two stars dancing to it (the others resting); and at the end of this duo section, having the first air repeated with all the instruments and stars, continuing this pattern until all the said stars have danced two by two – but not having had the actual number, and this information being essential (if indeed Your Most Serene Highness takes pleasure in this kind of interspersed arrangement as I mentioned), I have in consequence put off doing it until I know; and in order to find out, I have written to Signor Giovanni Battista the dancer, so that he can give me the exact number through my brother.
>
> Meanwhile, I have composed this piece, which I am now sending off to Your Most Serene Highness, for the shepherds and the stars . . .

This letter reveals the basic outline of the work, comprising *entrate* for the stars and shepherds, and two separate dances, one for the stars (in a ritornello/refrain form) and one for the shepherds. However, the overall structure of the entertainment remains unclear: indeed, Monteverdi himself does not yet know what would happen in the actual dancing. It seems that Duke Vincenzo was not yet as precise on the commission as he was to become on later occasions, as Monteverdi subsequently described in a letter of 21 November 1615 discussing his work on the *ballo Tirsi e Clori* (later included in the Seventh Book of madrigals of 1619). Here Monteverdi says that when the duke used to commission such works in six, eight or nine *mutanze*, he would 'give me some account of the plot, and I used to try to fit to it the most apt and suitable music and the metrical schemes [*tempi*] that I knew'.

Matters are more straightforward in the first two surviving *balli* combining singing with dancing in prints by Monteverdi: 'Lasciate i monti' from

Act I of *Orfeo*,[7] and the independent 'De la bellezza le dovute lodi', included in the 1607 *Scherzi musicali* (its dedication is dated 21 July). Both works are associated with Prince Francesco Gonzaga – he commissioned *Orfeo* and was the dedicatee of the *Scherzi musicali* – whose interest in sung *balli* was also to become apparent in 1608. 'Lasciate i monti' is, of course, part of an opera, but it only makes sense in the context of sung *balli*. In the 1609 score of *Orfeo* (also dedicated to Prince Francesco), it has a rubric explaining that this 'balletto' was sung to the sound of five *viole da braccio* (like *Gli amori di Diana ed Endimione*), three chitarroni, two harpsichords, a double-harp, a bass viol and a sopranino recorder.[8] Striggio provided three 6-line stanzas ($a^5a^5bc^5c^5b$). Monteverdi sets the first ('Lasciate i monti') in duple time in the manner of Gastoldi; the second stanza ('Qui miri il sole') is in a slower triple time ($C3/2$), with the text of the third stanza ('Poi di bei fiori') laid underneath. The succeeding instrumental 'Ritornello' (two statements written out) is in a faster $6/4$.[9] Again, duple time moves to slower and faster triple times on the Cavalieri model.

The 3-voice 'balletto' 'De la bellezza le dovute lodi' is more complex.[10] There are problems over the sources; it comes at the end of the *Scherzi musicali* after two pieces by Giulio Cesare Monteverdi, but that is no reason to suspect its attribution to Claudio, given that a *ballo* would normally come last in any print (as in Monteverdi's Seventh and Eighth Books of madrigals). The text has sometimes been attributed to Prince Ferdinando Gonzaga, a well-known poet and melomane, although there is more than a hint that it may be by Alessandro Striggio. We do not know whether this was a free-standing entertainment or a conclusion to a longer work: the fact that the text starts *in medias res* would seem to suggest the latter. Nor do we know what characters, or perhaps groups of characters (the repetitions in the music

7   I leave aside the problematic revised ending to *Orfeo* in the 1609 score, with a duple-time ritornello, duple-time final chorus ('Vanne Orfeo felice a pieno'; two 6-line stanzas in *ottonari*) and an instrumental 'moresca' in triple metre (but with the signature **C**). Certainly the *moresca* was danced, but there is no indication about the chorus.

8   'Questo Balletto fu cantato al suono di cinque Viole da braccio, tre Chittaroni, duoi Clauicembani, un'Arpa doppia, un contrabasso de Viola, & un Flautino alla vigesima seconda.'

9   The third stanza is omitted in the repetition of this unit later in the act. In fact, the overall structure is unclear and could be any one of the following: stanzas 1, 2, 3 (to the music of 2), ritornello; 1, 2, ritornello, 3, ritornello; or (most commonly performed) 1, 2, ritornello, 1, 3, ritornello. The first is most likely.

10 I discuss this piece in greater depth in 'New Light on Monteverdi's *Ballo delle ingrate*', pp. 72–4. Denis Stevens suggests (in 'Monteverdi's Earliest Extant Ballet') that it may originally have been in five parts rather than three, although his main argument, the missing thirds in cadential chords, would apply to most of the 3-part pieces in the 1607 *Scherzi musicali*.

suggest at least two groups in antiphony), are being represented: the text's
generic praise of beauty is quite extensive, but unspecific. But the verse and
music each offer a good example of the more extended schemes now possible for sung *balli*, for all their retention of earlier characteristics identified
above.

To use Monteverdi's terminology, the piece consists of an instrumental *entrata* and five (in the music, six) *mutanze* contrasted by poetic and
musical metre (see Table 6-1), with, as we have come to expect, sections in
duple time and others in slow and fast triple (see Ex. 6-1). The *versi sciolti* in
the fourth section ('Ben sallo Alcide il forte . . .') might suggest that this was
originally intended to be in some kind of recitative; the text adopts a more
narrative style to recount two examples of mythical gods affected by beauty,
first Hercules and then Mars. Monteverdi, however, maintains the dance style,
although he changes metre (at 'ond'ei cangiato stile') and hence moves into
a new musical section where Mars 'changed his style' on falling in love with
Venus; presumably this is conventional word-painting. The poetic metres are
those used, if in different ways, in Guarini's *Giuoco della cieca*. Both the metrical organization of the text and its content (with two references to 'canto'
and one to 'amorosi balli') suggest that the performance combined singing
and dancing simultaneously, albeit by different performers: in fact, it seems
likely (from a reference in the text to 'these proud, well-born souls concor-

Table 6-1 The structure of Monteverdi's 'De la bellezza le dovute lodi' (*Scherzi
musicali a tre voci* (Venice, Ricciardo Amadino, 1607), pp. 35–40)

Mutanza	Time-signature	Text incipit	Poetic metre
	C	[*Entrata*]	
1	C	De la bellezza le dovute lodi	predominantly *ottonari* (9 lines)
2	3/2[1]	È la bellezza un raggio	*settenari* (6 lines)
3	3	Chi di tal lume	*quinari* (8 lines)
4a	3/2	Ben sallo Alcide il forte	predominantly *versi sciolti* (*settenari* and the occasional *endecasillabo*; 8 lines)
4b	C	ond'ei cangiato stile	*versi sciolti* continue (4 lines)
5	3[2]	Dunque a lei, che di beltate	alternating *ottonari* and *settenari* with a final *endecasillabo* (6 lines)

[1] But the movement is by semibreve in the 3/2 sections, i.e., three semibreves per 'bar'.
[2] Shifts to C for cadence on final half-line ('. . . quest'amorosi balli').

Ex. 6-1 Monteverdi, 'De la bellezza le dovute lodi' (*Scherzi musicali a tre voci*
(Venice, Ricciardo Amadino, 1607)).

Claudio Monteverdi: Tutte le opere, ed. Malipiero, x, pp. 62–8.

[a] [Let us celebrate] the praises owed to beauty . . .
[b] Beauty is a ray of the heavenly [light . . .]
[c] The one who does not shine adorned with such light . . .

dant with our song', ll. 38–9) that the dancers were noblemen and noble-
women of the court. We do not know whether they danced to special choreography or just adapted generic dance-steps, but either way, presumably
they must have had some rehearsal with the music. Indeed, as we shall see

in 1608, the preparations for such *balli* involving courtiers could be quite extensive.

It would no doubt be worth comparing 'De la bellezza le dovute lodi' (and, indeed, Monteverdi's other *balli*) with contemporary dance treatises to clarify its structure and choreography. If it did in fact come at the end of some longer entertainment, it would fit with the trend in such entertainments in the north Italian courts. In February 1607, Simone Borsato, *gentilhuomo di camera* of Prince Alessandro Pico della Mirandola (a small town some 45 kilometres south-east of Mantua), contacted Alessandro Striggio about a *mascherata* in honour of Laura d'Este (the prince's wife) to be performed on 22 February during Carnival, for which he expected Monteverdi to write at least the *entrata* and *ballo*.[11] Borsato outlines the *intermedio*-like action in some detail: after a brief prologue (sung by a tenor with a voice like Francesco Rasi's), a mountain is drawn in by two dragons; Flora descends and proceeds through the hall to address Laura d'Este; the mountain opens to reveal a beautiful garden with six of Flora's handmaidens and six gardeners; the latter play instruments while the maidens leave the garden to the sound of a sung *entrata*; they present flowers to the princess while a madrigal is sung, and then they perform a sung *ballo* ('S'a questa d'Este valle'). It is not known whether Monteverdi ever composed this music: the commission must have come at an irksome time, given the last-minute preparations for *Orfeo*. But this kind of more extended *ballo* was to become a feature of Mantuan entertainments.

The Ballo delle ingrate *(1608)*

The year 1608 was busy for the north Italian courts, with no fewer than three dynastic marriages demanding the customary celebration: Prince Francesco Gonzaga of Mantua wedded Margherita of Savoy; Prince Alfonso d'Este of Modena, Isabella of Savoy; and Prince Cosimo de' Medici of Florence, Maria Magdalena of Austria. The coincidence of these festivities was not entirely planned: political and diplomatic uncertainties dogged all three weddings, which had been long in the making. It also created some difficulties in terms of securing the services of the artists and artisans required for court entertainment. These artists, in turn, benefited from an atmosphere of intense competition, as Florence and Mantua, in particular, sought to stage the most magnificent festivities in terms of spectacle and virtuosity.

The Mantuan celebrations in May–June 1608 included a play (Guarini's *L'idropica*) with extravagant *intermedi* by Gabriello Chiabrera, an

11   See Patuzzi, ' "S'a questa d'Este valle" '.

opera (Monteverdi's *Arianna*, to a libretto by Ottavio Rinuccini), a tournament, a mock naval battle on the lagoon, and two *balli* mixing dancing with dramatic action, one of which was Monteverdi's *Ballo delle ingrate* (again, to a text by Rinuccini).[12] It was a remarkable sequence of works that covered the gamut of genres and styles of courtly entertainment to project dynastic themes of royal love and divine favour. The consistent themes prompt the recurrence of characters in successive entertainments: Venere and Amore in *Arianna* and the *Ballo delle ingrate* (and, for that matter, in Gagliano's *Dafne* that preceded the festivities), Venere alone in the second of the *intermedi* for *L'idropica*, Arianna and Teseo in *Arianna* and in the tournament. This is conventional enough, although it also raises the possibility of intertextual references, wherein each entertainment may have drawn significance from its broader context.

Monteverdi later complained repeatedly about the amount of work involved in the 1608 festivities, which, he said, had almost killed him. The prologue (i.e., first *intermedio*) to *L'idropica* must have been fairly easy. Its text (the music is lost) is unremarkable, apart from the fact that, unlike the prologue to *Orfeo*, it follows the practice of the *intermedi* by introducing several characters within spectacular staging: thus there are four stanzas of *ottava rima* for Manto ('Ha cento lustri con etereo giro', presumably set in strophic variation), a chorus for five deities (the madrigal 'Pronte scendiamo a volo'), and five 4-line stanzas in *endecasillabi* for Imeneo ('Coppia real, che di sua mano insieme', again, presumably in strophic variation). *Arianna*, however, must have been harder work, in terms not just of its composition but also of various crises prior to its performance (discussed in Chapter 8). The *Ballo delle ingrate*, while on a smaller scale, also underwent revisions at a relatively late stage.[13] This was a fact of life when working for a court.

12 The official description of the 1608 Mantuan festivities was Follino's *Compendio delle sontuose feste*; most of the relevant passages regarding the specific entertainments are in Solerti, *Gli albori del melodramma*, *passim*, and a number appear in Fabbri, *Monteverdi*, trans. Carter, pp. 77–99, from which the translations below are taken save where noted.

13 We do not know precisely when it was decided to include the *Ballo delle ingrate* in the festivities. Solerti (*Gli albori del melodramma*, i, p. 92) suggests that it was in response to the meeting between the court artists and Duchess Eleonora on 26 February, when the entertainments were discussed and revisions (particularly to *Arianna*) agreed. However, Duke Vincenzo and Prince Francesco were then on the verge of leaving for Turin (if they had not done so already), suggesting that their *balli* were already planned at least in outline by that time. Duchess Eleonora was working hard to complete work on the entertainments in mid-March 1608; see the letters cited in Solerti, *Gli albori del melodramma*, i, p. 95. But Margherita's departure from Turin was repeatedly delayed by Duke Carlo Emanuele of Savoy, who was not averse to embarrassing the Gonzagas; see Mamone, 'Torino, Mantova, Firenze, 1608'.

The *Ballo delle ingrate* was performed on 4 June, and on the next day there was another *ballo*, Marco da Gagliano's *Il sacrificio d'Ifigenia* (text by Alessandro Striggio). Gagliano was a favourite of Prince Ferdinando Gonzaga; his new setting of Ottavio Rinuccini's *Dafne* was originally intended for the 1608 festivities but was performed in advance of them during Carnival, because of delays in the Mantua–Savoy negotiations. And there is no doubt that the two 1608 *balli* involved several levels of competition, between their patrons, Duke Vincenzo Gonzaga (the *Ballo delle ingrate*) and Prince Francesco, between Rinuccini and Striggio, and between Monteverdi and Gagliano. Indeed, Monteverdi later complained bitterly (writing on 2 December 1608) about the favour Gagliano had received. The relationship between these *balli* is important, not least because it helps explain one curious feature of the *Ballo delle ingrate*, that it is not a sung *ballo* in the by now conventional mould.

The *Ballo delle ingrate* (the 1608 libretto styles it 'Mascherata dell'ingrate') survives only in the version adapted for a much later performance (actual or intended) in Vienna, and published in Monteverdi's Eighth Book of madrigals, the *Madrigali guerrieri, et amorosi*, of 1638. Yet however much the music may have been revised, the poetic text is close enough to the one known to have been performed in 1608. It deals with the eternal punishment meted out to women who are 'ungrateful' in love, and thus provides a lesson in female ingratitude to counterbalance the male ingratitude demonstrated by Teseo in *Arianna*, performed the previous week (28 May). Venere and Amore visit Hades to discuss with Plutone the harsh fate of such ingrates forever burning in the fires of hell. He summons forth from the Underworld a band of them (according to Follino, eight pairs, in fact comprising eight women and eight men, including Duke Vincenzo and Prince Francesco).[14] They enter to the sound of an *entrata*, descend into the area in front of the stage designated for dancing, and then perform a formal (untexted) dance lamenting their sorry state. Plutone issues a sententious warning (eight quatrains in *endecasillabi*) to the ladies in the audience not to follow their example, and the *ingrate* continue the dance and then leave to the music of the *entrata*. But one *ingrata* remains on stage to sing a lament (*versi sciolti*, with a refrain) echoed by four other female spirits from the wings: 'Apprendete pietà, donne e donzelle' ('Learn pity, ladies and maidens').

Condemning ingratitude (whether male or female) as a threat to the power of Cupid's arrows was a widespread trope in courtly entertainments,

14   The preface to the piece in Monteverdi's Eighth Book refers just to eight 'anime ingrate'; he may or may not mean that each *ingrata* nevertheless has a male dance partner (hence, eight pairs as in 1608), or he may have reduced the number to make the piece appear less intimidating for a general market.

although the notion here of punishment for such ingratitude in the afterlife has more specific resonances, whether of Dante, of Boccaccio or, more intriguingly, of Ariosto. Boccaccio's ghost-story in the *Decameron* (fifth day, eighth story), concerning Nastagio degli Onesti's lesson to his intended bride against ingratitude, is well enough known. However, the links with a more obscure episode in Ariosto's *Orlando furioso* (XXXIV.11–43) are more striking.[15] Here the hero Astolfo pursues the harpies into the mouth of hell, where he encounters the ghostly spirit, Lidia, who has been condemned for eternity for being ungrateful in love. Her fate is shared by many other similar ingrates, including Daphne (ungrateful to Apollo), and also by men guilty of similar ingratitude (Jason, Theseus, Aeneas and Absalom), who are punished still more because their behaviour is even less excusable.[16] Lidia then goes on to explain her mistreatment of the warrior knight Alcestes, who eventually died of sorrow:

> Questa mia ingratitudine gli diede
> tanto martir, ch'al fin dal dolor vinto,
> e dopo un lungo domandar mercede,
> infermo cadde, e ne rimase estinto.
> Per pena ch'al fallir mio si richiede,
> or gli occhi ho lacrimosi, e il viso tinto
> del negro fumo: e così avrò in eterno;
> ché nulla redenzione è ne l'inferno.

'And my ingratitude such bitter pain / Inflicted on him that his spirit broke. / When he had pleaded many times in vain, / Illness confined him to his bed; he spoke / No more, and soon he died, by sorrow slain. / And now I weep and on my face the smoke / Has left a tinge that is indelible, / For no redemption can be found in Hell.'[17]

---

15 See Patuzzi, 'Da Ariosto al *Ballo delle ingrate*'; Carter, 'New Light on Monteverdi's *Ballo delle ingrate*'.

16 The presence of men in this list is intriguing; it also throws a slightly different light on attempts to provide a feminist reading of the *Ballo delle ingrate*, as in Gordon, 'Talking Back'. Further, the *Ballo delle ingrate* should be read in the context of Rinuccini's defence of ungrateful women in the so-called *Mascherata di donne tradite*, a series of nine *ottava rima* stanzas published in Rinuccini's *Poesie* (Florence, I Giunti, 1622; in Solerti, *Gli albori del melodramma*, ii, pp. 61–3). The female speaker here, addressing 'Cortesi donne', warns 'incautious, simple-minded women' of the 'sweet speech full of falsehood of false lovers' – 'Come a noi incaute e semplicette avvenne / ch'al parlar dolce e di fallacia pieno / de' falsi amanti . . .' – which causes them to forget the love of their homeland and to be left abandoned on desert shores ('che poi lasciate da gli amanti infidi / fummo in deserti abbandonati lidi').

17 *Orlando furioso*, XXXIV.43, trans. Reynolds, ii, p. 322.

Rinuccini knew his Ariosto – several quotations and allusions prove the point – even if he casts his story differently. The initial design of the *Ballo delle ingrate* seems to have comprised what is now its central episode: the entrance of the *ingrate*, Plutone's quatrains, and the exit (but not the final lament).[18] However, this outline was revised and extended in spring 1608 after, it seems, Monteverdi had set this central episode to music. Events are explained by a long letter from Alessandro Striggio to Prince Francesco Gonzaga of 22 April 1608, concerning the other 1608 *ballo*, *Il sacrificio d'Ifigenia*:[19]

Yesterday Your Highness's *balletto* [*Il sacrificio*] was rehearsed. It was danced very well, but the Lord Count Canossa and Signora Angusciola were somewhat offended, whenceforth in their place Signor Carlo Caffini and Messer Giovan Battista did it. The music which is recited has been rehearsed, but it needs a performance if it is to turn out perfectly as is desired. Signor Rinuccini, in imitation of Your Highness's invention, has himself, too, added many things to the *Ballo delle ingrate*, and he has Amore and Venere in dialogue on a cloud, and has La Florinda sing, who as the *ingrate* return to the Inferno will mingle with them and will appear as one of those who have danced, and will sing plaintively, abhorring the cause of their suffering. And all this has been added secretly perhaps for fear that Your Highness's *balletto* would appear more beautiful than the other. I have been advised of everything by Messer Marco [da Gagliano], and certainly I feel some resentment over this, only because I would not have wanted both the one and the other *balletto* to be done in the same manner. Thus if there had been more time, and if it had been certain that the lord duke's *balletto* [*delle ingrate*] was to be designed as a sung play, I would rather have been of a mind, with Your Highness's agreement, to change the invention: for what worries me is that Your Highness's *balletto* is to be the last entertainment that will be done. But whatever the case, I will not fail to ensure some change both in the *entrata* and in the instrumental music of the *ballo* that will be with the singing, even though I doubt that there will be the

18   This central episode was regularly seen as the core of the work. For example, the Este ambassador reported of the 1608 performance that 'one saw the Inferno burning, and from there came Plutone, but first Venere and Cupido appeared, who sang many verses and with Plutone made a scene in song'. In the preface to the *Ballo delle ingrate* in the Eighth Book of madrigals, Monteverdi refers just to this episode, although Venere and Amore are included in the list of 'interlocutori'.

19   The relevant portion of this letter is in Buratelli, *Spettacoli di corte a Mantova tra Cinque e Seicento*, p. 63; the version in Solerti, *Gli albori del melodramma*, i, pp. 96–7, has some errors (including the date); I have altered slightly, but with a significant new reading, my translation in Fabbri, *Monteverdi*, trans. Carter, pp. 84–5. Rinuccini was in Mantua at least by 21 April; see Solerti, *Gli albori del melodramma*, i, p. 95.

latter, because the design has been taken by Signor Rinuccini, who, having heard it the day before yesterday praised it greatly to me.[20] And I would also think it good that we should abandon the cloud on which it was decided to have Diana appear above her temple, unless Your Highness commands the opposite, and that this deity should appear in the most noble part of the temple sat in majesty to receive the sacrifice. I have also discussed this my idea with the lord prefect [the architect Antonio Maria Viani], who agrees with my opinion, so as not to do the same as will be done in the other *balletto*, where, as I have already said, Venere and Amore appear on a cloud.

This is an important letter, not least because it reveals that such works involving members of the court were somehow rehearsed, even if Prince Francesco, who eventually took part in the performance, was not present (he was currently in Turin). It also casts new light on the *Ballo delle ingrate* by virtue of its relationship to *Il sacrificio d'Ifigenia*.

 Il sacrificio involved a much more developed plot (drawn from Euripides' *Iphigenia in Aulis*); it is also more friendly to the ladies in the audience than the *Ballo delle ingrate*, and Follino emphasizes their presence to a far greater extent.[21] Its music is now lost, although one can gauge something of it from the text. Agamemnon has been ordered by an oracle to sacrifice his daughter Iphigenia, so that the winds may blow his fleet to Troy. The sacrificial procession enters from the rear of the auditorium, with priests, archpriests and a high priest accompanied by Agamemnon, Iphigenia, Ulysses and Achilles, plus ten knights (including Duke Vincenzo and Prince Francesco Gonzaga) and ten ladies (so, two more pairs than in the *Ballo delle ingrate*). There are various exchanges between the main characters, and poignant laments for Ifigenia ('Morir dunque pur deggio') and the chorus ('Chiuda gli occhi anco il Sole'). But as the sacrifice is about to begin, the goddess Diana calls a dramatic halt to the proceedings, prompting a chorus in praise of her clemency followed by a sung *ballo*. This, in turn, was followed by social

20 'Ma in tutti i casi non mancherò di procurar di variare e nell'entrata e nel suono del ballo, che sarà con canto, se bene di questo dubito che non vi sia per esser tolta la foggia dal signor Rinuccini, che havendolo sentito l'altr'hieri me lo lodò grandemente'. This is a point of some difficulty, given that it is unclear what 'questo' is (the *ballo* with singing or just the singing?).

21 See Solerti, *Gli albori del melodramma*, iii, p. 277: 'With the princesses descending from the platform [where they had viewed a *giostra all'uomo armato*] they had all the ladies enter court, where, having been given a very sumptuous collation, they then moved to the usual Teatro della Commedia to see the graceful *balletto* which had been prepared by the Prince [Francesco] of Mantua'. The text of *Il sacrificio* is in Follino, *Compendio delle sontuose feste*, pp. 142–9 (Solerti, *Gli albori del melodramma*, iii, pp. 275–83).

dancing. The text of the final *ballo* ('Vergine alma, che 'n Delo') is organized in a manner similar to 'De la bellezza le dovute lodi', incorporating much the same poetic metres. The rest of *Il sacrificio*, however, involves monologues and dialogues in straightforward *versi sciolti* (*settenari* and *endecasillabi*), suggesting that the music (at least in the solo sections) was predominantly in recitative.

Striggio's letter reveals that Rinuccini's first version of the *Ballo delle ingrate* was expanded quite late on, and in response to his hearing of the plans for *Il sacrificio d'Ifigenia*. Two things in particular concerned Rinuccini: that *Il sacrificio* incorporated dramatic action presented in musical recitative (the central episode of the *Ballo delle ingrate* involved just Plutone delivering his formal quatrains to the audience); and that there was a sung *ballo* at the end. This had already prompted Rinuccini to add 'many things' to the *Ballo delle ingrate*, including an opening dialogue for Venere and Amore on a cloud, and a closing lament to be sung by Virginia Andreini (Striggio uses her stage-name, La Florinda), who would appear on the exit of the dancing *ingrate*; presumably she did not dance because it would not have been appropriate for her to move in noble circles.[22] The former addition may also have extended to the exchanges between Venere, Amore and Plutone, and the brief interjection of the shades of the Underworld (or at least, it implied them, if they were added later still). Most intriguing, however, are Striggio's fears for the sung *ballo* planned for the end of *Il sacrificio d'Ifigenia*, given that Rinuccini, on hearing recently of its design (or seeing it in rehearsal), appears to have decided to combine singing with dancing in the *Ballo delle ingrate*. Rinuccini's original plan for the textless dancing of his *ingrate* may have taken its cue from Ariosto (Lidia is at first reluctant to tell her tale). But it seems that on the basis of his experience of *Il sacrificio d'Ifigenia*, Rinuccini was planning to change course.

There is a strong air of frustration, perhaps even panic, in Striggio's letter, written just one month before Margherita of Savoy eventually arrived in Mantua (on 24 May). He was unhappy with the turn of events, and indeed, reading between the lines, with the notoriously difficult Rinuccini. But in his concern that the final entertainment of the festivities, *Il sacrificio d'Ifigenia*, might be eclipsed by the *Ballo delle ingrate*, which was planned to come earlier, he appears willing to defer not so much to Rinuccini as to Duke Vincenzo Gonzaga, the promoter of the Rinuccini–Monteverdi *ballo*: thus he raises the

---

22 According to Follino, the lament was sung by 'one of the *ingrate* who had remained on the stage when the others descended to dance', suggesting that Virginia Andreini entered with the other *ingrate* but stayed on stage while they moved down to the auditorium to perform the dance. But Striggio's simple deceit seems more effective.

possibility of changes to the structure, music and staging of *Il sacrificio d'Ifige-nia*. However, Striggio and Gagliano – or perhaps Prince Francesco – appear to have held out against significant modifications to their own *ballo*. Thus in the final version of the *Ballo delle ingrate* performed in 1608, Venere and Amore did not appear on a cloud machine (rather, they stood at the mouth of the Inferno). As Follino describes, the *ingrate* also remained silent during their dance:

> They moved (but with great grief indicated by gestures) two by two in a pleasing descent from the stage, accompanying their steps with the sound of a great number of instruments which played a melancholic and plain-tive dance tune; and having reached the floor of the theatre, they did a *bal-letto* so beautiful and delightful, with steps, movements and actions now of grief and now of desperation, and now with gestures of pity and now of scorn, sometimes embracing each other as if they had tears of tenderness in their eyes, now striking each other swollen with rage and fury. They were seen from time to time to abhor each other's sight and to flee each other in frightened manners, and then to follow each other with threat-ening looks, coming to blows with each other, asking pardon and a thou-sand other movements, represented with such affect and with such naturalness that the hearts of the onlookers were left so impressed that there was no one in that theatre who did not feel his heart move and be dis-turbed in a thousand ways at the changing of their passions.

One wonders whether Rinuccini had pressed Follino to include so vivid an account precisely because he had, in the end, been denied the opportunity to put words to dance-music.

Nevertheless, the music for the central *ballo* follows a standard pattern, with two 16-bar strains (A, B) subject to metrical and some melodic variation: *Entrata* – A (time-signature, **C**); *Ballo* – A (**C**), A′ (3/2), B (**C**), B′ (6/4), B″ (3/2); [*Uscita*] – A (foreshortened; **C**). The music is in an old-fashioned five parts (C1, C1, C3, C4, F4 clefs),[23] for which the preface to the *Ballo delle ingrate* in the Eighth Book of madrigals specifies 'Cinque Viole da brazzo, Clavicembano e Chitarone', evoking the five *viole da braccio* used in part of *Gli amori di Diana ed Endimione*, and still more the scoring (with the same clefs) of 'Lasciate i monti' in *Orfeo*. This preface also allows that these instruments might be doubled according to the size of the performance space (*Li quali ustrimenti si radoppiano secondo il bisogno della grandezza del loco in cui*

---

23 For the 'missing' second part misplaced in the 1638 partbooks (and omitted in Malipiero's first edition of Monteverdi's complete works), see Stevens, '"Monteverdi Unclouded"'. Holman ('"Col nobilissimo esercitio della vivuola"', p. 583) argues that the *entrata* and *ballo* are for the older combination of one violin, three violas and one bass *viola* (*da braccio* or *da gamba*?).

devisi rapresentare). However, Follino mentions 'a large number of musicians playing both string and wind instruments', and notes that the dancing within the *Ballo delle ingrate* was accompanied 'by the sound of a great number of instruments'.

There are other difficulties in the *Ballo delle ingrate* as it survives, which in turn raise questions concerning Monteverdi's intention for the 1638 edition (or the materials on which that edition was based). The arrival of the *ingrate* is cued by a rubric in the score, and is commented upon by Venere and Amore, 36 bars before the instrumental *entrata* preceding the first dance. There is a sense of clumsiness in Plutone's final 3-line injunction (after the second dance), 'Tornate a 'l negro chiostro / anime sventurate; / tornate ove vi sferza il fallir vostro' ('Return to the black cloister, unfortunate spirits; return to where your fault forces you'). Nor is it clear how much of the dance-music is heard before Plutone's central quatrains. Follino appears to refer to two separate and distinct dances, the first before Plutone's speech and the second after – 'with the instruments taking up a new dance tune sadder than the other, those *ingrate* began another dance' – whereas the 1638 materials present just one extended dance before Plutone's speech. A rubric says that the *ingrate* first 'dance the *ballo* up to the middle' (*Danzano il ballo sino a mezzo*), and then, after Plutone has spoken, they take up the second part of the *ballo* (*Qui ripigliano le Anime Ingrate la seconda parte del Ballo al suono come prima*). The presentation of the *entrata* and dance music *en bloc* at the centre of the work may simply have been for typographical or related reasons, but the dance-music does not fall easily into two halves.

In part, these difficulties may have resulted from later revisions to the work, but they also give the impression of last-minute cutting-and-pasting. Monteverdi was forced to provide a significant amount of additional music at speed, much of which was new. But some, at least, of this music may have involved reorganizing what was already there. An example would seem to be provided by the *entrata* that covers both the entrance and the exit of the *ingrate* (Ex. 6-2). In the version printed in 1638, the *entrata* on its first hearing (when the dancers enter) comprises two straightforward 8-bar phrases, matching the eight dancers who could, of course, leave to entirely the same music. But according to the preface to the score, only seven dancers leave the stage, with one remaining to sing the lament: the *entrata* repeated at the end of the *ballo* therefore becomes truncated into two 7-bar phrases by the simple, if jolting, expedient of (effectively) cutting one bar in the middle of each phrase. This has sometimes been taken as a misprint and therefore ignored, although 7-bar phrases are found elsewhere in Monteverdi's instrumental music: there is another example in the *Ballo delle ingrate*, the (later?) sinfonia both preceding and occurring in the middle of Venere's 'Udite, donne, udite i saggi detti', and also one in the *Combattimento di Tancredi e Clorinda* (the sinfonia

Ex. 6–2: *Ballo delle ingrate.*

Monteverdi, *Madrigali guerrieri, et amorosi . . . Libro ottavo* (Venice, Alessandro Vincenti, 1638), *Basso continuo* partbook, pp. 73, 75 (upper part only).

preceding the 'Notte' stanza). In this specific case, however, the change appears to have been prompted by the revised ending comprising Virginia Andreini's lament, with Andreini entering surreptitiously and appearing to be one of those who had danced (so Striggio's letter suggests): thus in 1608 (when the dancers were doubled), while sixteen dancers entered, only fifteen appeared to leave (as seven 'pairs'), although all sixteen in fact did so.[24] Depending on one's point of view, the 7-bar phrases are either a stroke of genius or an act of desperate measure; given the pressures under which Monteverdi was working during this period, one suspects more the latter than the former.

It was no doubt the inclusion of a lament in *Il sacrificio* (did Virginia Andreini also play Ifigenia?) that prompted Rinuccini and Monteverdi to add the final lament for Andreini to the *Ballo delle ingrate.* It also allowed Andreini

24 Follino has all the *ingrate* leave after, not before, the lament: 'At the end of so beautiful a lament, they again entered the burning cavern, but in such a way that they appeared pushed by a great force.' The 1638 version has just the one *ingrata* remaining on the stage. The wording of Striggio's letter permits either possibility.

to confirm her skills in the dramatic performance of laments that were most obviously apparent in her 1608 performance in the leading role of Monteverdi's *Arianna*; the lament in the *Ballo delle ingrate* seems to have produced a similar tearful effect in the women of the audience (or so Follino says). But in the *Ballo delle ingrate* and *Arianna*, as in *Il sacrificio d'Ifigenia*, lament soon gave way to celebration. At the end of the *Ballo delle ingrate*, the scene seems to have changed to a garden, with singing and dancing nymphs and shepherds.[25] In the opera, Arianna's union with Bacchus is also marked by a sung *ballo* for two groups of soldiers, one dancing and one singing. The text, 'Spiega omai giocondo nume', has two 6-line stanzas ($a^8a^4b^8c^8c^4b^8$). According to Follino:

> There were seen to appear on the stage at the end of these words from the left-hand side of the scene Bacchus with the beautiful Ariadne, and Amor before them, surrounded in front and around by many pairs of soldiers girt with most beautiful arms, with proud crests on their heads. When they were on the stage, with the instruments that were within taking up the playing of a beautiful dance tune, one part of these soldiers performed a very delightful dance, weaving in and out in a thousand ways; and while these danced, another part of the soldiers began to accompany the sound and the dance with the following words.

Similarly, at least three of the *intermedi* accompanying *L'idropica* had sung *balli*. The Este ambassador was particularly struck by the end of the fourth *intermedio*, with 'a *moresca*, twelve with shield and ball, twelve with arrow and bow, twelve with darts and finally twelve with torches, who together and separately performed extraordinary *balletti*, which turned out beautifully, and all proudly dressed differently according to their team'.[26] And the *intermedi* concluded with a sung *ballo* by the gods and other allegorical figures to a text, 'Da quel dì, che l'auree strade' (five stanzas), in a form similar to that of the *ballo* towards the end of *Arianna*, $a^8a^4b^8c^8c^4b^8$. Certainly the Mantuan architect Gabriele Bertazzolo compared matters favourably with Florentine efforts in October 1608 precisely because of 'the *balli* and *moresche*, for here [in

---

25 Follino's account ends with the Inferno transformed into 'una bella e dilettosa prospettiva' ('a beautiful and delightful scene'). However, Federico Zuccari, in his *Il passaggio per l'Italia . . .* (Bologna, Bartolomeo Cocchi, 1608; in Solerti, *Gli albori del melodramma*, iii, pp. 235–40) describes 'un bellissimo giardino di rose e di fiori con molte Ninfe e Pastori a far graziose danze e allegre canzoni' ('a most beautiful garden of roses and flowers, with many nymphs and shepherds performing graceful dances and cheerful songs'); see Povoledo, 'Controversie monteverdiane', p. 372.

26 Solerti, *Gli albori del melodramma*, i, p. 101.

Florence] there were none, and in Mantua there were so many that at times
it would have sufficed, so to speak, to provide with them alone a spectacle
[worthy] of an entire comedy'.[27]

Tirsi e Clori *(1616)*

Monteverdi's involvement in *balli* for Mantua continued after he left Gonzaga
employment. One such entertainment, *Tirsi e Clori*, seems to have been
intended for the festivities celebrating the coronation of Duke Ferdinando in
January 1616 (another example, *Apollo*, of 1620 will be discussed in Chapter
8). In *Tirsi e Clori* the 'dramatic' action preceding the dancing is much simpler
than in *Il sacrificio d'Ifigenia* and the expanded *Ballo delle ingrate*, coming close
to what might have been the case for 'De la bellezza le dovute lodi' in the
1607 *Scherzi musicali*, if the latter was part of a longer work (see above). Tirsi
invites his beloved Clori to join a band of dancing nymphs and shepherds
and she agrees, prompting a sung *ballo* in praise of dancing (each stanza begins
with the invitation 'Balliamo' – 'Let us dance'). Monteverdi discusses the commission for *Tirsi e Clori* in his letter to Annibale Iberti of 21 November 1615,
where he notes that Ferdinando Gonzaga's request 'to set a ballet to music',
relayed by the Mantuan Resident in Venice, had been fairly imprecise (unlike
the commissions of Duke Vincenzo), but that Monteverdi had produced a
ballo of six *mutanze*, of which four had been written the previous summer.
The composer is willing to respond to Ferdinando's criticisms, should he want
'either a change of tune in this *ballo*, or additions to the enclosed movements
of a slow or grave nature, or fuller and without imitative passages'; he also
says that he could take 'no notice of the present words, which can easily be
changed, though at least these words help by the nature of their metre and
by the imitation of the melody'.

> But if by good fortune the enclosed should be to his liking, I would think
> it proper to perform it in a half-moon, at whose corners should be placed
> a chitarrone and a harpsichord, one each side, one playing the bass for Clori
> and the other for Tirsi, each of them holding a chitarrone, and playing and
> singing themselves to their own instruments and to the aforementioned. If
> there could be a harp instead of a chitarrone for Clori, that would be even
> better.

27   Carpeggiani, 'Studi su Gabriele Bertazzolo', p. 22: 'nelli balli et moresche, che qui
     non ve n'era nissuno, et in questo Mantova fu tanto, che alle volte basterebbe, per
     modo di dire, a far con essi soli un spetacolo di comedia intiera'. For the broader
     issues, see Carter, 'A Florentine Wedding of 1608'.

Then having reached the ballet movement after they have sung a dialogue, there could be added to the ballet six more voices in order to make eight voices in all, eight *viole da braccio*, a contrabass, a *spineta arpata*, and if there were also two small lutes, that would be fine. And directed with a beat suitable to the character of the melodies, avoiding overexcitement among the singers and players, and with the understanding of the ballet-master, I hope that – sung in this way – it will not displease His Most Serene Highness.

Monteverdi concludes with his usual request that the musicians should have sight of the piece for an hour before its performance.

We know from Monteverdi's letter of 28 November 1615 that Ferdinando had heard a small part of *Tirsi e Clori* with approval, but we have no details of the performance. The piece was subsequently published at the end of the Seventh Book of madrigals (1619; dedicated to Ferdinando's wife, Caterina de' Medici), although there are some discrepancies between the printed version and the comments in the 1615 letter. The *ballo* is certainly in six *mutanze*, as Monteverdi noted, but it is scored only for five voices (SSATB). However, doubling the soprano and tenor parts would produce the number of voices specified in the letter: that is, eight in all. If the soprano parts were taken by women, as the voice ranges suggest,[28] and if the singers danced (rather than members of the court), then this doubling would allow four women (the sopranos) each to have a male partner. The text is usually attributed to Alessandro Striggio, although the fact that Monteverdi wrote to Iberti, plus the composer's rather dismissive comments on the verse, suggests that he got it from elsewhere, perhaps in Venice. It is entirely in *senari* (i.e., 6-syllable lines), with five 8-line stanzas for Tirsi and Clori in alternation (stanza by stanza), then for the *ballo* itself five 6-line stanzas and a concluding quatrain.[29] Tirsi's ebullient triple-time writing (each of his three stanzas is a strophic variation) suits the mood, but Clori's recitative (again, her two stanzas are strophic variations) seems less appropriate, for all its pliant languor. The *ballo* itself alternates duple time and slow triple, also making some play of antiphonal effects, with passages for ATB repeated for SST. But the piece gives the impression of just going through the motions, as indeed Monteverdi's curiously indifferent remarks in his letter also suggest.

---

28   The ranges are: Tirsi, *d–f'*; Clori, *d'–f"*; C1, *c'–g"*; C1, *b'–f"*; C3, *d–a'*; C4, *c–g'*; F4, *E–c'*. These voice-types, including the wide-ranging alto, are not untypical of Monteverdi's Mantuan madrigals, at least some of which were designed to include women; see Carter, 'Singing *Orfeo*', p. 88.

29   The text in Solerti, *Gli albori del melodramma*, iii, pp. 289–91, is corrupt, with missing lines.

The later balli

Nevertheless, Monteverdi's subsequent correspondence with Striggio over *Apollo* suggests that the composer was to regain some enthusiasm for these kinds of works. This is also apparent in his later relations with the Habsburg court in Vienna. When Eleonora Gonzaga moved there in 1622 as the wife of Emperor Ferdinand II, she joined a court accustomed to large-scale music-making. Gabriele Bertazzolo made special note of the music during the banquets celebrating her arrival:

> In a corner of that large room had been built a platform which contained some 50–60 musicians, which was full, and as soon as the meal began, they started to sing and play with so many voices and instruments, and with such variety – now with full harmony, now with few voices, now with solo instruments, and now with verses more recited than sung – that it was a very pleasurable thing to hear. And so great is the pleasure that they say the emperor takes in music, that the expense of it is reckoned to amount to 60,000 florins each year.[30]

Bertazzolo's account is also full of references to social dancing, both in the German manner and, much to the emperor's delight, by his new wife in the Italian style. Eleonora seems to have been keen to bring Mantuan practices to Vienna; she also provided a safe haven for musicians leaving Mantua on the death of Duke Vincenzo II Gonzaga on 25 December 1627 and during the War of Mantuan Succession, including the Rubini brothers and other singers and instrumentalists. They seem to have aided the dissemination of Monteverdi's music north of the Alps, while the composer himself regularly sought favours from the empress and her husband.[31]

   The Eighth Book of madrigals (1638; dedicated to Emperor Ferdinand III) and the *Selva morale e spirituale* (1640–1; dedicated to Eleonora Gonzaga) become directly associated with these favours. A letter from Emperor Ferdinand II of 19 December 1633 suggests that Monteverdi had

30 Bertazzolo, *Breve relatione dello sposalitio* (1622), p. 64: 'In un cantone di quella gran Sala era fatto un palco, in cui capiva sino à cinquanta in sessanta Musici, che si trovò tutto ripieno, & subito che principiò la cena cominciarono à cantare, & suonare co*n* tante voci, & stromenti, e con tanta varietà, hora con piena armonia, hora con poche voci, hora con soli stromenti, & hora co*n* versi più tosto recitati, che cantati; che fù cosa molto gustevole da sentire; & è tanto il compiacimento, che dicono habbia l'Imperatore della musica, che si tiene ascenda la spesa d'essa ogn'anno à sessanta mila fiorini.' Monteverdi himself seems to have had some loyalty to the Habsburgs in this period; see Jonathan Glixon, 'Was Monteverdi a Traitor?'.

31 See Saunders, 'New Light on the Genesis of Monteverdi's Eighth Book of Madrigals'.

Ex. 6–3 (a) *Ballo delle ingrate*; (b) *Il ritorno d'Ulisse in patria*, I.5; (c) *L'incoronazione di Poppea*, II.2.

Monteverdi, *Madrigali guerrieri, et amorosi . . . Libro ottavo* (1638), *Basso continuo* partbook, p. 76; Vienna, Österreichische Nationalbibliothek, MS 18763, fol. 26v; Venice, Biblioteca Nazionale Marciana, MS 9963 (It. IV.439), fol. 55v.

[a] And while by your glances in the breast languishes mortally wounded the heart . . .

[b] I will punish their incautious pride: their moving ship . . .

[c] Friend, for a long time now have I armed my breast against the blows of fate.

---

already sent various pieces of music to Vienna, probably in connection with his attempt to gain a benefice that would, in turn, secure his Mantuan pension (this is one reason why the composer took holy orders in 1631–2). Several settings in the Eighth Book have strong Habsburg references, including the opening 'Altri canti d'Amor, tenero arciero', the virtuoso showpiece 'Ogni amante è guerrier, nel suo gran regno', and two *balli*, 'Volgendo il ciel per l'immortal sentiero'–'Movete al mio bel suon le piante snelle' and the revised *Ballo delle ingrate*. The poet of 'Altri canti d'Amor' is unknown, but the other works are to texts by Rinuccini, who had died in 1621 and therefore is most unlikely to have had a role in revising them for Viennese consumption ('Ogni amante è guerrier' and 'Volgendo il ciel' had originally been associated with Henri IV of France). But in fact the whole of the *Madrigali guerrieri, et amorosi*, with its themes of war and love, seems cast with more recent events in mind in the context of the Thirty Years War.

We do not know when the revised *Ballo delle ingrate* might have been performed in Vienna (the notion of a performance in 1628 derives from an error by Winterfeld). Both it and 'Volgendo il ciel' have been associated with the celebrations for the election of Ferdinand III as Holy Roman Emperor in December 1636 (before the death of Ferdinand II), and 'Volgendo il ciel' does indeed refer to an age of peace to be ushered in by the new King of the Romans ('un secolo di pace il sol rimena / sotto il re novo del Romano impero').[32] However, there is no evidence that they were performed then, or for that matter, at any other time. In the case of the *Ballo delle ingrate*, the topical Mantuan references in Rinuccini's libretto are replaced by Viennese ones (e.g., the Mantuan river Mincio becomes the 'Istro', i.e., the Danube). Plutone's music appears to have been rewritten (for a new singer?); the bass writing, with the range *D–d′*, seems much closer to that in *Il ritorno d'Ulisse in patria* and *L'incoronazione di Poppea* than in *Orfeo* (see Ex. 6-3). In addition,

---

32   For the dating, see Saunders, ibid., p. 189, who notes Seifert's suggestion (on the basis of a textual reference) that the Vienna *Ballo delle ingrate* cannot have been prepared before December 1635.

the instrumental sinfonia (G2, C1, C3, F4 clefs) in the opening scene for Venere and Amore, and also the ritornellos (G2, G2, F4 clefs) separating Plutone's stanzas, are in a more modern scoring and style,[33] even though the five-part *entrata* and *ballo* would seem to be original.

'Volgendo il ciel per l'immortal sentiero'–'Movete al mio bel suon le piante snelle' comprises two interconnected sonnets; the last line of the first is the same as the first of the second. 'Volgendo il ciel' is set as a recitative-like invocation for a 'Poeta' (the two quatrains and two tercets more or less in strophic variation, as was usual for sonnets); he receives a 'nobil cetra' (a lyre, represented by a chitarrone) and then a crown of laurels from one of the nymphs of the Danube, so as to pronounce the glories of Ferdinand III. The Poeta also delivers the first quatrain of the second sonnet, comprising the invitation to the nymphs to garland their brows with roses, to leave the bed of the river, and to move their fleeting feet to his fine sound. The following *ballo* is sung and danced to the second sonnet (the first quatrain of which thus gets repeated), divided into two parts (the octave and the sestet). It is mostly in slow triple time, apart from a duple-time opening *riverenza* and the closing cadence. The scoring (SSATB), and at times the style of writing, is similar to the *ballo* of *Tirsi e Clori*, although the structure is tauter: each section of the sonnet (two quatrains and two tercets) is set as a strophic variation, with adjustments for the fewer lines in the tercets, while within each section repetitive cadential formulas serve to create the impression of recurring ground basses. Above them, Monteverdi weaves vocal lines of remarkable variety to highlight different words in the text – the storms put to flight, the murmuring waves and the resounding echoes of praise for Ferdinand – in the manner of the duet 'Zefiro torna, e di soavi accenti' in the 1632 *Scherzi musicali*. The parts printed in 1638 contain unusually precise performance instructions, including how to stage the Poeta's invocation and the possibility of some dancing without singing between the first and second parts of the *ballo* which might comprise 'a canary, or *passo e mezzo* or other dance *ad libitum* without song' (*un canario o passo e mezzo od altro balletto a bene placito senza canto*) or perhaps a pair of 'little dances' (*un par di ballettini*) by the dancing-master. It is not clear whether these instructions are for the general reader of the *Madrigali guerrieri, et amorosi*, or whether they derive from (a copy of) the manuscript which Monteverdi sent to Vienna and thus are directed towards a proposed staging there. This reflects broader problems with the Eighth Book, where oddities, confusions and inconsistencies seem to

33 The sinfonia is more in keeping with the 4-part scoring of the instrumental music in the *Combattimento di Tancredi e Clorinda* – which Holman suggests ('"Col nobilissimo esercitio della vivuola"', pp. 586–7) in its original form was for violin, two violas and bass, and then partly revised for two violins, viola and bass.

derive not just from loose supervision of the printing process but also from the copy-texts given to the typesetter.

Monteverdi's last known (but lost) *ballo*, *Vittoria d'Amore*, to a text by Bernardo Morando, was performed in Piacenza on 7 February 1641;[34] presumably it reflects the composer's connection with the Farnese, stemming from 1627–8. It seems to have incorporated action in recitative and two (unsung) dances, the latter a battle-dance. But quite apart from these relatively independent *balli*, almost all of Monteverdi's theatrical works involved dancing in some shape or form. One of the many defects of Agnelli's *Le nozze di Tetide* (so Monteverdi wrote on 9 December 1616) was that 'the dances which are scattered through the fable do not have dance measures' (*non hanno piedi da ballo*); *Andromeda* (1620) appears to have had at least one sung–danced chorus of maidens – 'Il fulgore onde risplendono', in *versi sdruccioli* it seems – or so Monteverdi queried in his letter of 21 July 1618; one of the attractions of the revised *La finta pazza Licori* was that there would be 'a ballet in every act, each one different from the other, and in a fantastical style' (he wrote on 10 July 1627); and *Proserpina rapita* (1630) had at least two sung *balli* (see Chapter 8). Even *Il ritorno d'Ulisse in patria* (II.6) had a 'Greek dance' performed by eight moors ('Dame in amor', in *versi tronchi*), although the music does not survive. The exception is *L'incoronazione di Poppea* – unless the *coro di Amori* in the final scene involved some kind of dancing – but then, that work is exceptional in other ways, too.

There is also a broader point to be made. Just as the sung *ballo* could transgress numerous generic and other boundaries, so did such entertainments blur the dividing line between courtly life and courtly art in ways that were essential to the definition of the courtier and the court. The movement of dancers from stage to auditorium and back, and the participation of members of the court in the dancing, reinforced the notion that one could move in and out of formal entertainments in a seamless flow: a banquet could contain musico–dramatic interludes; a ball could precede, include or conclude a theatrical ballet; and even an opera could end with social dancing. Both of the *balli* staged in Mantua in 1608 reveal the point in different ways. The singers and dancers in *Il sacrificio d'Ifigenia* made their entrance from the rear of the auditorium, and although the dramatic action took place on the stage, the final *ballo* was done in front of it and was succeeded, so Follino recounts, by social dancing involving members of the 'audience'. The *Ballo delle ingrate* is even more intriguing. Follino describes it as a discrete event: the audience enters the theatre, takes its seats and is suddenly surprised by a 'strepito spaventoso' from drums underneath the stage, at which point the curtain rises and

---

34 See Solerti, 'Un balletto musicato da Claudio Monteverdi sconosciuto a' suoi biografi'; Fabbri, *Monteverdi*, trans. Carter, pp. 254–7.

the scene reveals the mouth of the Inferno, whence Venere and Amore appear. However, the Este ambassador reported that the piece was preceded by 'an ordinary large ball with *passi e mezzo* and galliards with positions', and it also seems to have been followed by more dancing.[35] The space in which the *Ballo delle ingrate* and *Il sacrificio d'Ifigenia* were performed was both theatre and ballroom, merging context, content and function. These entertainments presented powerful messages to their audiences; they also offer powerful lessons to modern scholars who dare to believe that there is more to early seventeenth-century music theatre than opera.

---

35   For the Este ambassador, see Solerti, *Gli albori del melodramma*, i, p. 102; I have slightly modified my translation in Fabbri, *Monteverdi*, trans. Carter, p. 93.

7

The *Combattimento di Tancredi e Clorinda* (1624)

In February 1612, Francesco Gonzaga became Duke of Mantua; on 30 July 1612, Monteverdi was summarily dismissed from service for reasons which remain unclear, although they seem to have included insubordination.[1] When he arrived in Venice in October 1613 to take up the position of *maestro di cappella* in St Mark's Basilica, he was glad to leave Mantua far behind. The conventional view, encouraged no doubt by our own political preferences, has Monteverdi much happier working for a republic rather than a court. However, he remained a Mantuan citizen and subject, and the Gonzagas kept a hold over him by virtue of the pension awarded by Duke Vincenzo but rarely if ever paid on time; the issue preoccupied Monteverdi until the end of his life (it is the subject of his last surviving letter, written in August 1643). Moreover, Francesco's successor (from December 1612), Cardinal (later Duke) Ferdinando, appears much to have regretted the loss of the composer. For his part, Monteverdi's duties in St Mark's distanced him from the world of the theatre, or so he wrote on 31 December 1615 and 9 January 1620, and he became adept at finding excuses for not responding speedily to Mantuan requests for stage music, ranging from his church commitments to headaches and the after-effects of blood-letting and purges. At times, however, he had no choice but to accede to his feudal lords, and at others he did so reasonably willingly if he saw favours within his grasp.

But Monteverdi's progress on theatrical works for Mantua in the 1610s was often desultory. He found numerous reasons not to engage with Scipione Agnelli's *Le nozze di Tetide*, at least so long as he thought it was an opera, and the patience of the court secretary Ercole Marigliani was sorely tried by Monteverdi's reluctance to finish setting his *Andromeda*, on which he

1   See Parisi, 'New Documents Concerning Monteverdi's Relations with the Gonzagas'.

worked more off than on from 1618 to 1620.[2] The only stage music that
survives from this period is *Tirsi e Clori* (1616) and the prologue to *La
Maddalena*, a *sacra rappresentazione* by the Mantuan *commedia dell'arte* player
Giovanni Battista Andreini, written for the festivities celebrating the wedding
of Duke Ferdinando Gonzaga and Caterina de' Medici and performed in
Mantua in March 1617. For this curious work, music was also provided by
Muzio Effrem, Salamone Rossi and Alessandro Ghivizzani.[3] Monteverdi's prologue, 'Su le penne de' venti il ciel varcando', survives as a single stanza of
music with a 5-part instrumental ritornello, the music to be repeated for the
other stanzas of the text.

However, one Mantuan request appears to have re-ignited
Monteverdi's interest in the stage. In March 1620 he was asked to send the
score of *Arianna* for a performance at Duchess Caterina's birthday celebrations in May. The composer went to the trouble and expense (reimbursed by
the Gonzagas, it seems) of having a copyist produce a new manuscript. Revisit-
ing his old masterpiece seems to have made Monteverdi realize what he was
missing, as he wrote to Striggio on 4 April when sending the last quires: 'If
I had had more time, I would have revised it more thoroughly, and even
perhaps greatly improved it. I shall not let a day go by without composing
something in this theatrical style of song [*in tal genere di canto rapresentativo*] –
and all the more willingly if you will make me worthy of it to a greater
extent with your beautiful verses.' The correspondence with Striggio over the
ballo Apollo from late 1619 to early 1620 demonstrates a similar increase in
creative energy. Monteverdi's renewed passion suggests that at least part of the
sense of the excitement of working in the theatre, extinguished by the
exhausting efforts of 1608, had now returned.

This enthusiasm also seems to have been encouraged by new developments in Venice. On 1 February 1620, Monteverdi told Striggio of the
success there of part of *Apollo*:

2   It was performed in Carnival 1620. The recently discovered libretto remains in
    private hands; see the brief discussions in Rosenthal, 'Monteverdi's "Andromeda"';
    Fenlon, 'Mantua, Monteverdi and the History of "Andromeda"'. The facsimile
    of the libretto promised by Rosenthal (p. 1 n. 2) seems never to have
    appeared.
3   The music was published in *Musiche de alcuni eccellentissimi musici composte per La
    Maddalena, sacra rappresentazione di Gio. Battista Andreini fiorentino* (Venice,
    Bartolomeo Magni, 1617). For Rossi's (comic) contribution, see Harrán, *Salamone
    Rossi*, pp. 179–84. The play was revised for performance in Vienna in 1629 to
    include a lament for Lucia Rubini, who played Maddalena; see Saunders,
    'New Light on the Genesis of Monteverdi's Eighth Book of Madrigals', p. 191.
    One wonders whether this was a *contrafactum* of the *Lamento d'Arianna*;
    compare the later examples noted in Bianconi, *Music in the Seventeenth Century*,
    pp. 210–11.

The *Lamento d'Apollo* has been heard by certain gentlemen here, and since it pleased them in the manner of its invention, poetry and music they think – after an hour of concerted music which usually takes place these days at the house of a certain gentleman of the Bembo family, where the most important ladies and gentlemen come to listen – they think (as I said) of having afterwards this fine idea of Your Most Illustrious Lordship's put on a small stage.

Monteverdi was also cultivating relationships with other Venetian noble families, including the Giustiniani, who ran a public theatre near S. Moisé and on whose behalf Monteverdi negotiated in late 1622 for the appearance in Venice of Andreini's *commedia dell'arte* troupe, the Fedeli;[4] S. Moisé later also saw Monteverdi's début on the Venetian operatic stage with the revival of his *Arianna* in late 1639 or early 1640. The composer's position placed him in high demand among Venetian institutions and individuals seeking occasional music-making. As Monteverdi explained to Striggio on 13 March 1620, such moonlighting was a significant and frequent source of additional income for the better Venetian musicians, and Antonio Goretti, writing to Enzo Bentivoglio on 18 February 1628, noted that Monteverdi earned 'twenty plus twenty ducats apiece' from Carnival entertainments.[5] The seemingly increasing tendency for Venetians to engage in theatrical activity, and also the fashion for musical soirées in private houses, apparently prompted the composer to redirect his attention to the stage.

Monteverdi associates no fewer than four works of the 1620s with these occasions: *Apollo*, the *Combattimento di Tancredi e Clorinda*, *Armida abbandonata* and *La finta pazza Licori*, to which one might add a fifth, *Proserpina rapita*. When Striggio approached Monteverdi in late April 1627 for theatrical music associated, it seems, with the planned festivities for the accession of Duke Vincenzo II Gonzaga, the composer suggested (on 1 May) one or other of *Armida abbandonata*, the *Combattimento* and *La finta pazza Licori*, each of which could 'serve as short episodes between other pieces of music' (*per episodietti fra altre musiche*). The phrase anticipates the title-page of the Eighth Book of madrigals, the *Madrigali guerrieri, et amorosi*, which contains 'some works in the representative genre which will act as short episodes among the songs without action' (*Con alcuni opuscoli in genere rappresentativo, che saranno per brevi Episodij frà i canti senza gesto*). It also provides an important context in which to view these curiously hybrid works.

4 See Monteverdi's letters of 21 October, 19 November and 3, 10 and 31 December 1622. *Pace* Stevens, Monteverdi is here dealing with Alvise (not Lorenzo) Giustiniani; see Mancini, Muraro and Povoledo, *I teatri del Veneto*, i/1, pp. 194–5.
5 Fabbri, *Monteverdi*, trans. Carter, p. 217.

The Combattimento di Tancredi e Clorinda[6]

Monteverdi makes matters clearer still in the separate preface to the *Combattimento* in the continuo part of the Eighth Book:

> *Combatimento di Tancredi et Clorinda* in music, as described by Tasso, in which, if it is intended to be done in the representative genre [*genere rapresentativo*], one will have enter unexpectedly (after some madrigals without action have been sung) from the side of the room in which the music is performed, Clorinda armed and on foot, followed by Tancredi armed on a *cavallo mariano*, and Testo [the narrator] will then begin the singing. They will perform steps and gestures in the way expressed by the oration, and nothing more or less, observing diligently those measures, blows and steps, and the instrumentalists [will perform] sounds excited and soft [*suoni incitati, & molli*], and Testo delivering the words in measure, in such a way that the three actions come to unite in a unified imitation. Clorinda will speak when appropriate, Testo silent; and similarly Tancredi. The instruments — that is, four *viole da braccio*, soprano, alto, tenor and bass, and a *contrabasso da gamba* which continues with the harpsichord — should be played in imitation of passions of the oration. Testo's voice should be clear, firm and with good delivery, somewhat distanced from the instruments, so that the oration may be better understood. He must not make *gorghe* or *trilli* anywhere other than in the song of the stanza which begins 'Notte'. For the rest, he will deliver the words according to the passions of the oration.
>
> In this manner (now twelve years ago) it was performed in the palace of the Most Illustrious and Most Excellent Signor Girolamo Mozzenigo [Mocenigo], my particular lord, with all refinement, given that he is a knight of excellent and delicate taste, and in carnival time, since it was an evening pastime, in the presence of all the nobility, who remained moved by the emotion of compassion in such a way as almost to let forth tears; and [the audience] applauded it for being a song of a kind no longer seen nor heard.

There are some obscurities here: we still do not know for sure what a 'cavallo mariano' is (presumably some kind of imitation horse), and Monteverdi's claim

---

6   The following discussion draws on my 'The Composer as Theorist?'. This will also have a companion piece (in preparation), 'In Search of the Text of Monteverdi's *Combattimento di Tancredi e Clorinda*', where I discuss a range of bibliographical, typographical and philological problems in the sources, arguing that the materials of the *Combattimento* distributed through the 1638 print (broadly speaking, vocal and instrumental parts in the partbooks, and a full score in the *Basso continuo* book) reflect different redactions of the piece, with the full score being somewhat removed from the composer.

that the piece had been performed twelve years previously is a slip – according to the preface to the Eighth Book the *Combattimento* was done in Carnival 1624 (so, perhaps 1624–5)[7] – unless his text was in fact written in 1636, perhaps as part of a package of materials sent to the Habsburg court in Vienna in that year.

The preface to the Eighth Book itself is a dense, closely set, one-page statement that is the composer's longest theoretical essay since the materials associated with the Artusi–Monteverdi controversy of some thirty years before, including the postface to the Fifth Book of madrigals (1605) and the 'Dichiaratione' (by his brother, Giulio Cesare) appended to the *Scherzi musicali a tre voci* (1607).[8] The *Combattimento* is central to this preface, and also to the book as a whole: no other single work by Monteverdi receives such extensive discussion from his pen. Here Monteverdi claims that the *Combattimento* was his first significant experiment in the so-called *concitato genere* (the coinage 'stile concitato' is incorrect), and again he recounts the praise it received from its noble audience at its première in Mocenigo's palace. He also explains how it emerged from his thoughts on the different musical *generi* – the 'aroused', 'soft' and 'temperate' (*concitato*, *molle* and *temperato*) – and on how modern music had plenty of examples of the soft and the temperate *generi*, but none of the aroused one:

> After reflecting that in the pyrrhic measure the tempo is fast and, according to all the best philosophers, used warlike, agitated leaps, and in the spondaic the tempo slow and the opposite, I began, therefore, to consider the semibreve, which, sounded once, I proposed should correspond to one stroke of a spondaic measure; when this was reduced to sixteen semiquavers and restruck one after the other, and combined with words expressing anger and disdain, I recognized in this brief sample a resemblance to the affect which I sought, although the words did not follow in their metre the rapidity of the instrument. To obtain a better proof, I took the divine Tasso, as a poet who expresses with the greatest propriety and naturalness in his oration the passions which he wishes to describe, and I selected his description of the combat of Tancredi and Clorinda, which gave me two contrary passions to set in song, war – that is, supplication – and death. In the year 1624 it was heard by the best citizens of the noble city of Venice

---

7   Depending on which style of dating is used, whether modern (the year begins on 1 January), Venetian (1 March) or *ab incarnatione* (25 March). Carnival traditionally ran from St Stephen's Day (26 December) to the beginning of Lent.

8   The preface to the Eighth Book is most recently translated in Strunk, *Source Readings in Music History*, iv, pp. 157–9; for convenience, I use this translation below, with minor modifications. The more important of the Artusi–Monteverdi materials are in ibid., pp. 18–36.

in a noble room of my own patron and special protector the Most Illustrious and Most Excellent Signor Girolamo Mocenigo, a prominent cavalier and among the first commanders of the Most Serene Republic; it was received with much applause and praised.

The *Combattimento di Tancredi e Clorinda* focuses on the final battle between the Christian Tancredi and the pagan Clorinda in Canto XII (stanzas 52–62, 64–8) of *Gerusalemme liberata*, the grandiose romance epic of the First Crusade (1099) by Torquato Tasso (1544–95), first published in 1581. The text, as is usual for Italian epic, is in *ottava rima*, stanzas of eight *endecasillabi* rhyming ABABABCC. The story is also typical. Despite the religious divide, Tancredi has fallen in love with Clorinda at a distance, but when they meet on the battlefield she is in armour, and he does not recognize her. They fight, Tancredi wins, and as she lies dying, Clorinda forgives her killer and asks him to baptize her. As Tancredi removes her helmet, he realizes with horror what he has done; Clorinda dies happily with a vision of her soul ascending to heaven. Events are narrated by a narrator (Testo), although Tancredi and Clorinda have short passages of speech, and the battle is in effect played out through the instrumental accompaniment for strings and continuo, with their rich panoply of warlike sound-effects (see Table 7-1).

For all the reportedly tearful applause granted the *Combattimento* at its première, the work has not had such happy fortunes in the eyes of posterity. Although there are parallel examples of dialogues (some with narrator) in contemporary songbooks,[9] the larger scale of the *Combattimento*, the fact that it was somehow staged, and the dominant role allocated to Testo, have conspired to grant the work an awkward position in the Monteverdi canon. In terms of genre, several authors can say what it is not:[10] Denis Arnold takes it as 'neither opera nor *intermedio*', while for Nino Pirrotta it is 'not a secular oratorio, nor is it an opera, a ballet, or a tournament, though it has something of the features of all these genres'. But no one can say quite what it is – Arnold's 'dramatic scene', Pirrotta's '*intermedio*, but probably performed without a set' and Werner Braun's 'theatralische Kammerszene' are problematic – and most would probably end up agreeing with Paolo Fabbri, calling

---

9   As Whenham notes in his important *Duet and Dialogue in the Age of Monteverdi*, i, p. 203. See also my discussion of Giovanni Felice Sances's dialogue-setting of Guarini's 'Tirsi morir volea' in his *Cantade . . . a doi voci. . . . Libro secondo. Parte seconda* (Venice, Magni, 1633), in 'New Songs for Old?', pp. 73–5.

10 For these and other assessments, see Arnold, *Monteverdi*, p. 108; Braun, *Die Musik des 17. Jahrhunderts*, p. 159; Chafe, *Monteverdi's Tonal Language*, pp. 234–46; Fabbri, *Monteverdi*, trans. Carter, pp. 188–91; Gallico, *Monteverdi*, p. 80; Leopold, *Monteverdi*, pp. 192–6; Pirrotta, 'Monteverdi's Poetic Choices', pp. 288–90; Whenham, 'The Later Madrigals and Madrigal-Books', p. 244.

it a 'hybrid'. Gary Tomlinson says almost nothing about the work in his extensive writings on Monteverdi, which is curious in the context of his broader argument: the *Combattimento* certainly can be made to fit his (generally negative) view of Monteverdi's decline into the flashy but sterile aesthetic of Marinism. But Tomlinson probably has too much invested in Tasso as progenitor of Monteverdi's 'heroic' style in the early madrigal books to be able to deal with this transformation of the poet under a Marinist scalpel. Eric Chafe allocates a significant role to the *Combattimento* in Monteverdi's formation of new tonal languages, in particular as regards the juxtaposition of major and minor 'keys', each with their various affective significances; he also warns against the 'present-day worship of structure', something that was less of a concern for Monteverdi, for whom 'an artwork was in some respects more an experience than an object'. Most authors also comment favourably on Monteverdi's virtuoso imitation of the sounds of battle, and on Clorinda's affecting baptism and death at the end of the work. But their overall view of the *Combattimento* is almost always tinged with qualification and, at times, regret. Pirrotta's view is (as usual) provocative: '*Il Combattimento* surpasses contemporary operas, which almost never succeeded in representing the actions of character as effectively as their affective reactions.' However, Arnold speaks for most in his conclusion: 'But in itself the *Combattimento* is not entirely a success, as the sympathy for its characters is rarely imparted to the audience.'

     One of the 'problems' of the *Combattimento* is precisely that it is so strongly embedded in Monteverdi's theorizing about the *concitato genere* that occupies the bulk of the preface to the *Madrigali guerrieri, et amorosi.* This theoretical framework may have sought to flatter Monteverdi's Venetian patrons, in particular Girolamo Mocenigo, or perhaps it was directed at Emperor Ferdinand III, the dedicatee of the Eighth Book; it may also have formed a part of the composer's continuing plans for a treatise on the *seconda pratica* and on the art of *melopoeia*. But either way, it looks better than it reads. The explanation of the different musical *generi* — the 'soft' (*molle*), 'temperate' (*temperato*) and 'aroused' (*concitato*) — is clear enough, as is the association between the *molle genere* with slow, spondaic rhythms, and the *concitato genere* with fast, pyrrhic ones. But problems start to emerge as Monteverdi pursues his Aristotelian attempt to create a taxonomy of the expressive and other functions of music: the three principal passions or affections of the soul ('Ira, Temperanza, & Humiltà ò supplicatione'); three types of voice ('alta, bassa, & mezzana'); three musical *generi* ('concitato . . . molle, & temperato'); three manners of (instrumental) performance ('oratoria, Armonicha, & Rethmica'; presumably following Plato's three parts of *melopoeia* — oration, harmony and rhythm); the three ways in which great princes use music in their royal chambers ('da Teatro, da camera, & da ballo'); and three *generi* (again, but here more

Table 7-1 Sections of the *Combattimento di Tancredi e Clorinda*

(Underlined passages indicate direct speech for Tancredi and Clorinda; items in italic are rubrics in the partbooks. Section titles in square brackets are those of the Pythic Battle after Pollux/Zarlino.)

Section	Action	'Key'	Insts.	*Genere?*
Introduction (52–53) [1. 'Rudimento, overo Esplorazione']	(52.1–2) Testo introduces the characters;	d		Temperato
	(52.3–4) Clorinda is searching for the entrance to Jerusalem.	d	x	
	Trotto di cavallo	D	x	Temperato–Concitato
	(52.5–7) Tancredi follows Clorinda;	D–G	x	
	(52.7–8) she challenges him; Tancredi responds;	G–F		
	(53.1–2) Clorinda agrees to fight;	G		
	(53.3–6) Tancredi dismounts; they prepare for battle.	C–G		
	passaggio bellicoso grave	G	x	
	(53.7–8) they circle each other like bulls spoiling for a fight.	G	x	
Invocation (54)	*Sinfonia – passaggio più ristretto*	g	x	Temperato/Molle
	(54.1–4) Testo invokes Night,	g		
	passaggio ristretto	B♭–g	x	
	(54.5–8) and he proclaims the continuing fame of Tancredi and Clorinda.	g		
Battle I (55–57) [2. 'Provocazione']	*Principio della Guerra*			
	(55–57) The battle commences . . .	G	x	Concitato
	. . . until the combattants grow weary.	g–d	x	
Interlude (58–61)	(58.1–2) They eye each other;	g		Temperato/Molle
	(58.3–4) night changes to dawn;	B♭		
	(58.5–7) Tancredi rejoices in Clorinda's wounds;	B♭–G		
	(58.7–59.4) Testo comments on the folly of pride that will come before Tancredi's fall;	a		

Table 7-1   *Continued*

Section	Action	'Key'	Insts.	*Genere?*
	(59.5–6) Tancredi and Clorinda eye each other and pause;	a–F		
	(59.7–8) Tancredi breaks the silence so as to discover Clorinda's name;	C–G		
	(60) <u>he notes that their deeds will pass unseen and forgotten – thus each should at least know the other's identity;</u>	d–a–d		
	(61) <u>Clorinda refuses to give her name and enrages Tancredi still more.</u>	D		
Battle II (62) [3. 'Iambico']	*Guerra*			
	(62) The fighting restarts with renewed violence.	G	x	Concitato
Clorinda's death (64–68) [4. 'Spondeo']	(64) Clorinda is mortally wounded;	V/E–A–D–G–E		Molle
	(65.1–2) Tancredi celebrates;	C–G		
	(65.3–8) Clorinda gains spiritual strength from her last words, which suggest her conversion;	e–B♭–a/A–D–G–d		
	(66.1–4) <u>She forgives Tancredi and asks him to baptize her.</u>	g–V/d	x	
	(66.5–8) Tancredi is moved to tears;	C/c–d		
	(67.1–4) he obtains water from a nearby stream and returns;	a–G/g–V/d		
	(67.5–8) he removes Clorinda's helmet, realizes who she is, and is struck dumb.	V/a–G/g–D–a		
	(68.1–7) Clorinda urges Tancredi to baptize her, which he does; she dies happily, seeming to say	F–a–F–G		
	(68.8) <u>that the heavens open and she goes in peace.</u>	V/a–d	x	
[5. 'Ovatione, o Saltatione']	[*Ballo*: 'Volgendo il ciel per l'immortal sentiero'–'Movete al mio bel suon le piante snelle']	[G]	[x]	

in the sense of genre; 'Guerriera, Amorosa, & rappresentativa'). Things become confused enough even without the glorious Freudian slip of attributing a quotation from Plato's *Republic* to his 'Rhetorica' (presumably, Aristotle's treatise on rhetoric).[11] And although the *Combattimento* is 'representative' in the sense that individual characters are allocated individual voices, it is perhaps not quite so theatrical as we are led to believe.

We do not know the extent to which the *Combattimento* might have been revised for publication in a similar way to the *Ballo delle ingrate*. In the Eighth Book, Monteverdi seems anxious to associate the *Combattimento* as printed there specifically with the première in Girolamo Mocenigo's palace in the mid-1620s – there may have been a diplomatic difficulty in including a work sponsored by a prominent Venetian patron in a collection otherwise so strongly located in a Viennese context – although it seems that the work was subject to a subsequent process of musical and textual revision, whether or not entirely by the composer himself. Similarly, it is not clear whether the theoretical scaffolding of the *Combattimento* was erected before or after its original composition, whether to reinforce its agenda or to take it in a new direction for its new dedicatee. In fact, the presence of *concitato*-like gestures in the vocal writing of earlier works by Monteverdi, including *Orfeo* and the *Lamento d'Arianna*, would suggest that they emerged gradually in the context of standard word-painting devices. But despite all these difficulties, the *Combattimento* certainly fits the conceptual and structural design of the Eighth Book, being the most overtly warlike of the 'canti guerrieri'. It also provides some manner of counterpart to the *Ballo delle ingrate* (concluding the 'canti amorosi'): the *Combattimento* has two low-voice roles (Testo, Tancredi) and one high-voice one (Clorinda), while the *Ballo delle ingrate* has one low-voice role (Plutone) and two high-voice ones (Venere, Amore; plus the chorus of spirits and the singing Ingrata).

Monteverdi may or may not have needed the advice of another poet in producing the text of the *Combattimento*, although some of the alterations cause problems that suggest his own rather than another's hand. The text-underlay in the full score in the *Basso continuo* partbook of the Eighth Book – which at times is quite distinct from the underlay of the partial score (minus the string parts) in the *Tenore primo* partbook (in effect, Testo's part, although the passages for Tancredi and Clorinda are also included) – received a fair amount of later editorial intervention, probably not by the composer and almost certainly with a view to getting closer to Tasso's original. But there remain numerous discrepancies between Monteverdi's text and the then

---

11   For more positive views of Monteverdi's preface, see Kurtzman, 'Monteverdi's Changing Aesthetic'; Ossi, *Divining the Oracle*.

standard editions of *Gerusalemme liberata*.[12] Some are minor variants of orthography and so on that do not significantly affect the meaning and, indeed, may have derived from a specific edition that Monteverdi was using, although a convincing exemplar has yet to be found. Most, however, seem prompted by Monteverdi (or his poet) having done a close comparison with Tasso's revision of this episode in *Gerusalemme conquistata* (XV.65–82), a reworking of the *Liberata* published in 1593 and designed to respond both to the widespread controversies concerning its 'impure' – that is, non-Tuscan – language and its inferiority to Ariosto's *Orlando furioso*, and also to emerging Counter-Reformation sensibilities. Monteverdi had already demonstrated a preference for the *Conquistata* over the *Liberata* in his last setting from Tasso's epic published before the *Combattimento*, Erminia's lament 'Piagn'e sospira, e quando i caldi raggi', which concludes the Fourth Book of madrigals of 1603 (*Conquistata*, VIII.6; the equivalent in the *Liberata* is 'Sovente, allor che sugli estivi ardori', VII.19). In the *Combattimento*, Monteverdi takes from *Gerusalemme conquistata* words, phrases and, at one point (54.1–4), a reordering of lines (but not the lines themselves).

Some of these borrowings seem fairly haphazard, but others are more thoughtful, such as where Monteverdi prefers readings in which Tasso rendered his mixed tenses more consistent (now using past tenses instead of historic presents) or otherwise improved his language. For the latter, 'Né vol Tancredi, ch'ebbe a piè veduto' ('Nor did Tancredi wish, seeing [his enemy] on foot . . .'; 53.3, following the *Conquistata*) is much better than the original 'Non vuol Tancredi, che pedon veduto', even if the meaning is more or less the same. Monteverdi also tends to favour the trend in *Gerusalemme conquistata* towards more action-filled description (for 53.7, he prefers the 'steps sluggish and slow' of 'e vansi incontro a passi tardi e lenti' over the nondescript 'e vansi a ritrovar non altrimenti'), which in turn offers greater opportunity for mimetic musical effects. Yet the composer seems not to have liked the stanza comparing the battle to the Aegean Sea struck by the Winds ('Aquilone o Noto') in either version of the poem (XII.63; XV.77), which he omitted entirely. Perhaps he felt a slight shiver, remembering his difficulties in

12 The most extensive discussion is in Gallarati, '*Il combattimento di Tancredi e Clorinda*', which also in effect demolishes Bruno Brizi's provocative and even salutary claim ('"Il lauro verde"', p. 21) that Monteverdi's redaction of the text of the *Combattimento*, including the borrowings from *Gerusalemme conquistata* discussed elsewhere in this chapter, derives from a single source reflecting a contaminated transmission of Tasso's poem. Brizi is right, though, about some minor points, such as ('"Il lauro verde"', p. 21 n. 11) the reading in 60.8 ('chi la mia morte o la mia vita honore' for 'chi la mia morte o la vittoria onore') also found in a Venetian edition of *Gerusalemme liberata* of 1625.

providing appropriate music for such atmospheric characters (and for sheep) in Agnelli's *Le nozze di Tetide* (see Chapter 8).

The textual variants in the *Combattimento* that cannot be traced back to the different versions of Tasso's poem are rather problematic, especially in the context of Monteverdi's supposed fidelity to his poetry according to the tenets of the *seconda pratica*. He handles well enough the alteration to the beginning (52.1–2), which is necessary to provide an immediate context for a piece divorced from its broader textual environment. Other changes, however, are more difficult to accept. For example, Monteverdi seems to have been concerned about the minimal direct speech for Tancredi and Clorinda: he omits the narrator's intervention in 61.6 ('indi riprese') to allow Tancredi to continue uninterrupted – thus the line is a *settenario* rather than the required *endecasillabo* – and he misconstrues 53.2, thereby bringing the narrator's 'e ferma attende' ('and she stands firm') into Clorinda's speech (turning it into an irregular imperative addressed to Tancredi, 'and stand firm'), which makes scant sense and also, in a subsequent attempt to solve the problem, produces conflicting readings. Line 53.5 has one syllable too few, and 57.3 one too many; in 55.3 Monteverdi alters the rhyme-word, breaking the regularity of the *ottava rima* pattern; and elsewhere some of the word-setting suggests misprisions of Tasso's meaning. All in all, Monteverdi's reading of the text does not seem entirely that of a literary sophisticate.

Monteverdi's emphasis on the nobility present at the first performance of the *Combattimento* – and the references to a patron who has provided the 'chiaro sol' and 'pieno teatro' called for by Tasso to celebrate the valorous deeds of his hero and heroine – places the work strongly in an aristocratic environment. Warfare was a fact of life in sixteenth- and early seventeenth-century Italy, and Monteverdi himself had experienced life on the battlefield as a member of the entourage of Duke Vincenzo Gonzaga on campaign in Hungary in 1595. War was also reflected in numerous forms of courtly entertainment, including the indoor or outdoor tournaments on foot, horseback or water which served the purposes of display, training and a means of aristocratic self-representation.[13] As we saw in Chapter 6, the preface of Emilio de' Cavalieri's *Rappresentatione di Anima, et di Corpo* (1600) also notes that stylized battle-dances were to be favoured in *balli*, *intermedi* and similar kinds of theatrical endeavour, on the grounds of their novelty and virtuosity; thus Rinuccini and Monteverdi included an example towards the end of *Arianna*, while others appeared in the *intermedi* for *L'idropica*.

But the musical representation of battle had further resonances reaching back to antiquity that, in turn, served to enhance the aristocratic associations of the *Combattimento*. Chapter 5 of the second part of Zarlino's by now

---

13   See the comments on tournaments in Carter, 'The North Italian Courts', pp. 40–3.

classic text on music theory, the *Istitutioni harmoniche* (Venice, Francesco de' Franceschi, 1558; Monteverdi owned a copy of the 1573 edition),[14] discusses 'Le materie che recitavano gli Antichi nelle lor canzoni: & di alcune Leggi musicali' ('The subjects which the ancients recited in their songs, and on some musical laws'). Zarlino offers an overview of the different kinds of texts associated with music in Classical Antiquity, including praises of the gods (e.g., the hymns of Orpheus), the illustrious deeds of victors in the Olympic Games and similar competitions (the odes of Pindar), and songs appropriate for weddings (Catullus), plus funeral orations, lamentations, love-songs suitable for banquets, prayers (such as those to ward off the plague), and subjects both tragic and comic. However, later in the same chapter, Zarlino plays down amatory subjects and associates music for banquets specifically with the praise of illustrious men, accounts of glorious deeds, and thence descriptions of battle. The archetypal such scene was the Battle of Apollo and the Python (i.e., the first part of the Daphne story), as described by Pollux. According to Zarlino, this

> was divided into five parts, of which the first was called 'Beginning, or Exploration', the second 'Provocation', 'Iambic' the third, the fourth 'Spondaic', and the fifth and last, 'Ovation, or Saltation'. The representation . . . was of the manner of the fight of Apollo with the dragon: in the first part was recited how Apollo examined and contemplated the site [to see] whether it was appropriate for the fight or not; in the second was explained the way adopted [by Apollo] to provoke the serpent to battle; in the third [was] the combat, and this part contained a manner of singing to the sound of the pipe called *odontismos*, since the serpent gnashed its teeth when struck by an arrow; in the fourth was recounted the victory of Apollo; and in the last was explained how Apollo celebrated his victory with dances and leaps.[15]

14 See Reese, *Music in the Renaissance*, plate 4 (after p. 366).
15 *Istitutioni harmoniche* (1558), p. 66: 'L'Argomento adunque di tal legge era la Battaglia di Apolline col serpente Pithone, il quale dà il nome alla favola; & il nome di tutta la cantilena era Delona; & forse fu cosi nominata: percioche Apollo nacque nella isola di Delo. Era questa legge (si come mostra Giulio Polluce) divisa in cinque parti, delle quali la prima nominavano Rudimento, overo Esploratione; la seconda Provocatione; Iambico la terza; la quarta Spondeo; Et la quinta & ultima Ovatione, o Saltatione. La rapresentatione (come hò detto) era il modo della pugna di Apollo col Dragone, & nella prima parte si recitava, in qual modo Apollo investigava, & contemplava il luogo, se era atto alla pugna, over non: Nella seconda si dichiarava il modo, che teneva a provocare il Serpente alla battaglia: Nella terza il combattimento; & questa parte conteneva un modo di cantare al suono del Piffero, chiamato ὀδοντισμός: conciosia che il serpente batteva li denti nel saettarlo: Nella quarta si raccontava la vittoria di Apollo: et nella ultima si dichiarava, come Apollo faceva festa con balli et salti, per la ricevuta vittoria. Non sarebbe gran maraviglia,

Giovanni de' Bardi had already provided a representation of this scene in the third of the 1589 Florentine *intermedi* (with music by Luca Marenzio; the dance has not survived), and it appeared in the Rinuccini–Peri *Dafne* (then reset by Marco da Gagliano). The *Combattimento* would seem to follow its plan (and also its sound-effects), at least through the first four parts. Thus we have the preliminary exploration of narrative, theatrical and (in the 'Notte' stanza) temporal space; then the 'Provocation', as Tancredi and Clorinda have their first skirmish and draw breath, whereupon Clorinda's refusal to reveal her name provokes Tancredi to renew the fighting; then the 'Iambic' battle itself; then the 'Spondaic' account of the mortal wounding of Clorinda, her baptism and death. Of course, this sequence is Tasso's rather than Monteverdi's. But the composer may have had some inkling of its operation, given that the first extended passage in the *concitato genere* (at 'Non schivar, non parar, non pur ritrarsi') – in what I would call the 'Provocation' – is only the 'Principio della Guerra',[16] whereas the 'Guerra' proper begins at the second (at 'Torna l'ira nei cori e li trasporta'). We also find within the accompaniment some of the sound-effects described by Zarlino, including the gnashing of teeth struck by arrows (the pizzicato effects marked by Monteverdi), although on string instruments rather than wind. The matching of the *Combattimento* to the Pythic Battle does not extend to a final 'Ovation, or Saltation'; nor could it, given its conclusion at Clorinda's imminent death. However, in the *Madrigali guerrieri, et amorosi*, the *Combattimento* is the penultimate piece of the 'canti guerrieri' and is indeed followed by a 'saltation', the *ballo* 'Volgendo il ciel per l'immortal sentiero'–'Movete al mio bel suon' in praise of Emperor Ferdinand III. This is not connected directly to the *Combattimento*, although the 'Poeta' who delivers the prologue to the *ballo* serves a similar function to Testo, and could plausibly be the same singer. But whether deliberately or no, Monteverdi seems to have found a manner of 'conclusion' for the *Combattimento* that satisfied a classical model. He also thereby emphasized still more its aristocratic agenda within the educative programme for a young prince that is one reading of the Eighth Book of madrigals.[17] Tancredi's victory teaches the arts of war, Clorinda's death the virtues of Christian piety, and

---

se gli antichi havessero saltato, et ballato, quando si recitava cotal legge: percioche usavano anco di saltare, & ballare nelle loro Tragedie, & Comedie; & a ciascuna di esse haveano accommodato il suo proprio modo'. Massimo Ossi has already associated this passage with the *Combattimento* in *Divining the Oracle*.

16   At least, in the instrumental parts contained in the *Alto secondo* and *Basso secondo* partbooks. For the section beginning 'Non schivar . . .', the *Tenore secondo* partbook (containing the third *viola da braccio* part plus Tancredi) has 'Principia qui la guerra'; the *Tenore primo* partbook (containing the vocal lines and continuo) has just 'Guerra'; the score in the *Basso continuo* partbook has nothing.

17   Chew, 'The Platonic Agenda of Monteverdi's *seconda pratica*', pp. 153–5, 157.

the *ballo* their inevitable consequences: the gaining of princely honour and glory.

This episode from *Gerusalemme liberata* was not a popular one for sixteenth- and early seventeenth-century madrigalists. Monteverdi had already set Tancredi's subsequent lament on Clorinda's death – 'Vivrò fra i miei tormenti e le mie cure' (XII.77–9) – in the Third Book of madrigals of 1592. But the *Combattimento* is very different, relying less on personal statement than on a lengthy description extending over sixteen *ottava rima* stanzas presented largely by a narrator who is the poetic voice (in effect, Tasso himself). No one seems to have set the battle scene before, although it is possible that Monteverdi was seeking to emulate similar 'battle' madrigals by composers such as Antonio Taroni and Giovanni Arrigoni (in turn, in the preface to the Eighth Book he mildly accused other composers of imitating him). But Clorinda's affecting baptism and death had prompted 5-voice madrigals by Tiburtio Massaino in 1587 (in his Third Book of 5-voice madrigals, setting XII.65–6) and Antonio Il Verso in 1619 (in his Fifteenth Book; XII.66–9 – Il Verso also sets Tancredi's lament in XII.75–7), and a solo-voice setting by Sigismondo d'India in 1621.[18] Monteverdi may have known Massaino in his early days in Cremona, but there is no apparent relationship between their settings; d'India would seem to have known Il Verso's setting (both composers were Sicilian), given the musical parallels between the two; and Monteverdi must certainly have known d'India's, given that he refers quite directly to it.

Monteverdi appears to have had some kind of difficult relationship with d'India in the 1620s; as we shall see (in Chapter 8), they were in competition to gain the commission for the music for the wedding festivities for Odoardo Farnese and Margherita de' Medici eventually held in December 1628. They may first have encountered each other in Mantua in or around 1608, when d'India was pursuing a peripatetic career through the north Italian courts. He was notoriously difficult and renowned for his inflated opinion of his own talents. But what might really have hurt was his creation as a Knight of St Mark, an honour awarded by the Venetian republic in March 1621 pursuant to a request (instigated by the composer) to the Venetian Collegio by d'India's patron, Prince-Cardinal Maurizio of Savoy.[19] This order was open to Venetian patrician families and also to non-aristocratic Venetians and

18 See the list in Vassalli, 'Il Tasso in musica e la trasmissione dei testi'. Massaino's and Il Verso's settings are included in *Antonio Il Verso*, ed. Bianconi, pp. xviii–xix (Massaino; 2ª parte only), 42–51.

19 See Whenham, 'Sigismondo d'India'. The singer Francesco Rasi had been nominated Cavaliere di San Marco on 3 July 1618; see Kirkendale, *The Court Musicians in Florence during the Principate of the Medici*, pp. 589–90. However, Rasi was a former collaborator of Monteverdi, and he died on 30 November 1621, so was less of an immediate threat.

Ex. 7-1 Sigismondo d'India, 'Amico hai vint'io ti perdon, perdona' (*Le musiche
. . . libro quarto*, 1621); *Combattimento di Tancredi e Clorinda.*

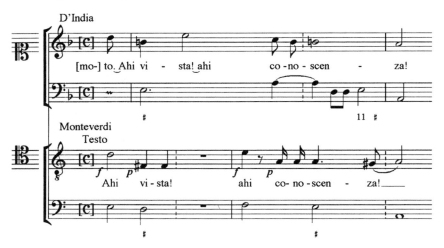

D'India, *Le musiche . . . a una et due voci . . . libro quarto* (Venice, Alessandro Vincenti, 1621), pp.
15–17; Monteverdi, *Madrigali guerrieri, et amorosi . . . Libro ottavo* (Venice, Alessandro Vincenti,
1638), *Basso continuo* partbook, pp. 19–43 (but string parts taken from partbooks).

Ah what a sight! Ah what recognition!

---

foreigners of distinction, and Monteverdi may have smarted to see d'India
parade the title 'Cavaliere di San Marco' on his subsequent publications, especially given his own position as *maestro di cappella* of St Mark's.

Perhaps, then, Monteverdi looked askance at 'Cavaliere' d'India's *Le
musiche . . . a una et due voci . . . libro quarto*, published in Venice in 1621 by
Alessandro Vincenti (later to be the printer of the Eighth Book). Certainly
he seems to have sought to outdo d'India's 'Amico hai vint'io ti perdon,
perdona', where Clorinda gives voice to her forgiveness of Tancredi, and the
narration (by the same voice) describes her baptism and her final words.[20]
There are close similarities between the two settings of the narrator's excla-
mation on Tancredi's discovery of Clorinda's identity (Ex. 7-1), and also of
Clorinda's final words, where the tonic in the voice grinds against the
dominant harmony in the continuo (Ex. 7-2). In the latter case, Monteverdi

20 D'India's *Le musiche . . . libro terzo* (Milan, Filippo Lomazzo, 1618) also contains
    solo-voice settings of Petrarch sonnets to which Monteverdi in effect later laid
    claim: 'Voi ch'ascoltate in rime sparse il suono' (set in the *Selva morale e spirituale*
    of 1640–1) and 'Hor che 'l ciel e la terra e 'l vento tace' (in the *Madrigali guerrieri,
    et amorosi*). One wonders whether d'India's inclusion of *Pastor fido* settings in his
    L'ottavo libro de madrigali a cinque voci (Rome, Giovanni Battista Robletti, 1624) was
    to compete with Monteverdi's own *Pastor fido* settings, particularly in his Fifth
    Book (reprinted by Bartolomeo Magni in Venice in 1620).

Ex. 7-2

Heaven opens; I go in peace.

Ex. 7-3

Ex. 7-3 *Continued*

Friend, you have won, I pardon you. May you now give pardon not to my body, which matters naught . . .

---

may also be quoting himself: Clorinda's cadence appears (in the same key and in much the same local context) in the fifth stanza of 'Possente spirto e formidabil nume' in Act III of *Orfeo*, on – perhaps significantly – the word 'vita'. No less revealing, however, are d'India's and Monteverdi's settings of Clorinda's speech (Ex. 7-3), which are in the same tonal-type, and where Monteverdi adapts and at times changes the sequence of d'India's affective gestures, even if there are significant differences (not least Monteverdi's expressive string chords). D'India uses the wide melodic intervals and chromatic harmonies that he claimed as early as 1609 (in the preface to his first book of *Musiche*) were his novel contribution to the expressive power of the 'new music'. Monteverdi is more measured, quite literally so in the spondaic rhythms of Clorinda's opening (a reference to the Pythic Battle on the one hand, and, as we shall see, to the *molle genere*), and he resists d'India's more extravagant word-setting. But at least d'India does not have to make a choice that is forced upon Monteverdi. According to Tasso, Clorinda only 'appeared' to say her final words ('dir parea'), which, rather, are inferred by the narrator from her peaceful countenance at the moment of baptism. Monteverdi gives the words directly to Clorinda; d'India can keep matters open.

The comparison with d'India also raises questions about the theoretical edifice constructed around the *Combattimento* in the preface to the

Eighth Book of madrigals. As we have seen, this is full of classicizing references, with quotations from Plato and Boethius cited in Monteverdi's support. Monteverdi's notion of three *generi* also derives from the tripartite division of musical ethoses into diastaltic, hesychastic and systaltic affections as described by Cleonides, Aristides Quintilianus and Bryennius, and transmitted through Renaissance and Baroque music theory in particular by Zarlino and by Giovanni Battista Doni (the latter was in direct touch with Monteverdi in an exchange of letters in 1633–4).[21] Monteverdi may also have recalled conversations on the battlefields of Hungary in 1595 with the Florentine patron Giovanni de' Bardi, who thereby may have transmitted some of the ideas of Girolamo Mei, the theorist who most influenced the thinking of the Florentine Camerata.[22] When writing to Doni on 2 February 1634, Monteverdi confessed himself confused by the main treatise to emerge from the Camerata's deliberations, Vincenzo Galilei's *Dialogo della musica antica, et della moderna* (1581), although the composer's division of the voice into high, middle and low, and his emphasis on rhythm as an affective indicator, seem to reflect some influence of Florentine thinking, for all that they are commonplaces. Presumably, however, he did at least glance at the treatise Doni seems later to have sent the composer following their correspondence, the *Compendio del trattato de' generi e de' modi della musica* (Rome, Andrea Fei, 1635).

In the preface to the Eighth Book, Monteverdi is clearest on the role of rhythm both to signify the *concitato genere* and to invoke its affect in the listener. He explains that the ancients used the fast 'tempo piricchio' for 'le saltationi belliche, concitate', and the 'tempo spondeo' for their opposite (and hence, presumably, to signify the *molle genere*). The pyrrhic foot (two short syllables) can be musically represented by taking one element of the spondee (two long syllables), that is, a semibreve, and dividing it into sixteen semiquavers which, when repeated one after the other and joined with words conveying 'ira e sdegno', will produce the desired result, even if the words cannot always keep up with the (instrumental) music. This explains the famous repeated semiquavers of the *concitato genere*. It also, presumably, confirms the setting of Clorinda's 'Amico, hai vinto' (Ex. 7-3) with its exaggerated spondees – doubly so, given the repeated minims in the voice and the semibreve chords in the instruments – as representing the opposite of the *concitato genere*, the *molle*. According to Renaissance theorists, however, diastaltic, hesychastic and systaltic ethoses (i.e., *concitato*, *temperato* and *molle*) could be represented not just by rhythm (from fast to slow) or by pitch level (high, middle, low), but also by melodic inflection – from 'strong' diatonic intervals to 'soft

21   See the extensive discussion in Hanning, 'Monteverdi's Three *genera*'.
22   For Monteverdi meeting Bardi in 1595, see my 'Artusi, Monteverdi, and the Poetics of Modern Music', pp. 180–1. For Mei, see Palisca, *Girolamo Mei*; idem, *The Florentine Camerata*.

and effeminate' chromatic ones – and by mode. Doni in particular associated the (ancient) Dorian mode with the hesychastic, the Phrygian with the diastaltic, and the Lydian with the systaltic.[23] In the preface to the Eighth Book, Monteverdi did not link his *generi* with specific modes (ancient or modern), although in the case of his *Proserpina rapita* of 1630 (discussed further in Chapter 8), the *concitato genere* was associated with the Phrygian mode, and the *molle* with the Lydian (and lament with the Mixolydian). In the case of the *Combattimento*, the notation of the passages in the *concitato genere* in 'G major' might be assimilated to some notion of recreating an ancient Phrygian mode: Mei, followed by Bardi, provides a precedent.[24] The fact that Testo begins the *Combattimento* so firmly on *a* also links that opening to a Mei–Bardi Dorian mode (where *a* is the central *mese* of the *e–e′* scale which Mei calls Dorian) – hence linking the Dorian with the *temperato genere* – although its harmonic context is that of a conventional (Renaissance) D-Dorian, the mode which Tasso himself claimed was most appropriate for epic.[25] However, it is more difficult to relate the 'G minor' tonal-type adopted by both d'India and Monteverdi for Clorinda's 'Amico, hai vinto' to any Lydian (or even Mixolydian) mode – for all that both the rhythm and the flat hexachord would seem to signify the *molle genere* – and the presence of this tonal-type also in the prologue-like 'Notte' stanza suggests a degree of confusion, given that this stanza would appear to be more *temperato* than *molle*. And even G major is ambivalent. The one surviving piece by Monteverdi that was given a secure ancient (rather than modern) modal identifier is the 'Parthenian canzonetta sung by the three nymphs in Lydian harmony – that is, in soft sound and suitable for children' – inserted in *Proserpina rapita*, 'Come dolce hoggi l'auretta' (later published in the Ninth Book of madrigals). It is in a pastoral G major which is neither Lydian (unless one stretches Boethius) nor *molle*.

Thus mode itself seems a less secure affective indicator in the *Combattimento* than other technical or stylistic features. In part, the difficulties are

23 See Chafe, *Monteverdi's Tonal Language*, pp. 237–8. However, other theorists substituted the Mixolydian for the Lydian, as in effect did the Venetian poet (and later collaborator with Monteverdi) Giulio Strozzi in describing Monteverdi's (and others') music for the Mass held by the Florentine community in Venice on 25 May 1621 commemorating the death of Grand Duke Cosimo II de' Medici; see Fabbri, *Monteverdi*, trans. Carter, p. 179. This Mass began 'with a most plaintive *sinfonia* apt to draw forth tears, nay excite grief, imitating the ancient Mixolydian mode formerly rediscovered by Sappho' (*con mestissima sinfonia atta a cavar le lagrime non che ad eccitar il dolore, imitando l'antico tuono missolidio già da Saffo ritrovato*).

24 Chew, 'The Platonic Agenda of Monteverdi's *seconda pratica*', pp. 161–3.

25 Tasso was highly ambivalent about epic's need for music, given such poetry's uniformity and avoidance of extremes. His association of epic with the Dorian mode reflects this call for moderation and also invokes classical precedent (in particular, Plato); see the representative passages from Tasso's dialogues in *Antonio Il Verso*, ed. Bianconi, pp. xvi–xvii.

caused by the attempt to mesh threefold taxonomies (high, middle, low; *concitato, temperato, molle*) with the affective and structural dualities chiefly available for expressive effect within late Renaissance and early Baroque systems, be they 'hard' versus 'soft' hexachords (*cantus durus, cantus mollis*) or emerging notions of major and minor. Both are achieved simultaneously in the *Combattimento* at a crucial point when the combatants take respite from their first skirmish and the music changes abruptly from G major (*durus*) to G minor (*mollis*). But in this squeezing of three into two, scant space is left for the *temperato genere*, just as, in the end, Monteverdi is left to speak (in the preface to the *Combattimento*) only of 'suoni incitati, & molli' ('sounds excited and soft'). And even where things should be clear, they are often not. Clorinda's final words (Ex. 7-2, above) move rapidly from *cantus durus* to *cantus mollis* (a major triad on E to one on B flat), yet end in what seems to be a more 'temperato' D minor; the rhythm is chiefly spondaic (so, *molle*); while in terms of vocal register Clorinda is given the highest notes in the piece (so, *concitato*, although this is presumably for 'celestial' word-painting). One might choose to read these seven bars as somehow summing up and resolving the affective and structural registers of the work as a whole. Or one might view them instead as a remarkable gesture, produced without the slightest regard for theoretical propriety, ancient or modern.

The chief problem of the *Combattimento*, however, lies in identifying its genre and function. By the 1620s, Tasso and *Gerusalemme liberata* had each achieved classic status – Monteverdi could refer to the poet as 'the divine Tasso', and others could speak of the 'Tuscan Virgil' – with the literary controversies of the 1580s and 1590s that had embroiled the poet and the poem more or less forgotten. Not for nothing do we find the incipient hagiographies of works such as Giovanni Battista Manso's oft-reprinted *Vita di Torquato Tasso*, first published in Venice by Evangelista Deuchino in 1621. Similarly, the poem could be mined for moral precepts and pedagogical exemplars, being cited in marginalia and glosses with the same authority and respect as the greatest literature both of the Renaissance and of Classical Antiquity. Thus Antonino Colluraffi's *Il nobile veneto* (Venice, Andrea Muschio, 1623) – a treatise for noble Venetian youths – is peppered with quotations from and references to Tasso (and also from Marino and from Guarini's *Il pastor fido*) on a par with those from Plato and Cicero: here (p. 148), 'la bella, e valorosa Clorinda' is held up as a model for how to train oneself as a soldier, with a reference to Tasso's description (*Gerusalemme liberata*, II.40) of how she developed her skills with spear and sword, trained herself to run, and engaged in hunting. Acting out episodes from Renaissance epic seems to have been a further educative tool: in 1600, the Tuscan poet Giovanni Villifranchi published *La fuga d'Erminia* and *Gli amori d'Armida*, both after Tasso, plus *La cortesia di Leone a Ruggiero*, after Ariosto, each 'ridotta in favola scenica' and dedicated to his young pupils.[26] Villifranchi's technique involves constructing dramatic action by inventing dialogue for characters who speak or are mentioned in Tasso, while also quoting as much as possible from Tasso's direct speech (the quotations are marked in inverted commas). The prologue to *Gli amori d'Armida*, delivered by 'Ombra del Tasso' (i.e., his 'ghost'), has Tasso proclaim his wish to live on in 'music' – which presumably means just poetry, given that there is no suggestion that Villifranchi's texts are meant to be sung – and also that his 'offspring' (i.e., his characters) are eager, nay desperate, to reach the stage.

Villifranchi's texts are less *favole sceniche* than a series of 'ragionamenti' (the term he uses instead of 'scene' to divide up each act). This in turn reflects several fundamental difficulties of turning epic into drama. One is the stately rhythm of the *ottava rima*, and another, the continuous presence of the narrating voice. Tasso himself had noted that the regularity of, and lack of variety within, *ottava rima* stanzas made them less capable of expressing emotional extremes and also less suited to musical setting: this is one reason why Monteverdi breaks up the verse to produce what comes close to musical prose. The fact that the predominant mode of epic is narration (Monteverdi says that events are 'described by Tasso') also makes the text less than auspicious for a dramatic setting, or at least, one that seeks to gives individual voice to its characters. Certainly, the work also contains all the elements that a good Aristotelian would call tragic – peripeteia, catastrophe and purgation – while, as Testo notes (58.7–8), Tancredi exhibits the pride that conventionally leads to a tragic fall.[27] But an equally good Aristotelian would have no difficulty with epic containing the parts and manners of tragedy (after all, many of Aristotle's precepts on tragedy derive from his analysis of Homer). And there

26 All three were published in Venice by Giovanni Battista Ciotti; they are dedicated (each on 10 November 1599) respectively to Paolo Maffei, Marc'Antonio Maffei, and Marcello and Ascanio Agostini. Although they were published with separate title-pages and dedications, they seem to have been conceived as a unit: the title-page of *Gli amori d'Armida* refers to the other two works, and its dedication promises more of the same, including dramatic treatments of Sofronia – which Villifranchi says is 'already born' (*già partorita*) – and of Clorinda (both after Tasso). The issue relates to the acting out of classical myths in the classroom to develop rhetorical fluency and appropriate models of behaviour; see Woods, 'Rape and the Pedagogical Rhetoric of Sexual Violence'. For other contemporary 'dramatic' (more or less) works based on Ariosto and Tasso, see Pieri, 'La drammaturgia di Chiabrera', pp. 412–13. The trend was in part a result of the loosening of the rules defining appropriate subject-matter for theatrical genres, and in part for the benefit of audience familiarity, a point made by Gabriello Chiabrera in connection with his tragedies *Angelica in Ebuda* (after Ariosto) and *Erminia* (after Tasso, although the action moves beyond *Gerusalemme liberata*).

27 The adherence of the *Combattimento* to Aristotelian principles of tragedy is a central plank of La Via, 'Le *Combat* retrouvé'.

remains one fundamental distinction: 'Epic poetry agrees with tragedy to the extent that it is a representation, in dignified verse, of serious actions. They differ, however, in that epic keeps to a single metre and is in narrative form.'[28]

Narrative frames were not unusual to opera, particularly by way of prologues establishing the premisses of a story to be told (*Orfeo*) or of a moral to be exemplified (*L'incoronazione di Poppea*). But in the case of the *Combattimento*, the bulk of the text belongs to Testo, with only a few passages of quoted speech that can feasibly be allocated to Tancredi and Clorinda. The fact that on discovering that the enemy he has mortally wounded is in fact his beloved Clorinda, Tancredi 'remained without both voice and movement' ('. . . restò senza / e voce e moto . . .') is an inconvenience, at very least – an opera would surely have allowed him to say something – and as we have seen, Clorinda should only 'appear' to utter her last, touching words. As for Testo, he stands in a curious (but typical, for epic) position in relation to these changing events. He variously tells the story, comments upon it, addresses the audience, apostrophizes (in the 'Notte' stanza), and even speaks to the characters themselves, in a fluid shifting of roles that relies on the acceptance of narrative conventions codified in a Renaissance literary environment. He can use the first-person plural when he speaks to or for the audience ('Oh nostra folle / mente'), but he is firmly denied the first-person singular, the 'I' that would make him a plausible character for the stage.[29] Some of the other textual changes, too, serve to alienate the work from any dramatic present, as with the shifts from the historic-present 'risponde' to the past-tense 'rispose' (52.8, 61.1). And Monteverdi's writing for Testo further renounces the expressive characteristics of voice, by way both of the musical constraints of the *concitato genere* (the declamation in fast-moving semiquavers) and of the composer's Aristotelian strictures on ornamentation (Testo 'must not make *gorghe* or *trilli* anywhere other than in the song of the stanza which begins "Notte" ').[30] Testo is, quite literally, a distant 'text' speaking of and for itself.

But while this might make for good (post-)structuralist theory, it scarcely nurtures a rewarding dramatic experience. One might perform the *Combattimento* as a work in the *genere rappresentativo*, but its status as representation is problematic in much the same way, if for different reasons, as the

28   Aristotle, *Poetics*, 5, in *Classical Literary Criticism*, trans. Dorsch, p. 37. For Aristotle's more detailed discussion of epic, see *Poetics*, 23–4 (trans. Dorsch, pp. 65–9).

29   Thus in the case of 54.5, Monteverdi prefers the *Conquistata* reading, 'Piacciati ch'indi il tragga . . .', over the *Liberata*'s 'piacciati ch'io ne 'l tragga . . .', removing the 'io'/'I'.

30   Compare Aristotle, *Poetics*, 24 (*Classical Literary Criticism*, trans. Dorsch, p. 69): 'The diction should be elaborated only in "neutral" sections, that is, in passages where neither character nor thought is in question, for diction that is too brilliant may obscure the presentation of character and thought.'

polyphonic version of the *Lamento d'Arianna* in the Sixth Book of madrigals (1614). As Giovanni Battista Doni's criticisms suggest, having Arianna lament in five voices is anachronistic within the context of a *stile rappresentativo* that had established new canons of verisimilitude: that is, that one voice should sing for one character in an appropriately emotional or even dramatic way, whether in the theatre or not.[31] But paradoxically, the narrative and representational strategies of the five-voice madrigal were no less well (and perhaps better) suited to epic than the newer styles for solo voice(s) and continuo; the alienated narrating 'text' could be delivered just as well by five voices as by one. It is significant that although Tasso was often set by Monteverdi in his early madrigal books, particularly the Third, there is no epic poetry in the Fifth, Sixth and Seventh. It was much more difficult to adapt epic to the new musical styles of the early seventeenth century: dramatic poetry was their *raison d'être*, and lyric poetry could be transferred easily given the straightforward nature of the poetic 'I' therein. If, as Pirrotta claims, the *Combattimento* surpasses contemporary operas because of its representation of action rather than mere reaction, it does so not because it is more operatic than opera; rather, it is because it belongs to a different, older genre where action had to be narrated rather than performed.

This in turn helps explain why the 'suoni incitati, & molli' of the instruments have such a significant role in the *Combattimento*. The 'suoni incitati' are famously exuberant, exploiting a full panoply of string effects that Monteverdi is careful to specify in the score. For the most part, these gestures are directly mimetic: a circular, regular motion in crotchets as Clorinda searches for entrance to the city; trotting, cantering then galloping motions for the 'Trotto del cavallo';[32] pacing minims as the combatants warily circle each other (a 'passaggio bellicoso grave'); *concitato* effects at the comparison with two fighting bulls; and the instrumental fireworks in the battle scenes (*concitato* semiquavers, fanfares, syncopations, rushing scales, etc.). These gestures tend to precede (later, coincide with) Testo's reference to what they imitate; there is one striking exception where Testo directly addresses the audience ('Odi le spade . . .'; 'Hear the swords . . .'), followed one bar later by representations of clashing weapons in the strings, whereupon Testo pointedly

---

31 The term 'genere rappresentativo' ('stile rappresentativo', etc.) is problematic, given that in the period it is variously applied to theatrical music (in both the strict and the general senses), *seconda pratica* madrigals, chamber songs and even certain types of sacred music; see my entry 'Stile rappresentativo' in *The New Grove Dictionary of Opera*, ed. Sadie, iv, pp. 543–4. For Doni's comments on the *Lamento d'Arianna* in his *Trattato della musica scenica* (1633–5), see Fabbri, *Monteverdi*, trans. Carter, p. 140 (and n. 30).

32 So called in the *Alto secondo* partbook (first *viola da braccio* part). The *Basso continuo* has 'Motto del cavallo'.

repeats 'Odi, odi le spade'; here Testo seems to speak less as Tasso than as the composer himself, doubtless to the audience's delight. In general, the instrumental writing is strikingly modern, and Monteverdi's admission (in the preface to the Eighth Book) that the performers could and should play according to the oration, harmony and rhythm is prophetic in opening the way to a semiotic of instrumental music. But their function is essentially conservative: the strings provide the mimetic gestures that would have been adopted by voices in a conventional sixteenth-century 'battle' chanson or madrigal.

Only twice do the instruments take different roles. The sinfonia preceding stanza 54 – the 'Notte' invocation – and the 'Passeggio' (in effect, the second half of the sinfonia) dividing this stanza into two invoke an operatic prologue even though we are *in medias res*, with instrumental music providing space for movement (literally, it seems, in the case of the 'Passeggio'): one is reminded of Marco da Gagliano's specification for the prologue to *Dafne* (given in Chapter 4), where Ovidio is to move gracefully in the instrumental passages between his stanzas.[33] The other case, however, is less obviously functional: at key moments in the action, Clorinda's speech is accompanied by string chords (66.1–4, 'Amico, hai vinto . . .'; 68.8, 'S'apre il ciel . . .') that seem designed to enhance the expressive effect – presumably these are the 'suoni . . . molli' – while also, perhaps, hinting at the sounds of the celestial paradise opening up to the character. 'S'apre il ciel . . .' must have been particularly affecting, given that the presentation of the instrumental parts in the partbooks (here provided with Clorinda's text and without barlines) suggest that it was sung in free time. The sound of strings was commonly associated with moments of pathos: Arianna's lament was performed to the sound of 'viole e violini' (so the Este ambassador said) – although we still do not know what they played – while in the case of Apollo's lament towards the end of Gagliano's *Dafne*, the stanzas were separated by string chords which Apollo mimed on his *lira* to the sound of four off-stage instrumentalists (again, see Chapter 4). The chords at Clorinda's 'Amico, hai vinto', marked to be done each with a single bow stroke dying away, seem part of this tradition. Indeed, were Testo to be holding a *lira da braccio* in the stance of a laurel-crowned poet (as with Gagliano's Ovidio), this and even the other instrumental effects of the *Combattimento* could be imagined as coming direct from him.[34]

---

33   The connection is made in Osthoff, 'Osservazioni sul canto della stanza che incomincia "Notte" nel "Combattimento" di Claudio Monteverdi'.
34   This may link to the surprising absence of a separate fourth *viola da braccio* part (the lowest) for the *Combattimento* in the 1638 partbooks: the player must read from either the *Tenore primo* partbook (Testo's part with bass line throughout) – guessing when to play with the other three *viole da braccio* – or from the *Basso continuo* partbook.

At this point, a number of other resonances emerge. Monteverdi's preface to the work sets an intriguing scene: the evening party in Mocenigo's palace is proceeding apace, with musical (and, one assumes, other) entertainment comprising chamber madrigals ('senza gesto'), when all of a sudden appear a woman in armour, an armed man on a 'cavallo mariano', and an unidentified third person who, after just one chord, begins to sing. And if, as Monteverdi seems to suggest, the instrumentalists were hidden from view (playing in a separate room), the effect must have been all the more startling. For those surprised Venetian nobles seeking to locate the sounds they were hearing, the most likely association would have been with the *cantastorie*, the itinerant ballad-singers who, for a price, would recite the heroic deeds of mythical heroes to simple poetic and musical formulas, weaving and extending their narratives for as long as the money lasted.[35] The *cantastorie* was also often featured accompanying himself on the *lira da braccio*. Thus the *Combattimento* brings into the aristocratic salon a form of 'popular' entertainment more often heard, so contemporary myth-making went, in Venetian squares.

Indeed, rather than attempt to view the *Combattimento* as an opera *manqué*, one might better locate it more securely in its original environment, that of a salon entertainment 'per passatempo di veglia' during Carnival. 'Veglia' can mean an 'evening party' or a more or less structured (semi-)dramatic work performed at such occasions, particularly in courtly or aristocratic circles. As an example of the latter, Francesco Cini's so-called 'veglia' *La notte d'Amore*, performed in a hall of the Pitti Palace during the 1608 Florentine wedding festivities, began with social dancing which was interrupted from the stage; the ensuing dramatic entertainment also provided further opportunities for group dancing as characters descended into the auditorium. On the other hand, Orazio Vecchi's 'madrigal-comedy' *Le veglie di Siena* (Venice, Angelo Gardano, 1604) is not dramatic in any significant sense; rather, Vecchi invokes

---

35 Silke Leopold (*Monteverdi*, p. 196) has already made the point. For the tradition (in particular, as regards Ariosto's *Orlando furioso*), see Haar, '*Improvvisatori* and their Relationship to Sixteenth-Century Music'. It usually involved the application to *ottava rima* stanzas of standard reciting formulas such as the *aria di Romanesca* (for each pair of lines). The technique is nowhere applied strictly in the *Combattimento*, although there are hints of it in parts of the work, such as the 'Notte' stanza (54), a strophic variation (4 + 4 lines) with harmonic patterns redolent of the Romanesca (presumably this was one reason for favouring *Gerusalemme conquistata* here, given that the stanza falls easily into two halves, unlike the equivalent stanza in the *Liberata*). There are also repetitive structures in the battle stanzas (55–7, 62) and Clorinda's 'Amico, hai vinto' (2 + 2 lines). For a counter-example, see Domenico Mazzocchi's dialogue-setting of the Olindo–Sofronia episode (*Gerusalemme liberata*, II) in his *Dialoghi e sonetti* (Rome, Francesco Zanetti, 1638), discussed in Gallico, 'Musicalità di Domenico Mazzocchi'. Here the narrator is called 'Tasso', and most of his text is delivered over standard reciting formulas ('aria de' sonetti', the Romanesca, etc.).

the 'games' associated in particular with the Sienese Accademia degli Intronati that would also seem to provide a proper context for the *Combattimento*. These more or less ritualized forms of pre- or post-prandial entertainment were fully documented in the Sienese Scipion(e) Bargagli's *I trattenimenti . . . dove da vaghe donne, e da giovani huomini rappresentati sono honesti, e dilettevoli giuochi: narrate novelle, e cantate alcune amorose canzonette* (Venice, Bernardo Giunti, 1587), a popular manual on how to stage-manage such occasions.[36] Bargagli (1540–1612) was closely associated with the Intronati (his academic name was 'Lo Schietto'), which sought to establish a reputation for aristocratic entertainment, whether by way of formal drama or through other kinds of social discourse and games. Each of the three parts of his treatise, representing three sample evenings, comprises quasi-academic disputations on standard themes, story-telling (Bargagli includes model *novelle*), word-games and, in conclusion, some musical activity: in the first part, a dialogue of nymphs and shepherds; in the second, the singing of (pseudo-improvised) *ottave rime* around an amorous theme; in the third, a *ballata* with dancing. Stefano Guazzi's widely reprinted *La civil conversatione* (Brescia, Vincenzo Sabbio, 1574) covers similar ground, moving beyond its guidelines for conducting conversations between individuals of different rank, position and gender, to (in the fourth part) a sample 'convito', where the participants eat, drink and speak well, improvising or reciting new poetry, and peppering their conversations with quotations from Petrarch and commentaries on historical exemplars.[37]

The tradition (or perhaps better, its literary representation) derives from Boccaccio's *Decameron* – whose model is invoked by Bargagli – as filtered through etiquette manuals such as Castiglione's *Il libro del cortigiano*. And even though Monteverdi's account of the soirée in Girolamo Mocenigo's palace in Venice in Carnival 1624 only mentions music, one can imagine that the host engineered other similar activities for his guests. The *Combattimento* would certainly provide an ersatz version of the role-playing typical of such occasions: it invokes a special form of story-telling; it plays both with words and with their musical representation (not least by means of the *concitato genere*); it leads (at least in the Eighth Book) to a *ballo*; and its content would provide material for further discussion along the lines of Bargagli's disputa-

36 Giunti reprinted it in 1592; there is a modern edition by Laura Riccò (Rome, Salerno, 1989). The text had in fact been written before 1569. Scipione's elder brother, Girolamo, was the author of the play *La pellegrina*, later performed at the wedding of Grand Duke Ferdinando I de' Medici and Christine of Lorraine in Florence in May 1589; he also wrote a widely reprinted *Dialogo de' giuochi che nelle vegghie sanesi si usano di fare* (Siena, Luca Bonetti, 1572).
37 For Guazzi's popular text, I consulted the edition issued in Venice by Giovanni Antonio Giuliani in 1621. For earlier Venetian examples of the practice, see the discussion in Feldman, *City Culture and the Madrigal at Venice*, pp. 102–8.

tions, such as whether the male lover should use prominence in arms or letters to achieve seduction, whether outer or inner beauty is more effective to attract a lover, whether love is best pursued openly or in secret, or, indeed, whether music can appropriately represent an epic poetic text. Indeed, in this sense the musicological debates still engendered by the *Combattimento* continue a tradition going right back to the work's première.

Armida abbandonata *(?1627)*

Monteverdi appears to have been enthusiastic enough about the *Combattimento* to attempt a similar (it seems) piece based on Tasso, the so-called *Armida abbandonata*. It is first mentioned in his letter to Striggio of 1 May 1627: 'I happen to have set many stanzas of Tasso – where Armida begins "O tu, che porte, parte teco di me, parte ne lassi", continuing with all her lament and anger, with Rinaldo's reply; and these perhaps would not be displeasing.' Here Monteverdi suggests that the piece has been completed, although on 18 September he refers (perhaps) to it as unfinished.[38] Subsequent references in letters of 25 September, 2 October and 18 December 1627, and 4 February 1628 chiefly concern copying a manuscript 'completely full of creases' (2 October) that eventually falls 'in the hands of the Most Illustrious Signor Mocenigo, my very affectionate and special master' (4 February).

The sorceress Armida, a favourite of subsequent opera composers, is one of the chief villains of *Gerusalemme liberata*. In a plot reminiscent of the Alcina–Ruggiero episode in Ariosto's *Orlando furioso* (1516), Armida lures the noble Christian Rinaldo away from his duty, seducing him to stay on her enchanted island until he is rescued by Carlo and Ubaldo. The passage to which Monteverdi refers begins in Canto XVI.40: 'Forsennata gridava: "O tu che porte / teco parte di me, parte ne lassi / . . ."' ('Mad, she cried out: "O you who take part of me with you, and leave part of me behind . . ."').[39] Armida seeks to halt Ruggiero's flight; Ubaldo reminds Ruggiero of his duty (41); Armida asks only to stand at Ruggiero's side in battle (42–51); Ruggiero denies her request and dismisses her (52–6); Armida breaks out in fury, curses him and then falls into a dead faint (57–60). This is presumably where Monteverdi's setting ended, although Armida subsequently renews her lament in stanza 63 ('Poi ch'ella in sé tornò, deserto e muto') prior to summoning

---

38 Here Monteverdi says that he has not 'completely finished *Aminta*', which Stevens (*The Letters of Claudio Monteverdi*, p. 369) takes to refer to the 1628 Parma music. However, Fabbri (*Monteverdi*, trans. Carter, p. 204) believes, probably correctly, that Monteverdi has made a mistake for *Armida*.

39 Curiously, this echoes Clorinda's first words in the *Combattimento*, XII.52 (ll. 7–8): 'ch'ella si volge e grida: "O tu, che porte, / che corri sì?". . .'.

her demons and flying to the Orient (68–75, the end of the canto). This section was a favourite quarry for late sixteenth-century madrigalists seeking texts variously representing love, rage and lament; it also contains Tasso's famous comparison of Armida preparing to address Ruggiero with the musician preparing to sing (53: 'Qual musico gentil, prima che chiara'). Thus Monteverdi had already set portions of Armida's curse (stanzas 59, 60, 63) for five voices in a sequence in his Third Book of madrigals of 1592 ('Vattene pur, crudel, con quella pace'). Assuming that Ubaldo's brief and irrelevant intervention (stanza 41) was omitted, the piece would set twenty *ottava rima* stanzas (the *Combattimento* has sixteen) and, like the *Combattimento*, would require three voices, for the narrator, Armida and Ruggiero. The similarity of casting suggests that Monteverdi may have been writing for the same singers. However, there is much more quoted speech here that could be given to the principal characters (ninety-four lines for Armida and twenty-eight for Ruggiero), diminishing the role of the narrator. One assumes that representing the opposites of 'lament and anger' worked in a similar way to the various opposites in the *Combattimento*, while the music for Armida must have produced an effect worthy of the *Lamento d'Arianna*. As we shall see, this music would also find a curious echo in Monteverdi's work for the 1628 Parma *intermedi*.

8

Approaching the lost works

A significant number of Monteverdi's theatrical works are known only through documentary references (in his letters and the like), or by way of partial sources (librettos, descriptions, etc.). While a few of these losses are relatively minor, others – such as the operas *Arianna* (1608), *Proserpina rapita* (1630) and *Le nozze d'Enea in Lavinia* (1641)[1] – are more to be lamented. Also, given that the bulk of the lost works date from the 1610s and 1620s, they might well provide several missing links between Monteverdi's earlier Mantuan theatrical works and those he later wrote for Venice. Without these links, if such they be, it is hard to produce a coherent account of his development as a composer for the stage, should coherence be at all achievable or even desirable.[2] Ironically, too, Monteverdi wrote much more about these works than about those that survive, chiefly because they usually involved long-distance collaborations. Yet failing some major discovery in some unexplored library – always a possibility – they will never see the light of day.

Some of Monteverdi's own references to particular stage projects are very vague indeed, such as an unspecified Carnival composition that could be performed in masks, which he mentioned to Alessandro Striggio on 26 February 1621. Others reflect just twinkles in his eye – including the suggestions (20 January 1617, 5 June 1627) that he might provide theatrical or similar music for Florentine wedding festivities (where Monteverdi may also have exaggerated matters to make a good impression) – or ill-formed plans on the part of his patrons and would-be employers. For the latter, we have seen (in Chapter 6) that Simone Borsato hoped that Monteverdi might write at least a sung *ballo* for a mascherata in Mirandola in February 1607; Prince

---

1 For the last, see Severi, *'Le nozze d'Enea con Lavinia'*. A study of this work will also figure prominently in Ellen Rosand's forthcoming *Monteverdi's Late Operas*.
2 The issue is explored provocatively in Degrada, 'Il teatro di Claudio Monteverdi'.

Francesco Gonzaga sent Striggio the text of a *ballo* (to be set by Monteverdi?) in early 1610; the composer may have been involved in plans for a *ballo* and other entertainments for the birthday celebrations of Duke Francesco Gonzaga and Margherita of Savoy on 7–8 May 1612; and his letters of 2 January and 1 May 1627 refer to a proposed theatrical entertainment that would seem associated with the accession of Duke Vincenzo II Gonzaga.[3] It is not clear that any of these proposals came to fruition. Conversely, while in Mantua, Monteverdi must have worked extensively on the tournaments, *balli* and comedies that, his brother said, had prevented him from penning a proper response to Giovanni Maria Artusi, even if we have few details of them. But there is reliable documentation for at least fifteen 'lost' theatrical works covering the period 1604–41, eleven of which definitely reached performance; of the remaining four, the status of two (*Gli amori di Diana ed Endimione*, 1604–5; *Armida abbandonata*, ?1627) is more doubtful, while two (*Le nozze di Tetide*, 1616–17; *La finta pazza Licori*, 1627) were unfinished – nay, hardly begun.

Monteverdi's comments on these lost works have proved invaluable to scholars seeking to construct the composer's views on theatrical and other music. They also reveal his eminently practical concerns. Monteverdi's first questions when reading a proposed text were if and how it might work on the stage; he regularly sought to know the singers involved so as to provide appropriate music according to their abilities; he was not averse to making quite precise suggestions to his librettist on matters of plot, structure and even poetic metre; and running as a leitmotif throughout the correspondence is the need for adequate time for composition and rehearsal, a lesson learnt while working on *Arianna*, which in turn is regularly cited as an example of how best to proceed in theatrical matters.

The correspondence concerning *Le nozze di Tetide* (1616–17) and *La finta pazza Licori* (1627) is particularly fruitful in this light. *Le nozze di Tetide* was a *favola marittima* submitted by the undistinguished poet Scipione Agnelli – author of the *sestina* 'Incenerite spoglie, avara tomba' in Monteverdi's Sixth Book of madrigals of 1614 – for the impending festivities in Mantua celebrating the wedding of Duke Ferdinando Gonzaga and Caterina de' Medici (they were married in Florence on 7 February 1617). When Monteverdi received the libretto in early December 1616, he made a number of criticisms of it (to Striggio on 9 and 29 December), including its problematic casting (too many low ensembles; too many sopranos and tenors), difficulties of instrumentation and staging, the feeble plot, the length of the speeches,

3   For the 1610 *ballo*, see Bertolotti, *Musici alla corte dei Gonzaga in Mantova dal secolo XV al XVIII*, p. 92; for the 1612 one, see Ademollo, *La bell'Adriana ed altre virtuose del suo tempo alla corte di Mantova*, pp. 197–8 n.

the scant number of dialogues, plus the fact that they chiefly required recitative and therefore would not provide attractive ensembles, and the poverty of the choruses, several of which, moreover, would have to be accompanied by wind instruments, producing an unpleasant effect. It seems from Striggio's own letters to the duke that he, too, was less than enthusiastic about the piece.[4] But Monteverdi's trenchant statements in the letter of 9 December 1616 have been taken as emblematic:

> How, dear Sir, can I imitate the speech of the winds, if they do not speak? And how can I, by such means, move the passions? Ariadne moved us because she was a woman, and similarly Orpheus because he was a man, not a wind. Music can suggest, without any words, the noise of winds and the bleating of sheep, the neighing of horses and so on and so forth; but it cannot imitate the speech of winds because no such thing exists.
>
> Next, the dances which are scattered throughout the fable do not have dance measures. And as to the story as a whole – as far as my no little ignorance is concerned – I do not feel that it moves me at all (moreover I find it hard to understand), nor do I feel that it carries me in a natural manner to an end that moves me. *Arianna* led me to a just lament, and *Orfeo* to a righteous prayer, but this fable leads me I don't know to what end. So what does Your Most Illustrious Lordship want the music to be able to do?

Monteverdi's (over?)reaction seems prompted in part by fear of having to produce something at speed, a condition endemic to court service but which he always resented. He did moderate his stance on discovering that Agnelli's text was intended as *intermedi*, rather than an opera. This may in part be due to his sense that the two genres had different requirements; after all, the winds had sung in one of the sets of *intermedi* associated with the 1598 performances of *Il pastor fido* (see Chapter 2). But it also made more feasible his idea of sharing the work out among several musicians (including the singers, he suggested on 9 December). On 6 January 1617 he claimed that he had set some 150 lines to music, coming close to finishing all the recitative soliloquies; he promised then to start on those containing florid song ('quelli che cantano di garbo'). However, the project had been abandoned by the time of Monteverdi's letter of 14 January, and although there were subsequent discussions of a replacement (see his letters of 20 and 28 January, and 4, 11 and 18 February), the Mantuan court seems to have stuck with more home-grown fare for the celebrations, including a revival of an opera (now lost) by Santi Orlandi, *La Galatea*, and Giovanni Battista Andreini's *sacra rappresentazione*, *La Maddalena*, with its prologue by Monteverdi.

4   Fabbri, *Monteverdi*, trans. Carter, pp. 150–1.

La finta pazza Licori is more enticing. Here the issue of imitation again comes to the fore, but in more creative ways, it seems. The death of Duke Ferdinando Gonzaga on 29 October 1626 prompted plans for festivities following the accession of Duke Vincenzo II, and as had become usual, Monteverdi was approached by Striggio for theatrical music. In his letter of 1 May 1627, the composer suggested *Armida abbandonata*, the *Combattimento di Tancredi e Clorinda*, and 'a little play [*operina*] by Signor Giulio Strozzi, very beautiful and unusual, which runs to some 400 lines, called *Licori finta pazza innamorata d'Aminta*, and this – after a thousand comical situations – ends up with a wedding, by a nice touch of stratagem'. On 7 May, he added to this list Rinuccini's *Narciso*, a libretto given to the composer by the poet (who had died in 1621) but which Monteverdi felt was impractical. In this same letter, however, Monteverdi told Striggio that Strozzi was prepared to expand his text to three acts if need be (eventually it reached five) and that it was essentially a showpiece for a virtuoso singer–actress such as Margherita Basile, sister of the famous Adriana. The notion of feigned madness was a standard topos of the *commedia dell'arte* going back at least to Isabella Andreini's well-known *La pazzia d'Isabella* of 1589, and accordingly, Monteverdi described (7 May) how the main character had to represent rapid shifts of emotions:

the imitation of this feigned madness must take into consideration only the present, not the past or the future, and consequently must emphasize the word, not the sense of the phrase. So when she speaks of war she will have to imitate war; when of peace, peace; when of death, death, and so forth.

And since the transformations take place in the shortest possible time, and the imitations as well – then whoever has to play this leading role, which moves us to laughter and to compassion, must be a woman capable of leaving aside all other imitations except the immediate one, which the word she utters will suggest to her.

The text would allow for 'a new kind of music, different from what has gone before' in the role of Aminta (so the composer said on 22 May), and it was also rich in contrasts for Licori (24 May):

my aim is that whenever she is about to come on stage, she has to introduce fresh delights and new inventions. In three places I certainly think the effects will come off well: first, when the camp is being set up, the sounds and noises heard behind the scenes and exactly echoing her words should (it seems to me) prove quite successful; secondly, when she pretends to be dead; and thirdly, when she pretends to be asleep, for here it is necessary to bring in music suggesting sleep.

However, Monteverdi again feared the problems of imitating non-verbal sounds: 'In some other places, however, because the words cannot mimic either gestures or noises or any other kind of imitative idea that might suggest itself, I am afraid the previous and following passages might seem weak.'

Monteverdi continued to whet Striggio's appetite in an almost weekly series of letters from June and July 1627, for all that Strozzi was proving slow to complete the revisions. On 10 July we discover that the feigned madness will begin in Act III (of the now 5-act version) and that there will be 'a ballet in every act, each one different from the other, and in a fantastical style'. Also, it seems that the piece provided opportunities for the newly emerging *concitato genere* and related instrumental styles seen in the *Combattimento di Tancredi e Clorinda*:

> It will now be up to Signora Margherita to become a brave soldier, timid and bold by turns, mastering perfectly the appropriate gestures herself, without fear or favour, because I am constantly aiming to have lively imitations of the music, gestures and tempi take place behind the scene [i.e., from the instrumentalists]. And I believe it will not displease Your Most Illustrious Lordship because the changes between the vigorous, noisy harmonies and the gentle, suave ones will take place suddenly so that the words will really come through well.

One wonders, then, why Monteverdi was so slow to write the music, unless it was just the usual fear of Mantuan ventures coming to naught. Although he says a great deal about his plans for it in his letters, he claims only to have more or less finished Act I (see his letters of 3 and 24 July), and even that is probably an exaggeration.[5]

Monteverdi often seems more eloquent in his letters about music that he never composed than about that which he did; in the latter case, his concerns are usually far more pragmatically to do with poetry, singers and staging. One wonders, in fact, whether guilt prompted by disinclination somehow encouraged him to feign creativity in other ways to satisfy his patrons, pending a stronger commitment to bringing a project to fruition. But even taking Monteverdi's comments on Licori at face value, one is left with problems of interpretation, given that here we are dealing with a special case, the imitation of madness. All this probably undermines Tomlinson's claim that the letters concerning *La finta pazza Licori* provide some kind of support for a newly emerging Marinist aesthetic in Monteverdi's Venetian works, one that

---

5 See Tomlinson, 'Twice Bitten, Thrice Shy'. The libretto of *La finta pazza Licori* does not survive, although Strozzi seems to have reused some of its thematic elements (but not its characters) in his libretto for Francesco Sacrati's *La finta pazza* (1641). We do, however, have another dramatic text by Strozzi from this period, *La gelosia placata*, set to music by Giovanni Rovetta and published in 1629; see Whenham, *Duet and Dialogue in the Age of Monteverdi*, i, pp. 207–16; ii, pp. 414–37. This is adapted from his 'anacronismo' *Il natal di Amore*, III.1.

laid an unwarranted emphasis on individual fragmented images. Typically, too, as the project started to falter the composer returned to basics. On 18 September 1627, he told Striggio that he shared his (unspecified) criticisms of it, which may have hinged on the too frequent presence on stage of the lead character (the issue recurs several times in the correspondence), and also, perhaps, on the fact that Strozzi's verse made too much use of strophic structures; either or both would explain Monteverdi's response that 'everything could have been kept going with some variation of the vocal line' (*con la variazione del canto*). The composer may well have been relieved when the project was tacitly dropped in late September 1627, not least because his plate was now full with work on music for festivities in Parma.

As for those theatrical works known to have reached performance, and despite the loss of their music, one can often tell a great deal about them from other sources. Here, chiefly because he was soon involved in practicalities, Monteverdi's letters can seem more reliable, even if they represent just one side of a dialogue and so must be treated with caution. Contemporary descriptions are problematic in other ways, given that by nature they are prone to exaggeration and distortion, and they also rely on rhetorical tropes that render vivid the account to the mind's eye, but distance it increasingly from reality. As for surviving librettos, the discrepancies between poetic and musical structures in Monteverdi's known works make it difficult to predict the likely outcome of his setting given verse to music. Yet for all the caveats, the results of any such speculation are intriguing enough to warrant further thought. Four case studies help prove the point.

Arianna *(1608)*

Monteverdi's second opera was the largest of the three works on which the composer worked for the festivities for the wedding of Prince Francesco Gonzaga and Margherita of Savoy in May–June 1608.[6] It has gained an almost

---

6   This section draws upon my 'Lamenting Ariadne?', which in some cases gives fuller details. Most of the relevant documents (except where noted) are given in Fabbri, *Monteverdi*, trans. Carter, pp. 77–99. The libretto is in Solerti, *Gli albori del melodramma*, ii, pp. 143–88, following the text in Follino, *Compendio delle sontuose feste* (1608), pp. 31–65. Solerti divides the libretto into a prologue and eight scenes, although these divisions have no contemporary authority. His edition misreads line 658 (*recte* 'Pietà mi scusi e sdegno'), omits a line after line 836 ('Ahi, che più d'aspe è sordo a' miei lamenti'), and contains an error in the line numbering. But I shall cite this edition, albeit with minor editing. There were several separate prints of the libretto (Mantua, Aurelio & Lodovico Osanna, 1608; Florence, I Giunti, 1608; Venice, Bernardo Giunti, Giovan Battista Ciotti & co., 1608; Venice, Gherardo & Iseppo

totemic status, partly because of the power of the one section of the music that survives, the famous *Lamento d'Arianna*, and partly because the composer regularly cited the opera in his letters, viewing it, it seems, as his greatest work for the stage. Not for nothing was he keen to see a performance of *Arianna* in Mantua in 1620 (which did not come to fruition); equally, when the composer took to the operatic stage in Venice, he did so with a revival of this opera. The lament survives in a number of sources, each variously distanced from the music heard in the opera, including manuscript sources of indeterminate date and two prints from 1623.[7] Monteverdi arranged it for five voices in his Sixth Book of madrigals of 1614, and he produced at least one *contrafactum*, as a 'Pianto della Madonna' (with the Latin text, 'Iam moriar mi fili') in his *Selva morale e spirituale* of 1640–1. The piece inspired numerous imitations, spawning an important sub-genre in recitative music for the theatre and the chamber. And in his letter to Giovanni Battista Doni of 22 October 1633, the composer specifically associated the piece with his arduous search for the 'via naturale alla immitatione' ('natural path to imitation'), on which he had found scant guidance in books, even in the writings of Plato.

The wedding festivities were originally intended to be held during Carnival 1607–8. Rinuccini arrived in Mantua on 23 October 1607, presumably bringing with him his libretto; Monteverdi did not have it when he met Prince Francesco Gonzaga on 9 October, and asked for the text(s) to be set for the festivities 'within seven or eight days'. On 20 December the poet was able to report to Striggio on the progress of the opera and on matters of casting; the music must also have been well in hand by the end of the year.[8] However, a serious problem arose in late February 1608 when the eighteen-year-old singer Caterina Martinelli, Monteverdi's pupil and intended for the part of Arianna, contracted smallpox; Martinelli had already distinguished herself in the performance of Marco da Gagliano's *Dafne* and in another unspecified work, both staged in Mantua towards the end of Carnival (probably in the week of 13–19 February), but she died on 7 (or perhaps 9) March. Meanwhile, on the morning of 26 February 1608 a meeting

Imberti, 1622; Venice, Angelo Salvadori, 1640; Venice, Antonio Bariletti, 1640). For the casting of the opera, which included Francesco Rasi as Apollo and Bacco, and perhaps Giovanni Gualberto Magli as a 'pescatore', see Annibaldi, ' "Spettacolo veramente da principi" ', p. 42.

7   Monteverdi's lament appeared in his *Lamento d'Arianna . . . con due lettere amorose in genere rapresentativo* (Venice, Bartolomeo Magni, 1623) and in *Il maggio fiorito: arie, sonetti, e madrigali, à 1.2.3. de diversi autori* (Orvieto, Michel'Angelo Fei & Rinaldo Ruuli, 1623). For the manuscripts, see Godt, 'I casi di Arianna'.

8   According to a letter from Ferdinando Gonzaga of 2 February (? = March) 1608, Monteverdi had by now finished the bulk of the music for *Arianna*; see Strainchamps, 'The Life and Death of Caterina Martinelli', p. 167.

to discuss the wedding entertainments was held between Duchess Eleonora Medici-Gonzaga, the prefect of the ducal buildings Antonio Maria Viani, the superintendent of the festivities Federico Follino, and Rinuccini and Monteverdi. Here it was noted that Duchess Eleonora had agreed with Rinuccini to enrich *Arianna* with additional action 'since it is quite dry' (*assai sciutta*).[9] It is not clear whether this agreement was reached at or before the meeting, although the wording implies that it was recent.

Martinelli's fatal illness prompted a frantic search for a replacement, including a singer from Florence (Margherita Romana) who turned out to be unsatisfactory, one in the service of Cardinal Montalto (probably Ippolita Recupito) who, it was claimed, could not possibly learn the role in time, and a singer from Bergamo whom Monteverdi recommended but who refused to come to Mantua.[10] In a mounting tide of panic, the Mantuans turned to Virginia Andreini, a famous *commedia dell'arte* actress and member of the Comici Fedeli, the troupe often engaged by Duke Vincenzo Gonzaga and which was to perform Battista Guarini's *L'idropica*, the main play at the festivities. Antonio Costantini reported on 15 March that Andreini had learnt the part of Arianna by heart in six days, singing it 'with such grace, and with such manner and affect' as to amaze everyone; he also noted the success of a try-out of the work the previous evening.[11] Events then proceeded at a more leisurely pace, in part because of the repeated postponement of the Mantua–Savoy wedding, due to diplomatic difficulties. But the première of the opera on Wednesday 28 May was by all accounts a triumph; and everyone noted the powerful effect of Arianna's lament, which, according to Follino, using the by now familiar trope, had moved each lady of the audience to shed 'some little tear' (*qualche lagrimetta*).

9 Striggio had already warned that a tragedy might be thought improper and inauspicious for such an occasion; see his letter to Duke Vincenzo Gonzaga of 5 March 1606 in Parisi, *Ducal Patronage of Music in Mantua*, p. 194 n. 92.

10 Margherita 'Romana' had arrived in Mantua by 2 March 1608; see Kirkendale, *The Court Musicians in Florence during the Principate of the Medici*, pp. 162, 339. For other Florentine singers in Mantua for the festivities, see Carter, 'A Florentine Wedding of 1608', pp. 99–100; contrary to common opinion, they did not include Settimia Caccini. As for the reluctant singer from Bergamo, this was not unusual, given that familial pressures were often brought to bear to prevent young women singers appearing on stage; compare the case discussed in Carter, 'A Florentine Wedding of 1608', pp. 101–2.

11 Costantini's letter is transcribed complete in Besutti, 'The "Sala degli Specchi" Uncovered', p. 460. Andreini's husband(!) received a necklace with medallion valued at 210 *scudi* for her performance; such payment in kind was not unusual for court service, as Monteverdi himself experienced when given a necklace for the dedication to Caterina de' Medici, Duchess of Mantua, of his Seventh Book of madrigals. For Andreini's payment and later echoes of her role, see Besutti, 'Da *L'Arianna* a *La Ferinda*'.

The lament has attracted a great deal of attention in the scholarly literature: Gary Tomlinson proclaims it a supreme example of poetry and music united to rhetorical and dramatic effect, and Suzanne Cusick offers a powerful reading of it as a (mis)appropriation of music's new-found power to move the soul while constructing and controlling gendered discourse.[12] However, less attention has been paid to Rinuccini's libretto as a whole. The action concerns the consequences of the Cretan Ariadne having aided the Athenian Theseus to kill her half-brother, the Minotaur, in the labyrinth at the palace of Ariadne's father, King Minos. Ovid's *Metamorphoses* (VIII.169–82) gives a compressed account of Theseus in the labyrinth, the flight to Dia (Naxos), Ariadne's abandonment to lament her fate, and the arrival of Bacchus and Ariadne's apotheosis. Rinuccini is necessarily more expansive (for the moment, I follow Solerti's scene divisions). After the prologue delivered by Apollo, scene 1 has Venere (Venus) announce to Amore (Cupid) the imminent arrival on Dia of Teseo and Arianna fleeing to Athens; she declares that Arianna will be abandoned by her ungrateful lover. Amore promises to inflame Teseo with still more passion to prevent his departure, but Venere has a different plan: Bacco (Bacchus) has been summoned, and Amore should make him love Arianna instead. Venere leaves and Amore makes himself 'invisible' to oversee the following action. In scene 2, Teseo and Arianna arrive with soldiers and decide to rest from their travails. Arianna is sad for her betrayal of her father but asserts her love for Teseo. She leaves to find shelter to sleep, and a rather bucolic chorus of fisherfolk provide a song comparing the stars in the sky to the eyes of a beautiful woman ('Fiamme serene e pure'). In scene 3, Teseo agonizes over his intended abandoning of Arianna (we are not told when that decision was made), but is encouraged by his Consigliero (Counsellor), who says that honour must conquer love and that Arianna cannot be an acceptable queen for the Athenians. The chorus heralds the arrival of dawn ('Stampa il ciel con l'auree piante'). In scene 4, Arianna returns, having been unable to sleep: she is troubled with foreboding, despite the comfort offered by her companion Dorilla, and decides to go to the port to find Teseo. The chorus praises the rural life, ending with a plea that Teseo might not forget Arianna ('Avventurose genti'). In scene 5, a messenger (Nunzio Primo) relates to the chorus his sighting of an unnamed woman (but obviously Arianna) arriving at the seashore, discovering Teseo's departure and lamenting her fate. The chorus sympathizes with Arianna and again praises the rural life, free of the cares of the city ('Misera giovinetta'). In scene 6, Arianna and (later?) Dorilla return; this is the scene containing the famous lament. Fanfares are then heard in the

---

12 Tomlinson, 'Madrigal, Monody, and Monteverdi's "via naturale alla immitatione"';
Cusick, '"There was not one lady who failed to shed a tear"'.

distance, and they go to the shore in the hope that Teseo has turned back. The chorus compares the force of male and female eloquence, expressing the hope that Teseo will indeed return ('Su l'orride paludi'). In scene 7, a second messenger (Nunzio Secondo) recounts the arrival not of Teseo but of Bacco, who has taken pity on Arianna. In scene 8, their union is celebrated by a sung *ballo* ('Spiega omai, giocondo nume'), followed by the appearance of Amore and (from the sea) Venere, while Giove (Jupiter) speaks from on high. Bacco offers to make Arianna immortal in the heavens, crowned with stars.

This text must reflect the revisions agreed with Rinuccini at or before the meeting with Duchess Eleonora on 26 February, probably including the opening scene for Venere and Amore (although Rinuccini refers to the casting of Venere in his letter of 20 December 1607) and the finale involving the appearance of the gods; both scenes would have helped provide action, spectacle and divine intervention so as to soften the duchess's criticisms of the libretto.[13] Thus the chorus beginning scene 8, 'Spiega omai, giocondo nume', could in fact have been intended to conclude scene 7, and hence the opera as a whole prior to the addition of the finale (which causes the libretto to end, unusually, with a speech by Bacco). Although 'Spiega omai, giocondo nume' (the 'nume' is Apollo, called 'Re del giorno' in the second stanza, l. 1074) was eventually sung and danced by a chorus of Bacco's soldiers, it could just as well be delivered by the generic chorus of fisherfolk. However, even discounting those additions, anomalies remain, not least the six effectively end-of-'scene' choruses instead of the standard five found in Rinuccini's *Dafne* (1608 version; there are four in the original), *Euridice* (1600) and the undated *Narciso*, and also, of course, in Striggio's *Orfeo*. This is striking, given Rinuccini's apparent intention to cast *Arianna* as a 'tragedia rappresentata in musica'. His insistence on the generic label – unprecedented in librettos – is entirely appropriate on other grounds, including the noble characters and plot, and the work's adherence to the unities of time (in effect, twelve hours from dusk to dawn), action and place. But if this were a tragedy in the statutory mould, one would expect five main choruses (four separating the 'acts' and a final comment), not six. However, one of these six choruses does in fact stand out from the rest: unlike the others, 'Misera giovinetta' (at the end of scene 5) is not given the centred heading 'CORO' or the like in the 1608 librettos, it consists of only two strophes, not the four or five found elsewhere (except the last chorus, which is exceptional for being a sung *ballo*), and its mixture of *settenari* and *endecasillabi* is more fluid. This chorus is then followed (again, unusually) by three lines for Nunzio Primo as he announces Arianna's return from the seashore. Its non-standard format raises questions about its place in Rinuccini's scheme.

The two messengers' narrations also create difficulties. In the first (scene 5), Nunzio Primo describes how Arianna, on the seashore, 'laments the broken promise, laments the wicked departure of an unfaithful lover' ('Piange la rotta fede, / piange l'empia partita / d'un amante infedele'; ll. 668–70). She stands on a rock, sees the departing ships of Teseo's fleet, runs to the water's edge to berate her lover, and throws herself into the sea, only to be rescued by fishermen who bring her back to shore and revive her, whereupon she renews her plaint. In scene 6, Arianna returns from the seashore and delivers her lament (punctuated by sympathetic remarks from the chorus) as she affirms her wish to die, until her hopes are restored by the sound of trumpets and drums from the beach. Then (scene 7) Nunzio Secondo enters to relate a striking turn of events. Bacco has arrived to see Arianna still filling the air with her deep sighs and plaints. Moved, he asks her why she is weeping; she tells him of Teseo's infidelity, and Bacco offers her his hand instead. At that point (Nunzio Secondo continues), the heavens open to reveal Amore in glory, with gold raining down from the skies. The narration concludes with Nunzio Secondo announcing the arrival on stage of Arianna and Bacco – 'ecco gli sposi, ecco i reali amanti' ('here the bride and groom, here the royal lovers') – which is also a clear reference to the wedding party in the audience.

Two points follow. First, Arianna's lament (in scene 6) has already in effect been described to the chorus by Nunzio Primo in scene 5: it follows much the same sequence of rhetorical and dramatic gestures as the narration, and indeed has some of the same words quoted by the messenger. Second, Nunzio Secondo's narration picks up precisely where Nunzio Primo's left off, with Arianna on the shore still bemoaning her fate. Arianna's lament is redundant; we have, almost literally, heard it all before. Also, she should not still be sighing and weeping on the shore (so Nunzio Secondo relates in scene 7) if she has just gone back there hope in heart, on hearing the trumpets and drums heralding the arrival of a fleet (so scene 6 describes). Thus it seems at least possible that some or all of scene 6, including Arianna's famous lament, was a later addition to Rinuccini's original scheme, further prompting the unusual chorus at the end of scene 5, plus Nunzio Primo's announcement of Arianna's arrival on the stage, and creating other difficulties that the poet never quite ironed out. Not for nothing did Monteverdi and others treat the lament as separate, and separable, from the main action. In short, *Arianna* seems to have been subject to a process of re-drafting based on a 5-part classical design that became diluted as a result of various external and other pressures placed upon Rinuccini in late 1607 and early 1608,

Table 8-1   A probable 5-scene organization of *Arianna*

(Scene numbers follow Solerti; suggested later additions are indented in italic.)

Prologue	Apollo
	(Scene 1) Venere/Amore (no chorus at end)
1	(Scene 2) Teseo, Arianna, Consigliero, Coro di Soldati [e di Pescatori]
	. . . final chorus: 'Fiamme serene e pure' (four 6-line stanzas; *settenari* and *endecasillabi*)
2	(Scene 3) Teseo, Consigliero, Messaggero, Coro di Pescatori
	. . . final chorus: 'Stampa il ciel con l'auree piante' (4-line refrain and three 8-line stanzas in scheme R–S1–R–S2–R–S3–R; *ottonari*)
3	(Scene 4) Arianna, Dorilla, Coro di Pescatori
	. . . final chorus: 'Avventurose genti' (four 6-line stanzas; *settenari* and *endecasillabi*)
4	(Scene 5) Nunzio Primo, Coro [di Pescatori]
	chorus 'Misera giovinetta' (two 9-line stanzas; settenari and endecasillabi) plus Nunzio Primo's announcement (3 lines) of Arianna's arrival
	(Scene 6) Arianna, Dorilla, Coro [di Pescatori] *(= Lamento d'Arianna and subsequent dialogue)*
	. . . final chorus: 'Su l'orride paludi' (five 6-line stanzas; *settenari*)
5	(Scene 7) Nunzio Secondo, Coro [di Pescatori]
	. . . final chorus (Scene 8): 'Spiega omai, giocondo nume' (sung *ballo*: two 6-line stanzas; *ottonari* and *quaternari*)
	chorus reallocated to a Coro di soldati di Bacco, leading to speeches (versi sciolti) for Coro, Amore, Arianna, Coro, Venere, Giove, Bacco

specifically as regards scenes 1 and 8 (probably) and 6 (possibly); the result is clear in Table 8-1.[14]

The question that follows, then, is why the lament might have been added. Certainly it is justified by classical sources, including Ariadne's letter to Theseus in Ovid's *Heroides* (X), and Catullus' Poem 64 (ll. 52–264); in the latter, the telling of Ariadne's story is inspired by the embroidery on the coverlet of the marriage bed of Peleus and Thetis (hence the association

---

14 Table 8-1 is supported by attempts to bring the finished text back into a standard format. Bujić ('Rinuccini the Craftsman') discusses a Croatian translation (1633) of *Arianna* with five acts: the divisions occur precisely at the choruses ending Solerti's scenes 2, 3, 4, 6; Act V is Solerti's scenes 7–8. Scene 5 (ending with 'Misera giovinetta') is Act IV scene 1.

of Ariadne with weddings). The partial roots of Arianna's lament in Ovid's letter help explain why Monteverdi published the music with two *lettere amorose* in 1623. Rinuccini was also influenced by Giovanni dell'Anguillara's oft-reprinted translation (and expansion) of Ovid – *Le metamorfosi di Ovidio, ridotte . . . in ottava rima* (Venice, Giovanni Griffio, 1561) – which adds a long lament for Arianna (VIII.92–150), declared to be modelled on the lament of Olimpia in Ariosto's *Orlando furioso* (X.20–34; in turn derived from the Ariadne of the *Heroides*). The genealogy of Rinuccini's lament explains some of its inconsistencies, including Arianna's improbable claims about being abandoned on a deserted island and under threat from wild animals (common to Olimpia and to the Ariadnes of the *Heroides* and Catullus), even though Rinuccini's Dia is clearly inhabited and, indeed, rather civilized, with comforting fisherfolk at every turn. But this genealogy also explains the lament's standard topoi and structures. Like Olimpia's, it offers a patriarchal lesson on the perils of female (mis)behaviour,[15] even if that might be softened by the admonitions against (female) ingratitude that also figured in the 1608 Mantuan festivities, not least in the *Ballo delle ingrate*, and also by the well-known end of the tale, with Theseus punished for his misdeeds by inadvertently causing the death of his father, Aegeus: 'Thus bold Theseus, as he entered the chambers of his home, darkened with mourning for his father's death, himself received such grief as by forgetfulness of heart he had caused to the daughter of Minos' (Catullus, Poem 64, ll. 246–8). The lament also marks a point of transition. Arianna speaks just before dawn, that characteristic period of introspection where things untenable and inexpressible in the harsh light of day may be given voice. She is seen on various other boundaries – between land and water, maidenhood and marriage – her lament acting as a rite of passage. And for that matter, she ends up with a far better husband than Teseo could ever be, while her last words in the opera pronounce a moral truly appropriate to an early seventeenth-century royal wedding: 'blessed is the heart that has a god for comfort' ('beato è il cor che ha per conforto un Dio'; l. 1090). Her union with Bacco is sanctioned not just by Amore, Venere and Giove, but also by Apollo, the sun-god invoked in the last chorus, who thereby (given his presence in the prologue) brings things full circle.

15 This is the reading in Cusick, '"There was not one lady who failed to shed a tear"', which offers a range of contemporary views of the Ariadne story. The following discussion of rites of passage also draws upon MacNeil, 'Weeping at the Water's Edge'. However, one should not underestimate the potential for entirely contrary readings. The moral in a later prologue for *Arianna* (Solerti, *Gli albori del melodramma*, ii, p. 188), perhaps for a performance before nuns (perhaps in Florence in 1614), is particularly perverse: Ariadne's tale reveals how worldly affairs can be scorned to gain divine reward.

But there may have been another factor influencing the insertion (if such it was) of the lament. Commentators moved by its power have failed to note just how unusual is its length, and how it runs counter to the general reluctance to have women sing extensively, if at all, on the stage. Hitherto, lead operatic female roles (whether or not sung by women) were fairly limited: of the 445 lines of text in the Rinuccini/Peri *Dafne*, the title-role has just 22 (30 in the 1608 revision); Euridice in the Rinuccini/Peri *Euridice* has just 27 lines out of 790; and the same character in the Striggio/Monteverdi *Orfeo* has a mere 12 lines out of some 650. Arianna, in contrast, has 146 lines out of some 1100, a proportion exceeded only by Aurora in Chiabrera's *Il rapimento di Cefalo* (89 lines out of 658). Moreover, Arianna's lament (84 lines) is by far the longest single piece for a female role (and a female voice) in the repertory to date; even Orfeo's lament in Act V of *Orfeo* has only 50. The young Caterina Martinelli would have been hard pressed to take the part. Yet if it was a later addition, perhaps associated with Duchess Eleonora's judgement of *Arianna* as being 'quite dry' (noted on 26 February), Rinuccini could scarcely have contemplated manipulating so long a scene while Martinelli lay gravely ill with smallpox (from about 22 February): by the 29th, the singer Francesco Campagnolo was complaining rather churlishly about wasting his time, given that everything relating to *Arianna*, including the rehearsals, had been put on hold.[16] Nor would Rinuccini have altered the libretto while Mantuan officials were so desperately trying to find a replacement after Martinelli's death in early March. Things were moving quickly: by 10 March the Florentine singer had been considered and rejected, and Duchess Eleonora had written to Bergamo. And if Virginia Andreini had learnt the part of Arianna in six days by 14 March (so Costantini reported on the 15th), she must have been given the music on or before the 8th. This was not the time to consider an extended lament, still less to write its text and music. It seems more plausible that the addition was made (and the music composed) only after it was certain that Virginia Andreini would be taking on the role, when things settled down as the court artists and players awaited the long-delayed arrival of the bride from Turin.

Indeed, it is also possible that Virginia Andreini did not just enable the lament to be added but positively encouraged it. Andreini had already established a formidable reputation, not least by way of her performance in the title-role of her husband Giovanni Battista Andreini's *La Florinda* in 1606, a play designed as a vehicle to demonstrate her thespian skills, and from which she earned her stage-name. Significantly, it incorporates a long lament (reportedly sung) in Act IV scene 5 ('Ben à ragion, dev'io lagrime e preci'). In turn, Arianna later became a popular character among *commedia dell'arte* actresses.

---

16   In a letter to Prince Francesco Gonzaga; see Strainchamps, 'The Life and Death of Caterina Martinelli', pp. 166–7.

The notion that Andreini encouraged, or even required, Rinuccini and Monteverdi to capitalize on her fame and skill by incorporating a lament in *Arianna* is an attractive one. Further, it is tempting to suggest that the prominence granted the lament was due specifically to the presence in the cast of a professional actress – rather than a court singer – for whom, by long practice, rhetorical empowerment was less of an issue on the contemporary stage. And it is even possible that the unusual structures of Rinuccini's text – in particular its inbuilt repetitions noted by Tomlinson – and hence Monteverdi's discovery of his 'via naturale alla immitatione' were a result of first-hand experience of Andreini's manner of recitation.[17]

Yet with or without Andreini's influence, the lament and its aftermath must follow a prescribed course. As more light is shed both figuratively and literally on Arianna's condition, she returns to more constrained modes of feminine behaviour, increasingly adopting the corollary of female constancy, a womanly silence.[18] Although Arianna curses Teseo, she then retreats behind the conventional trope of denial, muting her imprecations: 'it is not I who let loose the harsh words: my suffering spoke, grief spoke; my tongue spoke, yes, but not my heart' ('non son quell'io che i feri detti sciolse: / parlò l'affanno mio, parlò il dolore; / parlò la lingua sì, ma non già 'l core'; ll. 846–8). More telling still, Nunzio Secondo (ll. 1032–5) describes how, when Bacco arrived and spoke to Arianna, she 'fell silent in modesty and bowed her head to the ground' ('tacque modesta e chinò a terra il ciglio'; l. 1032), blushing delicately. The chorus comments immediately on this more seemly behaviour: 'O courteous silence, the more silent by far the more eloquent' ('Oh silenzio cortese, / quanto tacito più, vie più facondo!'; ll. 1036–7). Thus Arianna's final reward is gained by denying her right to speak. She gets caught on the horns of what would fast become a typical operatic dilemma: the need to admire and respond to female eloquence coexisting with an exhortation in favour of female silence.

Apollo *(1620)*

Monteverdi wrote to Striggio on 9 February 1619 concerning an unnamed *ballo* required for performance in Mantua; in his letter of 7 March, it emerges

---

17 Godt ('I casi di Arianna', pp. 330–3) suggests that Monteverdi's original (now lost) 1608 score used some kind of schematic approach to the notation of rhythm, leaving matters freer for the performer.

18 Cusick ('"There was not one lady who failed to shed a tear"', pp. 32, 35–6) refers to the 'self-silencing' of Arianna, and hence the 'death to the self that was her proper destiny in the marriage ideology of early modern Europe'. The issue, with its profound implications for female eloquence, also underpins Heller's argument in *Chastity, Heroism, and Allure*, pp. 137–41, on which my following remarks rely.

that the text is by Striggio himself and that plans had been postponed so that the composer now had more time to write the music. Then there were the usual delays. On 19 October Monteverdi announces his plan to come to Mantua later in November to present the Seventh Book of madrigals to its dedicatee, Caterina de' Medici, Duchess of Mantua, and also to give Striggio 'the greater part (if not all)' of what he now calls the 'eclogue' (*egloga*); on 13 December he promises to complete the work as soon as the Christmas festivities at St Mark's are concluded; on 9 January 1620 he sends the 'Lament of Apollo' – the first indication of the subject-matter – and promises more music by the next post, also making suggestions for additional strophic verse for Amore to provide musical contrast, and asking what type of *ballo* will come at the end; on 16 January he sends the beginning of the work; on 1 February it emerges that there has been some confusion about whether *Apollo* is to be performed, but that Monteverdi will send all or almost all of the rest of the music by the next post, although he is still uncertain whether the final *ballo* is to involve singing; on 8 February he encloses 'the other remaining pieces of music for Your Most Illustrious Lordship's very fine and beautiful eclogue', although some music for the river-god Peneo (Peneus) is still to be written, even if Monteverdi can now get down to it, given that he knows that it is to be sung by Giovanni Amigoni; on 15 February (the same day that Monteverdi sent the 8-voice piece that was his final contribution to Marigliani's *Andromeda*) he sends the music for Peneo, which is composed *alla bastarda*, and also some left-over music for Apollo, promising that the 'little symphonies' (*sinfoniette*) will be in the next post; and on 22 February he sends the sinfonia for Amore and another for the *entrata*, also finding excuses not to come to Mantua for the performance. In his letter of 8 March we discover that the work was a success; it was also repeated, again with praise, some time in July 1620 (so he wrote on the 24th).

This sequence of letters is typical of Monteverdi when in working mode; he would write once a week in time for the post to Mantua, while the schedule of deliveries from Mantua to Venice made it possible to reply by return. In effect, *Apollo* seems to have been composed in just under two months (January–February 1620), suggesting that Monteverdi could work reasonably quickly when required (and when convinced that a performance was likely); he was helped (he said on 1 February) by the fact that the piece was very short and that he had had time to digest it. The apparent order of composition is also revealing in that it follows the scheme suggested in the discussions over *Le nozze di Tetide*: Monteverdi worked piecemeal, starting with the recitative soliloquies, including a *Lamento d'Apollo* (presumably on the pattern of the *Lamento d'Arianna*), then on the dialogues, a song for Amore, a florid song (the *alla bastarda* setting for Peneo), and finally the instrumental music. This appears to have been his normal strategy. In the case of

Marigliani's *Andromeda*, on which Monteverdi worked sporadically between 1618 and early 1620, he seems to have started with the music for the messengers (see his letters of 21 April and 21 July 1618); the last piece he sent (on 15 February 1620) was 'the 8-part song'. In the *intermedi* for Marigliani's *Le tre costanti*, the composer worked chiefly on the 'canti rappresentativi' (and for just two of the *intermedi*). And on 10 September 1627 Monteverdi told Striggio that he had already composed almost half of one *intermedio* for the Parma festivities 'and shall compose it easily because they are almost all soliloquies [*soliloqui*]'. The more generic recitatives could be composed relatively quickly, and at a distance, while in the case of choruses and dances, they were best done on site so that they could be arranged according to the space and (if necessary) the movement of the stage machines (so Monteverdi suggested in his letter of 17 April 1621 concerning *Le tre costanti*). The florid songs, on the other hand, needed knowledge of the specific singer involved. In the case of *Apollo*, this is why Monteverdi waited to write the music for Peneo, taken by the virtuoso bass, Giovanni Amigoni. But presumably Monteverdi knew from the outset who would sing the role of Apollo (Francesco Rasi or Francesco Campagnolo?) if he was able write a lament for him, and although Monteverdi's letters do not register the fact (or the role), he may have had another familiar collaborator in Virginia Andreini as Dafne.[19]

Apollo's ill-fated love for Daphne, caused by Cupid's irascible response to Apollo's vainglorious praise of his own powers as an archer in the battle against the Python, was the subject of the first opera, the Peri–Rinuccini *Dafne* (1598), and Monteverdi knew Gagliano's new setting of 1608. The story is taken largely from Ovid's *Metamorphoses*. Smitten by love, the god pursues the nymph who, to escape his clutches, is metamorphosed into a laurel tree, prompting Apollo to lament his foolhardiness and to consecrate himself to art. The Monteverdi–Striggio *Apollo* seems to have followed the broad outlines of the tale, adding to the characters the river-god Peneo (Peneus was Daphne's father), who sings just once in the piece (so the composer says on 15 February 1620). It is unclear, and Monteverdi himself seems to have been uncertain, just how the final *ballo* was to fit in the whole. On 9 January 1620 he asked Striggio to tell him 'what type of ballet [*che forma di ballo*] will have to go at the end', and on 1 February he noted that

19 Rasi, aged forty-six, was still active; see Kirkendale, *The Court Musicians in Florence during the Principate of the Medici*, p. 594. Campagnolo remained in contact with the composer; see Monteverdi's letters to Striggio of 13 March 1620 and 2 January 1627. As for Andreini, on 22 April 1623, she wrote perhaps to Striggio (Archivio Gonzaga, *busta* 2761, no. 216) referring to 'that feeble service which I then did for you who deigned to have me do [the role of] Dafne in your most gracious *balletto*' (*quella debile servitù ch'allor io le feci che si degnò farmi far la Dafne nel suo gentilissimo balletto*); see Buratelli, *Spettacoli di corte a Mantova tra Cinque e Seicento*, p. 230 n. 131.

You have only to let me know – once the verses are finished – what more I have to do, because if you wanted the *ballo*, and one sung, let Your Most Illustrious Lordship send me the words, for which I shall try (in setting them) to invent something in the metre that you give me; but should there be one metre in all the verses, I shall certainly change the tempo from time to time.[20]

Monteverdi does seem to have felt the need for some kind of conclusion to the work, as he suggests in this same letter in connection with a proposed performance in Venice (we do not know whether it took place), following a successful hearing of the *Lamento d'Apollo* there: 'If I have to compose the *ballo* for this, would Your Most Illustrious Lordship send me the verses as soon as possible? But if not, I shall add something of my own invention so that such a fine work of Your Most Illustrious Lordship's can be enjoyed.' The fact that Monteverdi later sent an *entrata* (on 22 February) suggests that there was indeed a *ballo*, although he may or may not have written the music for it, especially if it was not sung.

 The traditional place for dancing in the Apollo tale was in the battle with the Python, but if Amore enters only after Apollo's lament (as it appears from the letter of 9 January), then the piece probably did not include this first stage of the story, which in turn means that the text probably took a fair amount for granted (the tale was well enough known). Also, the letters seem to suggest that the *ballo* came at the end, after Apollo's lament and a song (presumably of celebration) for Amore, marking his entrance (we do not know when Peneo appeared). Therefore the *ballo* may just have continued the theme of the triumph of Cupid, or perhaps of Art (another conventional reading of the Apollo myth), and it was probably not integrated into the action as in the expanded *Ballo delle ingrate*. Nevertheless, *Apollo* appears to take over several elements of that work, with soliloquies and dialogue in recitative, a lament, and a prominent role for bass.

 But there are other issues prompted by Monteverdi's comments on the role of Amore. In his letter of 9 January he makes a striking suggestion to Striggio:

At the place where Amore begins to sing, I would think it a good idea if Your Most Illustrious Lordship were to add three more short verses [*versetti*] of like metre and similar sentiment, so that the same tune [*aria*] could be repeated (hoping that this touch of gladness will not produce a bad

20 Stevens (*The Letters of Claudio Monteverdi*, p. 167) misleadingly translates 'ché, se volesse il ballo e cantato' as 'if you wanted the ballet to be sung as well'. The 'principio del ballo', which Monteverdi sent Striggio on 16 January 1620, was presumably the beginning of the piece and not of its final *ballo*.

effect when it follows – by way of contrast – Apollo's previous doleful mood), and then go on as it stands, changing the manner of expression in the music, just as the text does [*mutando modo di parlare, l'armonia, come parimente fa l'orazione*].

The close association of *armonia* and *orazione*, the latter meaning the delivery of the text rather than the text *tout court*, was a central tenet of the *seconda pratica*. But here matters appear to take a different twist. Following Apollo's lament (in 'doleful mood'), Striggio seems initially to have provided a recitative for Amore beginning with three short lines (presumably *settenari*), prior to a shift in the rhetoric, presumably as Amore moved from celebration to some kind of comment. Monteverdi saw the opportunity to add three similar lines to the opening, to produce a strophic aria. The composer's claim that the harmony would therefore change its 'manner of speaking' (to translate him literally), in keeping with a change in the oration, may refer to Amore's song or to what occurs immediately after – presumably a reversion to recitative – or, for that matter, to both. But while shifts in harmony may match shifts in oration, here harmony and oration are no longer directly equivalent in the manner of the *seconda pratica*; rather, their relationship is both mediated and modified by the possibility of using different musical structures and styles. Also, and again as Monteverdi's comments suggest, Amore's song would provide both contrast and emphasis by crystallizing a particular sentiment. As we shall see in this and subsequent chapters, the issue is explored still further in Monteverdi's later stage works.

To these two musical styles in *Apollo* – recitative and aria – was then added a third, the florid song sent on 15 February:

> I am sending Your Most Illustrious Lordship the song of Peneo and the three little verses for Apollo which had slipped my mind. This song of Peneo I have composed in such a manner – like *alla bastarda* – because I know how effective such a style is when Signor Amigoni sings it. It will also serve to provide a change from the other songs [*canti*], and the distinction will appear greater if such a deity sings only once.

Virtuosic *alla bastarda* singing, involving elaborate ornamentation and passage-work over a wide vocal range, was particularly associated with bass singers. The notion of florid song for supernatural characters also harks back to the *intermedi*, and of course to *Orfeo*. Monteverdi seems to have continued the tradition in the prologue to the tournament *Mercurio e Marte*, staged in Parma in December 1628, wherein Settimia Caccini, as Aurora, 'singing the following verses with superhuman grace and an angelic voice, made the air resound and filled the entire theatre with sweetest accents', so that 'among the 10,000 people seated in the theatre, there was no one, however feeble of judgement, who did not grow tender at the trills, sigh at the sighs, become ecstatic at the ornaments, and who were not stupefied and transfixed by the miraculous beauty and song of a heavenly siren . . . '.[21] The music for the gods in *Il ritorno d'Ulisse in patria* is also close to what seems to be described here.

The 1628 Parma festivities

However, a different role sung by Settimia Caccini in Parma provides a more significant illustration of the changing roles of aria in this period. The wedding of Duke Odoardo Farnese and Margherita de' Medici, eventually celebrated in Florence on 11 October 1628 and in Parma in December, had been long in the planning (since 1615), and had been subject to a number of political vicissitudes, including the substitution of two proposed brides.[22] On 10 September 1627, Monteverdi acknowledged receipt of the commission for the entertainments from the impresario in charge, Marchese Enzo Bentivoglio from Ferrara, a prominent patron well known for his involvement in court and civic spectacle. But Monteverdi had been intriguing for the commission for at least a month before news of it appears in his letters. Also on 10 September, Monteverdi told Striggio of the commission and said that 'about six or seven applied for the appointment'; they seem to have included Sigismondo d'India from Turin, Domenico Mazzocchi from Rome, and Antonio Goretti, Alessandro Ghivizzani and possibly Giovan Battista Crivelli. However, Ghivizzani and Goretti also appear to have campaigned on behalf of Monteverdi, and the latter eventually became Monteverdi's assistant on the project. Ghivizzani's support was useful because he was the husband of the virtuoso singer who was to be the star of the show, Settimia Caccini. On the other hand, Goretti, a music-lover and instrument collector, had known Monteverdi for some thirty years: the performances of Monteverdi's madrigals in Ferrara in November 1598 which had led to the Artusi–Monteverdi controversy took place in his house. Monteverdi seems once more to have been fired with the renewed enthusiasm for the theatre typical of him in the 1620s,

21 From Buttigli's *Descritione dell'apparato* (1629), in Fabbri, *Monteverdi*, trans. Carter, p. 219.
22 The principal discussions of the 1628 Parma festivities are Lavin, 'Lettres de Parme (1618, 1627–28) et débuts du théâtre baroque'; Reiner, 'Preparations in Parma'; Nagler, *Theatre Festivals of the Medici*, pp. 139–61; Fabbri, *Monteverdi*, trans. Carter, pp. 206–19; Mamczarz, *Le Théâtre farnese de Parme*. Most of the Bentivoglio correspondence now appears in Fabris, *Mecenati e musici*. The texts of the prologue, *intermedi* and tournament, originally printed separately, are edited in Solerti, *Musica, ballo e drammatica alla corte medicea dal 1600 al 1637*, pp. 411–518. The following discussion draws upon my 'Intriguing Laments', where fuller details can be found.

which also caused him some embarrassment with Striggio, who, so the letters suggest, was starting to suspect him of double-dealing. The composer may also have enjoyed working for a duke again. For all his apparent satisfaction with life in Venice (so he regularly told Striggio), Monteverdi was not averse to the prospect of working at another court: he was strongly attracted by the idea of moving to work for Prince Władisław (later, King Władisław Sigismund IV) of Poland in 1623;[23] and we have already seen his eagerness (partly for the ulterior motive of his pension) to forge links with the Habsburgs. He reported that he was delighted with his reception in Parma, and, much to the consternation of the Procurators of St Mark's, he engineered at least three extended stays there, from late October to mid-December 1627, mid-January to March 1628, and for the performances themselves. During the second of these stays, he also wrote a madrigal for two castratos (Antonio Grimano and Gregorio Lazzarini), a bass and various instruments, for a Carnival *mascherata* based on the theme of Jason and the Argonauts.

His main competitor for the Parma commission was Sigismondo d'India, whose path had already crossed Monteverdi's. D'India had been dismissed in 1623 from his position as *maestro di musica da camera* to Carlo Emanuele I, Duke of Savoy, because (he claimed) of malicious gossip from courtiers, and had then pursued a roving career in Modena and Rome. After making preliminary contact with Bentivoglio on 26 August 1627, d'India sent him on 2 September two sample works to demonstrate his theatrical abilities, a *Lamento d'Armida* and a *Lamento di Didone*. In the letter sent with this music, he also noted that he had been involved in finishing the music for Mazzocchi's opera *La catena d'Adone* (performed in Rome on 12 February 1626) because of the inadequacies of its composer, and that the *Lamento di Didone* was an ideal vehicle for Settimia Caccini, whom Bentivoglio might hear sing it in Florence. The choice of texts is revealing: Monteverdi was currently working on *Armida abbandonata*, and a Dido was indeed to appear in the 1628 *intermedi*. D'India's *Lamento d'Armida* is lost, although his *Lamento di Didone*, to a text by the composer himself, was published, together with other laments for Jason and Olimpia, in his *Le musiche . . . da cantarsi nel chitarrone, clavicembalo, arpa doppia, & altri stromenti da corpo . . . libro quinto* (Venice, Alessandro Vincenti, 1623).[24] D'India's previous collection of songs, *Le musiche . . . a una et due voci . . . libro quarto* (Venice, Alessandro Vincenti, 1621), had also included laments for Apollo and for Orpheus, again echoing Monteverdi

23 See Parisi, 'New Documents Concerning Monteverdi's Relations with the Gonzagas', pp. 503–7.
24 The *Lamento di Didone* is in d'India, *Le musiche a una e due voci*, ed. Joyce, ii, pp. 295–304. Like the *Lamento d'Arianna*, it was also arranged for five voices (the alto part is in Modena, Biblioteca Estense, F1530).

(whose *Lamento d'Apollo* had recently been heard in Venice); this is also the book with the setting of Clorinda's death-scene from *Gerusalemme liberata*, discussed in Chapter 7. These laments are largely expressive recitatives in the manner of Monteverdi's *Lamento d'Arianna*, which was published twice as a chamber monody in the same year as d'India's *Le musiche . . . libro quinto*.[25] D'India's choice of style can hardly be coincidental. Mazzocchi's *La catena d'Adone* had been notable for its introduction of so-called 'mezz'arie' which 'break the tedium of the recitative' (*rompono il tedio del recitativo*).[26] D'India told Bentivoglio on 2 September, however, that he felt that Mazzocchi's reliance on 'canzonette' had been detrimental to the whole. The argument thus starts to hinge on the respective roles of recitative and aria in theatrical composition. D'India's conservative stance was clear, but the 1628 Dido, to Monteverdi's music, seems to have gone in a different direction.

The odds were against d'India, who was famously unpopular with musicians, largely because of his inflated ego, or so Goretti said to Bentivoglio in a letter of 13 August that sought to pre-empt and prevent his appointment. Ghivizzani also entered the discussion, claiming that he was as good a composer as d'India, and that his wife, Settimia Caccini, would sing only Monteverdi's music. Thus it was almost inevitable that Monteverdi would gain the commission for the prologue (*Teti e Flora*, by Claudio Achillini) and five *intermedi* (by Ascanio Pio di Savoia, Enzo Bentivoglio's son-in-law) for Tasso's *Aminta*, which would be performed in a temporary theatre erected in the courtyard of S. Pietro Martire in the confines of the ducal palace on 13 December 1628. He was also to provide music for the large-scale tournament *Mercurio e Marte* (again, by Achillini), to mark the long-delayed opening of the Teatro Farnese on the 21st. This comprised over 1,000 lines of verse, so Monteverdi wrote on 4 February 1628 (exaggerating only slightly, to judge by the printed text). Planning the tournament also gave him yet another opportunity for his curious, perhaps temporizing, musings on the difficulties of representing unusual situations in music. As he wrote to Bentivoglio on 18 September 1627,

> I have, however, taken a quick glance at the Months and how they speak, and I have also looked at Discord. I have also thought a little about the

---

25 Another *Lamento d'Arianna* (to a text by Marino) was also published by
    Bartolomeo Magni in 1623, in Pellegrino Possenti's *Canora sampogna*; while
    Francesco Costa's setting of Rinuccini's text (there are also numerous others)
    appeared in his *Pianta d'Arianna: Madrigali e scherzi . . . a voce sola* (Venice,
    Alessandro Vincenti, 1626). For the broader repertory, see Porter, '*Lamenti recitativi
    da camera*'.
26 The comment comes from a note in the score of *La catena d'Adone* (Venice,
    Alessandro Vincenti, 1626); see Reiner '"Vi sono molt'altre mezz'arie . . ."';
    Gianturco, 'Nuove considerazioni su *il tedio del recitativo* delle prime opere romane'.

representation of the aforementioned Discord, and it seems to me that it will be a little difficult. The reason is this: since the Months have to sing together in mellow harmony – and I shall seek out the kind that will provide the most plausible representation of each – I am going to assign the opposite kind of music to Discord (I mean opposite to that which is suitable for the Months). I cannot for the moment think of anything else but to have her declaim in speech and not in music.

This however is a first thought, which I wanted to let Your Most Illustrious Excellency know about, so that with your most refined judgement you can assist my ability the better to serve Your Most Illustrious Excellency's pleasure, which I desire with all my heart. Yet I would not deny that those speeches of the aforementioned Discord might be intensified by music; that is, she would have to speak just as if she were actually singing, but this singing of hers would not, however, be based on any instrumental harmony, and this (it seems to me) would be the way to represent Discord.

The Parma festivities were the most onerous theatrical endeavour of Monteverdi's career. He must have been hard pressed, even with the capable assistance of Antonio Goretti, whose responsibility was to make fair copies of the music and generally chivvy along a composer too much inclined to lengthy discussion and post-prandial naps. Monteverdi also needed to be on site to manage the often recalcitrant singers,[27] to co-ordinate the rehearsals, and to resolve the conflicting demands of music and staging, and in particular, where to position the instruments – eventually, in a box in front of the stage – so as to be heard by the singers and yet not interfere with the machinery. Given the huge amount of music to compose both for the *intermedi* and for the tournament, it is quite remarkable that he had completed four of the *intermedi* by the end of November 1627 (so Goretti told Bentivoglio in his letter of 20 November), even if Goretti's earlier hope (expressed to Bentivoglio on 5 November) that all five would be finished before Christmas proved too optimistic. It was also no doubt fortunate that, as usual with princely weddings, delays in the negotiations led to postponement of the festivities. As for the performances, the circumstances were less than happy.

---

27 On 28 October 1627, Antonio Goretti told Enzo Bentivoglio that 'these singers are a pretentious bunch, to the extent that we are amazed'; see Fabbri, *Monteverdi*, trans. Carter, p. 209. Goretti also complained about Settimia Caccini to Bentivoglio on 2 November 1627 – 'she is unlikely to have the success one believes, since she does not let the words be understood well' (*non debba fare quella riuscita che si crede, non lasciando bene intendere le parole*) – and discussed plans to bring in her elder sister, Francesca (who had recently remarried and was living in Lucca), although the two are 'mortal enemies' (*nemiche mortali*); see Mamczarz, *Le Théâtre farnese de Parme*, pp. 463–4.

According to the Florentine courtier Luigi Inghirami, the wedding guests suffered from the December snow, fog, rain and freezing temperatures.[28] In the courtyard theatre with its thin canvas roof, few paid serious attention to *Aminta*; indeed, the ducal party left to take refreshment during the third act. The play was too well known and thus regarded as an unwise choice; and the actors found it hard to project their speeches above the coughing and sneezing in the audience, and the sound of feet stamping to keep warm. Yet Inghirami roundly praises the stage machinery, and notes that the prologue, *Teti e Flora*, was performed 'with rare music and exquisite voices, this being the work of Monteverdi, today the best musician of Italy' (*con musiche rare e voci squisite, essendo composizione di Monteverdi, oggi il migliore musico d'Italia*).

Monteverdi's involvement in *intermedi* dated back at least to the 1598 performance of Guarini's *Il pastor fido*, and he had composed music for those associated with Guarini's *L'idropica* in 1608. Similarly, he was not averse to Agnelli's *Le nozze di Tetide* once he discovered that it was not to be an opera, even making some constructive suggestions about its conclusion (so he wrote to Striggio on 6 January 1617) in terms of adding a sung *ballo*, with

> a canzonetta in praise of the most serene princely bridal pair, the music of which could be heard in the heaven and earth of the stage, and to which the noble dancers can dance, since a noble ending of this kind seems to me suitable to a noble scene such as I have proposed. And if at the same time you could accommodate to a dance measure the lines which the Nereids have to sing (to the tempo of which you could make expert dancers dance gracefully), it seems to me that it would be a much more suitable thing.

More recently, Monteverdi had been involved in the *intermedi* for Ercole Marigliani's comedy *Le tre costanti*, staged on 18 January 1622 during the festivities for the wedding of Eleonora Gonzaga and Emperor Ferdinand II. Plans for the wedding (performed by proxy on 21 November 1621) had been made with some secrecy and the celebrations were meant to be subdued, although according to Gabriele Bertazzolo's description of the events,[29] Duke Ferdinando Gonzaga felt that it was inappropriate to pass over the occasion in silence, so at short notice he had arranged, for successive days, a ball, a comedy with fifty machines in the *intermedi* (before an audience of 5,000), and then a firework display (one of Bertazzolo's specialities). Monteverdi's

---

28 Inghirami wrote four letters reporting on the festivities to Archduchess Maria Magdalena in Florence; see Minucci del Rosso, 'Le nozze di Margherita de' Medici con Odoardo Farnese Duca di Parma e Piacenza'.

29 See Bertazzolo, *Breve relatione dello sposalitio* (1622; the dedication to Carlo Gonzaga, Duke of Nevers, is dated 22 February 1622). For the *intermedi*, relevant extracts are in Fabbri, *Monteverdi*, trans. Carter, pp. 181–2.

involvement in the commission seems to have begun in March 1621 (so the notice was not so short): on the 5th, he wrote to Duchess Caterina acknowledging a request to send unspecified music to Marigliani, and on 17 April he confirms to Marigliani that he was to work only on certain 'canti rappresentativi', 'since with regard to certain others (which ought to have a definite order and duration for as long as the machines are operating), you have been pleased to give this task to those gentlemen composers who are on hand'; he also notes that he has until September to produce the music. Surprisingly true to his word – presumably because he was expecting the Duchess of Mantua to support the admission of his son, Massimiliano, to study in Bologna – on 10 September he sent part of the third *intermedio* to Marigliani, and on 27 November he tells the duchess that he had sent Marigliani the music for the *licenza* by the previous post; he also offers further help 'in the matter of scoring for the instruments in symphonies and in the various vocal dispositions'.

The broad theme of the 1622 *intermedi* was the conflict of Heavenly and Earthly Love, seen in the tales of Hercules and Omphale (after Act I; a garden scene), Neptune and Amphitrite (after Act II; a sea scene), Boreas and Oreithyia (after Act III; rocky mountains and aerial scenes), and Pluto and Proserpine (after Act IV; the Inferno and the Elysian Fields), ending with a triumph of Heavenly Love. According to Bertazzolo:

> The third *intermedio* was staged among rocky mountains, from which there seemed to appear thick clouds. In their middle was imitated with so artful a manner a torrent, which left the onlookers doubting whether it was feigned or no. The story which served for this *intermedio* was the love of Boreas for Oreithyia. But because he raped her through the wiles of Cupid, he could not reach his end until an honest betrothal between them was fixed by Hymen on the order of Heavenly Love. One saw in this *intermedio* a dance of flying winds, during which it snowed endlessly. And once the winds had left, Apollo calmed the air, who on a chariot drawn by four steeds brought a most beautiful splendour; and thus the *intermedio* ended.

Then

> The *licenza* after the last act of the comedy represented a triumph of Cupid accompanied by a multitude of lovers, who made a most beautiful dance. Meanwhile, the triumphal [Heavenly] Love appeared from heaven accompanied by the Graces, Mars, Apollo, Mercury and Venus, all in their machines in due proportion and in their separate places. Love called on Jove to revenge the outrage and arrogance of Cupid, whence he, appearing in majesty in a large heaven, with a large following of gods and carried forward by a large eagle, cast a lightning bolt at Cupid, who suddenly

disappeared beneath the stage, and with Jove, the Graces and all the other deities singing the praises of Heavenly Love, Cupid's followers repeated the same praise, and the *licenza* ended.

At a further signal from the trumpets, there descended from heaven a large coat of arms of the most august house of Austria, surrounded by four eagles, the sign of the most serene house of Gonzaga, and by six orbs entwined with them, representing the arms of the most serene house of Tuscany. There also arose from the earth a large tablet, on which was a motto 'Aeterno stabunt tempore' ['They will stand for eternal time'], and the entertainment was ended, leaving all most comforted by the admirable spectacle.

Although the Parma *intermedi* had similar features, they seem to have been more operatic in design, such that Monteverdi was concerned (in his letter to Bentivoglio of 25 September 1627) that they would not suit a large space and an *intermedio*-type staging. Their subjects were Ruggiero and Bradamante, Dido and Aeneas, Diana victorious over Venus and Cupid, Jason and the Argonauts, and the appearance of the four continents and the gods (prefacing a brief tournament itself heralding *Mercurio e Marte*). This combination of themes typically exploited mythology, classical sources (Virgil) and Renaissance epic (Ariosto and Tasso), to generate the range of princely encomiums, spectacular settings (landscape, sea scene, inferno, the heavens) and stage machines conventional of the genre.[30] But the texts consist primarily of soliloquies (see Monteverdi's comment to Striggio on 10 September 1627) and dialogues, with none of the large choruses or sung *balli* conventionally associated with *intermedi*. In that sense, at least, each *intermedio* comes close to being an operatic episode.

The second *intermedio* merits closer study, not least because of the apparent, if partial, precedent of d'India's sample lament. Monteverdi seems to have begun work on it early in the proceedings: in his letter to Bentivoglio of 18 September 1627, he says that he is hoping to send 'the intermezzo of *Dido* in its entirety' on the forthcoming Saturday, although on 30 October he admits that it is still not finished.[31] The story comes from Virgil, with accre-

---

30   A number of the stage effects used in Parma in 1628 drew on entertainments planned for the original opening of the Teatro Farnese in 1618, including in the second *intermedio* the appearance of the dragon and the descent of Iris (although Dido and Aeneas were not part of the subject-matter). This second *intermedio* also seems to have some connection with a set of *intermedi* by Battista Guarini, reworking Tasso's Armida story, which Guarini provided for Enzo Bentivoglio(!) in 1612; see Carter, 'Intriguing Laments', p. 53 n. 44.

31   However, on 24 October 1627 the stage designer Francesco Guitti reported to Bentivoglio that the Carthage set was almost complete; see Mamczarz, *Le Théâtre farnese de Parme*, p. 125.

tions drawing upon Ariosto and Tasso. The scene represents Carthage in the process of construction, with the sea in the distance. Aeneas enters with Achates; Mercury descends to urge Aeneas to fulfil his destiny in Italy (l. 16); Aeneas wishes to take farewell of Dido, and Mercury tells Achates to lead the fleet offshore to await Aeneas' arrival; Ascanius looks forward to triumphs in Italy (l. 81); Fame descends with two trumpets in hand and accuses Aeneas of treachery (l. 127); Dido argues with Aeneas (l. 151); Juno expresses her sympathy for Dido (l. 212); Dido enters with Aeneas' sword in hand and accuses her lover, who makes his escape flying overhead on a dragon (l. 238); Dido curses Aeneas, laments her fate, and resolves to die (l. 294); and Iris descends on a cloud to pronounce the moral of the tale to the ladies of the audience, that is, to beware the fate of 'wretched Dido' (ll. 362–74).

This conclusion is conventional enough both within the *intermedio* tradition and in terms of contemporary perceptions of Dido. Similarly, the accretions to Virgil sit squarely within this theatrical context and serve to increase the scenic possibilities: witness the descent not just of Mercurio (following the *Aeneid*) but also of Fama, Giunone and Iride. Enea's escape by dragon is part of the same trend, but it also evokes other resonances: Mercurio arranges the dragon's appearance 'dal mauritano Atlante' (l. 73), a reference to the African necromancer in Ariosto's *Orlando furioso* who also appears in the first of the 1628 *intermedi*. Other comments by Mercurio further associate 'effeminato Enea' (l. 16) with those famous Renaissance heroes seduced from the path of duty by women–magicians, Ariosto's Ruggiero and Tasso's Rinaldo. Didone, on the other hand, is explicitly equated with Rinaldo's captress, the pagan Armida. When she curses Enea, her invective keeps returning to 'Vattene pur . . .' ('. . . fellone', '. . . o crudo', etc.): the poet seals the reference to Armida's 'Vattene pur, crudel, con quella pace' (*Gerusalemme liberata*, XVI.59) with a direct quotation, 'tanto t'agitarò quanto t'amai' ('I will harass you as much as I loved you'), which recurs as a refrain.[32] Monteverdi had already set Tasso's text in his Third Book of madrigals of 1592, and presumably it formed part of the now lost *Armida abbandonata*. But the association of Didone with Armida is still more striking, given d'India's two laments submitted to Bentivoglio on 2 September 1627. It also turns Virgil's heroine into a type much closer to one late Renaissance notion of the feminine: the lamenting, perhaps mad, woman betrayed and abandoned by her lover.

Monteverdi himself remarked (to Bentivoglio on 25 September 1627) on the 'many and varied speeches' (*molte e variate orazioni*) in the Parma

---

32   The quotation is extended in the second strophe: 'Nova furia co' serpi, ove sarai, / tanto t'agitarò quanto t'amai' (ll. 304–5; compare Tasso's 'Nova furia, co' serpi e con la face / tanto t'agitarò quanto t'amai' in *Gerusalemme liberata*, XVI.59).

intermedi,[33] and in the second *intermedio* this variety extends even to the verse structure in several striking ways. In particular, the 7- and 11-syllable *versi sciolti* typical of stage recitative (and of d'India's text for his *Lamento di Didone*) are interspersed with regular strophic units, often with refrains. The text of the first part of the *intermedio* includes strophic structures for Ascanio (three stanzas mixing *settenari* and *quinari* with a final *endecasillabo* refrain; one is reminded of Telemaco in *Il ritorno d'Ulisse in patria*, II.1), Fama (three stanzas of *endecasillabi* and *settenari*), Didone (two *ottava rima* stanzas) and Giunone (four stanzas of *endecasillabi*, each ending with a *quinario*). The second half (from l. 238) is still more involved. Here Didone has a series of strophic texts: 'Ferma tu pure, o mio Signore, il volo' ('Stay, o my lord, your flight') in four 7-line stanzas (separated by freer speeches for Enea), each with the refrain 'O core del mio cor, riedi, deh riedi' ('O heart of my heart, return, ah return'); 'Vattene pur, fellone' ('Go then, villain'), in four 6-line stanzas, each with the refrain 'tanto t'agitarò quanto t'amai' taken from *Gerusalemme liberata*; and then 'Ma l'empio se n'è gito' ('But the wicked one has gone'), with the refrain 'Ché più tardo a morire?' ('Why do I delay my death any longer?'), the verse of which starts as if strophic but then dissolves into looser structures. To be sure, refrains were by no means unusual in laments, and Dido's speeches shift conventionally enough from accusation, to curses and remorse, to resignation. But in terms of structure, at least, this is no *Lamento d'Arianna*, nor, for that matter, a *Lamento di Didone* as d'India construed it.

In fact, the text suggests a different model. Some time before 1614, Ottavio Rinuccini had written a lament for a nymph abandoned by her lover, 'Non havea Febo ancora', of which Monteverdi included a setting (titled *Lamento della ninfa*) in the *Madrigali guerrieri, et amorosi* of 1638; there had been earlier musical settings by Antonio Brunelli (in 1614, for solo voice and continuo), Girolamo Kapsberger (in 1619, for two voices and continuo) and Giovanni Battista Piazza (in 1633, for solo voice and continuo).[34] The content of Rinuccini's poem is conventional enough: a narrator sets the context (and the time, just before dawn, as with Arianna), the nymph laments, and the narrator concludes with a moral against placing too much faith in love. But the structure is unusual: ten 4-line stanzas in *settenari piani* and *tronchi*, each with an additional refrain in *ottonari tronchi* ('Miserella, ah più, no, no, / tanto giel soffrir non può'; 'Wretched girl, ah no, no, no more can she suffer such coldness'). In Monteverdi's miniature scene, the narration (for three shepherds) is

---

33 Stevens translates 'orazioni' as 'soliloquies', although it is likely that Monteverdi means it in a broader sense (see the discussion of *Apollo*, above), perhaps even extending to different modes of musical speech.

34 For the sources and Piazza's setting (of just the first stanza), see Carter, '*Possente spirto*'. Kapsberger's setting is transcribed in Whenham, *Duet and Dialogue in the Age of Monteverdi*, ii, pp. 332–3.

in a declamatory duple time, while the nymph's central lament – labelled 'rappresentativo' in the Eighth Book and directed to be sung freely to match the emotion (*al tempo dell'affetto*) – is in triple time over a ground bass repeating a descending tetrachord, the emblem of lament.[35] In this central episode, the shepherds continue to pass comment (via the refrain), but it is the solo nymph who holds centre-stage.

In the *Lamento della ninfa*, the use of aria for the nymph instead of recitative has been construed as an overly feminized rhetoric of seduction or as a signifier of madness.[36] The singing of strophic canzonettas had long been associated with madness in the contemporary theatre. For example, in the *commedia dell'arte* performance of *La pazzia d'Isabella* in 1589, a prototype of dramatic mad scenes, Isabella Andreini 'as a madwoman went running through the city, stopping now one person and now another, and speaking now in Spanish, now in Greek, now in Italian and many other languages, but all without reason, and among other things she began to speak French and to sing certain canzonettas in the French style . . .'.[37] Monteverdi, too, had recently considered the representation of (feigned) madness in the theatre while working on *La finta pazza Licori*. In his letter to Striggio of 22 May 1627, confirming the decision to set Giulio Strozzi's libretto, he said that he would encourage the poet ('as is my habit') to enrich his text with 'varied, novel and diverse scenes' and 'other novelties', so that 'each time [Licori] comes on stage she can always produce new moods and fresh changes of music [*novi gusti e nove differenze di armonie*], as indeed of gestures'. Didone, too, appears to go mad as she is directed to leave 'furiosa' to commit suicide. Representing madness required a loosening of the conventional constraints upon genres and styles appropriate for particular character-types. This not only served the cause of verisimilitude but also provided a convenient justification

---

35 The term derives from Rosand, 'The Descending Tetrachord', but note the caveat in Carter, 'Resemblance and Representation', p. 129. For other laments involving strophic or otherwise structured verse, see the discussion in Holzer, *Music and Poetry in Seventeenth-Century Rome*, pp. 52–60, 307–21; idem, ' "Sono d'altro garbo . . . le canzonette che si cantano oggi" '.

36 Principally in McClary, 'Excess and Frame'.

37 Giuseppe Pavoni, *Diario . . . delle feste nelle solennissime nozze delli serenissimi sposi il sig. duca Ferdinando Medici e la sig. donna Christina di Lorena* (Bologna, Giovanni Rossi, 1589), pp. 29–30, cited in Fabbri, 'On the Origins of an Operatic Topos', p. 164: 'come pazza se n'andava scorrendo per la cittade, fermando or questo ed ora quello, e parlando ora in spagnuolo, ora in greco, ora in italiano, e molti altri linguaggi, ma tutti fuori di proposito, e tra le altre cose si mise a parlar francese et a cantar certe canzonette pure alla francese'. See also MacNeil, 'The Divine Madness of Isabella Andreini'. Fabbri charts the whole range of signifiers of madness in seventeenth-century opera: unusual musical behaviour figures prominently.

for musical variety and, indeed, excitement, as women gave voice to sounds transgressing the boundaries of decorum.

The burning question, of course, is how Didone's texts were set to music, and to what extent they might have provided 'new moods and fresh changes of music' on the model of *La finta pazza Licori*. Her strophic texts with refrains strongly imply that the poetry requires a musical style in some way more structured than recitative, which may have been achieved by a more formal arioso style, perhaps involving strophic variation, and/or by invoking duple-/triple-time aria styles; contemporary Venetian songbooks provide a range of such possibilities.[38] The notion that Monteverdi made at least some reference to aria styles in his writing for Didone would certainly be consistent with his remarks on Licori, with the idea that he was somehow responding to a challenge from d'India, and also with apparent trends both in Venetian secular music and in his own later works, as aria, and the musical styles associated with it, increasingly gained aesthetic credibility as a significant means of emotional arousal.

Proserpina rapita *(1630)*

Proserpina rapita was Monteverdi's first wholly theatrical work to be written within and for a Venetian environment and known to have been completed and performed.[39] It was commissioned by Girolamo Mocenigo, patron of the *Combattimento di Tancredi e Clorinda*, to celebrate the wedding on 16 April 1630 of his daughter Giustiniana to Lorenzo Giustiniani (of the family on whose behalf Monteverdi had negotiated with Giovanni Battista Andreini in 1622). According to Girolamo Priuli,

> Ser Girolamo Mocenigo . . . held a most solemn and extraordinary banquet for the relatives and friends, with truly royal trappings, giving them in the meal that was prepared meat and fish, and cold and hot dishes – all that

---

38 I discuss a representative example, Giovanni Pietro Berti's 'Da grave incendio oppresso', from his *Cantade et arie . . . libro secondo* (Venice, Alessandro Vincenti, 1627), in 'Intriguing Laments', pp. 59–61. Vol. 6 of *Italian Secular Song 1606–1636*, ed. Tomlinson, contains facsimiles of a number of other Venetian songbooks with useful examples.

39 See Abert, *Claudio Monteverdi und das musikalische Drama*, pp. 130–1; Zoppelli, 'Il rapto perfettissimo' (discussing a contemporary account by Girolamo Priuli); Fabbri, *Monteverdi*, trans. Carter, pp. 221–3. The libretto survives in two editions, the first of 1630 and a second of 1644 (*Proserpina rapita, drama di Giulio Strozzi, honorato già di musica dal Monteverde. Seconda impressione* (Venice, Pietro Miloco)). I have only been able to consult the latter, but except for the title-page it would seem to contain the same text as the first.

could be offered – with four or five servings of confections, both regaling the dishes and as *intermedi* between one and the other courses. After this meal there was dancing until the 24th hour [i.e., sunset], and then in the evening with torches there was recited and represented in music (something the like of which had never been seen) *Il rapimento di Proserpina*, with most perfect voices and instruments, with aerial apparitions, scene changes and other things, to the astonishment and wonder of all those present. The banquet was held in the house where he lives and which he owns on the Calle delle Rasse on the lower floor, and on the upper floor owned by Messer Gritto there was represented the play which was invented by Signor Giulio Strozzi, Florentine, a virtuous person living in this city, and the music was the work of Monteverde, famous *maestro di cappella* of the ducal chapel, and the French Dukes of Roan and Candales were there with singular satisfaction and also equal admiration.

Giulio Strozzi had been associated with Monteverdi at least since 1621 – they were both involved in the commemorations by the Florentine community in Venice of the death of Grand Duke Cosimo II de' Medici – and they had collaborated on *La finta pazza Licori*, when Monteverdi noted to Striggio (on 7 May 1627) that Strozzi was 'desiring beyond all measure to see it set to music by me, and rejoicing to see his most honoured works clothed with my modest music'. Strozzi was also the author of the sonnet–cycle *I cinque fratelli*, set by Monteverdi in honour of the visit to Venice of the new Grand Duke of Tuscany, Ferdinando II, and his brother in 1628.

A libretto of *Proserpina rapita* was published by Evangelista Deuchino on the day of its performance (so says the dedication from Deuchino to Girolamo Mocenigo). The precise location may have been the same as that of the *Combattimento di Tancredi e Clorinda*, although the room now seems to have been set up as a proper theatre: Deuchino's dedication refers to scenery by Gioseppe Schioppi (i.e., Giuseppe Alabardi) and choreography by Girolamo Scolari, and both the libretto and Priuli's account suggest a significant number of scenic effects that, whether separately or together, would seem to go beyond the capacities of a simple salon. The printed libretto contains a number of direct and indirect references to music, and also to the staging, but just a small part of the music survives, the 3–voice canzonetta 'Come dolce hoggi l'auretta' published in Monteverdi's posthumous Ninth Book of madrigals (1651).

There are no act or scene divisions in the libretto, but the action falls (by virtue of entrances and exits) into a prologue, twelve scenes and an epilogue. The plot elaborates upon the well-known story of Pluto and Proserpine and is yet another of the mythical rapes associated with wedding entertainments destined both to proclaim the power of love and to set proper

bounds on female behaviour: the tale had already been told in the first of the
1608 Mantuan *intermedi* (with music by Salamone Rossi), and also in the
fourth of those of 1622.[40] After a chorus urging the descent of the curtain,
and the prologue delivered by Imeneo (Hymen), Proserpina is seen in a
pastoral setting (in Sicily), accompanied by the nymphs Aretusa and Ciane
(scene 1). They sing of the delights of nature, but Proserpina is uneasy in her
heart (for reasons as yet unclear); Ciane urges them to gather flowers but
Proserpina fears being bitten by a snake. Pachino and his companion Anapo
appear singing a hymn to love (scene 2); Pachino is enamoured of Proserpina, but she scorns him (scene 3) and he is left to lament his fate (scene 4).
Anapo asks why he is weeping and urges him to seek intercession from on
high (scene 5), but Pachino decides instead to invoke Plutone (scene 6), who
appears as the earth rumbles (scene 7). Plutone promises to free Pachino from
his love for Proserpina (because she is worthy of a divine consort), and does
so by turning him into a mountain at the touch of his sceptre, promising that
his soul will live in Elysium. He then sees Proserpina coming and hides to
admire her beauty from a distance. Venere appears in a cloud with Amore
(scene 8); she urges him to strike Plutone with a dart. Proserpina, Ciane and
Aretusa remark on the darkening sky, and Aretusa urges four shepherds to
dance while they sing (scene 9). Aretusa sees a god emerging from Mount
Etna; it is Plutone (scene 10). Aretusa flees; Ciane tries to defend Proserpina
but is turned into a spring (*fontana*). Proserpina resists Plutone but then
submits to her fate; Plutone orders the gates of Hades to open and the
infernal spirits to pay homage to his new queen. Anapo complains about the
terrible darkness and other inauspicious auguries (scene 11); Pachino (now a
mountain) and Ciane (a spring) call out to him and urge him not to be sad,
for they are in Elysium. Anapo seeks news of Proserpina so that he can tell
Ceres (Proserpina's mother); Ciane eventually reveals the story but urges
Anapo to keep silent; Anapo says that he cannot do so, and Pachino turns
him into a river – as a result, the three will be together for ever. Plutone
enters with Proserpina and says that now he has made her a woman in his
bed, she can take the sceptre and diadem to become Queen of Hades (scene
12). Proserpina vows obedience to him; Plutone says that he must leave on
other business, but that Proserpina should stay for the celebrations. Anapo,

40   It was also the subject of Giulio Cesare Monteverdi's only opera, *Il rapimento di
     Proserpina* (libretto by Ercole Marigliani), staged by Prince Francesco Gonzaga in
     Casale Monferrato on 29 April 1611; see the extracts from the *Breve descrittione delle
     feste* . . . (Casale, Pantaleone Goffi, 1611) in Solerti, *Gli albori del melodramma*, i,
     pp. 157–61; Data, 'Il "Rapimento di Proserpina" di Giulio Cesare Monteverdi e le
     feste a Casale nel 1611'. Both the text and the music are lost, although from the
     description there would seem to be no relationship between this work and the
     1630 one save the subject-matter.

Ciane and Pachino sing in Proserpina's honour, introducing a dance of blessed spirits, and Proserpina invites the company to join her in the Elysian Fields. Imeneo has the *licenza*: the audience has seen Plutone soften, and he will no longer deal harshly with lovers – such is the power of women, who rule the world with their beauty.

In the first edition of the libretto, Strozzi calls the work an 'anatopismo',[41] although the term is dropped in the second edition, where *Proserpina rapita* is simply a 'drama'. He also fills his libretto and its associated performance instructions with a welter of Hellenistic references, in particular to the ancient modes, to classical poetic–musical genres and to instrumentation. Thus the libretto gives the following details: p. 6, 'Paranetic Acclamation with Phrygian harmony, enthusiastic, that is, aroused and vehement, sung in the theatre by two full choruses before the curtain fell' ('Scenda omai la cortina: e ché si tarda?', for two choirs; ABABCC, three stanzas); p. 7, the prologue 'sung by Imeneo and partitioned by a most lively sinfonia in choreographic rhythm, that is, in a dance-style; and Imeneo descends from the sky on a golden eagle full of roses, alluding to the arms of the wedding couple, Giustiniani and Mozzenigo' ('Dall'alta, augusta, adamantina rocca'; ABBA, seven stanzas); pp. 12–13, 'Parthenian canzonetta sung by the three nymphs with Lydian harmony, that is, in soft sound and suitable for children' ('Come dolce hoggi l'auretta'; $a^8b^{8t}a^4b^{8t}$, four stanzas); pp. 15–16, 'Pachino and Anapo come from afar singing together this beginning of a hymn to Love, which the Greeks called *prosodio*, and it was delivered by them while walking to the sound of an aulos, that is, of a pipe or other wind instrument' ('La pargoletta acerba'; abaB, four stanzas); p. 22, 'Pachino with Mixolydian harmony accompanied only by the *lira* players unfolds his lament called threnody by the ancient Greeks' ('Misero esempio di schernito amante'; *versi sciolti*); pp. 29–30, '*Ballo della crudeltà* danced by four shepherds and sung by the three nymphs to the full *lira [a piena lira]*' ('Il valor d'ogni beltà'; $a^{8t}b^8b^8a^{8t}$, four stanzas), preceded by an invitation to the dance by Aretusa; p. 34, 'Chorus of infernal deities – Minos, Eaco, Radamanto, Cloto, Lachesi and Atropo [Minos, Aeacus, Rhadamanthys, Clotho, Lachesis, Atropos] with six other spirits – who dance to their song an infernal dance sounded by the aulos players, or wind instrumentalists' ('Chi mai costei sarà'; three 6-line stanzas in *settenari piani* and *tronchi*); p. 42, 'Dance of blessed spirits' ('Su, su, beati amanti'; abbc', four

---

41 The meaning remains unclear, although Strozzi appears to have been fond of such Hellenistic titles: his earlier *Il natal di Amore* (a fourth edition was published in Venice by Evangelista Deuchino in 1629) was called an 'anacronismo'. The librettist of *Le nozze d'Enea in Lavinia* uses the term 'anatopismo' in one literal sense ('misplacement') when justifying his having figured Vulcan's forge in Latium (see *Composing Opera*, ed. Szweykowski and Carter, pp. 164–5). But it is hard to see what is misplaced in *Proserpina rapita*.

stanzas, with additional 3-line refrain). The *licenza* for Imeneo (p. 44) is also strophic ('Buona nuova, o mortali, han gli occhi vostri'; ABBA, three stanzas).

The classicizing tendencies are not unusual for Strozzi: his account of the music for the 1621 ceremonies commemorating Grand Duke Cosimo II de' Medici has similar references, as we saw in Chapter 7. But there is not much evidence that Monteverdi consciously altered his musical language to deal with them: the one surviving piece from *Proserpina rapita*, 'Come dolce hoggi l'auretta', is in a pastoral G major that may be 'in soft sound and suitable for children', but which is only tenuously Lydian, if at all. The classical framework may have had some impact on the instrumentation: the hymn to love accompanied by a 'pipe or other wind instrument'; the lament accompanied by *lira* players (presumably represented by viols or *viole da braccio*, as with the *Lamento d'Arianna*); the *Ballo della crudeltà* accompanied by the 'full *lira*'; the infernal spirits dancing to the sound of wind instruments. However, almost all of these conventional associations can also be found in, say, *Orfeo*.

The presence of such well-characterized musical episodes is further argument for the increasing ascendance of aria-related styles over recitative. These episodes also led Paolo Fabbri to suggest that *Proserpina rapita* may not have been sung throughout, although other indications in the libretto reveal that it was. Thus Proserpina, Aretusa and Ciane 'cantano unitamente' ('sing together') in scene 1 with a text in *ottonari* and *quaternari* (but not strophic), 'Dolce fiato, aura gentile' (p. 9), with the first seven lines repeated at the end. Elsewhere in the libretto there are other indications of ensembles. Thus scene 11 has a duet as Pachino and Ciane address Anapo (p. 37):

Pachino
Non ti doler, no, no.   Do not grieve, no, no.

Ciane
                    Non ti contristi   Do not be sad at
la perdita di Ciane.   the loss of Ciane.

Pachino/Ciane
                    Il nostro frale,   Our frail body,
che lasciar dovevamo un giorno   which we all must leave in the end one
    alfine,   day,
fece un cambio pregiato; e le   has made a precious exchange; and our
    nostr'alme,   souls,
d'una buia prigion per tempo   having left a dark prison for ever,
    uscite,
son fra le schiere degli Elisi   have been welcomed among the hosts of
    accolte.   Elysium.

Ciane, Anapo and Pachino then tell of their fate in what develops as a trio (p. 39):

Ciane	
In fonte . . .	Into a fountain . . .
Anapo	
In fiume . . .	Into a river . . .
Pachino	
In monte . . .	Into a mountain . . .
Tutti 3	
questa spoglia mortal si trasformò.	this mortal body has been transformed.
L'alma si' eterna in fra gli Elisi, e '1 frale	The soul is eternal in the Elysian Fields, and the frail
velo, ch'ella vestiva,	veil which clothed it
Ciane	
. . . in fonte . . .	. . . as a fountain . . .
Anapo	
. . . in fiume . . .	. . . as a river . . .
Pachino	
. . . in monte . . .	. . . as a mountain . . .
Tutti 3	
vive in terra immortale.	lives immortal on earth.

Also, the libretto makes use of poetic refrains that, as with the texts of the 1628 *intermedi*, presumably have strong musical implications. The trio for Proserpina, Aretusa and Ciane opening scene 1, 'Dolce fiato, aura gentile', is in an ABA form (at least, so the text suggests) with, in addition, the last two lines of each A section repeated. Pachino's lament in scene 4, 'Misero esempio di schernito amante' (in *versi sciolti*), has four appearances of 'Ma la bella crudel sen fugge intanto', the last at the end. In scene 12, Anapo's 3-line invitation to the *anime beate* to dance ('Su, su, beati amanti') becomes a refrain of the *ballo* itself. The most striking example, however, is Proserpina's petulant rejection of Pachino in scene 3 (p. 21):

No, ch'io non t'amo, no, né devo amarti,	No, I do not love you, no, nor must I love you,
discortese, che scacci	discourteous one, who chases
da' lor piaceri le donzelle, e vuoi	maidens from their pleasures, and do you wish

per forza esser'amato.	to be loved by force?
No, ch'io non t'amo no. Ché se non lasci	No, I do not love you, no. For if you do not cease
di seguirmi, importuno,	to follow me importunate,
la mia gran genitrice,	if my great mother,
Cerere di Saturno,	Ceres, born of Saturn,
se mai ciò di te sente	ever hears this of you,
potria farti dolente.	she could make you suffer.
No, ch'io non t'amo, no, no, no, no, no.	No, I do not love you, no, no, no, no, no.

Here the rhetoric, and even the vocabulary, would seem to anticipate Penelope in *Il ritorno d'Ulisse in patria* ('Non voglio amar, no, no / ch'amando penerò'; II.5). But Proserpina's argument with Pachino also takes on the legalistic rhetoric of a Nerone and Seneca, and she herself appears strongly as a Poppea-figure in her scorning of Pachino (she is Jove's daughter and will not mix with the likes of a mere shepherd), in her initially haughty treatment of Plutone, and then in her total submission to him, once she has gained the throne. As for Pachino, Anapo's instruction to him after his lament – 'Risvegliati meschino. / Torna, torna a te stesso' ('Wake up, wretch. Come, come to your senses'; p. 23) – turns him quite literally into an Ottone ('Otton, torna in te stesso', he sings in *L'incoronazione*, I.12).

But *Proserpina rapita* also looks backwards to more courtly traditions in terms of its subject-matter, its staging, as well as the prominence of dance. Perhaps that should not be surprising, given that the demands of a noble Venetian patron need not have been so different from those of a duke, although it does prompt some caution over too polarized a view of the potential differences between works produced in a courtly environment and in a republican one. There even seem to be some knowing references to *Orfeo* and to the *Ballo delle ingrate*. For the former, Proserpina refuses to pick flowers in the field because she fears being bitten by a snake (compare Euridice), while Ciane praises the delights 'In questo prato adorno' (p. 14; compare the two Pastori in Act II of *Orfeo*). For the latter, in scene 6 Pachino urges Plutone to 'see the cruelty of an ungrateful nymph so much loved by me' ('mira la crudeltà di ninfa ingrata / da me tanto adorata'; p. 25), while the subsequent appearance of Plutone, and then (in scene 8) of Venere and Amore (a dramatic irrelevance, given that Plutone has already fallen for Proserpina), also owes something to the prior work. These quotations and allusions may or may not be intended, although the explicit pun in Pachino's reference in the final scene to the world praising Proserpina 'su VERDI Arcadi MONTI' ('on the Arcadian mountains green'; p. 42) suggests a rather knowing literary sensibility on Strozzi's part.

The 'Parthenian canzonetta', 'Come dolce hoggi l'auretta', raises further interesting questions. While the G major 'in soft sound and suitable for children' may or may not be Lydian, it is certainly not the warlike G major of the *concitato genere* seen in the *Combattimento di Tancredi e Clorinda*. Eric Chafe would have this key become so resonant that, even without associated *concitato* gestures, the warlike connotation remains: hence, by his reading, the final duet of *L'incoronazione di Poppea*, 'Pur ti miro, pur ti godo', is not quite the simple love-duet most would assume, for it is in a key associated with 'the victory of Love over Virtue and Fortune', with Love as 'a force, allied to the predominant key of the Book Eight *guerriero* style'.[42] 'Come dolce hoggi l'auretta' prompts caution over so schematic a view of the evolution of Monteverdi's tonal language, and the drawing of semiotic implications therefrom. It might also offer a solution to another Monteverdi 'problem'. It has been argued, and is now almost universally accepted, that 'Pur ti miro' is not by Monteverdi but, rather, reflects the work of one of his colleagues who evidently collaborated on the production of *Poppea*, or at least on its revivals as reflected in the surviving manuscript sources. However, the central section of 'Pur ti miro' bears close similarities to the central section of 'Come dolce hoggi l'auretta' (Ex. 8-1); if 'Pur ti miro' is not by Monteverdi, it is a much closer imitation of him than is currently assumed.[43]

It is tempting to decipher in all these 'lost' works some sense of orderly transition from the techniques, forms and styles known to have been used in *Orfeo* to those in *Il ritorno d'Ulisse in patria*, and from 'court' opera to 'public' opera. That is probably a mistake, given that each of the works discussed here can variously be shown to have been conditioned by its particular circumstances, and thus is in some sense *sui generis*: *Arianna* is a strong case in point. On the other hand, however, changing poetic and musical conceptions of how best to represent drama on the stage in early seventeenth-century Italy can at times

---

42 Chafe, *Monteverdi's Tonal Language*, p. 324.
43 The arguments over 'Pur ti miro, pur ti godo' have been articulated most completely in Curtis, '*La Poppea impasticciata*' and are widely accepted; compare Rosand, *Opera in Seventeenth-Century Venice*, pp. 256 n. 18, 336. Anthony Pryer ('Authentic Performance, Authentic Experience and "Pur ti miro" from *Poppea*') offers a revisionist view, in part on methodological grounds, and in part because of a number of similarities between the first section of 'Pur ti miro' and other works by Monteverdi. These include the duet between Ulisse and Eumete in *Il ritorno*, II.2 (see Ex. 9-3(a)) and a passage in the Nerone–Lucano duet in *L'incoronazione*, II.5. To them one might add the Fortuna–Virtù duet in the prologue, and some of the music for Valletto and Damigella in II.4, and for Nerone and Poppea in III.5. In Ex. 8-1, Nerone's last note in bar 6 is usually read as *b'* (not *d''*, as given here) conforming to the later repeat of this passage. There are some corrections at this point in the manuscript, but the *d''* is perfectly clear.

Ex. 8-1 (a) Monteverdi, 'Come dolce hoggi l'auretta' (*Madrigali e canzonette . . . libro nono* (Venice, Alessandro Vincenti, 1651)); (b) *L'incoronazione di Poppea*, III.8 (original time-signature, 3).

Ex. 8-1 *Continued*

Claudio Monteverdi: Tutte le opere, ed. Malipiero, ix, pp. 61–2; Venice, Biblioteca Nazionale Marciana, MS 9963 (It. IV.439), fol. 106v.

[a] [How the breeze . . .] comes wantonly to kiss my [cheeks and breast.]
[b] *Poppea*: I am yours, my hope, say it, say, my hope, my idol . . . *Nerone*: Yours am I, say it, say; you are indeed my idol . . .

seem entirely independent of context, function and genre. For example, the one 'transitional' feature to emerge quite strongly in this chapter is the exploration of new dramatic and musical roles for aria and related styles which, in turn, become strongly identified with Monteverdi's later Venetian operas. Yet these new roles can be shown to have developed within *balli* (*Apollo*) and *intermedi* (Didone) as well as operas (*Proserpina rapita*), not to mention chamber madrigals (including the *Lamento della ninfa*), and also within rather than outside various courtly or similar environments, be they a carnival entertainment for Mantua, a wedding festivity for Parma or a musical evening in the house of a Venetian nobleman. There is no doubt that opera changed quite radically when it took to the 'public' stage in Venice in 1637. But Monteverdi's own response was probably as much one of consolidation as of moving in new directions.

9

Il ritorno d'Ulisse in patria (1640)

In general, Monteverdi scholars have set great store by the composer's first opera for the Mantuan court, *Orfeo*, and by his last for the new 'public' opera houses of Venice, *L'incoronazione di Poppea*. But this has tended to deflect attention from Monteverdi's first Venetian opera, *Il ritorno d'Ulisse in patria*. *Il ritorno* was slow to enter the Monteverdi canon, coming to the attention of scholars and performers chiefly, it seems, by way of Robert Haas's 1922 edition. Its authenticity was once a cause of some debate – the issues were explored and resolved chiefly by Wolfgang Osthoff in the 1950s – but *Il ritorno* now tends to be viewed more complacently. We have only one manuscript of the score (Vienna, Österreichische Nationalbibliothek, MS 18763), the uncertain provenance of which has caused scant musicological anxiety. Nor have the surviving copies of Giacomo Badoaro's libretto, with their divergent readings, excited much published comment. Moreover, the supposed 'moral' of the work – 'the rewards of patience, the power of love over time and fortune'[1] – seems both unproblematic and conventional. On the whole, *Il ritorno* is widely touted as a straightforward opera with a straightforward message.

That is a pity, not least because *Il ritorno* was Monteverdi's first attempt fully to come to terms with the new 'public' opera inaugurated in Venice in 1637. His seemingly late arrival on the Venetian operatic stage – Giacomo Badoaro took the credit for encouraging it – was already a matter of comment at the time, although he appears to have played various back-seat roles before entering the limelight with the revival of *Arianna* at the Teatro S. Moisè in the 1639–40 season. He now moved in a very different theatrical world. The Teatro S. Cassiano opened for opera in 1637, and it was quickly followed by the Teatro SS. Giovanni e Paolo (1639), the Teatro S. Moisè (1640) and the Teatro Novissimo (1641). This commercial expansion,

---

1 Rosand, 'Iro and the Interpretation of *Il ritorno d'Ulisse in patria*', p. 142.

and the competition that ensued, made their effects quickly felt: five new operas were staged in the three seasons following the opening of the Teatro S. Cassiano, and some fifty had been performed by 1650. The situation could not have been more different from the infrequent performances of court opera, while the production-line mechanisms now operating for opera in Venice had a significant impact on librettists, composers, performers, and even audiences, whose expectations became both predictable and, if tickets were to be bought, demanding. Yet it is dangerous to exaggerate the extent to which these factors actually transformed the nature of the works themselves. For example, *Il ritorno*, like *Proserpina rapita*, shares a number of features with court opera: a quasi-mythological subject, gods and allegorical characters, reasonably lavish scenery and stage machines (at least as much as *Orfeo* and *Arianna*), and a surprisingly large number of roles – even if, as we saw in Chapter 4, there were probably not as many singers as that number might suggest. The only feature of *Il ritorno* that most obviously reflects the presumed economic pressures on Venetian opera is the reduced instrumental forces (five string parts, it seems) needed to provide a relatively small number of sinfonias and ritornellos.

True, the opera has enough sex, gore and elements of the supernatural to satisfy the most jaded Venetian palate, while a ship turned into stone, Ulisse transformed in a flash of lightning and an eagle flying overhead must have impressed the gallery. The story, extracted from Homer's *Odyssey*, is also manipulated well enough to create a dramatic flow. In the prologue, Humana Fragilità (Human Frailty) acknowledges her submission to Tempo (Time), Fortuna (Fortune) and Amore (Cupid), as the following drama will reveal. Act I opens in Penelope's palace in Ithaca, as she awaits the return of her husband Ulisse (Ulysses) from the Trojan wars. She cannot be consoled by her nurse Ericlea (Eurycleia). Melanto (Melantho), a maid, and Eurimaco (Eurymachus), a shepherd, comment on the pains yet pleasures of their own love. Nettuno (Neptune), supported by Giove (Jupiter), condemns the rescue of Ulisse by the Feaci (Phaeacians). They have brought him back to Ithaca, leaving him sleeping on the beach. As a punishment, Nettuno turns their ship into a rock. Ulisse awakes and believes himself to have been abandoned. Minerva enters, disguised as a shepherd, and tells Ulisse that the island is his home. To his amazement, she reveals herself and tells him to bathe in a sacred fountain, which will transform him into an old man, enabling him to enter his palace unrecognized and outwit Antinoo (Antinous), Pisandro (Peisander) and Anfinomo (Amphinomus), the suitors (Proci) who have insinuated themselves into the offices of state and are seeking his wife's hand. Meanwhile, Minerva will bring back Ulisse's son Telemaco (Telemachus) from Sparta. Ulisse rejoices. In the palace, Melanto urges Penelope to forget Ulisse and love another. Out in the fields, Eumete (Eumaeus), a shepherd faithful to Ulisse, is tending his flocks and arguing with the social parasite Iro (Irus), when Ulisse, now disguised, enters and warns Eumete of the imminent return of his sovereign.

In Act II, Minerva brings Telemaco on her chariot. Eumete welcomes the prince and presents the old man who, he says, has news of his father's return. A firebolt descends from heaven to reveal Ulisse in his true form. Father and son are joyfully reunited, and they plan their return to the palace. Melanto and Eurimaco discuss Penelope's continued devotion to Ulisse. The suitors enter to pursue their advances, but Penelope staunchly resists. Eumete announces the imminent return of Telemaco and Ulisse, and the suitors are disconcerted. They plot to kill Telemaco, but the sight of Giove's eagle flying overhead warns them against the plan, and they decide instead to redouble their wooing of Penelope. Minerva outlines to Ulisse a plan to remove the suitors, and Eumete attests to Penelope's continuing fidelity. Ulisse is happy, and he and the shepherd plan to go to the palace. Meanwhile, Telemaco discusses with Penelope his recent travels. Antinoo and Iro meet Eumete and Ulisse, now disguised as a beggar. Antinoo treats them badly and Ulisse is provoked to fight Iro, thrashing his fat adversary. Penelope orders that the beggar be made welcome. The suitors redouble their efforts to gain her favours with rich gifts. She proclaims that she will marry whoever manages to string Ulisse's great bow. The suitors agree willingly, but all three fail the test. The beggar asks to enter the competition, while renouncing the prize, and succeeds in stringing the bow. Invoking Minerva's protection, Ulisse looses arrows at the suitors, killing them all.

In Act III, Iro grieves for his colleagues in a splendid take-off of a lament scene. Penelope refuses to believe Eumete's claim that the beggar who bent the bow was indeed Ulisse, and even Telemaco cannot convince her. Minerva and Giunone (Juno) decide to plead with Giove on Ulisse's behalf. Nettuno is pacified, and choruses of celestial and maritime spirits praise the new accord. Ericlea ponders how best to behave towards Penelope, who still refuses the assurances of Eumete and Telemaco. Even when Ulisse enters in his true form, she fears a trick. Ericlea claims that it is indeed Ulisse: she has seen him in his bath and recognized a scar. But Penelope is finally convinced only when Ulisse correctly describes the embroidered quilt on their nuptial bed. Husband and wife are rejoined in a blissful love-duet.

The sources

As I argued in Chapter 4, the casting and layout of the Vienna score of *Il ritorno* suggest that it is in some sense a conflation of two previous 5-act versions of the opera (the issue hinges in part on the changed clef for the role of Eumete); it also preserves traces of the original 5-act division. It seems reasonable enough to assume that an opera performed at least ten times during its first season, then taken on tour to Bologna by Benedetto Ferrari and Francesco Manelli, then revived (unusually) in Venice in the 1640–1 season, would have undergone some alteration, whether or not by Monteverdi, to accommodate changes of cast and other practical exigencies. One issue is the extent to which the process might be reconstructed by comparison of the score with the nine surviving manuscript librettos, at least one of which (Venice, Museo Civico Correr, MS Cicogna 564) would seem to have significant seventeenth-century authority.[2] Cicogna 564 must have been prepared with some reference to a score – quite apart from a second or subsequent layer of corrections derived from the Vienna score or its archetype – even though it seeks to present some kind of 'literary' text (for publication, it would seem from the fulsome dedication to the composer). Thus although its 'a due' and (for the Proci) 'a tre' indications may be a librettist's instruction, the layout of the text for at least some of the duets suggests prior knowledge of the music. For example, Cicogna 564's version of the duet for Ulisse and Telemaco in II.3 follows Monteverdi's setting, rather than reflecting what might plausibly be assumed to be a more conventional 'poetic' layout (see Table 9-1). The fact that the same does not occur in, say, the final duet for Ulisse and Penelope (III.9) is perhaps revealing (see Table 9-2). Here, indeed, the lack of congruence between the score and Cicogna 564, plus the fact that Cicogna 564's layout is not particularly poetic (and, in one case, awkwardly reverses the word-order), may suggest that Cicogna 564 preserves the outline of a different musical conclusion to the duet. A parallel example is Melanto and Eurimaco's 'De nostri amor' concordi' in I.2, which in Cicogna 564 is given just to Melanto. If my broader point about Cicogna 564 reflecting some knowledge of a score is correct, then Ellen Rosand's argument concerning Monteverdi's 'powerful brand' of musical editing of Badoaro's libretto – made by comparing the score with the libretto in Cicogna 564 – needs some modification in the light of the possibility that Cicogna 564 had already, as it were, been edited musically.

However, Cicogna 564 does have a longer version of the text than the Vienna score, perhaps because it is prior to it in the *stemma* of the work or because it reflects some later attempt on the part of the librettist, or someone else, to set the record straight. The libretto's Act V (the score's Act III) is the exception: here the two sources follow each other quite closely,

2   See most recently Rosand, 'The Bow of Ulysses', pp. 377–8 n. 4. Rosand promises a much fuller study of the sources for *Il ritorno* in her forthcoming *Monteverdi's Late Operas*; my remarks here can thus only be regarded as provisional. In allocating some priority to Cicogna 564, I follow her lead (in 'Iro and the Interpretation of *Il ritorno d'Ulisse in patria*', pp. 142 n. 3, 148 n. 18). It must date at least from after the première, given that the dedication refers to ten performances of the work to date.

Table 9-1   *Il ritorno*, II.3: versions of the duet between Ulisse and Telemaco

Cicogna 564, fols. 23r–23v (passages in square brackets not set in score)	'Poetic' version
Telemaco O padre sospirato . . .	*Telemaco* O padre sospirato, genitor glorioso, t'inchino, o mio diletto.
Ulisse O figlio desiato . . .	*Ulisse* O figlio desiato, pegno dolce amoroso, ecco ti stringo al petto.
Telemaco genitor glorioso . . .	
Ulisse pegno dolce amoroso . . .	
Telemaco t'inchino, o mio diletto.	
Ulisse [ecco] ti stringo [al petto].[1]	
Telemaco Filiale dolcezza . . .	*Telemaco* Filiale dolcezza a lacrimar mi sforza.
Ulisse Paterna tenerezza . . .	*Ulisse* Paterna tenerezza il pianto in me rinforza.
Telemaco a lacrimar mi sforza.	
Ulisse il pianto in me rinforza.	
a due Mortal tutto confida e tutto spera, che quando il ciel protegge natura non ha legge: l'impossibile ancor spesso s'avverra.	*Telemaco/Ulisse* Mortal tutto confida e tutto spera, che quando il ciel protegge natura non ha legge: l'impossibile ancor spesso s'avverra.

[1] In the score, this line is compressed and taken into the previous one – thus '[T] t'inchino, [U] ti stringo, [T] o mio diletto' – with additional repetitions.

Table 9-2 *Il ritorno*, III.9: a comparison of the score
and libretto (Cicogna 564, fol. 47v) versions of the
ending of the duet for Ulisse and Penelope

Score	Cicogna 564
Ulisse Non si rammenti più de' tormenti: . . .	*Ulisse* Non si ram[m]enti più di tormenti: tutto è piacer.
Penelope Sì, sì, sì, vita, sì, sì.	
Ulisse tutto è piacere, tutto è piacer.	
Penelope Sì, sì, sì, vita, sì, sì. Fuggan dai petti dogliosi affetti: . . .	*Penelope* Fuggan dai petti dogliosi affetti: tutto è goder.
Ulisse Sì, sì, sì, core, sì, sì.	
Penelope tutto è godere, tutto è goder.	
a due Del piacer, del goder venuto è 'l dì. (Sì, sì, sì, vita, sì, sì, sì, core, sì, sì.)	*a due* Venuto è 'l dì . . .
	Penelope del goder . . .
	Ulisse del piacer . . .
	Penelope sì, sì, vita . . .
	Ulisse sì, sì, core . . .
	a due sì, sì, sì.

suggesting that the text of this part of the opera, at least, was fixed early on. In the previous acts, some of the apparent cuts may reflect original compositional decisions made by Monteverdi: one example is the shortening and restructuring of Penelope's opening lament. Others may instead reflect action at the production stage, where one might expect not just cuts but also late insertions to solve particular problems encountered in rehearsal or performance. This probably explains the two lines for Penelope added at the opening of I.10, which are necessary to get her on the stage. Among the ambiguous examples is the case of Iro in II.12. In Cicogna 564, he, too, participates in the test to string Ulisse's bow, and just as the Proci have appealed to their respective sources of inspiration (Amor, Mars and Penelope's beauty), so Iro invokes Bacchus to aid his strength (of course, he fails). This provides a further comic moment for this comic character (a *parte ridicola* according to the score's rubric to III.1), although one can see why either Monteverdi or a producer might have wanted to cut the passage: it slows the pace of the action leading to the death of the suitors, while Iro needs to escape the slaughter and return for his mock-lament at the opening of Act III.

Other cuts make good editorial sense: the score tends to reduce Badoaro's excessive descriptions or pseudo-philosophical peregrinations (particularly on beauty). But some are downright problematic. Thus in I.2, the shortened conclusion of the discussion between Eurimaco and Melanto (partly replaced by a reprise of the duet 'Dolce mia vita sei') removes an essential explanation of why they are conspiring together, plus references to the theme of food (and thus, indirectly, to Iro) and to the debate of honour versus love. In this extract from Cicogna 564 (fols. 9r–9v), the text in italic is omitted from the score (there are also further cuts later in the scene):

Eurimaco	*Eurimaco*
Se Penelope bella	*If beautiful Penelope*
non si piega alle voglie	*does not yield to the wishes*
de' rivali amatori,	*of the rival lovers,*
mal sicuri staranno	*insecure will be*
i nostri occulti amori.	*our secret love.*
Melanto	*Melanto*
Biasma il cibo in altrui bocca digiuna,	*The mouth which is fasting blames the presence of food in others,*
e detesta il piacere	*and he detests pleasure*
chi non gionge al godere.	*who does not reach happiness.*
Eurimaco	Eurimaco
Tu dunque t'affatica,	So, work hard,
suscita in lei le fiamme,	arouse in her the flames [of love],

percosso pietra ancora darà[?] faville.	*a stone when struck will still give sparks.*
Persuadi al diletto,	*Persuade her to delight,*
ch'in alma anco modesta	*for even in a modest soul*
così congiund'amor, Amor s'innesta.	*when love is joined, Amor sows its seed.*
Melanto	*Melanto*
Honor, crudo tiran d'alme più sciocche,[3]	*Honour [is] a cruel tyrant of souls who are more foolish,*
chi le sue leggi osserva	*he who observes its laws*
nega l'arbitrio human, sprezza natura:	*denies human judgement, scorns nature:*
ché legge di capricio è mal sicura.	*for a capricious law is scarcely secure.*
Ritenterò quell'alma	I will attack that soul
pertinace ostinata	stubborn and obstinate
(etc.)	*(etc.)*

Another example is the omission in II.9 of Minerva's instruction to Ulisse that he should kill the suitors; the action otherwise has scant justification in the opera, for all the Homeric precedents.

Reading Il ritorno

These kinds of substantive omissions raise two seemingly contradictory, but not mutually exclusive, possibilities: that the redactor of the Vienna score (whether or not Monteverdi) was catering either for an audience who knew the story very well, or for one that did not care much about it. One might say the same of other features of the libretto. There is none of the studied care to introduce characters and settings found in, say, *Orfeo*. The title of the opera is revealing enough, but the prologue is not. And the very opening of Act I gives us scant information about whom we are seeing on stage and where. It is also ungrammatical (unless line 2 should read 'terminate'):

Di misera Regina	Of a wretched Queen
non terminati mai dolenti affanni.	grieving suffering unending.
L'aspettato non giunge,	He who is awaited does not arrive,
e pur fuggono gli anni.	and yet the years fly by.
La serie del penar è lunga,	The tide of suffering is long, ah too
ahi troppo;	much so;
a chi vive in angoscie il Tempo è	for whomever lives in anguish, Time
zoppo.	is lame.

---

3 The libretto originally had 'Amor essendo tirran d'altri più scioche'; the revision produces an intriguing, and rather libertine, reversal of the argument.

Only in line 14 does our 'wretched Queen' start to mention the Trojan War; 'he who is awaited' is revealed as Ulisse only in line 24; and we discover Penelope's name only much later in the scene. Her nurse does introduce herself as 'Infelice Ericlea / nutrice sconsolata' at her first entrance, but in I.2, Melanto sings an entire song before Eurimaco reveals her name (and Eurimaco himself is not named until II.4), and so the pattern continues through the act; even Eumete does not declare his identity in I.11 (although Minerva mentions him in I.9), while Iro is named only after his speech mocking the faithful shepherd (in I.12). This leads to a more naturalistic playing out of the drama (so too, incidentally, does the absence of messengers' narrations), drawing upon models in the contemporary spoken theatre, although it does create some potential for confusion: *Orfeo* is far less allusive. Of course, the reliance on stock character-types, aided by costume and standard rhetorical gestures, would aid the knowing audience in their task of understanding what was being played out: lamenting queens, ageing nurses, dallying lovers and rustic shepherds were common enough on the Venetian operatic stage. But to follow *Il ritorno* properly in the theatre requires some prior knowledge of Homer's *Odyssey*, plus the attentive reading of a synopsis and/or a libretto; it would be typical of the time for one or both to be printed for the first performances, although none survives. Either that, or one gives up and just sits back to enjoy the show. No doubt contemporary audiences variously did both.

But Monteverdi and Badoaro could not afford to alienate their audience entirely, and direct references to those in the auditorium (for example, Minerva's address to 'voi stolti mortali', 'you foolish mortals', in I.7) are designed to grab the attention. And as with any operatic audience, its more knowledgeable members could have drawn a great deal from *Il ritorno*. Melanto's aphorism in I.2 (deleted from the score) on the foolishness of honour, a 'cruel tyrant', strikes a libertine stance with which different members of the audience might or might not have agreed, and which is played out across the broader canvas of the opera as Penelope wrestles between love and honour, and between the blandishments of the Proci and her fidelity to the memory of Ulisse. Other themes draw upon what seem to have been standard topics for debates in Venetian academies and salons. Is it better to woo a woman with fine words or to buy her with rich gifts?[4] Are beautiful

---

4   See 'Perche si paghino le Donne de' congressi amorosi' ('Why Women are Paid for Amorous Congresses'), in Loredano, *Bizzarie academiche* (1676; the first edition was published in Cremona in 1640), part 2, pp. 49–55, especially p. 52: 'Non ama la Donna senze interesse. Non si dona in preda a che non dona. Perche l'acquisto de' cuori feminili si guadagna con la profusione dell'oro' ('A woman does not love without self-interest. She does not give herself as booty to one who does not give. Therefore the purchase of feminine hearts is gained by the profusion of

women to be trusted or mistrusted? Should one live in the fields or in the city? Must a wife stay constant to her absent husband? Is love best earned by singing or weeping?[5] These and similar topics were common arguments in the Accademia degli Incogniti (of which Badoaro was a member), that group of free-thinking Venetians who had profound practical and philosophical influences on early Venetian opera.[6] *Il ritorno* is placed squarely in the context of the Incogniti in Badoaro's dedication to Monteverdi in Cicogna 564, which makes prominent mention of fellow members Pietro Loredano and Gasparo Malipiero. Federico Malipiero also refers to the opera in his *La peripezia d'Ulisse, overo La casta Penelope* (Venice, Giovanni Battista Surian, 1640); this Malipiero later produced a translation of the *Iliad*, *L'Iliada d'Omero trapportata dalla Greca nella Toscana lingua* (Venice, Paolo Baglioni, 1642), dedicated to the leader of the Incogniti, Giovanni Francesco Loredano, and promised one of the *Odyssey*, which seems never to have appeared. Thus when in I.8 Minerva tells Ulisse that he must pass through Ithaca in disguise – 'Incognito sarai' – presumably the audience would have made the connection. Telemaco in effect delivers an Incognito-style history lesson on the Trojan War (in II.11), where his remark that everything was justified by the ravishing looks of Helen of Troy is angrily put down by Penelope's dismissive comment on the perils of beauty and the dangers of love. Mercurio's traditional Lenten message (and Venetian opera was traditionally a pre-Lenten entertainment), that all human endeavour is vain because we turn to dust, was removed from the Vienna score 'for being melancholic' (a nice Incognito gesture?).[7] Yet the gods put in sufficient appearances to present a reassuringly conventional message: that all undertakings on earth are subject to divine intervention, but that the gods themselves have a duty to be merciful and to reward human endeavour.

Although these broader themes and topics are scattered throughout *Il ritorno*, there are further cues for a more strongly directed reading of the work. The copy of the libretto in Cicogna 564 contains a different prologue, delivered by Fato (Fate), Fortezza (Bravery) and Prudenza (Prudence). It proclaims the power of fate over men, and the uselessness of bravery and

---

gold'). Thus in *Il ritorno*, the Proci's final strategy to win Penelope is to buy her love with gold: 'Amor è un armonia, / sono canti i sospiri, / ma non si canta ben se l'or non suona; / non ama chi non dona' ('Love is a harmony, the sighs are songs, but one does not sing well if gold does not ring forth; he who does not give does not love').

5   For the celebrated 'Contesa del canto e delle lagrime', see Rosand, 'Barbara Strozzi', pp. 278–80.
6   For the Accademia degli Incogniti and Venetian opera, see Rosand, 'Seneca and the Interpretation of *L'incoronazione di Poppea*'; eadem, *Opera in Seventeenth-Century Venice*, pp. 37–40; Fenlon and Miller, *The Song of the Soul, passim*; Heller, 'Tacitus Incognito'.
7   The text of the deleted III.2 is in Rosand, 'Iro and the Interpretation of *Il ritorno d'Ulisse in patria*', pp. 160–2.

prudence without the support of fate, before anticipating the events of the opera to come: that Ulisse will overcome travails and dangers, that he will be supported by Minerva, that he will reach his homeland safely and will regain his wife, and that Nettuno will be placated.[8] This focus on Ulisse returns in the final lines of the libretto (not set in the score). In a concluding strategy rather similar to that of *Proserpina rapita*, Ulisse announces that he must leave to offer sacrifice on the altar of Minerva, whereupon he invites the Ithacans to sing the praises of their king and queen. But the Ithacans concentrate instead on their hero, reversing the argument of the libretto's prologue:

Pugnan spesso coll'huom fortuna e sorte,	Fortune and Fate often fight against man,
spesso si vede il destin disdegnato,	often one sees Destiny become angry,
ma cade la fortuna, e anche il fato,	but Fortune is defeated, and also Fate,
se s'arma di virtù l'huom saggio,	if a wise, brave man arms himself
e forte.	with virtue.

Yet so direct a prologue would not have suited the taste of the librettist of *Le nozze d'Enea in Lavinia*:

The prologue of the ancient tragedies was understood as all the instructive part of the tale before the song of the chorus, but since then it has become the practice to have it in some way detached, with those characters who have no place in the remainder of the work. However, to it remains its function of opening up the subject somewhat and not to reveal it completely. For this I wanted to represent the ghost of Creusa, judged by me to be very apposite to such an end, but having noted that as well as being just one continuous voice, her appearance at the beginning would have been very impoverished, I have added Virtue with three other ghosts invited by her to come and enjoy Aeneas' nuptials . . . And if it should appear that with these ghosts the beginning is melancholic, I say that perhaps it does not stand badly in this way so as to make all the greater the passage to the rejoicing of the end, just as in the case of a sad ending it is better to start with happiness, so that the fall turns out more pitiable. Also, although these are ghosts of the dead, they are nonetheless happy, coming from the Elysian Fields, and they sing very joyfully.

8 It is not clear why this prologue was abandoned (if it was). However, secular 'fate' was a tricky concept to get past the church censors in Venice (and indeed anywhere else in Counter-Reformation Italy). See, for example, the dedication of Federico Malipiero's *L'Iliada d'Omero* (1642), where Malipiero adds the standard caveat that words such as 'fate' and 'destiny' have been changed for being contrary to the Catholic faith.

The prologue of the score of *Il ritorno*, then, opens up, but does not completely reveal, a different subject. Here Humana Fragilità introduces in succession her three principal oppressors, Tempo, Fortuna and Amore. The rhetoric, and even the message, are those of the spiritual or moral dramas that were gaining in popularity in Italy in this period; indeed, the text (but not the music) of Monteverdi's prologue would not be out of place in the first example of the genre, Emilio de' Cavalieri's *Rappresentatione di Anima, et di Corpo*, performed in Rome in early 1600. No one can escape Time, who, though lame, has wings; Fortune is deaf and blind, dispensing riches and titles at her whim; while the blind archer Amor cannot be withstood. Humana Fragilità ends with the slightly feeble claim that it is vain to believe in the lame and the blind, although her three oppressors conclude the prologue stating how they will make man suffer.

The perils of Time, Fortune and Love become embedded in Penelope's speech that opens Act I (hence her reference to Time being lame in 1.6, given above) and, indeed, in the events of the opera as they impinge upon her. Thus one consequence of the change from the libretto's prologue to that of the score is a shift in emphasis away from Ulisse in favour of Penelope, who thus becomes empowered, temporarily at least, in ways similar to Arianna, and to some extent by the same means: a lament. That she makes an uncomfortable heroine entirely typifies the difficulties inherent in representing powerful women on the Venetian operatic stage, for all that powerful female singers were now in high demand. Some may feel that she does not act entirely honourably towards the Proci (which is the case also in Homer), and that her interminable reluctance to accept proof of Ulisse's identity from Eumete, Telemaco and even her nurse Ericlea renders Act III rather tedious. It should also be remembered that one strand of the classical reception of Penelope had her more chased than chaste:[9] in other versions of her story she succumbs to one (Amphinomus) or all of the suitors, and also bears illegitimately the god Pan. Yet her undeniable stage presence has a compelling effect; it extends the themes and topics of the opera in such a way that they can

---

9   This is also the general view held of women: compare Eurimaco's 'E pur udii sovente / la poetica schiera / cantar donna volubile e leggiera' (II.4: 'And yet I have often heard the poets' band call woman inconstant and flighty'). The Incogniti could argue in much the same way. For Penelope, compare also the doubts sown in Ariosto's *Orlando furioso* (XXXV.27). In a curious passage, St John the Evangelist invokes the power of poets who, given the right patronage, will readily spread lies (trans. Reynolds, p. 342): 'Homer makes Agamemnon win the war; / The Trojans cowardly and weak he shows. / Although the suitors so persistent are, / Penelope is faithful to her spouse. / But if for truth you are particular, / Like this, quite in reverse, the story goes: / The Greeks defeated, Troy victorious, / And chaste Penelope notorious.'

appeal to all members of the audience of whatever sex; and it also provides a narrative thread that in turn thematicizes the genre of opera itself.

As with *L'incoronazione*, any postmodern appeal to polyvalency in *Il ritorno* might be seen simply as a convenient escape from the need to fix one pre-eminent reading of the work, whether consonant with its historical context or rendered somehow transcendentally cohesive. But such an appeal can equally well be grounded in the commercial demands of public opera, where implicating a plurality of readings at different levels made (indeed, makes) sound cultural and financial sense. It also raises as yet unasked questions about the predominant constitution of opera house audiences in this period, whether male or female, young or old, foreign or native. Each represented section of society would no doubt read these operas differently, according to their predilections.[10]

Signifier and signified

No less grounded, but equally problematic, are the changing roles of music on the stage, as would appear from comparing *Il ritorno* with Monteverdi's earlier dramatic works. The careful positioning of (near-)diegetic arias and similar set pieces in *Orfeo*, which thus distinguished song from musical speech, shifts in favour of more fluid, and often quite rapid, movement between the various styles now available to the theatrical composer. This increasing fluidity, also traceable in the 'lost' works discussed in Chapter 8, in turn suggests a degree of acceptance of the musical conventions of opera on the part of audiences, chiefly, one assumes, by virtue of their increasing familiarity with the genre, and of newly emerging expectations of its desired aesthetic and other effects. Singing, rather than just musical 'speaking', is now both natural and inevitable.

As Rosand notes, Monteverdi exploited every opportunity for song in Badoaro's libretto (as cued either by the structure or by the content of the text), and indeed created others. She points in particular to the composer's use of refrain structures in I.8–9 (Ulisse's recurring 'O fortunato Ulisse') and III.8 (Ericlea's solo scene, with its four statements of a musical refrain, each time to new text). In the latter case, at least, the setting may owe more to the libretto than Rosand suggests – in particular, by way of the *versi tronchi* – but her point is still a good one: Monteverdi does seem to have been concerned to render more cohesive the rather disparate styles emerging in

---

10 Some suggestive hints of the sociological issues are provided in Bianconi and Walker, 'Production, Consumption and Political Function of Seventeenth-Century Opera'. However, this remains a topic ripe for research.

Venetian opera, which helps explain his refrains and also his use of passages
in triple time to provide a musical and emotional focus for a scene. Much
the same could be said of the refrains (this time in recitative) in Penelope's
opening lament, following the trend for text repetition in the *Lamento
d'Arianna*. Here the text would seem to have been quite radically reshaped
by Monteverdi: the bulk of Penelope's final passage in the score, with its
repeated emphasis on the theme of returning ('Torna il tranquillo al mare'),
is placed in the middle of the scene in the libretto, and Monteverdi's reorga-
nization of the text leads more naturally to a climax. However, even here the
thrice-recurring 'Torna, deh torna Ulisse' and the poignant repetition of
'tu sol del tuo tornar perdesti il giorno' would seem to have been cued at
least partly by Badoaro.

But these gestures have affective as well as structural significance.
Here Monteverdi exploits a vocabulary of text-expressive devices drawn in
part from his previous dramatic music, and still more from his more recent
chamber madrigals. Penelope's 'tu sol del tuo tornar perdesti il giorno' is
strongly reminiscent of Orfeo's 'Rendetemi il mio ben, Tartarei numi' (also
a refrain) in *Orfeo* (Ex. 9-1), not to mention the opening of the *Lamento
d'Arianna*, while the appearances of the fast-repeated semiquavers and fanfare
figures of the *concitato genere* at references to battle or the like – most obviously at the end of Act II, when Ulisse kills the suitors – derive from the
Combattimento di Tancredi e Clorinda. Signifiers taken from the madrigals include
close canons between voice and bass to indicate some kind of opposition or
struggle (Ex. 9-2); descending tetrachord ground basses (or variants thereof),
whether major for joy (Eumete and Ulisse's 'Dolce speme i cor' lusinga' in
II.2; see Ex. 9-3(a), below), or chromatic for the pains of love (Melanto and
Eurimaco's 'Dolce mia vita' in I.2); and the syncopated *ciaccona* patterns that
musically 'console' Iro in his soliloquy in III.1 (at the refrain 'chi lo consola').[11]
So powerful are these topoi that even the briefest reference to them fixes the
meaning, as with the one or two statements of the descending major tetrachord in Eumete's 'son delizie dell'huom' (in praise of pastoral 'delights') at
the end of I.11, or his 'e pur sei giunto al fine' celebrating Telemaco's return
in II.2. Many of the song-types in *Il ritorno* also draw upon techniques developed in the solo songs and duets of the 1632 *Scherzi musicali*: compare parts
of the latter's 'Eri già tutta mia' with Amore's 'Dio de' dei feritor' in the prologue, or 'Maledetto sia l'aspetto' with Minerva's 'Cara lieta gioventù' in I.8.
Even the flexible shifting between musical styles characteristic of the opera
draws upon lyric conventions in the chamber madrigals of the Seventh and
Eighth Books, where the place of simple recitative tended to be more
restricted for generic and functional reasons.

11   Rosand, 'Operatic Madness', p. 263.

Ex. 9-1 (a) *Orfeo*, III; (b) *Il ritorno d'Ulisse in patria*, I.1.

Monteverdi, *L'Orfeo, favola in musica* (Venice, Ricciardo Amadino, 1609), p. 66; Vienna, Österreichische Nationalbibliothek, MS 18763, fol. 10v–11r.

[a] Restore to me my beloved, gods of Tartarus.
[b] you alone have lost the day of your return.

The strongest signifier is triple time itself. This can be used for conventional word-painting at words suggesting mutability ('cangiare', 'to change') or circularity ('tornare', 'to return'). It can imitate the sounds of joy ('ridere', 'to laugh') or just express its general state, as in Ulisse's refrain 'O fortunato Ulisse' in I.8–9, Eumete's 'O gran figlio d'Ulisse' in II.2, or the Proci's 'Lieta, soave gloria' in II.12. Finally, it can provide rhetorical and emotional emphasis independent of any mimetic function. These various uses of triple time had been fixed at least since Monteverdi's Seventh Book of madrigals of 1619,[12] and in the case of *Il ritorno* we have already seen the trend at the opening of Act II (discussed in Chapter 3). Moreover, such appearances

Ex. 9-2 Monteverdi, 'Armato il cor d'adamantina fede' (*Madrigali guerrieri, et amorosi . . . Libro ottavo* (Venice, Alessandro Vincenti, 1638)), Tenor 2 and bass; (b) *Il ritorno*, Prologue; (c) *Il ritorno*, I.5.

Claudio Monteverdi: Tutte le opere, ed. Malipiero, ix, pp. 28–9; Vienna, Österreichische Nationalbibliothek, MS 18763, fols 6r, 23v.

[a] I will fight against heaven and fate . . .

[b] against my arrow . . .

[c] [Human liberty] dares all, braves all . . .

12 See Carter, 'Resemblance and Representation'; idem, '"Sfogava con le stelle" Reconsidered'.

Ex. 9-3 *Il ritorno*: (a) II.2; (b) II.3.

Ex. 9-3 *Continued*

Vienna, Österreichische Nationalbibliothek, MS 18763, fols 56v–57r, 61r.

[a] *Eumete*: Sweet hope charms hearts . . . *Ulisse*: Good news delights every soul . . .

[b] *Telemaco*: Oh sighed-for father . . . glorious progenitor . . . I bow to you . . . *Ulisse*: Oh desired son . . . sweet burden of love . . . I embrace you . . .

---

of triple time can range from small segments in the context of the recitative, to longer passages, to clearly partitioned sections that probably warrant the term 'aria', whether or not they are arias in the technical sense of a strophic setting of strophic poetry.

For the last, however, vestigial canons of verisimilitude remain. The quasi-formal arias and duets in Act I make the point clear, while a comparison of this list with that of the most strongly structured texts in *Il ritorno* given in Table 3-1 reveals Monteverdi's search for additional points of musical and emotional focus (the texts marked with an asterisk below do not appear in Table 3-1):

(I.2)   Melanto, 'Duri e penosi'; Eurimaco, 'Bella Melanto mia'* . . .
          Melanto/Eurimaco, 'Dolce mia vita sei'*
(I.6)   Feaci, 'In questo basso mondo'
(I.8)   Minerva, 'Cara e lieta gioventù'; Minerva/Ulisse, 'Ninfe serbate'
(I.9)   Ulisse, 'O fortunato Ulisse'*
(I.10)   Melanto, 'Ama dunque, ché d'Amore'
(I.11)   Eumete, 'Colli, campagni e boschi'*
(I.12)   Iro, 'Pastor d'armenti può'
(I.13)   Eumete, 'Come lieto t'accoglio'

The sequence, and its careful positioning scene by scene, is revealing. As with nurses (Ericlea in III.8), lower-class lovers can sing; indeed, I.2, for Melanto and Eurimaco, is a veritable catalogue of different aria and duet styles, for all that the text is primarily in *versi sciolti*. So, too, can shepherds, when extolling the delights of Arcadia: in I.12 Iro pokes fun at Eumete for having done precisely that (in I.11), and Iro's pointed musical parody of the pastoral clichés in turn suggests that opera has gained the maturity for self-mockery. In the case of Minerva, her song in I.8 would seem to reflect her disguise as a shepherd more than her status as a god; when she adopts the latter role, in III.6, her musical language changes to the rather archaic style of florid song – harking back to the Florentine *intermedi* (as in Ex. 2-1) – that quite strikingly alienates all the gods in *Il ritorno* from the musical present, as if they had no place in the modern operatic world. Slightly more problematic is the case of Ulisse, who, as a noble character (but no famous mythical musician), probably should not 'sing' as much as he does. His first appearance in I.7 invokes a nice harmonic parallel with Penelope's in I.1 (C minor, with the voice starting on E♭) and is impeccably sober, with arching recitative lines reminiscent of *Orfeo*, in particular the beginning of Act V. However, he soon takes on other musical idiolects, notably, but not exclusively, when he is in disguise; indeed, the act of singing accentuates the dissimulation.[13] The difference between his second duet with Eumete in II.2 ('Dolce speme i cor' lusinga'), when Ulisse is disguised and singing with a shepherd, and his duet with Telemaco in II.3 is striking (Ex. 9-3): although Telemaco can himself sing songs when flying through the air in Minerva's chariot, when father and son are united their musical language must stay within the bounds of a different propriety. But even so, Ulisse's propensity to song, while endemic to the genre, does create problems for him. Thus when he enters in his real form to greet his wife in III.10, his lyrical effusion ('O delle mie fatiche') would seem to be one reason why Penelope is suspicious of him ('incantator o mago' – 'enchanter or magician' she calls him), and Ulisse's attempts to persuade her of his identity must extend beyond his description of the quilt on their nuptial bed, to adopting a more appropriately restrained musical style.

Penelope

Penelope's remark is revealing, focusing the issue still further in ways that become almost thematic for and of *Il ritorno* as a whole.[14] Indeed, Penelope's insistence on 'speaking', rather than 'singing', is one of the most striking features of *Il ritorno*, exposing once more the dramatic and aesthetic dilemmas that lie at the very heart of the opera. We first see her right at the opening

---

13 The point is made in Rosand, *Opera in Seventeenth-Century Venice*, pp. 120–1.
14 My argument here is drawn from Carter, '"In Love's harmonious consort"?', with some modifications.

of Act I, establishing her considerable presence with a recitative lament that vies with the *Lamento d'Arianna* in expressive power and dramatic effect. In this overwhelming context of recitative, Penelope's one brief shift to an aria style at 'Torna il tranquillo al mare' ('Calm returns to the sea') seems no more than a nostalgic hankering for the joys of the past, when she did indeed know how to sing.

Penelope has been able to resist one of Humana Fragilità's oppressors in the prologue, Tempo. Events in the opera will show her also avoiding the Proci's riches and other blandishments offered by Fortuna. However, Amore – 'blind archer, winged, naked: no defence or shield can withstand my arrow', he says in the prologue[15] – poses a different threat, and one that will besiege Penelope throughout the opera. In I.1, Penelope makes clear her objections to the 'amor impuro' which was the chief cause of the Trojan War, and in I.10 she cites Theseus and Jason as exemplars of the dangers of love. But Amore's blandishments become readily apparent early on in the opera: in I.2 Melanto and Eurimaco sing their love-songs in a mellifluous triple time, its first extended appearance in the opera proper. In the prologue, Fortuna, Amore and (in the final trio) Tempo had each appropriated triple-time aria styles; but in the opera itself this is the musical language of love. The lesson seems drawn from the *Madrigali guerrieri, et amorosi* of 1638, the first piece of which, 'Altri canti d'Amor, tenero arciero', opens in a lyrical triple time ('Let others sing of Love'), with love's sweet blandishments then represented by drooping suspensions over a descending (minor) tetrachord ground bass. The message is clearer still in the opera. 'Ama dunque, ché d'Amore / dolce amica è la beltà' ('Love, then, for beauty is a sweet friend of Love') sings Melanto (twice) in a seductive triple time (I.10);[16] 'Ama dunque, sì, sì, / dunque riama un dì' ('Love then, yes, yes, then love again one day') sing Pisandro, Antinoo and Anfinomo (three times), again in triple time, in II.5 (Ex. 9-4(a)).[17] Not for nothing do the suitors proclaim in Act II scene 8 that 'Amor è un'armonia / sono canti i sospiri' ('Love is a harmony, sighs are songs'), singing in solemn 3-part harmony.[18]

---

15 'Cieco saettator, alato, ignudo, / contro il mio stral non val difesa o scudo.'
16 For the second appearance of Melanto's 'refrain', Cicogna 564 provides a second stanza, 'Fuggi pur del tempo i danni / tosto vien nemica età' ('Yet flee the losses of time, age the enemy comes soon'). This may also relate to the expunging of references to Penelope's beauty, discussed elsewhere in this chapter.
17 The second statement is omitted in Cicogna 564.
18 In Cicogna 564, the suitors' speech begins 'Sono canti i sospiri', with 'Amor è un armonia' a later insertion. This is, of course, all grist to my mill. Compare also the dedication to Barbara Strozzi's *Diporti di Euterpe, overo Cantate et ariette a voce sola* (Venice, Francesco Magni, 1659), in Rosand, 'Barbara Strozzi', p. 280 n. 118: 'Queste harmoniche note . . . son lingue dell'Anima, ed istromenti del Core' ('These harmonic notes . . . are tongues of the Soul, and instruments of the Heart').

Ex. 9-4 *Il ritorno*, II.5.

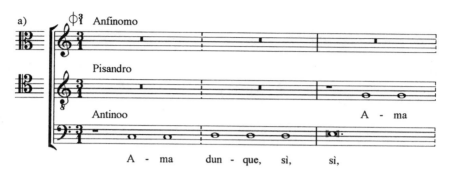

Ex. 9-4 *Continued*

Vienna, Österreichische Nationalbibliothek, MS 18763, fols 65v–66r (voices only), 66v, 71v.

[a] Love then, yes, yes, then love again one day.
[b] I will not love, no, no, for in loving will I suffer.
[c] I will not love, I will not, I will not. As a piece of iron wavers in doubt [between two magnets . . .]

For Penelope, however, 'canti' ('songs') all too easily become 'incanti' ('enchantments') – Eurimaco makes the pun in I.2 – and thence 'bugie' ('lies'; compare Penelope's brief shift to triple time at 'questo di tua bugia' in III.10). Her few passages in triple time are all conventional, as at 'cangia il piacer in duolo' (I.10: '*changes* pleasure into grief'), 'Concedasi al mendico la prova' (II.12: 'Grant the beggar the test', prompted presumably by the *sdrucciolo* accentuation of 'Concedasi'), and 'gioco' (III.5: 'plaything'). But victorious over Time and Fortune, she cannot afford defeat at the hands of Love. So, too, she must not give way to aria: just as Penelope encloses herself within her palace and within her chastity, she is no less enclosed in the joyless world of recitative. 'Non dee di nuovo amar / chi misera penò; / torna stolta a penar / chi prima errò' ('She should not love again who has suffered wretched; only a fool comes back to suffer after a first mistake'), she says to Melanto (I.10) in a bare recitative to a text that in most circumstances Monteverdi would have been happy to style as an aria, a homely moral in *versi tronchi*. His reluctance to allow Penelope to sing in structured triple and duple time is still more apparent in Act II scene 5. Here Penelope's response to the suitors' 'Ama dunque, sì, sì' is a foot-stamping refrain, 'Non voglio amar, no, no' ('I will not love, no, no') that denies its status as aria even as it runs its petulant triple-time course (Ex. 9-4(b)). By the third statement (Ex. 9-4(c)), Penelope seeks comfort in her familiar recitative, again despite Badoaro's *versi tronchi* later in the passage.

Penelope's recitative is surely the 'normal' language for so serious a character; indeed, some might claim it to be the most ennobling aspect of her music. But while we might not expect Arianna to sing an aria, given the dominant role of recitative in the earliest operas, by the early 1640s matters have changed significantly. In a context where aria as a medium of expression is both a norm and an expectation, denying a character access to such expression takes on a dramatic significance. Thus one might read Penelope's commitment to recitative as a gesture no less arid than her refusal to acknowledge the 'obvious' (at least to Melanto, Ericlea and the suitors) solution to her problems: she is alone and so must love and sing anew. Her faithfulness to the absent Ulisse is depicted as an obduracy that contravenes the laws of nature. In I.2, Melanto promises to 'revive that heart which honour has made as hard as diamonds' ('ritoccherò quel core / ch'indiamante l'honore'), while in II.4, Melanto says that Penelope has a 'cor di sasso' ('heart of stone'). The question of nature and the natural becomes still more prominent in II.5, where the suitors invoke horticultural images to represent love – the vine (Pisandro), the cedar (Anfinomo) and ivy (Antinoo).[19] By their account, the result of Penelope's inflexibility can only be an 'unnatural' sexual frustration. She reacts bitterly to Telemaco's description of the charms of Helen of Troy (II.11), and her test for the suitors (made from her lips, not her heart, she says) to fire Ulisse's bow is ripe for Freudian analysis. But Penelope's situation gets worse still. Trapped by the conflicting demands of heart and mind, and by the pressures of peers and circumstance, she eventually succumbs to emotional paralysis, unable to react even to the death of the suitors: 'Dell'occhio la pietate / si risente all'eccesso, / ma concitar il core / a sdegno et a dolore / non m'è concesso' ('My eyes do feel pity to the extreme, but to arouse my heart to anger or grief is not permitted me'; III.3). Even the evidence of Ulisse's return offered by her servant Eumete and her son Telemaco cannot arouse her from a catatonic state of disbelief. Still more notable is Ulisse's initial failure to convince her that he is indeed her husband. Eumete, she says (III.4), is 'stolto e cieco' ('foolish and blind'), accusing him of the failings she has previously attributed to Love. But in fact she herself is now made to seem foolishly blind to the truth.

Penelope's increasing passivity begins early in the opera: not for nothing is her first scene (I.1) her longest. In part, one suspects, this is because

19 In Cicogna 564, Penelope responds: 'L'edra, il cedro, e la vite / altre leggi non han, che di natura; / ogni suo pregio oscura / bella donna e regina, / s'a natura s'inchina' ('The ivy, the cedar and the vine have no other laws than nature's; [but] a beautiful woman and a queen blots out all her worth if she inclines to nature'). She is deprived of this defence in the score.

of the fear that she herself – and her womanhood – could threaten the potency of the messages she is meant to convey. In the libretto, her opening lament is longer still, and one of its themes, that her beauty is fast fading (and therefore that she fears her ability to arouse desire in Ulisse), is entirely missing from the score. Similarly, subsequent (often extended) references to Penelope's physical beauty, and hence her sexuality, are systematically expunged from the text set by Monteverdi. Such a strategy had its advantages: the Incogniti were clear that beauty could all too easily be an instrument of deceit (Loredano quoted Tasso: 'Beauty is an infamous monster, an unworldly monster, heaven's scourge with which to beat the world').[20] It also defused the potentially damaging comparison with those beautiful women so condemned in Monteverdi's *Ballo delle ingrate* because they 'ungratefully' deny love. But all this makes the resolution of the opera, which requires the reawakening of Penelope as a sentient woman, much more problematic. Indeed, Penelope's need to recover herself becomes specifically a matter of reviving her sexuality: only thoughts of Ulisse naked (as Ericlea sees him in the bath) and of her marriage bed – the site of sexual pleasure, for all its virginal quilt – show her some way out of the psychological crisis into which she has been manipulated (or has manipulated herself).

It is curious, if typical, that Penelope's fate is ignored by all the characters in *Il ritorno*. That Melanto, Eurimaco and the suitors treat her as literally a commodity comes as no surprise. But the gods, who have the power to resolve the plot, say absolutely nothing about her: when Giunone intercedes with Giove (compare Proserpina and Plutone in *Orfeo*), then Giove with Nettuno, the arguments are made entirely on Ulisse's part. Even Eumete and Telemaco explode in frustration (III.9): Penelope is 'Troppo incredula, / troppo ostinata' ('Too incredulous, too stubborn') – remarks worthy of a Melanto. As for Penelope herself, confused as she is (or as she is forced to be), she sees her acknowledgement of Ulisse as a choice between Love and Honour.[21] Finally, she picks Love, prompting a drastic reversal in her role. Having spent the whole opera resisting, so to speak, the blandishments of triple time, in the final scene she gives herself to them body and soul. Badoaro provides a straightforward recitative in 11- and 7-syllable *versi piani*: 'Hor sì ti riconosco, hor sì ti credo / antico possessore / del combattuto core' ('Now, yes, I recognize you, now, yes, I believe you, former possessor of my besieged heart'). But Monteverdi sets this in an excited triple-time aria style (Ex. 9-5). Penelope returns to musical recitative only to confirm her decision:

20   Fenlon and Miller, *The Song of the Soul*, p. 35 n. 14.
21   III.10: 'Creder ciò ch'è desio m'insegna [Cicogna 564 has the more plausible 'm'invita'] Amore; / serbar costante il sen comanda honore' ('Love teaches [invites] me to believe what is [my] desire, but honour commands my breast to stay constant').

'Honestà, mi perdoni: / dono tutto ad Amor le sue ragioni' ('Honesty, forgive me: I give all the arguments to Love'). Ulisse senses the change and meets her on this new ground, urging Penelope in a seductive triple time, again to 'recitative' verse: 'Sciogli la lingua, sciogli / per allegrezza i nodi. / Un sospir,

Ex. 9-5 *Il ritorno*, III.10, Penelope.

Vienna, Österreichische Nationalbibliothek, MS 18763, fol. 128r.

Ex. 9-6 *Il ritorno*, III.10, Penelope.

Vienna, Österreichische Nationalbibliothek, MS 18763, fols 128v–129r.

Shine bright, o heavens; renew your flowers, o fields . . .

un ohimè la voce snodi' ('Unloose your tongue, unloose for joy the knots.
Let your voice loose forth a sigh, an alas'). Penelope knows full well that 'sighs
are songs' (she heard the Proci?), and she looses forth the most stunning aria
in the opera, 'Illustratevi o cieli' (Ex. 9-6). Significantly, the instruments join
the voice in celebratory refrains. Penelope's song is an ecstatic moment of
emotional release as she once more learns to sing the language of love. But
if that love chosen by Penelope towards the end of *Il ritorno d'Ulisse in patria*
is pure, honourable and allied to constancy, the fickle Cupid advocated by
Melanto, Eurimaco and the suitors will live to fight another day.[22]

22   As Rosand notes in 'Iro and the Interpretation of *Il ritorno d'Ulisse in patria*',
     pp. 162–3.

10

L'incoronazione di Poppea (1643)

Monteverdi's last opera would seem to be everything that *Il ritorno* is not. The characters of *L'incoronazione di Poppea* and their actions are famously problematic; the opera's messages are at best ambiguous and at worst perverted; the sources are mixed; and the surviving materials present profound difficulties of chronology and attribution. Given the pressures that must have been placed upon those working in the Venetian 'public' opera houses – to work quickly, to meet and exceed audience expectations, to sell tickets and so forth – and the necessarily fluid concept of the musical 'work' that ensued, it is reasonable to suggest that at least some of the various difficulties of *L'incoronazione* are the norm rather than the exception, and indeed, that those operas which do seem more straightforward are in fact just more successful at hiding their problems. But there is something distinctly uncomfortable about an opera that would seem to be tainted in just about every way other than in the consummate artistry of its music, one that both repels and attracts with equal fascination.

The tone is set even in the prologue (the following synopsis follows the Venice manuscript). Fortuna (Fortune), Virtù (Virtue) and Amore (Cupid) dispute their respective powers. Amore claims to be master of the world, as the story of Nerone (Nero) and Poppea (Poppaea) will prove. At the opening of Act I, Ottone (Otho) arrives at Poppea's house and sees Nerone's soldiers outside, asleep. He realizes that his beloved is together with Nerone and curses her faithlessness. The soldiers wake and complain about their job and the decline of Rome. Nerone and Poppea enter: they take a sensuous farewell as Poppea emphasizes her love for him and seeks to guarantee their marriage. She is left alone with her nurse, Arnalta, to discuss tactics and ignores Arnalta's commonsense warnings, for Amore is on her side; Arnalta is left to grumble at her mistress's folly. Ottavia (Octavia), Nerone's wife, acknowledges her humiliation, while her own nurse (Nutrice) suggests that she should take a lover. The philosopher Seneca, shown in by Ottavia's page, Valletto, urges restraint and appeals to her dignity: Valletto responds by mocking Seneca's pedantry. As Seneca reflects on power and the transitory nature of life, Pallade (Pallas Athene) warns him of his impending death: Seneca welcomes the news. Nerone debates his plans concerning Ottavia and Poppea with Seneca, who urges reason, but Nerone is inflamed to anger. Poppea enters to calm him down, suggesting that Seneca must be killed. Ottone confronts Poppea over her infidelity, but she dismisses him. He tries to come to his senses ('Otton, torna in te stesso') and vows revenge. Then he turns to Drusilla, who has always loved him, and swears that he will favour her over Poppea.

In Act II, Seneca praises stoic solitude. Mercurio (Mercury) appears, warning him again of death, which the philosopher accepts happily. Liberto, a freedman, enters with Nerone's command: Seneca must die by the end of the day. He welcomes his fate, despite the urgings of his companions, and they leave to prepare the bath in which he will open his veins. The tension is broken by a flirtatious scene between Valletto and Damigella. Nerone and Lucano (Lucan) celebrate the news of Seneca's death with wine and song, praising Poppea's beauty. Ottone rededicates himself to Poppea, whom he still loves, but Ottavia orders him to assume female garb and kill her. He cannot refuse. Drusilla delights in her love for Ottone, and Ottavia's nurse wishes that she were in her place. Ottone enters and explains his plan for murdering Poppea; Drusilla gives him her clothes. Meanwhile, Poppea rejoices in Seneca's death and prays for Amore to support her. Arnalta lulls her to sleep as Amore watches overhead. Ottone, dressed as Drusilla, enters and tries to kill Poppea, but he is prevented by Amore. She wakes and gives the alarm as Ottone escapes. Amore proclaims his success.

Act III opens with Drusilla joyfully anticipating Poppea's death, but she finds herself arrested for the attempted murder – Ottone was wearing her clothes – and Nerone sentences her to death. Ottone in turn confesses his guilt, despite Drusilla's persistent attempts to protect her beloved, and Nerone banishes them both, a punishment they accept with glad heart. Ottone's implication of Ottavia has given Nerone the excuse he needs, and he banishes her, too. Nerone and Poppea rejoice now that the last obstruction to their marriage has been removed. Ottavia enters and, in a lament, bids a halting farewell to Rome. Arnalta revels in the exaltation of her mistress as empress. Nerone crowns Poppea, and the consuls and tribunes pay homage. Amore proclaims his triumph to his approving mother, Venere (Venus). Nerone and Poppea have a final ecstatic duet.

A fascination with *L'incoronazione* seems to have emerged early on, if we can believe the extent of the surviving materials for the opera (see Table 10-1). There are two printed librettos, seven in manuscript, two musical scores, and the *scenario* (synopsis) printed for the première at the Teatro SS. Giovanni e Paolo in the 1642–3 season. One of the printed librettos (*LN*) and one of

Table 10-1   Surviving materials of *L'incoronazione di Poppea*

(After Chiarelli, '*L'incoronazione di Poppea* o *Il Nerone*'; Fabbri, 'New Sources for "Poppea" '.)

Librettos:
Printed:

LN   *Il Nerone overo L'incoronatione di Poppea* (Naples, Roberto Mollo, 1651)

LV   *L'incoronatione di Poppea*, in Busenello, *Delle hore ociose* (Venice, Andrea Giuliani, 1656)

Manuscript:

F   *La coronatione di Poppea*, Florence, Biblioteca Nazionale Centrale, Magliabechi VII.6

R   *La coronatione di Poppea*, Rovigo, Biblioteca dell'Accademia dei Concordi, Silvestriana 239

T   *La Popea* (on the outer binding: *L'incoronatione di Popea*), Treviso, Biblioteca Comunale, Rossi 83

U   [untitled], Udine, Biblioteca Comunale, Fondo Joppi 496

U^f   *La coronatione di Poppea*, Udine, Biblioteca Comunale, 55 (prologue and Act I scenes 1–4 (part) only)

V   *La Poppea*, Venice, Museo Civico Correr, Cicogna 585

W   *Nerone* (in modern hand), Warsaw, Biblioteka Narodowa, BOZ 1043

Scores:

Vp   *Il Nerone* (on binding, originally 'Monteverde'), Venice, Biblioteca Nazionale Marciana, MS 9963 (It. IV.439) (Acts I and III copied by Francesco Cavalli's wife in the early 1650s; contains additional annotations by Cavalli)

Np   [untitled], Naples, Conservatorio di Musica S Pietro a Majella, MS Rari 6.4.1 (associated with 1651 Naples performance?)

Other material:

SV   *La coronatione di Poppea* (Venice, Giovanni Pietro Pinelli, 1643); *scenario*

---

the scores (*Np*) would seem to be associated with a touring version of *L'incoronazione* presented in Naples in 1651 by the Febiarmonici; the other score (*Vp*) was also copied in the 1650s in circles close to Francesco Cavalli. Most of the librettos, on the other hand, would generally seem to be associated with a more 'literary' transmission of the text, including Busenello's final approved version in his collected works, *Delle hore ociose*, of 1656 (*LV*); one important exception is the recently discovered libretto in Udine (Biblioteca Comunale, Fondo Joppi 496; *U*) which, according to Paolo Fabbri, reflects a reading close to the (now lost) original score. But most of these sources are located at some temporal distance from the première; their relationship to what was originally composed and heard in early 1643 is therefore problematic. For that matter, the composer's own name was thought to have been first associated with *L'incoronazione* only in the much later, and error-ridden,

'Le memorie teatrali di Venezia' in Cristoforo Ivanovich's *Minerva al tavolino* (Venice, Nicolo Pezzana, 1681), at least until the discovery of *U*, which mentions Monteverdi in its colophon (although the date of this manuscript remains unclear). And there are other well-known difficulties. The text of the final duet for Nerone and Poppea was used in a revival in Bologna in 1641 of Benedetto Ferrari's *Il pastor reggio* (first performed in Venice in 1640; the music is now lost), and in an entertainment (1647) by Filiberto Laurenzi; it is not included in *LV*, which ends with the triumphal proclamation of the Coro di Amori, 'e in ogni clima, in ogni regione / si senta rimbombar "Poppea e Nerone"' ('and in every clime, in every region, let there resound "Poppea and Nerone"'). The score also includes music almost certainly by other composers. The opening sinfonia is reworked in Cavalli's *Doriclea* of 1645, and instrumental music in the consul scene in III.8 appears in a touring version (1644–5) of Francesco Sacrati's *La finta pazza* (first performed in Venice in 1641). Alan Curtis also argues, on the grounds variously of notation and of musical style, that at least the final scene (III.8) and the parts for Ottone, if not other sections of the opera, are by one or more other hands, probably including those of Sacrati and Ferrari.[1] But as with *Il ritorno*, we still lack a full collation of the materials for *L'incoronazione* that would permit a thorough reconstruction of their *stemma(e)*; moreover, the impact of any such collation on a full and proper edition of the opera, whether based on *Vp*, *Np* or a conflation of the two, has not yet been realized. As a result, one cannot yet sustain the commonly held assumption that *Vp* somehow presents a more 'authentic' version of the opera, closer to the 1643 original (for all that *Vp* dates from the 1650s), and, in turn, that the variants in *Np* are increasingly 'inauthentic'. Indeed, those not infrequent places where *U* is nearer to *Np* than *Vp* leave the matter entirely open.

　　Nor is it clear whether these issues reflect a workshop approach to the original composition of *L'incoronazione* – after all, Monteverdi was now in his mid-seventies, a good age by any reckoning – or subsequent accretions and revisions after the composer's death. However, a fair amount of the opera as it survives rings reasonably true as Monteverdi; there are often close parallels between its music and that of *Il ritorno* (see Ex. 10-1), particularly, and curiously, as the opera progresses, and most of the latter part of Act II and much of Act III seem very close indeed, as is the music for the gods and allegorical characters. And although the bulk of the final scene (III.8) would

1　See Curtis, '*La Poppea impasticciata*', and also the preface to his 1989 edition of the score. However, reference must still be made to Osthoff, 'Die venezianische und neapolitanische Fassung von Monteverdis "Incoronazione di Poppea"'; idem, 'Neue Beobachtungen zu Quellen und Geschichte von Monteverdis "Incoronazione di Poppea"'; and Chiarelli, '*L'incoronazione di Poppea o Il Nerone*'.

Ex. 10-1 (a) *Il ritorno d'Ulisse in patria*, I.2; (b) *L'incoronazione di Poppea*, I.4;
(c) *Il ritorno*, I.8; (d) *L'incoronazione*, I.9; (e) *Il ritorno*, II.3; (f) *L'incoronazione*, III.5.

Ex. 10-1 *Continued*

Ex. 10-1 *Continued*

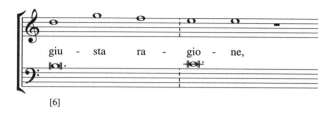

[6]

(Il ritorno) Vienna, Österreichische Nationalbibliothek, MS 18763, fols 16v–17r, 38v, 63r;
(L'incoronazione) Vp, fols 15v, 37v, 92v.

[a] It would be a lie if I, praising you, did not love you . . .

[b] Sire, you always see me, or rather, you do not see me . . .

[c] [of an outraged] goddess such is the anger.

[d] in spite of you, regardless of the people, and of the senate, and of Ottavia,
and of heaven, and of hell . . .

[e] Go to your mother, go! Step to the palace . . .

[f] for the repudiation [of Ottavia] you now have good reason . . .

appear to be by another composer – it also feels very disjointed, suggesting
several stages of revision – it may even be possible (as we saw in Chapter 8)
to redeem the final duet for Nerone and Poppea as being, if not by
Monteverdi, then at least a very plausible imitation of him. These problems
of authorship, however, need not be too disruptive, except for those who –
probably unreasonably – want to hear a single composer's voice in this work.

Some problems of interpretation

The difficulties over the sources – and also those associated with the apparent 'message' of *L'incoronazione* – would not be so disconcerting if we did not
have so much to invest in Monteverdi's last opera. Inevitably, we would like
to see in it a grand artistic statement summing up almost forty years' involvement in the theatre, an authoritative pronouncement on the human condition, and even, perhaps, some kind of oracular vision of the future. But
L'incoronazione is neither *Die Zauberflöte* nor *Falstaff*, and Monteverdi's apparent fascination with the antics of a degenerate Roman emperor and his
schemingly seductive mistress does not quite fit our bill. The situation is akin
to another morally problematic opera, Mozart's *Così fan tutte*, the last of his
three comic operas to librettos by Lorenzo da Ponte, and it is not surprising
that recent critical strategies for dealing with *L'incoronazione* have been quite
similar to those adopted for *Così*. The easiest solution is to blame anyone or
anything other than the composer, be it the librettist (both Busenello and da

Ponte have come in for a fair degree of disapproval), contemporary taste or, indeed, the commercial and other pressures under which these works were produced. Thus as early as 1908, Vincent d'Indy used the 'inferiority of the verse' (*cette infériorité du poème*) to explain the weaknesses of much of the music in *L'incoronazione*, and hence to justify his cuts; he also admitted, however, that some of the comic scenes anticipate Mozart, although for musical quality he preferred the death of Seneca and Ottavia's Act III lament. The more difficult solution is to find some new set of documents hinting at one or more meanings that remain otherwise hidden, except to the initiated: we shall see some examples for *L'incoronazione* below. But either way, Monteverdi and Mozart are absolved, and we renew our faith in music that remains achingly beautiful in spite of, rather than because of, its text.

In the case of *L'incoronazione*, the stakes are raised still higher by the fact that it is often claimed to be the first surviving 'historical' opera, in the sense of presenting 'real' characters from the past, rather than the gods of classical mythology, the shepherds of a fictive Arcadia, or the quasi-mythological heroes of classical or romance epic. Where this leaves the hagiographic Roman operas supported by the Barberini in the early 1630s – are saints' lives not 'historical'? – or how we should account for the presence of Amore in *L'incoronazione* as, in effect, a *deus ex machina* are interesting questions. But history, we assume, requires some kind of fidelity to the facts of previous ages, and also seeks to offer lessons for self-improvement: we learn from our pasts to make sense of our presents and to determine our futures. However, this places a significant, perhaps unreasonable, burden upon reading *L'incoronazione*. For example, were its characters different in name, time and place, their actions would not be unusual for a contemporary comedy or a (slightly later) comic opera: two young lovers resist arranged, unhappy marriages and the interference of a busybody elder tutor to find true bliss. Even death or exile for the 'bad' characters were not unreasonable outcomes in contemporary comic scenarios, at least if we are to believe the story-lines in contemporary *novelle* (whose influence on Venetian opera remains to be explored). Imperial Rome, however, would seem to bear a weightier moral burden, at least if its decline and fall is to pass the gimlet scrutiny of an Edward Gibbon.

Busenello felt scant allegiance to the 'facts' of history, or so he suggests in the *Argomento* prefacing *LV*:

> Nero, enamoured of Poppaea, who was the wife of Otho, sent the latter, under the pretext of embassy, to Lusitania so that he could take his pleasure with her – this according to Cornelius Tacitus. But here we represent these actions differently. Otho, desperate at seeing himself deprived of Poppaea, gives himself over to frenzy and exclamations. Octavia, wife of Nero, orders Otho to kill Poppaea. Otho promises to do it; but lacking the

spirit to deprive his adored Poppaea of life, he dresses in the clothes of Drusilla, who was in love with him. Thus disguised, he enters the garden of Poppaea. Amor disturbs and prevents that death. Nero repudiates Octavia, in spite of the counsel of Seneca, and takes Poppaea to wife. Seneca dies, and Octavia is expelled from Rome.[2]

His historical sources include Tacitus' *Annals* (XIII–XVI), Suetonius and Dio Cassius, and also the pseudo-Senecan tragedy *Octavia*. But Busenello has reordered and reconstituted historical events: the beginning of Nero's relationship with Poppaea in AD 58 and the transfer of Otho to Lusitania that same year; Nero's marriage to Poppaea and the exile (then death) of Octavia in AD 62; and the death of Seneca for involvement in the Pisonian Conspiracy against the emperor in AD 65. Also waiting in the temporal wings are Nero's murder of Poppaea in AD 65, his own suicide in AD 68, and Otho's brief assumption of the imperial throne in AD 69, plus, as we shall see, the death of Lucan, also as a result of the Pisonian Conspiracy in AD 65. To argue that, for all Busenello's manipulation of fact (presumably, by poetic licence), he nevertheless seeks out some version of historical truth depends on the notion of an adherence to Tacitist principles, whereby the motivations of characters can be kept distinct from, and indeed are often disguised by, their actions; and thus, that it is the task of the historian to delve behind appearances.

Tacitism has regularly been invoked to explain *L'incoronazione* in the context both of the Accademia degli Incogniti – whose leader, Giovanni Francesco Loredano, was the dedicatee of a commentary on Tacitus by Pio Mutio published in Venice in 1642 – and of the Venetian republicanism that is regularly seen to lie at the heart of the opera.[3] Tacitus' ultra-cynical view of historical events, actions and people in the Roman Empire was at once condemned as the ultimate in Machiavellian manipulation and praised for the insights it offered into corrupt administrations. Similarly, if less reasonably, the members of the Accademia degli Incogniti have been painted as sceptical libertines extolling a peculiarly Venetian brand of (im)morality. Yet Loredano himself was a respected Venetian senator and literary figure, whose intentionally 'witty' and 'bizarre' discourses – published with such titles as *Scherzi geniali*

2   The *argomento* is given in the preface (p. xxii) of Curtis's 1989 edition of the score. Curtis also gives relevant extracts from *SV* at the head of each scene. The libretto itself is in fact delicately ambiguous on whether Ottone and Poppea are actually married. As Tacitus makes clear, the original relationship between Otho and Poppaea was itself adulterous (she was married to Rufrius Crispinus, by whom she bore a son). Nor, incidentally, was Nero's extra-marital liaison with Poppaea his first.
3   The 'republican' reading was first advocated by Rosand in her pioneering 1985 article on Seneca. Loredano was the dedicatee of *Considerationi sopra il primo libro di Cornelio Tacito di Don Pio Mutio, milanese* (Venice, Marco Ginammi, 1642).

and *Bizzarie ac(c)ademiche* – have perhaps been treated with less levity than they deserve. One might say the same for Venetian operas in general, which were, after all, entertainments for Carnival. Also, if the Incogniti were so free-thinking, it is hard to see how the entirely respectable *Il ritorno* could come from another Incognito pen (Badoaro's).[4] But it has always been accepted that Tacitus' brand of imperialism, when read correctly, strongly served the cause of republicanism – the mode of good government for which Venice claimed both priority and pre-eminence – while the Incogniti, whatever their stance, tended to support, rather than undermine, the system. Thus Mutio's commentary on Tacitus, dedicated to Loredano, opens with a paean of praise of Venice's good government. As a result, the 'enemy' of republican Venice becomes Imperial, and by extension modern, Rome (and Venice–Rome relations were famously problematic even before the Interdict of 1606–7), whose sins become displayed and satirized on the operatic stage. Quite apart from the excesses of Nerone and Poppea, this further explains much of the undoubted polemic in the opera: the Soldati's complaints in I.2 about impending military catastrophe (this was, of course, the period of the Thirty Years War, when 'Armenia' was truly in rebellion and 'Pannonia' up in arms); Seneca's argument with Nerone in I.9 over what might be justified according to reason of state (*ragione di stato*) and what by imperial whim;[5] and even the strong statements against the court and its false behaviour, delivered by the Soldati in I.2, Arnalta in II.10 and Ottone in II.12. It also invokes our own historical knowledge of the fates of the real Nero, Poppaea and Otho – and, for that matter, of Seneca who, as Liberto predicts in II.2, lived on in his writings long after the passing of the Roman Empire – even if one might reasonably ask to what an extent an operatic subject should be judged by our awareness of events extraneous to it. In the end, one is encouraged to believe the Soldati in I.2 – 'Sia maledetto Amor, Poppea, Nerone, / e Roma, e la milizia' – that Amore, Poppea, Nerone and even Rome (and the military; they are soldiers, after all) are cursed for ever.

It has also been hard to accept at face value the apparent message of the prologue to *L'incoronazione*, so different from those of *Orfeo* and *Il ritorno*. That Fortuna and Virtù must in the end succumb to Amore could just be a conventional trope to motivate the action, much as the characters Amore and Fortuna would proclaim submission to Destino in Cavalli's *Ormindo* (1644, to a libretto by Giovanni Faustini). Also, Fortuna does not do badly in the opera:

4 A point made in Degrada, 'Il teatro di Claudio Monteverdi', p. 277. Degrada also
   cautions against too much attention on the Incogniti, particularly at the expense of
   its individual members; he feels that Busenello in particular has been mistreated by
   scholars not paying enough attention to the librettist's own writings.
5 The Venetians themselves were often accused of using *ragione di stato* as a justification
   for misdeeds; see Bouwsma, *Venice and the Defense of Republican Liberty*, p. 503.

Poppea has both love and fortune fighting on her side (she says in I.4), and Drusilla submits herself to fortune in III.4, even if Ottone is painted (by Poppea in I.11) as fortune's victim. But Virtù certainly takes a fall, and the debate in *L'incoronazione* seems heavily weighted in favour of Amore. This might be (and has been) explained in the Neoplatonic light of a possible ascent from earthly to heavenly love; and the fact that in II.11 Busenello has Amore cite the last line of Dante's *Paradiso* – 'Amor, che move il sol e l'altre stelle' ('Love, who moves the sun and other planets') – must be significant.[6] But with what we think we know of Nero and Poppaea, things do not augur well.

Even that does not quite satisfy our need to find some good in the opera's characters and actions. Much of the debate has hinged on Seneca, who was viewed historically, and is represented in the opera, in seemingly contradictory ways. On the one hand, according to the Soldati in I.2 and Valletto in I.7, he is the hypocritical pedant and corrupt beneficiary of Nero's misdeeds. On the other, he is the noble Stoic who views the world and its ways with admirable constancy even in the face of death, and who alone of all the characters is able to converse with the gods (Pallade and Mercurio). Rosand accepts the presence of both Senecas in the opera's libretto (and in contemporary Venetian historical discourse), although she argues that Monteverdi's noble, passionate music rescues the character from opprobrium. The chief problem of investing so much moral authority in Seneca, thus determining a reading of the opera as a whole, is the fact that he dies less than half-way through, in II.3, creating a moral vacuum thereafter. It is partly the need to find a 'hero' who survives to the end of the opera that seems to have prompted Iain Fenlon and Peter Miller (in *The Song of the Soul*) to transfer the virtues of Senecan constancy to Drusilla; her noble behaviour in Act III to protect her beloved Ottone makes her, as Nerone himself claims (in III.4), a paragon of her sex and an ideal example of the virtue of constancy (and he repeats 'la tua costanza' to emphasize the point). But Drusilla is not quite the newly inserted character (drawn from Ariosto's *Orlando furioso*) that Fenlon and Miller claim: the 'real' Drusilla was the unsavoury daughter of Agrippina the Elder.[7] Nor is she entirely innocent – she is complicit in the attempted murder of Poppea – while Nerone's acclamation does not come from the most trustworthy of sources. However, Drusilla's own appeal to the virtue of friendship, one of the very few cases in the opera where a character addresses the audience directly (another is Arnalta in II.10), becomes associated with a

6 For the broader issues, and also the quotation, see Ketterer, 'Neoplatonic Light and Dramatic Genre in Busenello's *L'incoronazione di Poppea* and Noris's *Il ripudio d'Ottavia*'.
7 See Heller, 'Tacitus Incognito', p. 63 n. 74.

further theme in Act III, that of clemency.[8] The fact that the erotic and even (im)moral temperature of the opera cools down significantly in the final act – even Poppea no longer plays the sex-kitten – must be at least partly because, with Seneca out of the way, the lovers' case was won as soon as Ottavia and Ottone colluded in murder. But Ottavia, Ottone and Drusilla are now so guilty that even the most ardent Venetian republican would understand their being put to death. Nerone's clemency, at least within the opera, becomes a surprising exemplar of (good) royal behaviour and goes some way to making the ending of the work more palatable. It also suggests that not all of Seneca's lessons were lost on his imperial pupil.

The most recent candidate (proposed by Wendy Heller) for rescuing *L'incoronazione* for some kind of moral cause is Lucano.[9] But he is even more problematic. He appears in just one scene of the opera (II.5), in which he and Nerone celebrate Seneca's death and sing extravagant praise of Poppea's beauties. The 'real' Lucan (Seneca's nephew) had been an intimate of Nero but had fallen out with him (in AD 64); the estrangement affected the completion of Lucan's epic poem, *Pharsalia*, concerning the defeat of Pompey by Caesar at Pharsalus that effectively marked the end of the Roman Republic. *Pharsalia* has thus been read as a strongly anti-imperial, pro-republican text. Certainly that was the view taken by Alberto Campani in his contemporary Italian translation of Lucan's poem, *Farsaglia, poema heroico di M. Anneo Lucano di Corduba* (Venice, Giacomo Sarzina, 1640), which has a dedication (dated 12 September 1639) to Loredano, a prefatory poem consecrating the glories of republican Venice, and also a biography of Lucan. Lucano's presence in *L'incoronazione*, then, can be read as yet one more allusion to a better, republican world, free of imperial corruption. But there remains the slight problem of reconciling this reading with Lucano's single appearance in a scene with Nerone that would seem to be an epitome of orgiastic excess (so it is often performed), and one, moreover, in what might also be perceived as a strongly homoerotic context. It might better serve Heller's cause to realize the most likely target of this scene. One reason for Nero and Lucan's falling out, so Campani tell us, was their engagement in a poetry contest in which Lucan

---

8 In III.3, Drusilla says 'O voi ch'al mondo vi chiamate amici, / deh specchiatevi in me: / questi del vero amico son gl'uffici' ('O you who in the world call yourselves friends, ah mirror yourselves on me: these are the duties of a true friend'). For a preliminary exploration of this theme, and of Drusilla's virtue based on love contrasted with Seneca's based on the intellect, see Giuntini, 'L'Amore trionfante nell'"Incoronazione di Poppea"'.

9 See Heller, 'Tacitus Incognito'. She deserves the credit for bringing Lucan into the frame; a spoken version of her paper preceded my 'Re-Reading *Poppea*', where I focus on Lucan and the paradoxical encomium, discussed further, below. Heller (p. 88) also refers to Campani's translation of Lucan and its prefatory poem, but does not use his biography of the poet.

was awarded the prize. The echoes in II.5 seem quite strong, especially given the apparent changes to the libretto (whether or not by Monteverdi) that redistribute to Lucano text allocated to Nerone, reducing the latter to stuttering incoherence ('ahi, ahi, ahi, ahi destin!'). As a result, in this contest of 'amorosi canzoni', Lucano outdoes Nerone in poetic extravagance, rhetorical eloquence and even musical prowess. The point becomes still clearer when one considers the subject (again, according to Campani) of Lucan's poem that defeated Nero's, the story of Orpheus.[10]

But Lucan's *Pharsalia* may offer a better clue for any reading of *L'incoronazione*. The poem starts with a long encomium in praise of Nero, the grotesque extravagance of which hardly squares with Lucan's presumed republican tendencies. Accordingly, in the Renaissance (when Lucan was widely read) this fawning eulogy was generally construed as a masterpiece of irony. It was also taken as one model for a rhetorical genre that gained some currency during the sixteenth and seventeenth centuries, the so-called paradoxical encomium, an exercise in praising that which cannot be praised. Erasmus' *Moriae encomion* (*Praise of Folly*, 1509) was one in a long line of paradoxical encomia written for rhetorical training and amusement and covering a number of standard topics, one of which was, precisely, the praise of Nero (others include madness and the French pox).[11] Girolamo Cardano's (1501–76) *Neronis encomium* is one example; another is Henri de Boulay's *Il Nerone difeso di Luciano*, published in 1627 by the Venetian printer Evangelista Deuchino as the third of *Tre discorsi del Signor Henrico De Bullay, gentil'huomo francese*. De Boulay was a Frenchman earning his living in Venice as a tutor to young members of the nobility – a context also relevant, it seems, to the *Combattimento di Tancredi e Clorinda* – and his fanciful dialogue thus offers both rhetorical training and moral precepts. It is set in the Underworld, with Nero summoned before the judge Minos for his crimes, and specifically for the

---

10 Campani recounts the story in his biography of Lucan. His source remains unclear; the episode does not appear in Suetonius' *Life of Lucan*. Nero's poem was on Niobe, whose famous arrogance, like Poppaea's, also came to a sticky end.

11 Compare George Chapman, *A Iustification of a Strange Action of Nero; in burying with a solemne funerall, one of the cast hayres of his mistresse Poppaea. Also a iust reproofe of a Romane smell-feast, being [a translation of] the fifth Satyre of Iuvenall* (London, Thomas Harper, 1629); and S. S., *Paradoxes, or Encomiums in the praise of: Being Lowsey; Treachery; Nothing; Beggery; the French Pox; Blindnesse; The Emperor Nero; Madnesse* (London, W. N., 1653). The latter condemns (p. 21) 'that very Seneca who wrot[e] so much in the praise of temperance, and fortitude, yet lived like an absolute epicure, and dyed like an effeminate coward'. In the preface, the author claims that 'I have attempted by a kind of novel Alchemy to turn Tin into Silver, and Copper into Gold'; of these paradoxes 'there hath none more intricate, been discussed, and canvased, among the Stoicks in Zenos Porch, [and] if thy sense besot not thy understanding, I do not doubt a welcome'.

murder of his mother Agrippina. In response to Minos' questioning, Nero asks for Seneca to be called as a witness, at which point the emperor presents an extraordinary defence of his life: his immoral excesses can be blamed on his family, on his poor upbringing and on destiny; his actions were justifiable by reason of state and indeed were approved by the Roman senate; and his erstwhile tutor Seneca (also responsible for his poor upbringing) both encouraged and was complicit in his crimes and benefited materially from them. Nero also draws to Minos' attention his own good points – including his artistic talents – and his military and architectural achievements for the glory of Rome and the Empire. But it is the attack on Seneca that provides the focus of De Boulay's text, which goes further than most in accusing the philosopher not just of luxury and wantonness, but also of sexual excess (with Agrippina, among many others), and of murder for political gain. De Boulay's Nero belittles Seneca's learning (in the manner of Valletto) and argues that, all in all, if Seneca had been of a different cast, things might not have turned out as they did.

Of course, none of this is to be taken seriously. If that were not apparent from the text – which is surprisingly persuasive – and its offence against common sense, it is so from De Boulay's title, *Il Nerone difeso di Luciano*. The dialogue masquerades as an Italian translation of a text in defence of Nero by the Greek poet Lucian, which is sufficient to anchor both the genre and the mode of the piece. It is written in the manner of Lucian's *Dialogues of the Dead*, a number of which focus on similar Underworld scenarios, and like much of Lucian, it is intended to be read satirically. For the Renaissance, Lucian, Juvenal and others established a sophist–satirical mode that gained some popularity in Italian and north European political and moral tracts, especially those attacking the monarchy, the Church or intellectuals.[12] Lucian himself vehemently attacked the Stoics in his writings, and Socrates, Seneca's great predecessor in noble suicide, receives harsh treatment in *Dialogues of the Dead*, IV (which may in turn have influenced De Boulay's criticisms of Seneca). Lucian also advocated 'the way ordinary men live' (*Menippus*, IV), in the face of the vanity of human endeavour and the mutability of fortune; thus his is the voice of the Soldati in *L'incoronazione*, I.2. His cynicism, plus the strong whiff of anti–establishment subversion (his writings were on the *Index librorum prohibitorum*), must have struck a chord in Venice, and especially within the Accademia degli Incogniti.

Lucian certainly makes his presence felt in the librettos of Monteverdi's late operas. His *The Parasite* has direct bearing on the treatment of the character Iro in *Il ritorno d'Ulisse in patria*, and the dispute between Fortuna, Virtù and Amore in the prologue to *L'incoronazione di Poppea* is a

---

12   The standard text remains Robinson, *Lucian and his Influence in Europe*.

Lucianic topos. No less linked to Lucian is the fact that not one single character of *L'incoronazione* (not even Seneca, as we have seen) stands out unequivocally as a paragon of virtue. But while it may be useful to politicize the references to Lucian, Lucan and others as indicative of Venetian republican political and social theorizing, or at least one strain thereof, one must remember that paradoxical encomia and other satirical genres cut both ways: they may have moral or political points to make, but they also exhibit a delight in rhetoric for its own sake. And there is some merit in dissecting *L'incoronazione* with just such a double-edged blade, as a paradoxical encomium either of Nero and Poppaea or, more intriguingly, of the Love (false and politically dangerous) that the Incogniti were to denounce in a different context as 'a plague and a defect, not an affect, of the heart', and which appears so prominently in the prologue and throughout the opera.[13] Thus Amore's victory over Virtù may, perhaps should, be read paradoxically. Indeed, one might go further and see *Il ritorno* and *L'incoronazione* as counterpointing each other in terms of presenting different faces of love, whether 'true' (constant Penelope) or 'false' (debauched Poppaea), as a textual and musical debate typical of so many within the Accademia degli Incogniti, an exercise *in utramque partem disputare* that was a basic feature of rhetorical training and of academic discussion. Whether such debates were to be taken seriously is an entirely different matter.

But however one reads *L'incoronazione* – as reprehensible smut, elegant paradox, or indeed carnivalesque subversion – one cannot deny the sheer artistry of Busenello's libretto. He draws upon the conventions and also the structures of contemporary tragedy and comedy to build scenes that lead to carefully calculated climaxes, and successions of scenes that produce a dramatic framework that is both cogent and powerful: the daring juxtaposition of the death of Seneca with a frivolous love-scene for a page (Valletto) and his girlfriend (Damigella) is just one obvious example. It is striking, too, that all this takes place within a structure that adheres to the unities of action and time: the opera takes place within the twelve hours from dawn to dusk (Nerone, Seneca and Ottavia each note how various events will happen by the end of the day), and Busenello is careful to mark the passing of time, even to the extent of having Arnalta explain in II.10 that, although Poppea is to sleep in the garden, this is just an afternoon nap ('è luminoso il dì, sì come suole, / e pur vedete addormentato il sole'; 'the day is light, as is usual, and yet you see the sun falling asleep' – a play on Poppea as the sun).

---

13 See the preface to *Novelle amorose de' Signori Academici Incogniti publicate da Francesco Carmeni, segretario dell'Academia* (Venice, Heredi del Sarzina, 1641), fol. [A4]v: 'è una pesta, & un difetto, non un'affetto del cuore'. For other Incogniti statements on love, see Fenlon and Miller, *The Song of the Soul*, p. 35.

Busenello exhibits startling rhetorical skill in the debate between Nerone and
Seneca in I.9. He also demonstrates a secure grasp of the amorous psycho-
babble of Marinist verse: the scenes for Nerone and Poppea draw heavily
on the witty tropes of contemporary love-poetry and thus provide concrete
lessons in the poetic language of love, to be matched, in turn, by Monteverdi's
music.

'Amor è un'armonia'

According to Giovanni Francesco Loredano,

> Love is a child of harmony, and therefore I have seen those lovers who
> wish to give rise to it in their beloveds sing, but not release tears, which
> are unworthy of man and which would be more apt to produce laughter
> instead of Love.[14]

Like the Proci in *Il ritorno*, Loredano affirms the indissoluble association of
love and harmony. In the prologue to *L'incoronazione*, triple-time writing is
associated with dissipation (Fortuna: 'Dissipata, disusata, / abborrita, malgra-
dita') and corruption (Fortuna: 'I privilegi e i titoli vendesti'), but most
strongly, and not inconsistently, with love (Amore: 'Riveritemi, / adoratemi').
In the opera, the theme is taken up with a vengeance. If Penelope takes time
to learn the musical language of love, Poppea knows it right from the start,
and her propensity towards song threatens to overwhelm *L'incoronazione* in
swathes of glorious melody.

Again there remain vestiges of diegetic verisimilitude: Arnalta accuses
Poppea (II.10) of singing too much and too often about her wedding ('Pur
sempre sulle nozze / canzoneggiando vai'), while, according to Valletto (I.6),
Seneca's philosophical musings are just so many songs. But while Valletto's
criticism is pointed up by a musical reference to the *ciaccona*, an archetypal
dance-song, Arnalta's has no word-painting whatsoever: song is a serious
matter for Poppea. And the songs she sings are much more developed than
anything in *Il ritorno*. Although generally in *L'incoronazione* we still find a flexible shifting between what one might call recitative, arioso and aria, arias
increasingly become separate entities, often articulated by opening (but less
frequently, closing) instrumental ritornellos that act more as structural markers

---

14 Loredano, *Bizzarie academiche* (1676), part 1, pp. 217–18: 'Amore è figliuolo
    dell'harmonia, e però quegli amanti, che vorrebono farlo nascere nelle loro amate
    hò ben io veduti cantare, ma non versar lagrime, indegne dell'huomo, e che
    sarebbero atte a produrre il riso in vece d'Amore'. This is from the 'Contesa del
    canto e delle lagrime' discussed in Rosand, 'Barbara Strozzi', pp. 278–80; compare
    also Fenlon and Miller, *The Song of the Soul*, p. 39.

than to fulfil any functional role, such as catering for stage movement. Also, as triple time becomes common coinage, we see the newer forms of duple-time aria-writing that had started to emerge in Monteverdi's Seventh Book of madrigals (although 'Qual honor di te fia degno' in *Orfeo* is an important precedent) and in the 1632 *Scherzi musicali*.

Poppea's arias allow her to dominate the stage and also to manipulate Nero, her strongly phrased lines contrasting markedly with his more languid efforts. There is something dangerous about a female character so prone to song: the Clori of *Tirsi e Clori* stayed more decorously within the limits of recitative, while Penelope in *Il ritorno*, as we have seen, staunchly resists the blandishments of aria. In the case of Poppea, however, song becomes a matter of erotic power and control. In I.3, for example (and as we saw in Chapter 3), her duple-time response, 'Signor, sempre mi vedi' (Ex. 10-1(b)), to Nerone's triple-time 'In un sospir che vien' reveals firmly who holds the reins in their relationship, and elsewhere Monteverdi gives the strong impression of Poppea seizing control of her music by way of lyrical effusions, repetitive refrains and even the *concitato genere* (I.5 provides good examples of all three). This is largely the composer's doing. In I.12, the second scene in the opera for Nerone and Poppea, the text is in *versi sciolti* throughout, without even any partial cues for aria (such as sequences of *versi tronchi* or focused conceits). But although Poppea begins in a languid recitative, she soon moves into short passages of triple time ('Di questo seno i pomi', 'Di queste braccia'), with breathless off-beat gasps and sighs, then a much longer outpouring ('Signor, le tue parole son sì dolci . . . sul cor i baci', covering eleven lines of verse), and finally what is in effect a song of exultation ('A speranze sublime il cor innalzo' over a 4-bar ground bass heard twice), before returning to recitative for her crafty insinuations against Seneca. Here Nerone is more bound to recitative, although he cannot in the end resist turning to triple time himself at 'Ma che dico, o Poppea?' ('But what do I say, o Poppea?'). Here, ten lines of verse are presented over a 2-bar ground bass, repeated with variation and transposition, as Nerone proclaims Poppea's present and future glory in her own musical language.

Nerone appears surprised at the effects of Poppea's musical rhetoric upon him ('Ma che dico, o Poppea?'). For all the musical fame of the 'real' Nero, one might in turn wonder about Nerone's own propensity to song, which might seem a sign of his lack of moral fibre. The resulting gender issues have a strong impact on any reading of *L'incoronazione*: while women might reasonably resort to songful wiles as a tool of seduction, men are usually meant to be made of sterner stuff. And although we might somehow expect Nerone to be feeble-minded, the matter comes to a head in any reading of the unfortunate Ottone. His cause is lost from the outset, not only because he is being cuckolded by the Emperor of Rome, but also because his musical language

Ex. 10-2 *L'incoronazione*, I.1, Ottone.

Vp, fol. 6v.

And so I return here, as a line to the centre, as fire to the sphere, and as a
stream to the sea . . .

is entirely inappropriate for anyone aspiring to be a man of action. At his
very first appearance in I.1 (Ex. 10-2), his opening bar, 'E pur io torno', might
seem to be recitative, but it soon moves into a more formal triple time (despite
the *endecasillabi*). If that were not enough to emasculate Ottone – and we
have no idea at all why he should be singing an aria[15] – the repetitive bass,

15   In classical terms, however, this is an example of a *paraclausithyron*, a lover's song in
     front of the closed door of the beloved; see the broad discussion of Ovidian and
     other tropes in *L'incoronazione* in Ketterer, '*Militat omnis amans*'. Nerone and

the flaccid trills and the fact that the melody gets monotonously 'stuck' on a single note (following the text) further disempower the character. It is hard to feel much sympathy for him. His whining laments become tedious, and he treats Drusilla shamefully both as he makes love to her at the end of Act I ('Drusilla ho in bocca, ed ho Poppea nel core'; 'Drusilla is on my lips, and Poppea in my heart'), and as he involves her (II.9) in the attempt on Poppea's life. Even where we might expect our compassion to be aroused, when Ottavia blackmails him to murder her rival (in II.7), the point is weakened by the fact that Ottone had already resolved to kill Poppea (in I.12; although, typically, he repents that decision in II.6), and also because, as Ottone admits, he becomes hoist by the petard of false courtly gallantry: he promises Ottavia that he will do anything to help her, but then claims that this was just out of conventional politeness. But for all that Ottone is pusillanimous, his chief defect is that he has adopted a feminized musical mantle long before he dons Drusilla's dress to kill his beloved.

Loredano would no doubt have included Ottone among those men who sing for love. But Ottone is no match for Poppea, a point made even before their first and only encounter in I.11, the scene which, in turn, sets the seal on their relationship. The idea that I.11 should in effect turn into a singing contest must have been Busenello's: this scene is constructed of seven 6-line stanzas (aBaBCC), the first six alternating between Ottone and Poppea, and the last split between them (two lines each, then one each, although Poppea starts the final line early by way of interruption). Monteverdi responds by setting the first six stanzas in strophic variation (the last, divided stanza is in recitative), although Poppea's melodies are regularly more expansive, rhythmically tauter and more goal-directed. The composer may not have had a choice about one factor that has a decisive effect on the characterization here: with Ottone effectively as an alto and Poppea as a soprano, for each set of stanzas to fit within their respective ranges (roughly, a fourth apart) they must be in a different key, Poppea's in C minor and Ottone's in G minor (at some stage his stanzas were transposed to A minor, presumably to suit a new singer). This gives Poppea the upper hand, and still more so when her last solo stanza moves up a tone to D minor. By the end of the scene, Ottone cannot even form a perfect cadence to conclude his speech (Ex. 10-3). The Naples score tries to rescue the situation with a sympathetic reaction from Arnalta (who has been watching from the side), but to little avail. It is hardly surprising that Monteverdi seems in the end to have lost interest in the character: Ottone's part in the murder scene in II.12 is fairly feeble, and he all but disappears as a significant musical presence in Act III.

Poppea's entrance in I.3, on the other hand, invokes the medieval *alba* as two lovers part at dawn.

Ex. 10-3 *L'incoronazione*, I.11.

Vp, fol. 48v.

Ottone: Is this the reward for my love? *Poppea*: Say no more, I am Nerone's.

Seneca

If, in the case of the male characters of *L'incoronazione*, triple time is the language of love fulfilled (Nerone) or failed (Ottone), that leaves the other important male in the opera, Seneca, in a difficult position. Casting him as a bass would seem on balance to grant the character a certain *gravitas*: his would seem to be the bass voice traditionally associated with the gods (compare Caronte and Plutone in *Orfeo*, Plutone in the *Ballo delle ingrate*, Nettuno in *Il ritorno* and, for that matter, Mercurio in *L'incoronazione*), rather than with potentially comic figures (Antinoo in *Il ritorno*). Seneca appears appropriately serious when he first enters in I.6, and his initial excursions into triple time seem prompted largely by the demands of poetic accentuation ('Ringrazia la fortuna') or word-painting (the face's 'beauty' in 'La vaghezza del volto, i lineamenti'). But Monteverdi also gives him a worrying tendency to engage in vapid musical gestures, whether to support his words (a melisma on 'faville', 'sparks') or even to contradict them (more than three bars of running semiquavers on the definite article 'la' of 'la bellezza'). In effect, the composer pre-empts Valletto's own criticism of Seneca's sentential dicta, that they are just 'songs', and once that negative judgement has been made, it is hard for us to know how best to read his subsequent effusions. Presumably Monteverdi later seeks to use aria styles for Seneca to indicate resolve – as with 'Venga la morte pur . . .' ('Let death come . . .') in response to Pallade in I.8, in duple time over a 2-bar ground bass stated five times – and a serene acceptance of fate (on several occasions in II.1–2). But the seeds of doubt have been sown, and despite Rosand's eloquent pleading of Seneca's musical case, the music itself remains ambivalent.

The issue inevitably comes to a head, but remains frustratingly unresolved, in II.3, where Seneca prepares for death, surrounded by his Famigliari. Seneca's triple-time opening might seem prompted by the accentuation of the text ('Amici, è giunta l'ora'; 'Friends, the hour has come'), but Monteverdi's repetitions ('Amici, amici, è giunta, è giunta l'ora') make it suspiciously like yet another of his songs; and either way, this is not quite what one might expect of an impending suicide. The three Famigliari respond with what seems to be some kind of lament, based on the contrapuntal treatment of an ascending chromatic tetrachord ('Non morir, Seneca, no'; 'Do not die, Seneca, no'), then a further contrapuntal passage based on a descending diatonic idea ('Io per me morir non vò'; 'For myself, I would not die'), then (after a ritornello) two stanzas of a songful celebration of the joys of life ('Questa vita è dolce troppo'), before reversing the sequence ('Io per me morir non vò', 'Non morir, Seneca, no' and the ritornello, the last now seeming very out of place). The sequence of musical items has shades of the symmetrical structures of Act I of *Orfeo*, while 'Questa vita è dolce troppo' and its preceding ritornello echo Orfeo's 'Vi ricorda, o boschi ombrosi' in Act II, whether or not just because of the shared poetic metre (*ottonari*). 'Non morir, Seneca no', however, would seem on the face of it to be more serious in intent, as would better fit the apparent nature of the scene.

But the musical semiotic is at best ambiguous. The scoring of the Famigliari (alto, tenor, bass) recalls that of the Proci in *Il ritorno*, and 'Non morir, Seneca, no' is a chromatic reworking of the Proci's diatonic 'Ama dunque, sì, sì' in *Il ritorno*, II.5 (see Ex. 9-4(a)). This is also the typical scoring of the *giustiniana*, a Venetian popular genre in which three old men conventionally complain of their failure in love; Monteverdi wrote several pieces that invoke the genre. We are thus disposed to take the Famigliari with a pinch of salt. Ex. 10-4 illustrates the problem. Their ascending chromaticism was certainly associated with seriousness: the motif appears worked in the same contrapuntal way (but for five voices) in the motet 'Christe, adoramus te' which Monteverdi published in 1620. But the same motif, for much the same three voices as the Famigliari, also appears in a canzonetta that seems more *giustiniana*-like, 'Non partir, ritrosetta' in the *Madrigali guerrieri, et amorosi* of 1638. Here the male voices complain at the departure of their beloved, who ignores their laments – a situation not dissimilar to the Famigliari and Seneca, were it not for the fact that 'Non partir, ritrosetta' is obviously parodic and designed for fun. Seneca's death should not be a laughing matter, and yet the music offers at least the potential for it to be taken less than seriously. It is

Ex. 10-4 (a) *L'incoronazione*, II.3, Famigliari (voices only); (b) Monteverdi, 'Christe, adoramus te' (in Giulio Cesare Bianchi, *Libro primo de motetti in lode d'Iddio nostro signore a una, due, tre, quattro, cinque, e à otto voci con il basso generale . . . con un altro à cinque, e tre à sei del Sig. Claudio Monteverde* (Venice, Bartolomeo Magni, 1620)); (c) Monteverdi, 'Non partir, ritrosetta' (*Madrigali guerrieri, et amorosi . . . Libro ottavo* (Venice, Alessandro Vincenti, 1638)).

Ex. 10-4 *Continued*

Ex. 10-4 *Continued*

Vp, fol. 58r; *Claudio Monteverdi: Tutte le opere*, ed. Malipiero, xvi, pp. 428–9; ibid., viii, p. 307.

[a] Do not die, Seneca . . .
[b] for through Your cross [You redeemed the world.]
[c] You do not hear my laments, ah you flee . . .

not surprising that this scene seems to have been omitted in at least some seventeenth-century performances.

Vp, Np *and* Ottavia

In the end, it may be unreasonable to expect the music of *L'incoronazione*, or of any Venetian opera of the 1640s, to bear its semiotic burdens with the clarity of the later Baroque period. Genres, forms and styles were still in flux, and the erratic transitions characteristic of these works make it hard to pin things down. This is both their charm and their difficulty. Yet one can detect even in the sources various degrees of nervousness about how *L'incoronazione* might properly be read by contemporary audiences. The unknown author of the synopsis in *SV* takes his task seriously enough – even the simplest synopsis directs interpretation – to steer several matters in Seneca's favour, working harder on the character's behalf than seems warranted by the score.[16] Similar motives would appear to prompt various intriguing differences between *Vp* and *Np* (see Table 10-2). These differences have tended to be downplayed in the literature on *L'incoronazione*, chiefly because of the presumed inferiority of *Np*. Yet one need not take a stand on the priority of *Vp* versus *Np*, or on their respective authority, to explore the way in which their variants might reveal contemporary perceptions of several apparent problems in this work.

The fact that many of the additions in *Np* also appear in *LV* suggests that they were somehow sanctioned by Busenello as prompting an effective reading of his libretto. Some (such as in II.4, II.5, III.3 and III.4) simply expand upon the prevailing dramatic situation. Others, however, seem designed to foster a different slant. For example, the longer version of the problematic final scene places still more emphasis on the role of Amore as the guiding hand of events in the opera, bringing further to fruition the prophecy of the prologue. Other changes affect our view of individual characters. If we felt inclined to sympathize with Poppea – and she is, of course, a highly attractive character, at least for most male members of any audience – then the change in I.4 makes her seem much more grasping and indecorously confident that her scheming will be successful. The addition to I.12 places Ottone's fate in a broader context (the fickleness of women) and attracts some sympathy for him from at least one character on the stage, Arnalta, if only to have that turned into a comic point. The modifications in II.1–3, on the other hand, focus greater attention on Seneca's virtues, first as Liberto proclaims him a divine example (and Nerone, in contrast, the epitome of wickedness) and then as Seneca himself reassures his followers and sets up the touchstone of constancy.[17] The point is emphasized in Busenello's additional scene (in *LV*) representing the apotheosis of Seneca; this may have been dropped for reasons of staging or casting, although there is also a curious parallel with the abandoned scene in *Il ritorno* (III.2) for Mercury and the shades of the suitors, despite the fact that Seneca's is hardly 'maninconica'.

16 Carter, 'Re-Reading *Poppea*', pp. 192–3.
17 On tonal grounds, this longer version of Seneca's final speech would seem to be part of the original conception of the scene; see Carter, 'Re-Reading *Poppea*', p. 189.

Table 10-2   Substantive variants in *Np* and *LV* compared with *Vp*

(Scene numbers are those of *Vp*.)

Np	*LV*
I.4: longer version of Poppea's opening ('Speranza, tu mi vai'), wherein Poppea pronounces that she has in effect been crowned empress of Rome (ed. Curtis, Appendix II.1).	As *Np*.
I.11: at end of scene, additional 5 lines for Ottone (complaining of the untrustworthiness of beauty) and 8 for Arnalta expressing sympathy for Ottone and remarking that she would not be so cruel to a lover who pleaded thus to her (ed. Curtis, App. II.2).	As *Np*.
II.2: additional lines for Liberto (and further repeat of the refrain 'Mori felice') noting that Seneca will attain divine status while wicked Nerone will never be admitted into heaven (ed. Curtis, App. II.3).	As *Np*.
II.3: additional lines for Seneca after the chorus of Famigliari, exhorting them not to weep for him and to wipe the unworthy stain of inconstancy from their breasts (ed. Curtis, App. II.4).	As *Np*.
	[II.3a]: additional scene for Seneca and a Coro di Virtù welcoming him into heaven (given in Carter, 'Re-Reading *Poppea*', p. 202).
II.4: longer concluding duet for Valletto and Damigella playing on the theme of love-bites (ed. Curtis, App. I).	As *Np*.
II.5: longer duet for Nerone and Lucano, and additional stanza for Nerone's 'Son rubin preziosi' (ed. Curtis, App. II.5–6).	As *Np*, but lines further divided between Petronio and Tigellino, two more intimates of Nerone's court.
[II.5a]: solo scene for Ottavia reflecting on her condition (ed. Curtis, App. II.7).	
	[II.5a]: scene for Nerone and Poppea renewing their protestations of love.

Table 10-2   *Continued*

Np	LV
II.7: on Ottone's departure at end of scene, 18 lines for Ottavia proclaiming vengeance and rejoicing in the death of 'wicked' Poppea (ed. Curtis, App. II.8).	First 5 lines of *Np* only.
	II.12: additional lines for Ottone as he contemplates murdering Poppea.
III.3: additional 4 lines for Drusilla ('Quest'alma, e questa mano / . . . / Non cercar più, la verità ti dico') moved (with different music) from III.4 (where it is also present in *Np* and *Vp*; ed. Curtis, p. 204).	As *Np*, but these lines do not appear in III.4.
III.4: additional line for Littore (in C1 clef!) as he tells Ottone and Drusilla to go to perdition (ed. Curtis, App. II.9).	As *Np*.
III.6 is for Arnalta; III.7 is for Ottavia (as in *Vp*).	III.6 is for Ottavia; III.7 is for Arnalta.
III.8: much expanded version of the central Amore episode (with the Coro di Amori; ed. Curtis, pp. 243–56), also with a duet for Nerone and Poppea, 'Su, su Venere ed Amor' (ed. Curtis, App. II.10). For full details of the various versions of this scene, see Curtis, '*La Poppea impasticciata*', pp. 36–7.	Largely as *Np*, but without 'Su, su Venere ed Amor'. The text ends with Amore's exaltation of Nerone and Poppea.

While these additions might be considered as clarifications, the revisions that appear to have occurred in the middle of Act II seem to have had a different impulse. Despite the taut structure of Busenello's libretto, it does have some loose ends. For example, it is surprising not to find a scene for Nerone and Poppea in Act II, even if little remains for them to do, other than renew their declarations of love (Poppea has already secured the repudiation of Ottavia in I.4, and the death of Seneca in I.12). Accordingly, *LV* contains just such a scene immediately after the one for Nerone and Lucano, in a sequence that softens the homoerotic overtones (if, indeed, they are) of the former scene, and reminds us of the chief focus of the opera. That this scene was never (it seems) set to music may have to do with its dramatic redundancy – although the lovers' repeated references to eyes and breath reinforce several topoi of the opera – or perhaps with the fact that it would create further problems of stage movement in a scene-complex that is already awkwardly configured, with no overlapping entrances and exits. At this same point in the opera, however, both *LV* and (still more) *Np* also try to deal with the most obvious 'loose end': Ottavia. Her treatment here and elsewhere merits some discussion.

Tacitus paints Octavia as a relatively minor figure in history's grand scheme, although he describes quite poignantly (towards the end of *Annals*, XIV) her exile and death in AD 62, aged twenty. Other classical sources also show her in a positive light, including the pseudo-Seneca *Octavia*, where Octavia is repudiated by Nero in favour of Poppaea but is reinstated after ferocious protests from the people of Rome that leave him whimpering in Octavia's arms. According to Tacitus (*Annals*, XIII.16), she tended to keep silent over Nero's actions, hiding her every emotion, which would not be quite appropriate for someone on the operatic stage. But even the Ottavia of *Vp* seems not quite to fulfil the expectations of her position in the drama, of her role for a star-singer (Anna Renzi), and of her place in the sympathies of the audience. We see her just three times in the opera: at her entrance in I.5–6, where she laments her fate; in II.7, as she blackmails Ottone to murder Poppea; and in III.7 (or 6), as she bids a sad farewell to Rome. Her opening scene invokes the obvious precedent of Penelope's first appearance in *Il ritorno*, I.1 – in both cases we have a queen escorted by her nurse and lamenting her treatment at the hand of fate, by way of a husband whose interests lie elsewhere – and the music is similar (as are the opening words). But Ottavia looks back to an even more illustrious predecessor, Arianna: Ottavia's lament goes through much the same textual and musical tropes, even to the point where she calls for the gods to punish Nerone but then immediately repents her impiety. Our support for Ottavia would seem to be assured when (in I.6) she refuses to follow Nutrice's advice to take a lover – men can be forgiven for adultery but women not – and prefers to live her life in suffering; it is confirmed still more by her remarkably equanimous responses to Seneca's rather inane advice to rejoice in her misfortune (and also to Valletto's merciless teasing of the philosopher), where she simply asks him to speak on her behalf to the senate while she offers prayers at the temple. Ottavia's farewell scene in Act III would also seem to press all the right emotional buttons. That hers is not the happy exile of a Drusilla is clear from her stuttering opening, her brave instruction to the oarsmen (Ex. 10-5),[18] and her final heartrending farewell to her family and to Rome.

Thus far, Ottavia presents the case for the 'miserable sex' of women ('O delle donne miserabil sesso', she says in I.5) that counterpoints Ottone's

---

18 I give this passage in full because it caused Curtis some problems in his edition, as indeed did the rest of this scene; performers would benefit from consulting *Vp* at this point.

Ex. 10–5 *L'incoronazione*, III.7, Ottavia.

Re - mi - ga - te,   <re - mi - ga - te,>   re - mi - ga - te hog - gi mai, per-

ver - se gen - ti,   Al - lon - ta - nar - mi,   <al - lon - ta - nar - mi>

da-,   da-,   da - gli a - ma - ti   li - di.___

[6]   [4   #]

Vp, fol. 98v.

Now row, wicked ones, to distance me from these beloved shores.

(and the Incogniti's) more conventional claims about women's inherent imper-
fection (see the opening of I.12).[19] Yet in between these two representations
of an empress pliant and abused, we have (in II.7) Ottavia the vengeful
harridan, capable of blackmailing Ottone to commit murder. Nothing we
have seen up to this point (or that we read in Tacitus) suggests that Ottavia
is capable of such an act – even if Nutrice had suggested various strategies
for revenge in I.5 – or that she will carry it out. Indeed, the process of transformation is never articulated by Ottavia or any other character; the last we
heard, she was on her way to the temple. Ottavia's sudden shift may be necessary for the resolution of the plot, but it does leave us nonplussed, which
perhaps explains why both *LV* and *Np* seek to resolve the issue through an
additional speech for Ottavia at the end of II.7. Here she rejoices in
vengeance, denounces the wicked Poppea, proclaims an end to Nerone's

19   See Heller's study of Ottavia, and in particular of I.5, in ' "O delle donne miserabil
     sesso" '.

tyranny and, as an afterthought (but harking back to her final words in I.6), expresses her concern for the welfare of Rome. By this reasoning, murdering Poppea is as much a matter of *ragione di stato* as it is of personal vendetta (*LV* gives lines 1–5 only):

Vattene pure: la vendetta è un cibo	Go then: vengeance is a dish
che col sangue inimico si condisce.	flavoured with an enemy's blood.
Della spenta Poppea su 'l monumento,	On the tomb of the dead Poppea,
quasi a felice mensa,	as at a happy banquet,
5 prenderò così nobile alimento.	shall I take such noble nourishment.
Mora, mora la rea,	Let the guilty one die, die,
mora, mora Poppea,	let Poppea die, die,
già, già la punta del coltel la svena.	already, already the knife's point opens her veins.
Scellerata Poppea,	Wicked Poppea,
10 verrà teco in sepolcro ogni mia pena;	all my suffering will go with you to your tomb;
risanarà il mio duolo	my grief will be healed
del tuo sangue odiato un sorso solo.	by a single drop of your hated blood.
Gioirò vendicata,	I will rejoice avenged,
nascerà il mio seren da la tua morte;	my serenity will be born of your death;
15 e uccisa te, o malnata,	and with you killed, o misbegotten one,
non sarà più tiranno il mio consorte,	my consort will no longer be a tyrant,
e tornerà giocondo	and happiness will return
il popolo, il senato, e Roma e 'l mondo.	to the people, to the senate, to Rome and to the world.

This is not the Ottavia of I.5–6. But at least here is a character-type that we can recognize: the woman bent on vengeance. Medea provides the obvious precedent, especially given the cannibalistic overtones. But presumably most republicans would have agreed with the sentiment (and with the implied revision of history), even in the mouth of a woman.

Np, however, does still more service to Ottavia by way of a solo scene between Nerone's and Lucano's II.5 and Ottone's soliloquy in II.6

(the latter is thereby delivered as an aside). It does not necessarily aid our understanding of Ottavia's transformation, even if it introduces the violent side of her personality that then comes to the fore in the addition to II.7. But it does allow her a powerful dramatic moment, enabling her to hold the stage on her own (only Seneca and Ottone are granted a similar privilege), in an impassioned speech rendered cohesive by a partial refrain (in italics below):

	Eccomi quasi priva	Here am I almost deprived
	dell'impero e 'l consorte,	of empire and of my consort,
	ma, lasso me, non priva	but, alas, not deprived
	del ripudio, e di morte.	of repudiation and of death.
5	*Martiri, o m'uccidete,*	*Suffering, oh kill me,*
	o speranze alla fin, non	*o hopes at an end, do not afflict me.*
	m'affliggete.	
	Neron, Nerone mio,	Nerone, my Nerone,
	chi mi ti toglie, oh dio,	who takes you away from me,
		oh god,
	come ti perdo, ohimè,	how do I lose you, alas,
10	cadde l'affetto tuo, mancò la fè?	how did your affection decline,
		your faith fall lacking?
	Poppea, cruda Poppea,	Poppea, cruel Poppea,
	se lo stato mi togli,	if you take the state from me,
	se de' miei regni e d'ogni ben	if you deprive me of my kingdoms
	mi spogli,	and all my fortune,
	non me ne curo, no, prendil'in	I do not care, no, take it in peace,
	pace,	
15	ch'io cedendoli a te, credi che	for in giving them to you, believe
	sono	that I do so
	fuor d'ogni strazio rio, priva di	without any painful suffering,
	lutto;	without grief;
	nulla pretendo e ti concedo il	I claim nothing, and grant you
	tutto.	everything.
	Ma non mi negar, no,	But do not deny me, no,
	il mio sposo gradito,	my beloved spouse,
20	rendimi il mio marito,	give my husband back to me,
	lasciami questo sol, soffri a	leave me this alone, grant this
	ragione,	reasonable request:
	se mi togli l'imper', dammi	if you take the empire from me,
	Nerone.	give me Nerone.
	Speranze, e che chiedete?	*Hopes, so what do you ask of me?*
	se disperata son, non m'affliggete.	*As I am desperate, do not afflict me.*

25 Disumanata cor, barbaro seno,	Inhuman heart, barbarous breast,
Neron, Poppea, tiranni,	Nerone, Poppea, tyrants,
cagione de' miei danni,	cause of my injuries,
farò che 'l ferro giunghi	I will act so that the sword manages
a recider lo stame	to cut out the root
30 d'un affetto impudico, un petto	of a shameful love, of an infamous
infame.	breast.
Così fia che riposi e non deliri,	Thus you [i.e., Ottavia] will gain
	rest and not rave,
che vendicata offesa a chi	for avenging an offence to
d'oprarla	whoever achieves it
o di trattarla è vaga;	or arranges it is delightful;
disacerba la piaga,	it soothes the wound,
35 mitiga il duol, e fuor d'ingiuria	lessens the pain, and covering the
ascosa,	hidden injury
rende la cicatrice più gloriosa.	makes the scar all the more
	glorious.
Ma, che parlo, che tento?	But what do I say, what do I
	suggest?
Uccidemi tormento,	Kill me, torment,
laceratemi o pene,	lacerate me, o pains,
40 straziatemi martiri,	torture me, suffering,
soffocatemi voi caldi sospiri.	suffocate me, you heated sighs.
Memorie, e che volete?	*Memories, so what do you want?*
O lasciate i pensieri, o	*Either leave aside your thoughts or*
m'uccidete.	*kill me.*

As far as we can tell from *SV*, this was not the Ottavia heard at the first performance of *L'incoronazione*. But one can well imagine that the singer of *Np*'s (or its source's) Ottavia (whether or not Anna Renzi) would want a grand scene in the middle of Act II similar, it seems, to Renzi's solo lament as Deidamia in Sacrati's *La finta pazza* (1641; II.6),[20] just as the altered sequence of III.6 and 7 may reflect her wish not to be upstaged by Arnalta. This would not be the first time that a particular feature of Monteverdi's works for the stage is better explained by some such practical reason than by a broader appeal to a grand interpretative design.

Again, the character-type is recognizable, as is the sequence of thought, from self-pity (lines 1–6), to a curiously regressive expression of love for Nerone (Poppea can have everything but him; 7–24) and the threat of vengeful murder (25–36), then the usual retreat ending in grief-filled resig-

20 See Curtis, '*La Poppea impasticciata*', p. 32.

nation (37–42). But if the sequence is (again) Arianna's, the emphasis on the refrain seems closer to Didone's lament in the second of the 1628 *intermedi* (discussed in Chapter 8). The composer of the music (Curtis suggests Sacrati, although Monteverdi is not entirely impossible) does what might plausibly have been done there, setting the discursive text in a passionate recitative and the refrain in a lyrical triple time (the first two appearances marked to be followed by a ritornello) that unifies the scene (the first part of the refrain is given in Ex. 10-6). It is significant that the refrain makes strong reference to the descending (minor) tetrachord in two statements of its (almost) ground bass; there is also another brief passage in triple time in the scene, again over two statements of a shorter ground bass, at 'Non me ne curo, no'. This is striking, not least because it is one of just two occasions when Ottavia sings in triple time in the entire opera; the other example is in I.5, where Ottavia complains of Nerone lying in Poppea's arms ('in braccio di Poppea'), with a Penelope-like passage that denies its triple-time status even as it articulates it. One might plausibly read both cases as Ottavia appropriating and

Ex. 10-6 *L'incoronazione*, additional scene in *Np* (between II.5 and II.6), Ottavia.

Monteverdi, *L'incoronazione di Poppea*, ed. Curtis, p. 278.

manipulating a musical style more associated with Poppea. Yet the lyrical refrain in this added scene has further implications, granting Ottavia at least temporary access to the lyricism that so dominates the music of the other characters in the opera. Perhaps here, too, triple time means something serious. This scene might just be viewed as turning Ottavia into a conventional lamenting heroine,[21] but the consequences for the character are quite profound. The fact that Ottavia here articulates her position so forcefully makes her taking fortune by the hand with Ottone more effective, maybe even impressive. And by combining the textual and musical personalities of a Penelope, an Arianna, a Didone and eventually a Medea, this Ottavia embraces just about all the serious female character-types now prevalent on the seventeenth-century operatic stage.

My account of Monteverdi's music for the theatre has ranged far and wide through issues that might conventionally be viewed as belonging to separate musicological domains, whether focused on history, analysis or performance. Yet each of these domains necessarily informs the others: any analytical reading must be situated in some kind of historical context, while both historical and analytical understanding will falter if it fails to take account of performance circumstances. As I have also tried to show, musicologists ignore other disciplines at their peril: much of what happens in Monteverdi's stage music is determined at least by the arts of poetry on the one hand, and of the theatre on the other, and to treat these works as somehow purely, or even supremely, 'musical' is fundamentally to miss their point. And if nothing else is clear from this study, it should at least now be apparent that Monteverdi's approach to theatrical composition must have been inherently pragmatic: he would have spent more time worrying about the demands of his singers or the staging than considering high-flown verities about the nature of art or life.

Here, at least, I have been true to Pirrotta's more localized notions of the 'problems' of Monteverdi's operas. Comparing my list of problems with those identified by Pirrotta, some are similar (the constraints of context), some are new (the influence of performers; the role of poetic structure), some are reconfigured (issues of genre), and some are taken in new directions (musical expression and representation) that, in turn, produce new problems. By virtue of my different approaches to context, function, genre, text and performance, we probably also disagree on the extent and nature of Monteverdi's successes and failures – the revised ending of *Orfeo* and the generic problems of *Arianna* worry me less than they did him – although we share a fascination with *L'incoronazione*. Like Pirrotta, however, I would be inclined not to view these works as marking some kind of progress towards an ideal union of music and

21   The point is Heller's; see ' "O delle donne miserabil sesso" ', p. 41 n. 70.

drama: they come from different times; they reflect different environments; they deal with different subjects; and they work in different ways. Nor can one claim that Monteverdi's stage works demonstrate an increasing maturity in, and control of, compositional or dramatic technique. But they do provide different perspectives on the matching of music to the structure and content of a poetic text, on the possible roles of text and music in the service of drama, and on the effects that performing such musical drama might have on the hearts and minds of an audience. They also each offer their own solutions to what must surely be the chief 'problem' of opera throughout its history, best expressed in a simple question: why should people sing?

This diversity is in turn a product of the extent to which Monteverdi's operas, *balli* and *intermedi* renegotiate the generic boundaries traditionally placed upon theatrical music in early seventeenth-century Italy, not only by mixing genres, modes and media but also by redefining theatrical and other spaces, and by creating complex relationships between performers and their audiences. One consequence is the need to privilege a fluidity of interpretation: we can and should gain a multiplicity of meanings from works that in the end are not amenable to the strongly directed readings that most post-Enlightenment critics would seek to place on them. Such ambivalence – perhaps polyvalence – suggests that at the heart of Monteverdi's music for the stage lies a simple pleasure in rhetorical play. This may be a counsel of post-modernist despair; it may be an authentic response to the practicalities of the seventeenth-century Italian stage; it may be also seen as exuberantly liberating for future approaches to Monteverdi's musical theatre.

These issues must in the end move far beyond the Monteverdian particular. Where my debt to Pirrotta is most apparent, if not yet sufficiently acknowledged, is in our shared view of the importance of aria and what it comes to signify in Monteverdi's theatrical works, and hence in opera as a whole. That shift from the specific to the general is possible because of opera's curiously consistent history. Few musical genres in the Western art tradition have their origins fixed with such precision. Moreover, few genres were subject to such intense theorizing about their *raison d'être* from the outset: the self-examination – at times violent polemic – characteristic of opera up to the present day began early in its history. This is in large part because opera and other forms of music theatre raise crucial questions concerning the aims and effects of music, drama, and indeed the arts in general, that cannot be ignored. These questions remain as pertinent today as they were to opera's first composers, librettists and audiences, and the history of music in the theatre is a history of repeated attempts – variously conditioned by time, place and circumstance – to find their response. Monteverdi's own solutions to the problems of opera, however those problems might be defined, are no less compelling in our time than they must have been in his own.

Appendix

Monteverdi's theatrical works

(Titles of works are those conventionally adopted in the literature; they do not always have contemporary authority. Genres follow the original sources or a plausible deduction therefrom; locations of performances are given only where reasonably secure. In cases marked ★ the music is entirely or mostly lost. For fuller details of sources and other information, see the relevant discussions in Fabbri, *Monteverdi*, trans. Carter, and elsewhere in this book.)

Title (genre)	Performance details	Librettist	Sources and other information	Mentioned in Monteverdi's letters (date given as day/month/year)
★*Gli amori di Diana ed Endimione* (*ballo*)	?Mantua, ?Carnival 1604–5		Choreography by 'Signor Giovanni Battista ballerino'.	12/04
Orfeo (*favola in musica*), SV318	Mantua, 24 February 1607; 1 March 1607	Alessandro Striggio jr.	Performed before the Accademia degli Invaghiti. Two editions of libretto published Mantua, Francesco Osanna, 1607. Score published Venice, Ricciardo Amadino, 1609, repr. 1615. Francesco Gonzaga requests a copy of the score, 12/10. For later performances, see Chapter 1.	24/8/09, 9/12/16

'De la bellezza le dovute lodi' (*ballo*), SV245			Music included in Monteverdi, *Scherzi musicali a tre voci* (Venice, Ricciardo Amadino, 1607, repr. 1609, 1615; Venice, Bartolomeo Magni, 1628)	
Arianna (tragedia in musica), SV291	Ottavio Rinuccini	Mantua (Palazzo Ducale), 28 May 1608; rev. Venice (Teatro S. Moisè), Carnival 1639–40	For the festivities celebrating the wedding of Prince Francesco Gonzaga and Margherita of Savoy. Three separate editions of the libretto published in 1608; there are several others, including two in 1640 for the Venetian revival. Part of the music (principally, Arianna's lament) survives in print (two editions of 1623; Monteverdi also published a 5-voice arrangement in his Sixth Book of madrigals of 1614) and in several manuscripts. Text and description in Follino, *Compendio delle sontuose feste* (1608). Francesco de' Medici requests a copy of the score from Duke Ferdinando, 12/13. There were also plans to stage it in Mantua in early May 1620 for the birthday celebrations of Duchess Caterina de' Medici-Gonzaga.	2/12/08, 6/11/15, 9/12/16, 6/1/17, 9/1/20, 17/3/20, 21/3/20, 28/3/20, 4/4/20, 18/4/20, 10/5/20, 11/7/20, 1/5/27, 23/10/33

Title (genre)	Performance details	Librettist	Sources and other information	Mentioned in Monteverdi's letters (date given as day/month/year)
★'Ha cento lustri con etereo giro', etc. (prologue [i.e., intermedio 1] for Battista Guarini, *L'idropica*)	Mantua (Palazzo Ducale), 2 June 1608	Gabriello Chiabrera	For the festivities celebrating the wedding of Prince Francesco Gonzaga and Margherita of Savoy. Text and description in Follino, *Compendio delle sontuose feste* (1608).	
Ballo delle ingrate, SV167	Mantua (Palazzo Ducale), 4 June 1608; rev. ?Vienna, ?1636	Ottavio Rinuccini	For the festivities celebrating the wedding of Prince Francesco Gonzaga and Margherita of Savoy. Music (revised) included in Monteverdi, *Madrigali guerrieri, et amorosi . . . Libro ottavo* (Venice, Alessandro Vincenti, 1638). Text and description in Follino, *Compendio delle sontuose feste* (1608).	
Tirsi e Clori (ballo), SV145	Mantua, January 1616		Music included in Monteverdi, *Concerto: settimo libro de madrigali* (Venice, Bartolomeo Magni, 1619)	21/11/15, 28/11/15

Title	Place/date	Author	Notes	Dates
Le nozze di Tetide (*favola marittima*)		Scipione Agnelli	Intended for the Mantuan festivities celebrating the wedding of Duke Ferdinando Gonzaga and Caterina de' Medici (married in Florence, 7 February 1617). Begun in December 1616 but abandoned by mid-January 1617.	9/12/16, 29/12/16, 31/12/16, 6/1/17, 14/1/17
'Su le penne de' venti il ciel varcando' (prologue for Andreini's *sacra rappresentazione La Maddalena*), SV333	Mantua (Palazzo Ducale), March 1617; rev. Vienna, 1629	Giovanni Battista Andreini	For the festivities celebrating the wedding of Duke Ferdinando Gonzaga and Caterina de' Medici. Music included in *Musiche . . . per La Maddalena* (Venice, Bartolomeo Magni, 1617). Vienna revival may have included a *contrafactum* of the *Lamento d'Arianna* as a *Lamento della Maddalena*.	
Andromeda (*favola in musica*)	Mantua (Palazzo Ducale), Carnival 1620 (between 1 and 3 March)	Ercole Marigliani	Libretto published Mantua, Fratelli Osanna, 1620. For the date of Carnival, see Fenlon, 'Mantua, Monteverdi and the History of "Andromeda"', p. 164.	21/4/18, 21/7/18, 22/3/19, 9/1/20, 16/1/20, 1/2/20, 8/2/20, 15/2/20 (Marigliani)
Apollo (*ballo*)	Mantua, Carnival 1620 (between 1 and 3 March); rev. Mantua, July 1620	Alessandro Striggio	Known chiefly from Monteverdi's letters.	9/2/19, 7/3/19, 19/10/19, 13/12/19 (Striggio), 9/1/20, 16/1/20, 1/2/20, 8/2/20, 15/2/20 (Striggio), 22/2/20, 29/2/20 (Striggio), 8/3/20, 24/7/20

Title (genre)	Performance details	Librettist	Sources and other information	Mentioned in Monteverdi's letters (date given as day/month/year)
*La contesa di Amore e Cupido, etc. (contribution to prologue, four intermedi and licenza for Marigliani, Le tre costanti)	Mantua (Palazzo Ducale), 18 January 1622	Ercole Marigliani	For the festivities celebrating the wedding of Eleonora Gonzaga and Emperor Ferdinand II. Text published Mantua, Aurelio & Lodovico Osanna, 1622. Description included in Bertazzolo, Breve relatione dello sposalitio (1622). Monteverdi wrote at least (parts of?) the third intermedio (on Boreas and Orithyia; after Act III) and the licenza (the triumph of Cupid).	5/3/21, 17/4/21, 10/9/21, 27/11/21
Combattimento di Tancredi e Clorinda, SV153	Venice (Palazzo Mocenigo), Carnival 1624(?–5)	after Torquato Tasso, Gerusalemme liberata, XII (with readings from Gerusalemme conquistata, XV)	Music included in Monteverdi, Madrigali guerrieri, et amorosi . . . Libro ottavo (Venice, Alessandro Vincenti, 1638).	1/5/27

Armida abbandonata		after Torquato Tasso, *Gerusalemme liberata*, XVI	Begun ?late 1626, although still unfinished by 18 September 1627 (letter to Striggio); ?completed shortly thereafter.	1/5/27, 18/9/27 (Striggio), 25/9/27 (Striggio), 2/10/27, 18/12/27, 4/2/28
La finta pazza Licori		Giulio Strozzi	Discussed with Striggio in mid-1627. Strozzi revised the original libretto, but Monteverdi probably composed very little, if any, of the score. Also styled *Licori finta pazza innamorata d'Aminta*.	1/5/27, 7/5/27, 22/5/27, 24/5/27, 5/6/27, 13/6/27, 20/6/27, 3/7/27, 10/7/27, 24/7/27, 31/7/27, 17/8/27, 28/8/27, 10/9/27 (Striggio), 10/9/27 (Marigliani), 18/9/27 (Striggio)
Gli Argonauti (mascherata)	Parma, (?5) March 1628	Claudio Achillini	Consisted of a madrigal performed by two castratos (Antonio Grimano and Gregorio Lazzarini), a bass and various instruments.	
Teti e Flora, etc. (prologue and five intermedi for Tasso, Aminta)	Parma, Courtyard of S. Pietro Martire, 13 December 1628	Claudio Achillini (prologue) and Ascanio Pio di Savoia	For the festivities celebrating the wedding of Odoardo Farnese and Margherita de' Medici. Description in Buttigli, *Descritione dell'apparato* (1629). Texts published separately (Parma, Seth & Erasmo Viotti, 1629)	10/9/27 (Bentivoglio), 10/9/27 (Striggio), 10/9/27 (Marigliani), 18/9/27 (Bentivoglio), 25/9/27 (Striggio), 25/9/27 (Bentivoglio), 30/10/27, 8/11/27, 18/12/27, 1/1/28, 9/1/28, 4/2/28, 9/3/30

Title (genre)	Performance details	Librettist	Sources and other information	Mentioned in Monteverdi's letters (date given as day/month/year)
Mercurio e Marte (tournament)	Parma, Teatro Farnese, 21 December 1628	Claudio Achillini	For the festivities celebrating the wedding of Odoardo Farnese and Margherita de' Medici. Description in Buttigli, *Descritione dell'apparato* (1629). Text published separately (Parma, Seth & Erasmo Viotti, 1629).	18/9/27 (Bentivoglio), 30/10/27, 9/1/28, 4/2/28
Proserpina rapita (anatopismo), SV323	Venice (Palazzo Mocenigo), 16 April 1630	Giulio Strozzi	For the festivities celebrating the wedding of Lorenzo Giustiniani and Giustiniana Mocenigo. Libretto published Venice, Evangelista Deuchino, 1630; repr. Venice, Pietro Miloco, 1644. One canzonetta ('Come dolce hoggi l'auretta') included in Monteverdi, *Madrigali e canzonette . . . libro nono* (Venice, Alessandro Vincenti, 1651).	
'Volgendo il ciel per l'immortal sentiero'–'Movete al mio bel suon le piante snelle' (*ballo*), SV154		Ottavio Rinuccini	Intended for Vienna after election of Emperor Ferdinand III (December 1636). Music included in Monteverdi, *Madrigali guerrieri, et amorosi . . . Libro ottavo* (Venice, Alessandro Vincenti, 1638).	

Il ritorno d'Ulisse in patria, SV325	Venice (?Teatro SS. Giovanni e Paolo), Carnival 1639–40; rev. Bologna, 1640; rev. Venice, Carnival 1640–1.	Giacomo Badoaro	Several MS copies of libretto (in five acts). Music survives in Vienna, Österreichische Nationalbibliothek, MS 18763 (in three acts)
★*Vittoria d'Amore* (*ballo*)	Piacenza, 7 February 1641	Bernardo Morando	Description by Morando published Piacenza, Giovanni Antonio Ardizzoni, n.d.
★*Le nozze d'Enea in Lavinia*	Venice, Teatro SS. Giovanni e Paolo, Carnival 1640–1		*Argomento e scenario* (Venice, n.p., 1640). Manuscript libretto survives in *I-Vnm* Dramm. 909.4.
L'incoronazione [*La coronatione*] *di Poppea*, SV308	Venice, Teatro SS. Giovanni e Paolo, Carnival 1642–3; rev. Naples, 1651	Giovanni Francesco Busenello	*Scenario* published Venice, Giovanni Pietro Pinelli, 1643. Music survives in Naples, Conservatorio di Musica S Pietro a Majella, MS Rari 6.4.1; Venice, Biblioteca Nazionale Marciana, MS 9963 (It. IV.439). For other sources, see Table 10-1.

Works cited

Editions of Monteverdi's music and letters

Claudio Monteverdi: Lettere, ed. Éva Lax, 'Studi e testi per la storia della musica', 10 (Florence, Olschki, 1994)

Claudio Monteverdi: Tutte le opere, ed. Gian Francesco Malipiero, 17 vols (Asolo, the author, 1926–42; 2nd rev. edn, Vienna, Universal Edition, 1954–68)

L'incoronazione di Poppea, facsimile of Venice, Biblioteca Nazionale Marciana, MS 9963 (It. IV. 439), 'Biblioteca musica bononiensis', IV/81 (Bologna, Forni, 1969)

L'incoronazione di Poppea, ed. Alan Curtis (London, Novello, 1989)

L'Orfeo, favola in musica (Venice, 1609), facsimile ed. Elisabeth Schmierer, 'Meisterwerke der Musik im Faksimile', 1 (Laaber, Laaber-Verlag, 1998)

L'Orfeo, ed. Denis Stevens (London, Novello, 1967; rev. 1968)

The Letters of Claudio Monteverdi, trans. Denis Stevens (London, Faber, 1980; rev. Oxford, Clarendon Press, 1995)

Other texts

Abert, Anna Amalie, *Claudio Monteverdi und das musikalische Drama* (Lippstadt, Kistner & Siegel, 1954)

Ademollo, Alessandro, *La bell'Adriana ed altre virtuose del suo tempo alla corte di Mantova* (Città di Castello, S. Lapi, 1888)

Aldrich, Putnam, *Rhythm in Seventeenth-Century Italian Monody* (New York, Norton, 1966)

Alm, Irene, 'Humanism and Theatrical Dance in Early Opera', *Musica disciplina*, 49 (1995), 79–93

Ancona, Alessandro d', *Origini del teatro italiano*, 2 vols (2nd rev. edn, Turin, Loescher, 1891)

Annibaldi, Claudio, '"Spettacolo veramente da principi": committenza e recezione dell'opera aulica nel primo Seicento', in *'Lo stupore dell'invenzione': Firenze e la nascita dell'opera; atti del convegno internazionale di studi, Firenze, 5–6 ottobre 2000,* ed. Piero Gargiulo (Florence, Olschki, 2001), 31–60

Ariosto, Lodovico, *Orlando furioso*, trans. Barbara Reynolds, 2 vols (Harmondsworth, Penguin, 1975)

Arnold, Denis, *Monteverdi*, 'The Master Musicians' (London, Dent, 1963); 3rd edn rev. Tim Carter (London, Dent, 1990)

Arnold, Denis, and Fortune, Nigel (eds), *The New Monteverdi Companion* (London, Faber, 1985)

Baker, Nancy Kovaleff, and Hanning, Barbara Russano (eds), *Musical Humanism and its Legacy: Essays in Honor of Claude V. Palisca* (Stuyvesant, NY, Pendragon Press, 1992)

Barlow, Jeremy, 'The Revival of Monteverdi's Operas in the Twentieth Century', in *The Operas of Monteverdi*, ed. John, pp. 193–203

Baroncini, Rodolfo, ' "Sinfonie et balli allegri": Functions, Genres, and Patronage of Instrumental Music at the Court of Mantua in the Early Seventeenth Century', *Italian History and Culture: Yearbook of Georgetown University at Villa Le Balze, Fiesole (Florence)*, 5 (1999), 29–70

Bertazzolo, Gabriele, *Breve relatione dello sposalitio fatto della serenissima principessa Eleonora Gonzaga con la sacra cesarea maestà di Ferdinando II imperatore* (Mantua, Aurelio & Lodovico Osanna, 1622)

Bertolotti, Antoni(n)o, *Musici alla corte dei Gonzaga in Mantova dal secolo XV al XVIII: notizie e documenti raccolti negli archivi mantovani* (Milan, Ricordi, [1890]; repr. Bologna, Forni, 1969)

Besutti, Paola, 'Da *L'Arianna* a *La Ferinda*: Giovan Battista Andreini e la "comedia musicale all'improviso" ', *Musica disciplina*, 49 (1995), 227–76

——'The "Sala degli Specchi" Uncovered: Monteverdi, the Gonzagas and the Palazzo Ducale, Mantua', *Early Music*, 27 (1999), 451–65

Besutti, Paola, Gialdroni, Teresa M., and Baroncini, Rodolfo (eds), *Claudio Monteverdi: studi e prospettive; atti del convegno, Mantova, 21–24 ottobre 1993*, 'Accademia Nazionale Virgiliana di Scienze, Lettere e Arti: Miscellanea', 5 (Florence, Olschki, 1998)

Bianconi, Lorenzo (ed.), *Antonio Il Verso: madrigali a tre (libro II, 1605) e a cinque voci (libro XV, opera XXXVI, 1619) con sei madrigali di Pomponio Nenna, Tiburtio Massaino, Ippolito Baccusi e Giovan Battista Bartoli*, 'Musiche rinascimentali siciliane', 8 (Florence, Olschki, 1978)

——*Music in the Seventeenth Century*, trans. David Bryant (Cambridge, Cambridge University Press, 1987)

Bianconi, Lorenzo, and Walker, Thomas, 'Production, Consumption and Political Function of Seventeenth-Century Opera', *Early Music History*, 4 (1984), 209–96

Bouwsma, William J., *Venice and the Defense of Republican Liberty: Renaissance Values in the Age of the Counter-Reformation* (Berkeley and Los Angeles, University of California Press, 1968)

Bowers, Roger, 'Proportional Notations in Monteverdi's "Orfeo" ', *Music & Letters*, 76 (1995), 149–67

Braun, Werner, *Die Musik des 17. Jahrhunderts*, 'Neues Handbuch der Musikwissenschaft', 4 (Wiesbaden, Athenion, 1981)

Brizi, Bruno, 'Teoria e prassi melodrammatica di G. F. Busenello e "L'incoronazione di Poppea"', in *Venezia e il melodramma nel Seicento*, ed. Maria Teresa Muraro, 'Studi di musica veneta', 5 (Florence, Olschki, 1976), 51–74

—— '"Il lauro verde": questioni relative alla trascrizione di testi polifonici del Cinquecento', in *L'edizione critica tra testo musicale e testo letterario: atti del convegno internazionale (Cremona 4–8 ottobre 1992)*, ed. Renato Borghi and Pietro Zappalà (Lucca, Libreria Musicale Italiana, 1995), 17–43

Bujić, Bojan, 'Rinuccini the Craftsman: a View of his *L'Arianna*', *Early Music History*, 18 (1999), 75–117

Buratelli, Claudia, *Spettacoli di corte a Mantova tra Cinque e Seicento*, 'Storia dello spettacolo: Saggi', 3 (Florence, Le Lettere, 1999)

Buttigli, Marcello, *Descritione dell'apparato fatto per onorare la prima et solenne entrata in Parma della serenissima d. Margherita di Toscana duchessa di Parma e Piacenza* (Parma, Seth & Erasmo Viotti, 1629)

Calcagni, Mauro, 'Monteverdi's *parole sceniche*', *Journal of Seventeenth-Century Music*, forthcoming

Canal, Pietro, *Della musica in Mantova: notizie tratte principalmente dall'archivio Gonzaga* (2nd edn, Venice, Giuseppe Antonelli, 1881; repr. Bologna, Forni, 1977)

Carpeggiani, Paolo, 'Studi su Gabriele Bertazzolo, i: Le feste fiorentine del 1608', *Civiltà mantovana*, 12 (1978), 14–56

Carter, Tim, *Jacopo Peri (1561–1633): his Life and Works* (PhD diss., University of Birmingham, 1980; repr. New York and London, Garland, 1989)

—— 'A Florentine Wedding of 1608', *Acta musicologica*, 55 (1983), 89–107

—— 'Artusi, Monteverdi, and the Poetics of Modern Music', in *Musical Humanism and its Legacy*, ed. Baker and Hanning, pp. 171–94

—— '"An air new and grateful to the ear": the Concept of *aria* in Late Renaissance and Early Baroque Italy', *Music Analysis*, 12 (1993), 127–45

—— '"In Love's harmonious consort"? Penelope and the Interpretation of *Il ritorno d'Ulisse in patria*', *Cambridge Opera Journal*, 5 (1993), 1–16

—— '*Possente spirto*: on Taming the Power of Music', *Early Music*, 21 (1993), 517–23

—— 'The North Italian Courts', in *Man and Music: the Early Baroque Era; from the Late 16th Century to the 1660s*, ed. Curtis Price (London, Macmillan, 1993), 23–48

—— 'Resemblance and Representation: towards a New Aesthetic in the Music of Monteverdi', in *'Con che soavità'*, ed. Fenlon and Carter, pp. 118–34

—— 'Intriguing Laments: Sigismondo d'India, Claudio Monteverdi, and Dido *alla parmigiana* (1628)', *Journal of the American Musicological Society*, 49 (1996), 32–69

—— 'New Songs for Old? Guarini and the Monody', in *Guarini: la musica, i musicisti*, ed. Angelo Pompilio, 'Connotazioni', 3 (Lucca, Libreria Musicale Italiana, 1997), 61–75

—— 'Re-Reading *Poppea*: Some Thoughts on Music and Meaning in Monteverdi's Last Opera', *Journal of the Royal Musical Association*, 122 (1997), 173–204

—— '"Sfogava con le stelle" Reconsidered: Some Thoughts on the Analysis of Monteverdi's Mantuan Madrigals', in *Claudio Monteverdi*, ed. Besutti, Gialdroni and Baroncini, pp. 147–70

—— 'Lamenting Ariadne?', *Early Music*, 27 (1999), 395–405

—— 'New Light on Monteverdi's *Ballo delle ingrate* (Mantua, 1608)', *Il saggiatore musicale*, 6 (1999), 63–90

—— 'Singing *Orfeo*: on the Performers of Monteverdi's First Opera', *Recercare*, 11 (1999), 75–118

—— 'Rediscovering *Il rapimento di Cefalo*', *Journal of Seventeenth-Century Music*, forthcoming

—— 'The Composer as Theorist? *Genus* and Genre in Monteverdi's *Combattimento di Tancredi e Clorinda*', in *Music in the Mirror: Reflections on the History of Music Theory and Literature for the 21st Century*, ed. Thomas J. Mathiesen and Andreas Giger (Lincoln, Nebraska, University of Nebraska Press, forthcoming)

Cesari, Gaetano, 'L'"Orfeo" di Cl. Monteverdi all'"Associazione di Amici della Musica" di Milano', *Rivista musicale italiana*, 17 (1910), 132–78

Chafe, Eric, *Monteverdi's Tonal Language* (New York, Schirmer, 1992)

Chew, Geoffrey, 'The Perfections of Modern Music: Consecutive Fifths and Tonal Coherence in Monteverdi', *Music Analysis*, 8 (1989), 247–73

—— 'The Platonic Agenda of Monteverdi's *seconda pratica*: a Case Study from the Eighth Book of Madrigals', *Music Analysis*, 12 (1993), 147–68

Chiarelli, Alessandra, 'L'incoronazione di Poppea o Il Nerone: problemi di filologia testuale', *Rivista italiana di musicologia*, 9 (1974), 117–51

Curtis, Alan, 'La Poppea impasticciata or, Who Wrote the Music to L'incoronazione (1643)?', *Journal of the American Musicological Society*, 42 (1989), 23–54

Cusick, Suzanne, '"There was not one lady who failed to shed a tear": Arianna's Lament and the Construction of Modern Womanhood', *Early Music*, 22 (1994), 21–41

Data, Isabella, 'Il "Rapimento di Proserpina" di Giulio Cesare Monteverdi e le feste a Casale nel 1611', in *Claudio Monteverdi*, ed. Besutti, Gialdroni and Baroncini, pp. 333–46

Davari, Stefano, 'Notizie biografiche del distinto maestro di musica Claudio Monteverdi, desunte dai documenti dell'Archivio storico Gonzaga', *Atti e memorie della R. Accademia Virgiliana di Mantova*, 10 (1884–5), 79–183

Day, Christine J., 'The Theater of SS. Giovanni e Paolo and Monteverdi's *L'incoronazione di Poppea*', *Current Musicology*, 25 (1978), 22–38

Degrada, Francesco, 'Il teatro di Claudio Monteverdi: gli studi dello stile', in *Claudio Monteverdi*, ed. Besutti, Gialdroni and Baroncini, pp. 263–83

Doni, Giovanni Battista, *Lyra barberina*, ed. Antonfrancesco Gori (Florence, Stamperia Imperiale, 1763)

Dorsch, T. S. (trans.), *Classical Literary Criticism* (Harmondsworth, Penguin, 1965)

Fabbri, Paolo, 'New Sources for "Poppea"', *Music & Letters*, 74 (1993), 16–23

—— *Monteverdi*, trans. Tim Carter (Cambridge, Cambridge University Press, 1994)

—— 'On the Origins of an Operatic Topos: the Mad-Scene', in *'Con che soavità'*, ed. Fenlon and Carter, pp. 157–95

—— and Pompilio, Angelo (eds), *Il corago, o vero Alcune osservazioni per metter bene in scena le composizioni drammatiche*, 'Studi e testi per la storia della musica', 4 (Florence, Olschki, 1983)

Fabris, Dinko, *Mecenati e musici: documenti sul patronato artistico dei Bentivoglio di Ferrara nell'epoca di Monteverdi (1585–1645)*, 'Connotazioni', 4 (Lucca, Libreria Musicale Italiana, 1999)

Feldman, Martha, *City Culture and the Madrigal at Venice* (Berkeley, Los Angeles and London, University of California Press, 1995)

Fenlon, Iain, *Music and Patronage in Sixteenth-Century Mantua*, i (Cambridge, Cambridge University Press, 1980)

—— 'Monteverdi's Mantuan *Orfeo*: Some New Documentation', *Early Music*, 12 (1984), 163–72

—— 'Mantua, Monteverdi and the History of "Andromeda"', in *Claudio Monteverdi*, ed. Finscher, pp. 163–73

—— 'The Origins of the Seventeenth-Century Staged *ballo*', in *'Con che soavità'*, ed. Fenlon and Carter, pp. 13–40

—— and Carter, Tim (eds), *'Con che soavità': Essays in Italian Opera, Song, and Dance, 1580–1740* (Oxford, Clarendon Press, 1995)

—— and Miller, Peter, *The Song of the Soul: Understanding 'Poppea'*, 'Royal Musical Association Monographs', 5 (London, Royal Musical Association, 1992)

Finscher, Ludwig (ed.), *Claudio Monteverdi: Festschrift Reinhold Hammerstein zum 70. Geburtstag* (Laaber, Laaber-Verlag, 1986)

Follino, Federico, *Compendio delle sontuose feste fatte l'anno MDCVIII nella città di Mantova, per le reali nozze del serenissimo prencipe d. Francesco Gonzaga con la serenissima infante Margherita di Savoia* (Mantua, Aurelio & Lodovico Osanna, 1608)

Fortune, Nigel, 'The Rediscovery of "Orfeo"', in *Claudio Monteverdi: 'Orfeo'*, ed. Whenham, pp. 78–118

Gallarati, Paolo, '*Il combattimento di Tancredi e Clorinda*: Monteverdi esegeta del Tasso', in *Torquato Tasso: cultura e poesia; atti del convegno Torino–Vercelli, 11–13 marzo 1996*, ed. Mariarosa Masoero (Turin, Paravia, 1997), 291–312

Gallico, Claudio, 'Musicalità di Domenico Mazzocchi: "Olindo e Sofronia" dal Tasso', *Chigiana*, 22 (1965), 59–74

—— *Monteverdi: poesia musicale, teatro e musica sacra* (Turin, Einaudi, 1979)

Gianturco, Carolyn, 'Nuove considerazioni su *il tedio del recitativo* delle prime opere romane', *Rivista italiana di musicologia*, 17 (1982), 212–39

Giuntini, Francesco, 'L'Amore trionfante nell'"Incoronazione di Poppea"', in *Claudio Monteverdi*, ed. Besutti, Gialdroni and Baroncini, pp. 347–56

Glixon, Beth L., 'Scenes from the Life of Silvia Gailarti Manni, a Seventeenth-Century Virtuosa', *Early Music History*, 15 (1996), 97–146

Glixon, Jonathan, 'Was Monteverdi a Traitor?', *Music & Letters*, 72 (1991), 404–6

Godt, Irving, 'I casi di Arianna', *Rivista italiana di musicologia*, 29 (1994), 315–59

Gordon, Bonnie, 'Talking Back: the Female Voice in *Il ballo delle ingrate*', *Cambridge Opera Journal*, 11 (1999), 1–30

Haar, James, '*Improvvisatori* and their Relationship to Sixteenth-Century Music', in Haar, *Essays on Italian Poetry and Music in the Renaissance, 1350–1600* (Berkeley, Los Angeles and London, University of California Press, 1986), 76–99

Hanning, Barbara Russano, 'Monteverdi's Three *genera*: a Study in Terminology', in *Musical Humanism and its Legacy*, ed. Baker and Hanning, pp. 145–70

Harrán, Don, *Salamone Rossi: Jewish Musician in Renaissance Mantua*, 'Oxford Monographs on Music' (Oxford, Oxford University Press, 1999)

Heller, Wendy, *Chastity, Heroism, and Allure: Women in the Opera of Seventeenth-Century Venice* (PhD diss., Brandeis University, 1995)

—— 'Tacitus Incognito: Opera as History in *L'incoronazione di Poppea*', *Journal of the American Musicological Society*, 52 (1999), 39–96

—— '"O delle donne miserabil sesso": Tarabotti, Ottavia, and *L'incoronazione di Poppea*', *Il saggiatore musicale*, 7 (2000), 5–46

Hill, John Walter, *Roman Monody in the Circle of Cardinal Montalto*, 2 vols (Oxford, Clarendon Press, 1997)

—— 'Toward a Better Theory of Recitative', *Journal of Seventeenth-Century Music*, forthcoming

Hitchcock, Wiley H. (ed.), *Giulio Caccini: 'Le nuove musiche' (1602)*, 'Recent Researches in the Music of the Baroque Era', 9 (Madison, Wisc., A-R Editions, 1970)

Holman, Peter, '"Col nobilissimo esercitio della vivuola": Monteverdi's String Writing', *Early Music*, 21 (1993), 577–90

Holzer, Robert R., *Music and Poetry in Seventeenth-Century Rome: Settings of the Canzonetta and Cantata Texts of Francesco Balducci, Domenico Benigni, Francesco Melosio, and Antonio Abati* (PhD diss., University of Pennsylvania, 1990)

—— '"Sono d'altro garbo . . . le canzonette che si cantano oggi": Pietro della Valle on Music and Modernity in the Seventeenth Century', *Studi musicali*, 21 (1992), 253–306

Hust, Gerhard, 'Claudio Monteverdi in Darstellungen und Wertungen der ersten Hälfte des 19. Jahrhunderts', in *Claudio Monteverdi*, ed. Finscher, pp. 249–69

India, Sigismondo d', *Le musiche a una e due voci: libri I, II, III, IV e V*, ed. John J. Joyce, 'Musiche rinascimentali siciliane', 9 (Florence, Olschki, 1989)

Ingegneri, Angelo, *Della poesia rappresentativa e del modo di rappresentare le favole sceniche*, ed. Maria Luisa Doglio (Modena, Panini, 1989)

John, Nicholas (ed.), *The Operas of Monteverdi*, 'E[nglish] N[ational] O[pera] Opera Guides', 45 (London, New York and Paris, Calder, 1992)

Kelly, Thomas Forrest, '"*Orfeo* da camera": Estimating Performing Forces in Early Opera', *Historical Performance*, 1 (1988), 3–9

—— *First Nights: Five Musical Premières* (New Haven and London, Yale University Press, 2000)

Ketterer, Robert C., '*Militat omnis amans*: Ovidian Elegy in *L'incoronazione di Poppea*', *Journal of the International Society for the Classical Tradition*, 4 (1998), 381–95

—— 'Neoplatonic Light and Dramatic Genre in Busenello's *L'incoronazione di Poppea* and Noris's *Il ripudio d'Ottavia*', *Music & Letters*, 80 (1999), 1–22

Kirkendale, Warren, *L'Aria di Fiorenza, id est Il Ballo del Gran Duca* (Florence, Olschki, 1972)

——— *The Court Musicians in Florence during the Principate of the Medici, with a Reconstruction of the Artistic Establishment*, ' "Historiae musicae cultores" biblioteca', 61 (Florence, Olschki, 1993)

Kurtzman, Jeffrey, 'Monteverdi's Changing Aesthetic: a Semiotic Perspective', in *Festa musicologica, in Honor of George Buelow*, ed. Thomas J. Mathiesen and Benito V. Rivera (Stuyvesant, NY, Pendragon Press, 1994), 233–55

La Via, Stefano, 'Le *Combat* retrouvé: les "passions contraires" du "divin Tasse" dans la représentation musicale de Monteverdi', in *La 'Jérusalem délivrée' du Tasse: poésie, peinture, musique, ballet; actes du colloque, musée du Louvre, 1996*, ed. Giovanni Careri (Paris, Klincksieck–Musée du Louvre, 1999), 111–58

Lavin, Irvin, 'Lettres de Parme (1618, 1627–28) et débuts du théâtre baroque', in *Le lieu théâtral à la Renaissance*, ed. Jean Jacquot (Paris, CNRS, 1964), 105–58

Leopold, Silke, *Monteverdi und seine Zeit* (Laaber, Laaber-Verlag, 1982), trans. as *Monteverdi: Music in Transition* (Oxford, Clarendon Press, 1991)

Leppard, Raymond, *Authenticity in Music* (London and Boston, Faber Music, 1988)

Loredano, Giovanni Francesco, *Bizzarie academiche* (Bologna, Gioseffo Longhi, 1676)

McClary, Susan K., *The Transition from Modal to Tonal Organization in the Works of Monteverdi* (PhD diss., Harvard University, 1976)

——— 'Constructions of Gender in Monteverdi's Dramatic Music', *Cambridge Opera Journal*, 1 (1989), 203–23; also in McClary, *Feminine Endings*, pp. 35–52

——— 'Excess and Frame: the Musical Representation of Madwomen', in McClary, *Feminine Endings*, pp. 80–111

——— *Feminine Endings: Music, Gender, and Sexuality* (Minnesota and London, University of Minnesota Press, 1991)

MacNeil, Anne, 'The Divine Madness of Isabella Andreini', *Journal of the Royal Musical Association*, 120 (1995), 195–215

——— 'Weeping at the Water's Edge', *Early Music*, 27 (1999), 407–17

Mamczarz, Irène, *Le Théâtre farnese de Parme et le drame musical italien (1618–1732): étude d'un lieu théâtral, des représentations, des formes; drame pastoral, intermèdes, opéra-tournoi, drame musical* (Florence, Olschki, 1988)

Mamone, Sara, 'Torino, Mantova, Firenze, 1608: le nozze rivali', paper presented at the Institute of Romance Studies, University of London, February 1997

Mancini, Francesco, Muraro, Maria Teresa, and Povoledo, Elena, *I teatri del Veneto*, i/1: *Venezia: teatri effimeri e nobili imprenditori* (Venice, Corbo e Fiore, 1995)

Matteini, Annamaria Testaverdi, *L'officina delle nuvole: il teatro mediceo nel 1589 e gli 'Intermedi' del Buontalenti nel 'Memoriale' di Girolamo Seriacopi*, 'Musica e teatro: quaderni degli Amici della Scala', 11–12 (Milan, Amici della Scala, 1991)

Minucci del Rosso, Paolo, 'Le nozze di Margherita de' Medici con Odoardo Farnese Duca di Parma e Piacenza', *La rassegna nazionale*, 21 (1885), 551–71; 22 (1885), 550–70; 23 (1885), 19–45

Monterosso, Raffaello (ed.), *Performing Practice in Monteverdi's Music: the Historic–Philological Background*, 'Instituta et monumenta', 13 (Cremona, Fondazione Claudio Monteverdi, 1995)

Nagler, Alois M., *Theatre Festivals of the Medici, 1539–1637* (New Haven and London, Yale University Press, 1964; repr. New York, Da Capo Press, 1976)

Neri, Achille, 'Gli "intermezzi" del "Pastor fido"', *Giornale storico della letteratura italiana*, 11 (1888), 405–15

Newcomb, Anthony, 'Girolamo Frescobaldi 1608–15', *Annales musicologiques*, 7 (1976), 111–58

—— *The Madrigal at Ferrara, 1579–1597*, 2 vols (Princeton, Princeton University Press, 1980)

Ossi, Massimo, 'Claudio Monteverdi's *ordine novo, bello et gustevole*: the Canzonetta as Dramatic Module and Formal Archetype', *Journal of the American Musicological Society*, 45 (1992), 261–304

—— *Divining the Oracle: Aspects of Claudio Monteverdi's 'seconda pratica'* (forthcoming)

Osthoff, Wolfgang, 'Die venezianische und neapolitanische Fassung von Monteverdis "Incoronazione di Poppea"', *Acta musicologica*, 26 (1954), 88–113

—— 'Zu den Quellen von Monteverdis "Ritorno di Ulisse in patria"', *Studien zur Musikwissenschaft*, 23 (1956), 67–78

—— 'Neue Beobachtungen zu Quellen und Geschichte von Monteverdis "Incoronazione di Poppea"', *Die Musikforschung*, 11 (1958), 129–38

—— 'Zur Bologneser Aufführung von Monteverdis "Ritorno di Ulisse" im Jahre 1640', *Österreichische Akademie der Wissenschaften: Anzeiger der phil. hist. Klasse*, 95 (1958), 155–60

—— *Das dramatische Spätwerk Claudio Monteverdis* (Tutzing, Hans Schneider, 1960)

—— 'Osservazioni sul canto della stanza che incomincia "Notte" nel "Combattimento" di Claudio Monteverdi: carattere e radici del genere', in *Monteverdi: recitativo in monodia e polifonia*, 'Atti dei Convegni Lincei', 124 (Rome, Accademia Nazionale dei Lincei, 1996), 59–80

Ovid, *Metamorphoses*, trans. M. M. Innes (Harmondsworth, Penguin, 1955)

Palisca, Claude V., *The Beginnings of Baroque Music: its Roots in Sixteenth-Century Theory and Polemics* (PhD diss., Harvard University, 1953)

—— *Girolamo Mei (1519–1594): Letters on Ancient and Modern Music to Vincenzo Galilei and Giovanni Bardi; a Study with Annotated Texts*, 'Musicological Studies and Documents', 3 (2nd edn, American Institute of Musicology, 1977)

—— *The Florentine Camerata: Documentary Studies and Translations* (New Haven and London, Yale University Press, 1989)

—— 'The First Performance of *Euridice*', in Palisca, *Studies in the History of Italian Music and Music Theory* (Oxford, Clarendon Press, 1994), 432–51

Parisi, Susan Helen, *Ducal Patronage of Music in Mantua, 1587–1627: an Archival Study* (PhD diss., University of Illinois at Urbana–Champaign, 1989)

—— 'New Documents Concerning Monteverdi's Relations with the Gonzagas', in *Claudio Monteverdi*, ed. Besutti, Gialdroni and Baroncini, pp. 477–511

Patuzzi, Stefano, 'Da Ariosto al *Ballo delle ingrate*: un itinerario di affluenze', in *Neoplatonismo, musica, letteratura nel Rinascimento: i Bardi di Vernio e l'Accademia della Crusca; atti del convegno internazionale di studi, Firenze-Vernio, 25–26 settembre 1998*, ed. Piero Gargiulo, Alessandro Magini & Stéphane Toussaint, 'Cahiers di "Accademia"' (Paris, Société Marsile Ficin, 2000), 73–81

—— ' "S'a questa d'Este valle": Claudio Monteverdi and a Hitherto Unknown *mascherata* of 1607', unpublished paper

Pickett, Philip, '*Armonia celeste*: Orchestral Colour and Symbolism in Monteverdi's *L'Orfeo*', in *Performing Practice in Monteverdi's Music*, ed. Monterosso, pp. 143–62

Pieri, Marzia, 'La drammaturgia di Chiabrera', in *La scelta della misura. Gabriello Chiabrera: l'altro fuoco del barocco italiano; atti del convegno di studi su Gabriello Chiabrera nel 350° anniversario della morte, Savona, 3–6 novembre 1988*, ed. Fulvio Bianchi and Paolo Russo (Genoa, Edizioni Costa e Nolan, 1993), 401–28

Pirrotta, Nino, 'Scelte poetiche di Monteverdi', *Nuova rivista musicale italiana*, 2 (1968), 10–42, 226–54; trans. as 'Monteverdi's Poetic Choices', in Pirrotta, *Music and Culture in Italy from the Middle Ages to the Baroque*, pp. 271–316

—— 'Teatro, scene e musica nelle opere di Monteverdi', in *Claudio Monteverdi e il suo tempo*, ed. Raffaello Monterosso (Verona, Stamperia Valdonega, 1969), 45–67; trans. as 'Theatre, Sets, and Music in Monteverdi's Operas', in Pirrotta, *Music and Culture in Italy from the Middle Ages to the Baroque*, pp. 254–70

—— 'Monteverdi e i problemi del melodramma', in *Studi sul teatro veneto fra Rinascimento ed età barocca*, ed. Maria Teresa Muraro (Florence, Olschki, 1971), 321–43; trans. as 'Monteverdi and the Problems of Opera', in Pirrotta, *Music and Culture in Italy from the Middle Ages to the Baroque*, pp. 235–53

—— *Music and Culture in Italy from the Middle Ages to the Baroque: a Collection of Essays* (Cambridge, Mass., Harvard University Press, 1984)

—— 'Forse Nerone cantò tenore', in *Musica senza aggettivi: studi per Fedele d'Amico*, ed. Agostino Ziino, 2 vols. (Florence, Olschki, 1991), i, pp. 47–60

—— (with Elena Povoledo), *Li due Orfei* (Turin, Eri, 1969; 2nd edn, Turin, Einaudi, 1975); trans. as *Music and Theatre from Poliziano to Monteverdi* (Cambridge, Cambridge University Press, 1982)

Porter, William V., 'Peri and Corsi's *Dafne*: Some New Discoveries and Observations', *Journal of the American Musicological Society*, 18 (1965), 170–96

—— '*Lamenti recitativi da camera*', in *'Con che soavità'*, ed. Fenlon and Carter, pp. 73–110

Povoledo, Elena, 'Controversie monteverdiane: spazi teatrali e immagini presunte', in *Claudio Monteverdi*, ed. Besutti, Gialdroni and Baroncini, pp. 357–89

Pryer, Anthony, 'Authentic Performance, Authentic Experience and "Pur ti miro" from *Poppea*', in *Performing Practice in Monteverdi's Music*, ed. Monterosso, pp. 191–213

Reese, Gustave, *Music in the Renaissance* (rev. edn, New York, Norton, 1959)

Reiner, Stuart, 'Preparations in Parma – 1618, 1627–28', *The Music Review*, 25 (1964), 273–301

—— ' "Vi sono molt'altre mezz'arie . . ." ', in *Studies in Music History: Essays for Oliver Strunk*, ed. Harold Powers (Princeton, Princeton University Press, 1968), 241–58

—— '*La vag'Angioletta* (and Others): i', *Analecta musicologica*, 14 (1974), 26–88

Robinson, Christopher, *Lucian and his Influence in Europe* (London, Duckworth, 1979)

Rosand, Ellen, 'Barbara Strozzi, *virtuosissima cantatrice*: the Composer's Voice', *Journal of the American Musicological Society*, 31 (1978), 241–81

—— 'The Descending Tetrachord: an Emblem of Lament', *The Musical Quarterly*, 55 (1979), 346–59

—— 'Seneca and the Interpretation of *L'incoronazione di Poppea*', *Journal of the American Musicological Society*, 38 (1985), 34–71

—— 'Iro and the Interpretation of *Il ritorno d'Ulisse in patria*', *Journal of Musicology*, 7 (1989), 141–64

—— *Opera in Seventeenth-Century Venice: the Creation of a Genre* (Berkeley, Los Angeles and London, University of California Press, 1991)

—— 'Operatic Madness: a Challenge to Convention', in *Music and Text: Critical Inquiries*, ed. Steven Paul Scher (Cambridge, Cambridge University Press, 1992), 241–87

—— 'The Bow of Ulysses', *Journal of Musicology*, 12 (1994), 376–95

Rosenthal, Albi, 'Monteverdi's "Andromeda": a Lost Libretto Found', *Music & Letters*, 66 (1985), 1–8

—— 'Aspects of the Monteverdi Revival in the 20th Century', in *Performing Practice in Monteverdi's Music*, ed. Monterosso, pp. 119–23

Rossi, Vittorio, *Battista Guarini ed 'Il pastor fido': studio biografico–critico con documenti inediti* (Turin, Loescher, 1886)

Sadie, Stanley (ed.), *The New Grove Dictionary of Opera* (London, Macmillan, 1992)

Saslow, James, *The Medici Wedding of 1589: Florentine Festivities as 'Theatrum mundi'* (New Haven and London, Yale University Press, 1996)

Saunders, Steven, 'New Light on the Genesis of Monteverdi's Eighth Book of Madrigals', *Music & Letters*, 77 (1996), 183–93

Schrade, Leo, *Monteverdi: Creator of Modern Music* (New York, Norton, 1950; repr. 1979)

Seifert, Herbert, 'Beiträge zur Frage nach den Komponisten der ersten Opern außerhalb Italiens', *Musicologica austriaca*, 8 (1988), 7–26

Severi, Maria Paola, *'Le nozze d'Enea con* [sic] *Lavinia': dal testo alla scena dell'opera veneziana di Claudio Monteverdi* (Recco, De Ferrari, 1997)

Solerti, Angelo, 'Un balletto musicato da Claudio Monteverdi sconosciuto a' suoi biografi', *Rivista musicale italiana*, 7 (1904), 24–34

—— *Gli albori del melodramma*, 3 vols (Milan, Sandron, 1904–5; repr. Hildesheim, Olms, 1969)

—— *Musica, ballo e drammatica alla corte medicea dal 1600 al 1637: notizie tratte da un diario con appendice di testi inediti e rari* (Florence, Bemporad, 1905; repr. New York, Broude Brothers, 1968)

Stattkus, Manfred H., *Claudio Monteverdi: Verzeichnis der erhaltenen Werke; kleine Ausgabe* (Bergkamen, the author, 1985)

Sternfeld, F. W., 'The Orpheus Myth and the Libretto of "Orfeo"', in *Claudio Monteverdi: 'Orfeo'*, ed. Whenham, pp. 20–33

—— *The Birth of Opera* (Oxford, Clarendon Press, 1993)

Stevens, Denis, '"Monteverdi Unclouded": a Ballet in Five Parts', *The Musical Times*, 101 (1960), 23

—— 'Monteverdi's Earliest Extant Ballet', *Early Music*, 14 (1986), 358–66

Strainchamps, Edmond, 'The Life and Death of Caterina Martinelli: New Light on Monteverdi's "Arianna"', *Early Music History*, 5 (1985), 155–86

Strunk, Oliver, *Source Readings in Music History*, rev. edn, iv: *The Baroque Era*, ed. Margaret Murata (New York and London, Norton, 1998)

Szweykowski, Zygmunt, and Carter, Tim (eds), *Composing Opera: from 'Dafne' to 'Ulisse errante'*, 'Practica musica', 2 (Kraków, Musica Iagellonica, 1994)

Tomlinson, Gary, 'Ancora su Ottavio Rinuccini', *Journal of the American Musicological Society*, 26 (1973), 240–62

—— 'Madrigal, Monody, and Monteverdi's "via naturale alla immitatione"', *Journal of the American Musicological Society*, 34 (1981), 60–108

—— 'Music and the Claims of Text: Monteverdi, Rinuccini, and Marino', *Critical Inquiry*, 8 (1982), 565–89

—— 'Twice Bitten, Thrice Shy: Monteverdi's "finta" *Finta pazza*', *Journal of the American Musicological Society*, 36 (1983), 303–11

—— *Monteverdi and the End of the Renaissance* (Oxford, Clarendon Press, 1987)

—— (ed.), *Italian Secular Song 1606–1636*, 7 vols (New York and London, Garland, 1986)

Vassalli, Antonio, 'Il Tasso in musica e la trasmissione dei testi: alcuni esempi', in *Tasso, la musica, i musicisti*, ed. Maria Antonella Balsano and Thomas Walker, 'Quaderni della *Rivista italiana di musicologia*', 19 (Florence, Olschki, 1988), 45–90

Vogel, Emil, 'Claudio Monteverdi: Leben, Wirken im Lichte der zeitgenössischen Kritik und Verzeichniss seiner im Druck erschienenen Werke', *Vierteljahrsschrift für Musikwissenschaft*, 3 (1887), 315–450

Walker, D. P. (ed.), *Les fêtes du mariage de Ferdinand de Médicis et de Christine de Lorraine, Florence 1589*, i: *Musique des intermèdes de 'La pellegrina'* (Paris, CNRS, 1963; repr. 1986)

Whenham, John, *Duet and Dialogue in the Age of Monteverdi*, 2 vols (Ann Arbor, UMI Research Press, 1982)

—— 'The Later Madrigals and Madrigal-Books', in *The New Monteverdi Companion*, ed. Arnold and Fortune, pp. 216–47

—— 'Sigismondo d'India, Knight of St. Mark', *Seventeenth-Century Music* [newsletter of the Society for Seventeenth-Century Music], 8/1 (1998), 2, 8–10

—— (ed.), *Claudio Monteverdi: 'Orfeo'*, Cambridge Opera Handbooks (Cambridge, Cambridge University Press, 1986)

Wilson, Alexandra, 'Torrefranca vs. Puccini: Embodying a Decadent Italy', *Cambridge Opera Journal*, 13 (2001), 29–53

Wistreich, Richard, '"La voce è grata assai, ma . . .": Monteverdi on Singing', *Early Music*, 22 (1994), 7–19

Woods, Marjorie Curry, 'Rape and the Pedagogical Rhetoric of Sexual Violence', in *Criticism and Dissent in the Middle Ages*, ed. Rita Copeland (Cambridge, Cambridge University Press, 1996), 56–86

Zoppelli, Luca, 'Il rapto perfettissimo: un'inedita testimonianza sulla "Proserpina" di Monteverdi', *Rassegna veneta di studi musicali*, 2–3 (1986–7), 343–5

Index of Monteverdi's theatrical works

Index of names, institutions and theatres